Taking Liberties

Ohio University Press Polish and Polish-American Studies Series

Series Editor: John J. Bukowczyk

Framing the Polish Home: Postwar Cultural Constructions of Hearth, Nation, and Self, edited by Bożena Shallcross

Traitors and True Poles: Narrating a Polish-American Identity, 1880–1939, by Karen Majewski

Auschwitz, Poland, and the Politics of Commemoration, 1945–1979, by Jonathan Huener

The Exile Mission: The Polish Political Diaspora and Polish Americans, 1939–1956, by Anna D. Jaroszyńska-Kirchmann

The Grasinski Girls: The Choices They Had and the Choices They Made, by Mary Patrice Erdmans

Testaments: Two Novellas of Emigration and Exile, by Danuta Mostwin

The Clash of Moral Nations: Cultural Politics in Piłsudski's Poland, 1926–1935, by Eva Plach

Holy Week: A Novel of the Warsaw Ghetto Uprising, by Jerzy Andrzejewski

The Law of the Looking Glass: Cinema in Poland, 1896–1939, by Sheila Skaff

Rome's Most Faithful Daughter: The Catholic Church and Independent Poland, 1914–1939, by Neal Pease

The Origins of Modern Polish Democracy, edited by M. B. B. Biskupski, James S. Pula, and Piotr J. Wróbel

The Borders of Integration: Polish Migrants in Germany and the United States, 1870–1924, by Brian McCook

Between the Brown and the Red: Nationalism, Catholicism, and Communism in Twentieth-Century Poland—The Politics of Bolesław Piasecki, by Mikołaj Stanisław Kunicki

Taking Liberties: Gender, Transgressive Patriotism, and Polish Drama, 1786–1989, by Halina Filipowicz

SERIES ADVISORY BOARD

M. B. B. Biskupski, Central Connecticut State University
Robert E. Blobaum, West Virginia University
Anthony Bukoski, University of Wisconsin-Superior
Bogdana Carpenter, University of Michigan
Mary Patrice Erdmans, Central Connecticut State University
Thomas S. Gladsky, Central Missouri State University (ret.)
Padraic Kenney, Indiana University
John J. Kulczycki, University of Illinois at Chicago (ret.)
Ewa Morawska, University of Essex
Antony Polonsky, Brandeis University
Brian Porter-Szűcs, University of Michigan
James S. Pula, Purdue University North Central
Thaddeus C. Radzilowski, Piast Institute
Daniel Stone, University of Winnipeg
Adam Walaszek, Jagiellonian University
Theodore R. Weeks, Southern Illinois University

Taking Liberties

*Gender, Transgressive Patriotism,
and Polish Drama,
1786–1989*

Halina Filipowicz

OHIO UNIVERSITY PRESS
ATHENS

Ohio University Press, Athens, Ohio 45701
ohioswallow.com
© 2014 by Ohio University Press
All rights reserved

To obtain permission to quote, reprint, or otherwise reproduce or distribute material from Ohio University Press publications, please contact our rights and permissions department at (740) 593-1154 or (740) 593-4536 (fax).

Printed in the United States of America
Ohio University Press books are printed on acid-free paper ♾ ™

24 23 22 21 20 19 18 17 16 15 14   5 4 3 2 1

Library of Congress Cataloging-in-Publication Data
Filipowicz, Halina.
 Taking liberties : gender, transgressive patriotism, and Polish drama, 1786–1989 / Halina Filipowicz.
   pages cm. — (Polish and Polish-American studies)
 Includes bibliographical references and index.
 ISBN 978-0-8214-2113-0 (hardback : acid-free paper) — ISBN 978-0-8214-2114-7 (pbk : acid-free paper) — ISBN 978-0-8214-4500-6 (pdf)
 1. Polish drama—History and criticism. 2. Patriotism in literature. 3. Gender identity in literature. 4. Theater—Poland—History. I. Title.
 PG7092.P37F55 2014
                891.8'52—dc3
                                            2014039260

For my parents—in memoriam.

For my sisters—as always.

Contents

Series Editor's Preface	ix
Acknowledgments	xi
Compass Points *A Prologue*	1
Introduction	15
1. Controversies over "True" and "False" Patriotism, 1786–91	46
2. Poland Unmanned? *Zofia Chrzanowska*	117
3. Is There Transgression in This Text? *Wanda, Queen of Poland*	143
4. No More Separate Spheres? *Emilia Plater*	166
5. Apocalypse Now? *Tadeusz Kościuszko*	193
6. Controversies over "True" and "False" Patriotism, 1941–89	227
Transformations *An Epilogue*	273
Notes	283
Plays Cited	349
Index	353

Series Editor's Preface

Publication of the Ohio University Press Polish and Polish-American Studies Series marks a milestone in the maturation of the Polish Studies field and stands as a fitting tribute to the scholars and organizations whose efforts have brought it to fruition. Supported by a series advisory board of accomplished Polonists and Polish-Americanists, the Polish and Polish-American Studies Series has been made possible through generous financial assistance from the Polish American Historical Association and that organization's Stanley Kulczycki Publication Fund, the Stanislaus A. Blejwas Endowed Chair in Polish and Polish American Studies at Central Connecticut State University, and the Kosciuszko Foundation, and through institutional support from Wayne State University and Ohio University Press. The series has also benefited from the warm encouragement of a number of other persons, including Gillian Berchowitz, M. B. B. Biskupski, the late Stanislaus A. Blejwas, Thomas Duszak, Mary Erdmans, Anna Jaroszyńska-Kirchmann, Brian McCook, James S. Pula, and Thaddeus Radzilowski, and from the able assistance of the staff of Ohio University Press. The series also has received generous assistance from a growing list of series supporters, including the benefactor Thomas Duszak, the contributor George Bobinski, and additional friends of the series including Alfred Bialobrzeski, William Galush, John A. and Pauline A. Garstka, Jonathan Huener, Grazyna Kozaczka, Neal Pease, and Maria Ziemianek. The moral and material support from all of these institutions and individuals is gratefully acknowledged.

John J. Bukowczyk

Acknowledgments

Back in the last century, I had the idea to stray from the beaten track and to write a book exploring absences and asymmetries in the available knowledge on Polish drama. I had just published a study of a major playwright, Tadeusz Różewicz, but for the new book I turned elsewhere—away from celebrated masterworks and canonized aesthetics. Over the course of the next decade, my project grew to a rather different monograph. Although the heart of this book is still drama, its overall subject has become more complex and multilayered: how dramatic writing has engaged with the problem of gendered dichotomies and the puzzle of transgressive patriotism. As I tracked the less familiar traditions of Polish drama and theatre, pored over a wealth of fascinating material ranging from parliamentary speeches to polemical pamphlets and verse broadsides, puzzled over the crossing paths of patriotism and transgression, and struggled to make sense of changing and often contradictory gender expectations, I had a lot of help along the way.

When I was just beginning research for my project, I was lucky enough to have many long, wonderful conversations with the late Roman Kaleta of Wrocław University, who enthusiastically supported my decision to take roads less traveled in Polish studies. He extolled the riches of the Ossolineum Library in Wrocław and introduced me to its staff and resources. He also shared his immense knowledge of the Polish Enlightenment and responded with delight rather than dismay to the idea that his archival research could be extended to shed new light on the problem of gender in eighteenth-century Poland. Although I disagree with him on some interpretive points, his work on textual misfits, contentious issues, and uncomfortable topics shunned by others was indispensable to my project. My admiration for and intellectual debt to his scholarship will be readily apparent.

Dobrochna Ratajczakowa, a faculty member at the Adam Mickiewicz University in Poznań and beyond much doubt the most distinguished scholar of Polish drama and theatre, provided a generous and inspiring exchange during the many years it took to research this book. The discussions we had about neglected dramatic genres, overlooked classics, and forgotten blockbusters led me to explore new perspectives on a field I thought I knew quite well. I also benefited from the conversations with the late Jadwiga Maurer, my long-ago mentor at the University of Kansas and a leading scholar in the field of Mickiewicz studies, from whom I received sage advice at crucial moments and insights that stuck with me for years. She heartily endorsed my project and kept me on track by inquiring every now and then if this was going to be the day for starting my voyage to the post office to send off the manuscript.

Many colleagues and friends—Adam Basak, Monika Blige, Jerzy Daniel, Maria Dębicz, Janusz Degler, Elwira Grossman, Leokadia Kaczyńska, Andrzej Karcz, Dariusz Kosiński, Anna Truszkowska Małecka, Elżbieta Małecka, Michael Mikoś, the late Krystyna Ruta-Rutkowska, Ewa Szymańska, and Anna Zacharska—sent me hard-to-find materials. The late Bogdan Czaykowski shared his collection of photocopies from the *Czerwony Sztandar*, a Soviet collaborationist newspaper published in Polish in Lwów (Lviv) during World War II. Equally generous were those colleagues who read parts or all of the manuscript and gave me feedback that was always valuable: Sibelan Forrester, Oleh Ilnytzkyj, and the anonymous readers for Ohio University Press. I thank them all.

Then there are the archivists and librarians, ever a scholar's guides. I did most of the research for this book over the course of many summers in the Ossolineum Library. I also worked in the Jagiellonian University Library in Kraków, the library of the Kraków branch of the Polish Academy of Arts and Sciences, theatre archives in Kraków, Warsaw, and Wrocław, and the Memorial Library at the University of Wisconsin in Madison where I teach. At all these libraries and archives, staff members responded to my numerous queries and requests with unfailing patience and promptness, even when all I had were vague and misspelled references ("I think his last name might have been Theatralski, a priest, perhaps, who wrote sometime in the eighteenth century"). I cannot thank them warmly enough for offering a congenial atmosphere in which to work and for providing me with so much courteous and expert assistance. I am particularly indebted to George Andrew Spencer, Bibliographer for Russian, East European, and Central Asian Studies at the Memorial Library, and Grażyna Rolak of the Early Imprints

Department at the Ossolineum Library for helping me track down some rare and obscure pamphlets from the eighteenth century. I was also fortunate to be able to obtain scanned copies of other eighteenth-century materials thanks to the generosity of Elżbieta Bylinowa, Dorota Krauze, Wanda Staszkiewicz, and Elżbieta Zygmuntowicz of the Warsaw University Library, while Robert Davis of Columbia University's Butler Library promptly sent me a scanned article whose existence I discovered only at the last minute.

I was privileged to try out different parts of my argument at several academic institutions. The conference "The Question of the 'Other' in Polish Literature and Culture" and a follow-up seminar, both of which Elwira Grossman organized at the University of Glasgow in April 1999, provided welcoming forums for the discussion of my work in its early stages. I am very grateful to Dr. Grossman, as I am to the colleagues who invited me to present excerpts from my project in one of the many shapes it inhabited in its slow progress to publication: David Goldfarb for the Slavic Department at Barnard College, Bill Johnston for the Polish Studies Center at Indiana University, Pia Kleber and Tamara Trojanowska for the University College Drama Program at the University of Toronto, Robert Pynsent for the School of Slavonic and East European Studies at University College London, and Richard Rudolph for the Center for Austrian Studies at the University of Minnesota. I am grateful especially for the opportunities these invitations afforded me to interact with audience members who sharpened my ideas and analyses with their comments and who raised more questions than I could possibly answer at the time. I hope that they will find in this book testimony to how much I valued their suggestions.

Funding for my research came from several institutions, but their resources often originate with the thousands of donors and taxpayers who contribute to endowments and research programs. I would like to thank these many anonymous benefactors who made my work possible. I began the research that led to this book while holding fellowships from the National Endowment for the Humanities and the American Council of Learned Societies. Travel grants from the International Research and Exchanges Board facilitated my archival work in Poland. At the University of Wisconsin in Madison, the Graduate School, the William F. Vilas Fellowship Fund, and the Center for Research on Gender and Women provided further financial support. A sabbatical enabled me to revisit the archives once my argument was in place.

My thanks also go to Gillian Berchowitz, director of Ohio University Press, and John Bukowczyk, editor of the Ohio University Press Polish and Polish-American Studies Series, for their interest and encouragement. I am indebted as well to the staff of the acquisitions department, who wrestled with my computer files with patience and ingenuity, and to managing editor Nancy Basmajian, who provided gracious assistance in the work involved in preparing this book for publication.

Much of the manuscript was handwritten, though not (as some of my colleagues suspected) with a quill pen. Although I had no research assistants—I have this stubborn conviction that reading the sources with my own eyes is the only way—Thomas Tabatowski performed much appreciated wizardry on my computer when I set out to type the handwritten sections.

During my research trips to Wrocław, the late Halina Dzieduszycka and the late Wojciech Dzieduszycki opened their home and their personal library to me. I am deeply grateful for their hospitality. I owe a special debt to Dr. Heather Potter of the Ophthalmology Department at the University of Wisconsin–Madison, who enabled me to see my project, literally, afresh.

Then there are countless debts that can hardly be put into words. They are due to my family—my most persevering intellectual colleagues, my severest critics, and my firmest supporters. This book is for them.

|l|

Earlier versions of short sections of this book were published in *Canadian Slavonic Papers / Revue canadienne des slavistes*, *Indiana Slavic Studies*, and *Theatre Journal*. Some of the material in chapter 4 originally appeared in *Engendering Slavic Literatures*, edited by Pamela Chester and Sibelan Forrester (Bloomington: Indiana University Press, 1996), as an article entitled "The Daughters of Emilia Plater." Chapter 5 derives some material from two articles: "Taming a Transgressive National Hero: Tadeusz Kościuszko and Nineteenth-Century Polish Drama," published in *The Great Tradition and Its Legacy: The Evolution of Dramatic and Musical Theater in Austria and Central Europe*, edited by Michael Cherlin, Halina Filipowicz, and Richard L. Rudolph (New York: Berghahn Books, 2003), and "Othering the Kościuszko Uprising: Women as Problem in Polish Insurgent Discourse," published in *Studies in Language, Literature, and Cultural Mythology in Poland: Investigating "The Other,"* edited by Elwira M. Grossman (Lewiston: Edwin Mellen Press, 2002). All of these materials have undergone many sea changes: they have been reconceptualized, augmented with new research, rewritten, and integrated into the book's larger argument.

As anyone who peruses my endnotes will discover, I have learned a great deal from those who preceded me. If I have failed to acknowledge my indebtedness in a particular case, it is inadvertently, and I ask indulgence. All translations are my own unless otherwise noted. I try to maintain gender-neutral language as far as possible, but it is sometimes evident that when the writers I discuss say "he," they do not mean "he or she." In these cases, I have felt obliged to follow their usage in order to avoid altering their sense.

All the customary caveats apply, which is to say that I have on occasion resisted excellent advice with my own readings of textual evidence.

Compass Points
A Prologue

> We live so fully enclosed in the circle of nationalism that we can hardly see beyond it.
> —John H. Schaar, *Legitimacy in the Modern State*

IF WORDS ARE ALSO DEEDS, as Ludwig Wittgenstein's aphorism reminds us, it is appropriate (and necessary) to give an account not merely of what plays are saying but of what they are doing in propounding their arguments.[1] Accordingly, one way to approach plays is to consider them as rhetorical performances in which stances are tried out for reasons that cannot be taken for granted at the outset. The challenge of such analysis and interpretation is compounded, on the one hand, by the Derridean interrogation of the transparency of language and, on the other, by the many forms of censorship that act on playwrights. With these points in mind, I propose to examine a rich array of plays by many authors, from Franciszek Dionizy Kniaźnin's *The Spartan Mother* (*Matka Spartanka*), staged by Izabela Czartoryska in 1786, to Anna Bojarska's *The Polish Lesson* (*Lekcja polskiego*), directed by Andrzej Wajda in 1988.

It may be helpful to know that *The Spartan Mother* features in Margaret R. Hunt's magisterial monograph, *Women in Eighteenth-Century Europe*, as one of the "heavily politicized cultural interventions" into the central debates of its time and place.[2] It may be intriguing to discover that Władysław Ludwik Anczyc's *Kościuszko at Racławice* (*Kościuszko pod Racławicami*, 1880), a source of frustration to modern critics, has made it to a list of the fifteen best plays ever written in the Polish language.[3] And it may be gratifying to find that my selection also includes a classic of Polish political satire: *The Return of the Deputy* (*Powrót posła*, 1791) by Julian Ursyn Niemcewicz, one of the most conspicuous stars of the Warsaw literary scene in the early 1790s. With this play, he made a major contribution to a vigorous exchange of rhetorical fire during what his contemporaries called the Polish Revolution of 1788–92.[4] The completion of *The Return of the Deputy* in November 1790 coincided with the publication in London, also in November 1790, of Edmund Burke's *Reflections on the Revolution in France* and Mary Wollstonecraft's rebuttal to Burke, *A Vindication of the Rights of Men*. While Burke denounced the upheavals taking place in France and depicted revolutionists as violators of royalty and womanhood, Niemcewicz, like Wollstonecraft, declared sympathy for the French Revolution. Performed with deliberate polemical intent at the Warsaw National Theatre in January 1791, *The Return of the Deputy* proved to be a bombshell with immediate and far-reaching political repercussions. Because its inflammatory content attracted massive attention, ranging from over-the-top enthusiasm to outrage and indignation, it would not be extravagant to say that few plays and theatrical performances anywhere and at any time had more direct or suggestive impact on their original audiences than the 1791 production of Niemcewicz's drama. However, much of the textual territory I want to explore remains uncharted in scholarship, even though many of the plays I propose to discuss, and not just *The Spartan Mother* or *The Return of the Deputy*, were successful at claiming a prominent place in public life in the past.

In Benjamin Bennett's pivotal phrase, the dramatic genre is "the memory and the conscience of literature."[5] I take this phrase to mean that one of the most significant achievements of dramatic writing is its ability to make plausible and convincing a broad range of conflicting conceptions and beliefs. To gain a fuller view of Polish drama and its engagement with political disagreement and conflict, I set out to recover a wide variety of plays, including those that have been sidelined or neglected in scholarly commentary. I began with the mid-eighteenth century when a demand for plays in print rose sharply in Poland, partly because of a rapid growth of the reading public, partly because of changes in reading habits, and partly because Enlightenment pedagogues and politicians enlisted drama as a forum for public debate. It also helps to recognize that residents of large areas of the country had only sporadic access to theatrical performance. It should not be particularly surprising, then, that plays were predominantly part of a burgeoning print culture. While some playwrights wrote explicitly for the stage, many others took advantage of the explosion of print culture and wrote with a readership in mind. Booksellers' advertisements, lending library records, inventories of private collections, and other sources of evidence, however fragmentary and frustrating, permit us to track in bold outlines the reading public's fascination with drama, which at times surpassed interest in the novel.[6] The surging demand for plays made dramatic literature a lucrative business for printers and booksellers. For example, Pierre Dufour, one of the largest printer-booksellers in Enlightenment Poland, brought out more than thirty plays between 1775 and 1779. His drama-publishing project was so successful that he launched a series entitled *The Polish Theatre* (*Teatr Polski*) in 1779. Over the next fifteen years, he published fifty-six volumes of *The Polish Theatre*, each volume consisting of up to five plays.[7]

Enjoying a large readership, the dramatic genre became a major venue through which the public was socialized into certain modes of belief and certain value orientations. This historical phenomenon, however, has eluded sustained investigation in Polish studies. To be sure, the work of leading playwrights and theatre practitioners has been extensively discussed, and the existing secondary literature contains a great deal of valuable scholarship on their achievements. But despite strong interest in Polish theatre and drama, a substantial body of material has yet to be fully acknowledged, examined, and documented.

Admittedly, it is almost impossible to resist the temptation to consider only those authors who for various reasons have entered the canon of academic culture and to leave out of consideration those who have failed to establish enduring reputations even though they developed a high profile in their own time as writers and public intellectuals. Although such oversights may be innocent, the almost exclusive focus on more familiar texts in the usual channels of scholarly commentary and curricular inclusion has had the effect of de-emphasizing the diversity of cultural practice in the past as well as generating some misleading epistemological assumptions. For example, it has nearly become an article of faith that a distinctively modern Polish culture emerged only in the Romantic era or that Poland's paradigmatic National Symbolic was forged single-handedly by Romantic poets such as Adam Mickiewicz.[8] Likewise, a Polish version of the myth of maternal virtue, known as the myth of the Polish mother, is presumed to have originated during Romanticism, in reaction to Poland's loss of independence in 1795 and necessarily via the cult of the Virgin Mary.[9] Such misapprehensions, sanctified by an earlier generation of commentators, have had remarkable staying power.

In response to these challenges, I turn to an archive of dramatic writing that has rarely been studied. I would like to retrieve this archive not only in the sense of dusty manuscripts and crumbling volumes that for the most part sleep undisturbed in libraries but also in the sense invoked by Michel Foucault when he sought to direct historical inquiry away from individual works to the discursive structures that support them.[10] I share Arlette Farge's sense that "the archives are always explosive."[11] They offer alternatives to generally accepted views and interpretations, complicating attempts at theorizing solely on the basis of established classics and other well-known materials. My purpose here is to make a case for the need to reevaluate the contribution made to Poland's cultural history by what might be called the other traditions of Polish drama and theatre—a plethora of material that, regardless of the "popular" or "elite" status of individual works, falls outside the purview of dominant critical paradigms and thus remains poorly understood. I have been inspired in part by John Ashbery's efforts to recover the less familiar traditions of American and English poetry. In one of his Charles Eliot Norton Lectures, presented at Harvard University in 1989–90, Ashbery said: "I myself value Schubert more than Pound or Eliot."[12] He meant David Schubert, not Franz Schubert, and one can imagine some members of his audience gasping.

Taking account of an overlooked or undervalued archive of dramatic writing, along with its vision of the thoughtways, interests, and desires of the public, has considerable implications for the widely accepted claim that the role of drama and theatre in the civic life of Polish society has been both vigorous and important. In Poland, according to this claim, plays and performances have repeatedly opened up possibilities of resistance and redress, thus confirming that drama and theatre can constitute a platform of activist and interventionist engagement, inspired by movements for political and social change. To put this another way, had the political role of drama and theatre been negligible in Poland, the level of concern it created among the authorities would be impossible to explain satisfactorily. I do not contest that the twists and turns of modern Polish history have strengthened the traditional significance of the stage as a magnification mirror for the circumstances that lie outside or that theatre and drama have enjoyed remarkable cultural authority in Polish society. But I argue that the engagement of Polish drama and theatre with politics cannot be explained solely through celebrated masterworks and canonized aesthetics. To allow a more complex picture, it is necessary to find room for the ignored spinster aunts and odd bachelor uncles of the nuclear family. They, too, participated in the broader dialogue on the social and political commitments of theatre and drama and had a hand in the shaping of idea(l)s and beliefs—sometimes even more insistently or subversively than their more acclaimed and more richly furnished relatives.

Given the sheer volume of plays that make up the other traditions, it is impossible to imagine any attempt to convey a sense of their range and depth without sacrificing one to the other. Rather than provide a general overview, then, I want to concentrate on a few topics only, chief among them an idea/phenomenon whose meaning is in dispute: patriotism.

For some users of the term, patriotism is synonymous with communitarian solidarity and a concern for the public good; for others, it is interchangeable with oppressive collectivism, crusading chauvinism, blindness to the darker aspects of the national past, sensitivity to slights to the national honor, and belligerent huffing by wavers of the national flag. Those for whom human life is communal to its roots might admire patriotism because it can lift individuals out of their narrow preoccupations and selfish interests; others will regard it with fear and loathing as "a cloak of deceit" and "an armor of righteousness" put on by cynical politicians intent on securing their goals.[13] While one person might say that patriotism is one of the important associative relationships that people develop and as such supplies the "strong common identification" that is necessary for a democratic political community to function, another will dismiss patriotism as nationalism's "bloody brother," each "characterized by exaggerated love for one's own collectivity combined with more or less contempt and hostility toward outsiders."[14] The conflict of opinion about patriotism has been best summarized by Alasdair MacIntyre: "At one end is the view, taken for granted by almost everyone in the nineteenth century, . . . that 'patriotism' names a virtue. At the other end is the contrasting view, expressed with sometimes shocking clarity in the nineteen sixties, that 'patriotism' names a vice."[15]

Although *patriotism* is a relatively new term that came into general use for the first time in the eighteenth century, the conception of allegiance to *patria* dates back to Greek and Roman antiquity.[16] Despite its long history, however, patriotism has rarely been the object of in-depth exploration in scholarship. In particular, only a handful of studies has considered it in relation to the circumstances of a specific time and place.[17] Moreover, although gender norms, or prescriptive standards of masculinity and femininity, have shaped assumptions about patriotic responsibilities, the interaction between patriotism and gender has scarcely been touched upon in existing scholarly accounts.[18] Admittedly, gender sometimes seems to be erased or invisible in patriotic discourse; on other occasions, however, it can be hypervisible as when the skills and qualities of women are celebrated over those of men (or vice versa). But invisible or hypervisible, gender can offer a lens through which to read how concepts of patriotism are constructed.

In the past, commentators tended to treat the concept of patriotism as timeless, monolithic, and self-evident. As Dustin Griffin points out, even those scholars who gave extensive attention to the subject of patriotism "largely . . . regarded it in unproblematic terms, as a 'universal' emotion," constant across time and space.[19] Given this general consensus, it would be reasonable to suppose that patriotism comes in a single, unambiguous form: love of *patria*. But to accept this assumption is to overlook the fact that while the term *patria* has outlived the old, classical world, its meaning has been far from stable.[20] Any attempt to understand patriotism inevitably and inescapably leads to the questions: What exactly is the *patria* that patriots claim to love? Are they lovers of *patria* in the sense of a geographic area, a polity, or a set of values and ideals? Is the object of their loyalty and devotion a community of their fellow citizens or (to invoke the ancient Stoics' understanding of *patria*) "the universal society to which all humans belong"?[21] And if *patria* refers to the patriots' native country, do they love their homeland "as it is, as it once was, or as it might be"?[22]

To compound the problem, the equation of the patriot with the dutiful son (or daughter) and patriotic obligations with the bonds of filial affection has become so ubiquitous that it seems almost indelicate to invoke John Adams who, in a series of essays published in the *Boston Gazette* in 1765, argued that those who seek separation from the mother country are not necessarily unpatriotic.[23] To compound the problem even further, Richard Price, who worked with a political club called the London Revolution Society, the revolution being that of 1688, made a historic case for a patriotism that contains strong universalist, even cosmopolitan strains. Price's "A Discourse on the Love of Our Country" (1789), best remembered today as the burning speech that provoked Burke's wrath in *Reflections on the Revolution in France,* begins with three crucial caveats. First, "our country" should not be understood in a purely geographical sense, but should be regarded as a corporate "community" of persons "bound together by the same civil polity" and "protected by the same laws." Second, "the love of our country" does not imply "any conviction of the superior value of it to other countries, or any particular preference of its laws and constitution of government." Third, "the love of our country" should not be confused with "that spirit of rivalship and ambition which has been common among nations." Patriots should love their country "ardently but not exclusively"; while performing the duty they owe to their country, they should also accept wider responsibilities as "citizens of the world" and in so doing "take care to maintain a just regard to the rights of other countries."[24] Price's idea of patriotism, in other words, rejects compatriot partiality or the widely and deeply held belief that we are permitted to show greater concern for compatriots than for strangers. In Price's view, being a patriot entails a moral obligation to, and solidarity with, all other human beings, who should be viewed as fellow citizens.

In recent scholarly literature, patriotism finds little favor.[25] Its critics consider the whole idea/phenomenon of patriotism as tired and passé. An odd relic of a bygone epoch, a stiffly unattractive, embarrassing, even offensive anachronism, it has nothing to offer to a much needed ethic for global citizenship. Or to be more precise, the era of globalization in which we are living, and particularly the erosion of national barriers through the rapid expansion of new communication technologies and transnational cultural networks, makes the notion of patriotic allegiance and obligation untenable. Yet there are also those commentators who recognize, on the contrary, that patriotism is far from becoming a useless fossil of a lost world. To them, the continuing appeal of patriotism is a cause for concern. The reasons for this concern are not hard to identify. While the emotional pull of patriotism in the sense of attachment to one's homeland, its people, and its cultural heritage (to mention only the most obvious forms) remains strong in the age of globalization and the attendant logic of placelessness, it is not unusual to see patriotic affection appropriated for the promotion of the "our country, right or wrong" idea, absorbed into chauvinist enthusiasms and exhortations, exploited for the veneration of the nation, or engaged to pay dividends for the politics of nationalism.[26] Terminologically, the slide of patriotism into nationalism is facilitated by a consistent tendency in the anglophone world "to sentimentalize the state by calling it *the nation*."[27] As the term *patriotism* is reconceptualized as "a mild, euphemistic alternative to 'nationalism,' 'national pride' or 'national loyalty,'" and the exclusionist rhetoric of the nation is dressed up as patriotic conviction, those who oppose chauvinist fervor and xenophobic bigotry are stigmatized as unpardonably disloyal.[28]

Considering that patriotism has often carried with it both racism and xenophobia, that patriotic sentiments are routinely co-opted for chauvinism and jingoism, and that the terms *patriotism* and *nationalism* are used interchangeably, it is hardly surprising that many commentators respond to patriotism "at best with embarrassment and at worst with downright hostility."[29] In 1946, Merle Curti defined patriotism as "love of country, pride in it, and readiness to make sacrifices for what is considered its best interest"; as such, he noted briefly, it "is related to nationalism."[30] Fifty years later, George Kateb identified patriotism as a dangerous, potentially lethal form of group membership and allegiance, driven by narcissistic commitment emanating from love of one's country:

> How can one love such a mottled or hybrid entity as a country, particularly when, as in a democracy, the country's people are (always by imputation and sometimes in fact) directly and indirectly responsible for the country's wicked policies? ... One does and sometimes should love persons "beyond good and evil," so to speak; but to love a country, an abstract entity capable of so much harm, especially to those outside, to those who are not fellow-patriots, but rather patriots of their own, if they are patriots at all—that is an unacceptable idea.... The evil done in the world by nationalism and patriotism, commonly abetted by racism or ethnocentrism, and often by religion as well, is immense.[31]

Kateb conceded that "patriotism may be mobilized for a good cause," but he darkly warned that "much more easily, it may be mobilized for an unjust one."[32]

The fact that a 2001 law, which gives the US government wide new powers to bypass fundamental civil liberties such as due process of law and protection from unwarranted searches and seizures, is named the Patriot Act has not boosted the reputation of patriotism. And the reputation of literature on patriotic themes has for decades been quite low because this body of writing is typically (and not unjustifiably) associated with stirring exhortations and panegyrical effusions. That said, I was intrigued to find, for instance, that *The Patriot's Calendar,* published in London in the 1790s, contained both the Magna Carta and the "Marseillaise."[33] Studies such as

Albert Goodwin's *The Friends of Liberty: The English Democratic Movement in the Age of the French Revolution* reminded me that the eighteenth-century roots of the term *patriotism* were in the defense of citizens' rights, the struggle against outrages of centralized power, and the fight against corruption in government. Accordingly, radical reformers in Britain between 1790 and 1850 "viewed themselves, initially at least, not as Chartists or Dissenters, socialists or trade-unionists, but as 'patriots' defending a familiar set of patriot concerns—liberty, property, and constitutional rights."[34] Focused on the "opposition to the increasingly centralized state and the growing capitalist economic order," their "patriot cause" was "*internationalist* in its leanings."[35] Thus, the patriot of *The Patriot's Calendar* stood for political equality, popular sovereignty, and social justice, rather than simply a romantic attachment to country.

Publications such as *The Patriot's Calendar* inspired my decision to revisit the concept of patriotism and to explore its equivocal and, at times, ambiguous meanings. Clearly, the perplexities and paradoxes that inhere in the question of patriotic beliefs, idea(l)s, allegiances, motives, intentions, aspirations, and commitments invite closer scrutiny. To be sure, there is no lack of commentaries arguing that patriotism welds together a strong sense of national identity with identification around a sense of the common good. But is this the only possible way to understand patriotism? Aren't a sense of national identity and a sense of the common good distinct and even in tension for some patriots? And isn't it reductive to link the exercise of patriotism to prideful admiration for the greatness of one's country rather than to the acknowledgment of its weaknesses?

To say that patriotism is a highly contentious yet oddly slippery category would be an understatement. This book begins with the recognition that patriotism is a notoriously promiscuous concept that seems to depend on a timeless conjunction of love and duty but carries multivalent meanings that have seldom been the object of a sustained analysis. Combining archival research with historical contextualization and critical theory, *Taking Liberties* is an attempt to elaborate a fresh approach to a complicated, contradictory, and often confusing idea/phenomenon known as patriotism. The core of my argument is that the porousness or elasticity of the concept of patriotism allows it to connect, converge, and cross-pollinate with other discourses and practices in unpredictable, even heretical ways. Through a series of engagements with the work of writers such as Kniaźnin and Bojarska, this study tracks some of the unorthodox interactions, exemplified here by the interplay between patriotism and transgression of social or customary norms, and it examines how and to what ends playwrights have grappled, either directly or obliquely, with a puzzling, seemingly absurd nexus between patriotic commitment and transgressive nonconformity. Although my project is situated in a particular historical context and steeped in local knowledge, its reach extends beyond its immediate subject and scholarly discipline. I hope to show that battles waged over the meaning and practice of patriotism; clashes between competing views of patriotic idea(l)s, principles, and concerns; controversies over "proper" and "improper" forms of rebellious insubordination; and attempts to distinguish the "true" patriot from the "false" not only illuminate the strong dependence of patriotism on local time and circumstance but also constitute rich terrain for investigating some of the broader issues—such as cultural memory and authority—that are at the center of debates in the humanities.[36]

This project began as an exploration of a vast trove of material bequeathed by those prolific generations between the mid-eighteenth and early twentieth centuries, contracted to focus on the 1880s and 1890s, and, finally, expanded to encompass the period between the mid-1780s and the late 1980s. I start, unconventionally, with Kniaźnin's *The Spartan Mother*, staged as a lavish private theatrical at an aristocratic court in June 1786, and end with Lech Wałęsa's public extravaganza-cum-masquerade, performed al fresco, on the site of an eighteenth-century battle, in May 1989. I made the decision to devote more chapters to the eighteenth century after I realized that the efforts in scholarship to locate the foundations of modern Polish culture in the Romantic period and to use Romanticism as a grid for conceptualizing the engagement of Polish literature with politics have been so successful that, paradoxically, they have diminished an entire era: the Enlightenment. The paradox (or the irony) here is that, for generation after generation, Polish political commentators have drawn their fundamental concepts and analogies from the tumultuous history of Enlightenment Poland and taught their lessons by referring to it.[37] Clearly, Poland's long eighteenth century has had an even longer afterlife, even though the hermetic view of the Polish Romantic age, of which Maria Janion has been the leading magus for many years, encourages us to believe that there was an irrevocable break between the Enlightenment and Romanticism in Poland. At a time when the

Enlightenment continues to be "one of the most debated themes of contemporary intellectual discourse,"[38] a reductive and misleading dichotomy—a conventional opposition of an Enlightenment of unoriginality, rationality, emotional restraint, and decorum versus a Romanticism of aesthetic daring, sublime emotionality, heroic individualism, and edgy, threshold-crossing subjects—dominates the thinking about Polish culture of the eighteenth and nineteenth centuries. Nowadays the meaning of the Polish Enlightenment has shrunk and narrowed so much that its cultural history appears uncontroversial, unproblematic, even boring. It is not particularly surprising, then, that the Enlightenment has become one of the most neglected periods in the poststructuralist discourse of Polish literary and cultural studies.[39] This neglect is unfortunate. For example, the fixation on the rationality of the Enlightenment misrepresents trends in eighteenth-century moral philosophy that resorted to the sway of the passions, the language of sentiment and feelings, and the heightened appreciation of sensibility. Moreover, although masculinity and femininity were key categories of Enlightenment thought, we know surprisingly little about the Polish Enlightenment's debate about gender.

I had planned to conclude this book with the last theatre season before World War I, but I decided to include more twentieth-century plays after I discovered, on one of my (all too) many furloughs from work on my project, Stefan Otwinowski's *Easter* (*Wielkanoc*). Drafted in 1943 and published by the Central Commission of Polish Jews in 1946, *Easter* is the earliest attempt in any language to depict the 1943 uprising in the Warsaw ghetto through the medium of drama. A wealth of scholarship has expanded our knowledge of literary and theatrical representations of the Holocaust, but when I set out to do research on *Easter*, I found that it had received scant critical attention. In the play, historical figures find modern counterparts, and events both past and present jostle one another. This in itself is not exceptional, but what still stands out is a puzzling conflation of the Jewish uprising of 1943 and the Polish insurrection of 1794. This conflation startled me, first by its seeming absurdity, then by its possible implications. I could not proceed with my project until I was clear in my mind about what the 1794 insurgency was doing in a play about the resistance of the Warsaw ghetto. *Easter* was an invitation to search for missing pieces of the puzzle, hidden in libraries. I found myself dealing with gaps, omissions, tense silences, censored traumas, buried anxieties, haunting "shadow" themes, thickening layers of significance, endlessly multiplying connotations, and no clear sense of closure. Madness may lie in that direction, but so too might a richer sense of Polish cultural history.

In a book that enables the other traditions of Polish drama and theatre to emerge from the shadows of condescension and neglect so that complications and contradictions of patriotic discourse can be examined, it is impossible to avoid the question: Why take up this topic *now*?

One reason is that in the age of boundless opportunities for global connectivity, transnational cultural traffic, and intensified hybridization it is still axiomatic that patriotism and allegiance to one's nation go together and that patriots should look to the well-being of their own nation and defend its core interests.[40] As the magic of national "we-identities" continues to hold sway in the ostensibly globalized postmodern culture, patriotic commitments are typically explained within a nationalist paradigm, and concepts such as cosmopolitan patriotism are viewed as a contradiction in terms.[41]

Another reason is that the problem of patriotism in Poland's "imagined community" (to use Benedict Anderson's indispensable phrase) has remained largely unexplored in scholarship.[42] That patriotism has been a dominant concept in "the cultural liturgy" of Polish society; that its persistent themes have been freedom and independence; and that its language has been one of moral absolutes, of self-sacrifice against self-interest—on these points there exists a strong consensus.[43] Additionally, it has become standard practice to attribute "a high voltage patriotism" to Poles and to invoke a parallel between the supreme sacrifice of Christ and the bloody ordeals endured by the martyred Poland.[44] It is hard to avoid the suspicion that such impassioned claims are sheer fustian that has more to do with rhetorical impact than with cool analysis. This kind of rhetoric has indeed caught the public attention, obscuring the fact that the semantic range of the term *patriotism* has encompassed, for example, defense of the rights and status of parliament, insistence on the contractual basis of government, concerns about the expansion of executive power, criticism of those who support a government without checks or oversight, demands for government accountability, struggles for the extension of human rights and civil liberties, and claims to equal educational opportunities. At a time when a narrow, nationalist motivation of patriotic allegiance is taken for granted, and patriotism is invoked to justify everything from flag-waving triumphalism and a celebratory nationalist historiography to arrant chauvinism and xenophobic bigotry, the nonnationalist or transnational conceptions of patriotism have vanished from the culture's radar. It seems that the time has come to bring them into view.

There is also a third reason for taking up the problem of patriotism now. Patriotism has become arguably the most polarizing term of public debate in postcommunist Poland, especially with regard to the memory of the Holocaust and the legacy of the communist period, but also with regard to the liberal tradition.[45] Many participants in the debate are either openly skeptical or unremittingly critical of what they construe as the liberal tradition's atomistic approach to society. They contend that it overestimates the individual as the bearer of value at the expense of values inherent in a community, and thereby it fails to inspire strong identification with, and enduring commitment to, the common good; instead, it encourages a clinical, amoral instrumentality in social relations. Convinced that it is imperative to assure the transmission and conservation of collectively held values, critics of the liberal tradition tout patriotic affection as the indispensable "'glue'" that can bind Poles together as a community, fostering both a shared sense of Polishness and an ethos of mutual indebtedness and mutual concern among individuals who are otherwise strangers to each other.[46] Just what this construction called Polishness means, what its role in the public sphere should be, and whether or not it stokes the fires of the national ego are questions that are hotly debated, but there is widespread agreement that Polishness has been shaped around the collective memory of a long history of foreign oppression and national resistance. Consequently, the most common understanding of patriotism has crystallized around a cluster of just a few associations: freedom fighting, battlefield heroism, honor (in particular, a rather kamikaze sense of honor), bloody glamor.[47] New parties that emerged after the collapse of communism in 1989 have become adept at using this abridged vocabulary in an attempt to broaden their electoral appeal and particularly to secure the support of voters who are alarmed over the growth of a liberal culture and concerned about the hollowness and corrosiveness allegedly inherent in individual liberalism. Some parties have gone so far as to insist that there should be a place for proper patriotic idea(l)s and traditions in school curricula, that the teaching of history in particular should impart "true" patriotism, and that more difficult and problematic aspects of the Polish past should be downplayed to facilitate a celebratory sense of Polish identity in the present.[48]

In theory, patriotism, at the very least, is capable of blurring the edges of party rivalry or animosity; in reality, its usefulness as the hard currency of party rhetoric and a tool of legitimation and persuasion has triggered new skirmishes in the unending combat between "true" and "false" patriotism. These skirmishes have escalated into a rancorous public controversy over whether the patriotic credentials of President Lech Kaczyński, who died in a plane crash in 2010, entitled him to be interred in Poland's most hallowed burial place, the Wawel Cathedral in Kraków, next to monarchs and national heroes. The polemics over President Kaczyński's enshrinement at Wawel have rekindled a bipolar commonplace that, on the one hand, self-proclaimed patriots are right-wing bigots prone to hysterical displays of nationalist sentiments and that, on the other, critics of patriotism are renegades guilty of a wanton abrogation of an intimate bond or an act of unpardonable disloyalty. In the rush of postcommunist Polish history, it is almost unavoidable to rehearse such overheated platitudes or to forget that patriotism has not been a monolithic and static concept, that patriotic commitments have not been the exclusive property of the political right, and that adherents of patriotism have not always been interested in the same political and social outcomes. At a time when patriotism is increasingly perceived in Poland (and elsewhere) as a sentiment associated with men and women who salute the flag, attend church, and become defensive when their country is criticized abroad, it is vital to supplement critiques of reductive presuppositions about patriotic allegiance and devotion with an investigation of a more complex, often paradoxical discourse of patriotism.

In the course of my research, I have acquired a richer appreciation of "raffish" writing, dramaturgical "bad" manners, rhetorical "ungrammaticalities," textual "oddities" and "aberrations," "preposterous" asynchronic quirks and singularities, "anomalous" effulgences, and many other ways in which the other traditions of Polish drama and theatre encourage us to stand back from some of the current assumptions and habits of thought about Polish cultural history and perhaps even to reconsider them. I hope to shed new light on a few old questions about cultural practice in the past, but this project might also help us better understand some of the dilemmas and disputes of our own time. Given that the term *patriotism* has become a handy label whose application reassures its users, turning questions into answers before they have even been asked, this is a timely moment to restore to view the complications and contradictions of the conceptual terrain of patriotism.

Introduction

I.

THIS BOOK TAKES UP a cultural puzzle and explores how and to what ends it has been thematized in dramatic writing. The puzzle arises from the interplay between, on the one hand, unswerving commitment and tireless devotion to a patriotic cause and, on the other, transgressive nonconformity. What interests me in particular is an intriguing moment when patriotism, commonly believed to be a self-explanatory orthodoxy, turns transgressive because some patriots do more than what all patriots are supposed ("supposed" as presumed; "supposed" as prescribed) to do. This moment involves a paradox that can be stated thus: while conscientiously fulfilling the patriotic mandate to serve their country selflessly and, if need be, to risk their lives for it, some deeply dutiful patriots flout public opinion, cross the bounds of "proper" patriotic activism, and subvert the social or customary norms of their time and place, and specifically the norms that draw on ideas about gender, class, and authority.

The transgressive nonconformity of these patriots may range from mildly contentious to flagrantly outrageous, from broadly troublesome to profoundly disturbing. Almost always, though, it is threatening to their contemporaries' fundamental assumptions about the value of social hierarchy. While guardians of the "proper" exercise of patriotism, suitably puzzled, alarmed, or outraged, shake their heads in disbelief, transgressive patriots insist that the idea of patriotism as a form of group membership and allegiance has serious limitations, not least since it may conceal various forms of unfreedom and injustice. While defenders of "true" patriotism, preoccupied with the dos and don'ts of patriotic activism, emphasize the need to maintain rigid, logically consistent boundaries around the concept of patriotism, transgressive patriots contend that such boundaries are highly problematic. From their standpoint, the practice of patriotism becomes ethically debatable and its potential success compromised if it relies on unquestioned or nonreflective attachments. Critical of invidious distinctions that justify an inequitable social order, transgressive patriots are determined to challenge the inherited discourse of social demarcation by eroding a dividing line between what is acceptably patriotic and what is necessarily transgressive.

Transgression in the sense of norm violation may be less provocative a concept today than it was in the past. But given the persistence of the norm as a category and the popularity of patriotism as a monologic discourse (not to mention the blurring of patriotism into nationalism or the appropriation of patriotic sentiments for chauvinist sloganeering, xenophobic bigotry, jingoistic huffing, and military muscle-flexing), the paradoxical nexus between patriotic commitment and transgressive nonconformity merits closer attention. My project here, then, is to give an overview of the historical contexts in which patriotism was imagined, corroborated, corrected, and disputed in modern Polish culture, to examine the fraught (yet illuminating) interaction between patriotism and transgression, and to consider how the paradoxical convergence of patriotic loyalty and devotion with transgression of social or customary norms was implicated in arguments for a wider recognition of democratic aspirations, including access to full citizenship.[1] With these aims in mind, I analyze textual examples (or cultural fragments, in Walter Benjamin's sense), chosen because they are particularly revealing of underlying ideological tendencies and tensions.[2]

To put it quite simply, my subject is a trope and a genre in which it thrived. The trope is the paradox of patriotism twinned with transgression. The genre is drama. At various points in my discussion, I also draw on other materials: theatrical and nontheatrical performance, parliamentary speeches, paintings, songs, poems, prose fiction, letters, memoirs, biographies, pedagogical treatises, conduct books, and printed ephemera of all kinds. But my primary concern is with the dramatic genre, "the memory and the conscience of literature" (to quote Benjamin Bennett again). Three major themes unite my discussion: controversies over "true" and "false" patriotism (along with disputes over credentials that set the "true" patriot apart from the pretender to patriotic virtue); contestations over class and gender boundaries; and imaginative attempts to extend the bounds of patriotic solidarity, to widen the meaning of "us," to stretch the "us" category in order to take in "not-us," and perhaps even to undo the whole opposition between "us" and "them."

In the chapters that follow, I present a series of case studies, drawing on a wide array of plays written over the course of more than two hundred years. Beginning with the recognition that one person's patriot can be another's transgressor and that the conceptual terrain of patriotism has been subject to ongoing revision and contest, I examine the cultural work performed by what might be called the drama of patriotism.[3] By cultural work, I mean the ways in which drama functions not only as a form of entertainment but also as a venue through which writers can attempt, under the epistemological and formal constraints of genre, to participate actively in the historically contingent processes of constituting, consolidating, or contesting the value and belief systems of their culture.[4] I do my best, of course, to provide a careful exegesis of the dramaturgical and rhetorical methods of thematizing and facilitating the emotion of patriotism, but I am at least as much interested in exploring the relations between plays and their social and political space in order to understand how they negotiate the strains and stresses of their local time and circumstance and perhaps also to gain a sense of the ways in which they maneuver (if they do) against circumstance.

It is no exaggeration to say that during the period covered in this book the question of patriotism was a veritable obsession in drama; it was taken up by numerous playwrights in a multitude of different ways. I have resisted the temptation to provide comprehensive coverage. My discussion reflects my decision to use a selective approach rather than try for an inclusive roundup or a fast-forward survey. The plays I have culled from a huge trove span a broad swathe of generic categories and of the attitudes expressed. This assortment includes neoclassical tragedy, satirical comedy, romantic comedy, *drame romantique,* music drama, melodrama, domestic drama, and thesis play, as well as several works that do not fit into any easily identifiable category in large part because they cross the line between "high-cultural" and "popular" genres.[5]

Only a few of the plays I discuss were performed with any frequency, but many enjoyed a large and passionate readership. They were serialized in newspapers and magazines and then reprinted in inexpensive editions, often in the flimsy little paperback form. The most famous of the plays I consider are Julian Ursyn Niemcewicz's *The Return of the Deputy* and Władysław Ludwik Anczyc's *Kościuszko at Racławice*. *The Return of the Deputy*, a trenchant comedy by one of the most gifted writers in the history of Polish political satire, has won acclaim as a pivotal contribution to a barrage of polemical literature that accompanied the battles fought in the 1788–92 Parliament, now known as the Four-Year Parliament, for reforms to modernize the Polish-Lithuanian Commonwealth.[6] *Kościuszko at Racławice*, arguably the finest of Polish *drames romantiques* and a runaway best-seller since its premiere in 1880, is the single most influential work about Tadeusz Kościuszko, the commander-in-chief of the 1794 insurrection, in all of Polish literature. In 1989, it returned to the stage to celebrate an overwhelming victory of Solidarity's candidates in a semi-free general election that ended the Communist Party's seemingly incontestable monopoly on political power.[7]

Many other plays I have selected for discussion enjoyed wildfire popularity in the past, but nowadays are footnotes at best in scholarly literature. Most scholars choose not to waste time on them on the simple grounds that these obscurities are tedious, unimaginative, and stale—in a word, boring. "But then," as Franco Moretti observes in his important work on how the archive might provide crucial material for the renewal of literary history, "are we so sure that boredom is boring?"[8] Admittedly, some of the plays are stiff, ponderous, or too long. But not many of them. It is as if their authors had been struck by lightning: their writing is electrified by the astonishing events they depict. And what they say about their world can be arresting and revealing.

II.

It might well be asked why this book begins with the latter third of the eighteenth century, the period of the high Enlightenment in Poland.[9] My answer is twofold. First of all, one can hardly overstate the centrality of the wider European movement we think of as the Enlightenment to the rise of modernity.[10] The impresarios of the Enlightenment promoted a vision in which a belief in the fundamental importance of liberty and happiness, in world-transforming progress and the perfectibility of society, and especially in education, was paramount. This vision helped create a framework for expanding women's social roles, without which nineteenth-century feminism would have been inconceivable.[11]

That said, it would be naive to maintain the once conventional view of the Enlightenment as an expansive, unruffled, serenely self-confident era of rationalism, toleration, and emancipation—the image memorialized in nineteenth-century historiography. Enlightenment discourse and practice demonstrated again and again their paradoxical capacity to absorb old hierarchies and boundaries and to construct new ones under the banner of the era's much-vaunted universalist orientation. For example, although both Enlightenment epistemology and Enlightenment political theory depended heavily on the idea of a uniform human nature, the Enlightenment was also a period of an intense scientific inquiry into the exact nature of difference between the sexes. Prior to the Enlightenment, the cultural and social world did recognize two genders, but this distinction was not grounded in scientific inquiry. To be sure, woman's nature was culturally "produced" in the absence of decisive scientific facts, and even, occasionally, in the teeth of evidence to the contrary. Physiologically speaking, however, woman was regarded not as the opposite sex, but only as a lesser or imperfect form of man. It was believed, for instance, that male and female genitalia developed out of the same anatomical structure and that woman's reproductive organs were an inverted version of the male genitals trapped within her body.

It was only the second half of the eighteenth century that brought a dramatic, if gradual, transformation in thinking about sex and sex difference, rooted in an aggressive scientism and a biologistic and medicalizing terminology. To identify, analyze, and explain sex (and gender) differences, new methods were developed. As Londa Schiebinger points out, "Anatomists and medical doctors investigated the body as a whole—each bone, organ, hair of the head, and nerve—for telltale signs of sexual differences."[12] It was "this new emphasis on understanding sexual difference in terms compatible with modern materialism" that constituted the Enlightenment revolution in sexual science.[13] As a result, "the older Galenic 'one sex' model, in which women were conceived as essentially the same as men but merely less perfect versions, gave way to the new 'two sex' model, a model of radical biological divergence"; in grounding sexual difference in every part of the body, the new model "played to Enlightenment sensibilities that *nature* prescribed the laws of society."[14] The authority of nature was invoked to explain the social role allocated to each sex, to justify the exclusion of women from political representation, and to legitimize an inequitable, male-dominated social and political order. "And nature," notes Joan W. Scott, "was a difficult authority to challenge."[15]

There was a certain irony in the fact that many centuries-old assumptions about women, which had often pandered to misogynistic attitudes, were "merely translated into the language of modern science" to legitimate what was already the traditionally narrow sphere of women's activities.[16] With new science also came new assumptions. Beginning in the eighteenth century, for instance, maternal love "was assumed to be a natural quality of women that, when cultivated, would motivate them to dedicate themselves to their children, and especially to the education of their daughters, which was their particular responsibility."[17] The new, modern woman, in other words, was defined largely by her maternal love and her delicate and tender disposition or her special gift for what was then known as sensibilité. It is thus hardly surprising that the subject of mothers, thick with such idealizations, would become one of the earliest and foremost targets of feminist critique.

As the historian Karin Hausen has observed in an article originally published in German in 1976, the full-fledged concept of "*Geschlechtscharakter* (character of the sexes)" emerged only in the eighteenth century; the ideology of sexual character, or innate, sex-specific character traits, would provide prescriptive guidelines for socially acceptable behavior for men and women from that time until well into the twentieth century.[18] Or, to put it somewhat differently, the Enlightenment science of sexuality helped undergird the doctrine of sexual complementarity, which in turn, as Schiebinger writes,

> provided an important ideological resolution to the new question of rights for women. The doctrine of sexual complementarity, which taught that men and women are not physical and moral equals but complementary opposites, functioned as an important supplement to nascent liberalism, making inequalities seem natural while satisfying the needs of European society for a continued sexual division of labor.[19]

Buttressed by Enlightenment science, the idea that women's activities ought to complement, rather than duplicate, the activities of men was reinforced by the concept of respectability. If a woman deviated from the norms of behavior prescribed for her sex, her femininity was in jeopardy, and femininity as a social construct was inseparable from respectability. Because of the distinctive cultural expectations directed toward women and the gendered dynamics by which such expectations were shaped, I am particularly interested, in this book, in exploring the role of women in the work of transgressive patriotism.

My second reason for beginning this book with the latter third of the eighteenth century is that the high Enlightenment marks a signal, arguably formative moment in the modern history of patriotism in Poland. By the early 1780s, the question of patriotic allegiance and commitment emerged as a matter of vigorous public debate, but the extension of the semantic range of patriotism was forged only gradually in the fires of factional conflicts, parliamentary polemics, and strident ideological warfare in the print media.[20] Patriotism embraced all the traditional arguments of the ideology of the nobility: the concern about the encroachment of the monarch on the nobility's traditional liberties and the need to defend the rights of Parliament against those of the crown. Its components also included an evocative but nebulous notion of love of country, the celebration of the great noblemen of Poland's past, and "a certain amount of xenophobia."[21] At the same time, patriotism was taking on new meanings and emphases. The modernization of the state and the desirability of popular involvement in politics, for example, were becoming more prominent themes. Allegiance to these commitments coexisted and competed with other allegiances and agendas such as the right of the Polish-Lithuanian Commonwealth to regulate its own affairs without interference from Russia, the expansion (or reduction) of the electoral franchise, the principle of equal justice for all, the enlargement of the army, the upgrading of female education, and a woman's right to select her conjugal partner—all of which were perceived by their advocates and supporters as patriotic concerns.[22] Because of the sheer variety of ways to define and test the patriotic stance (and of ways to cheat on a test), the term *patriotism* was often used in collocation with adjectives such as true, sincere, honest, and worthy. Scholarly attention in Polish studies has, however, bypassed some of the less obvious understandings of patriotism that were current in the past. It is time to bring them into sharper focus. In particular, an appreciation of the controversy over "true" and "false" patriotism, which caught fire in the late eighteenth century, is integral to a fuller understanding of subsequent disagreements about the meaning and practice of patriotism.

Prior to the Enlightenment, there was certainly no dearth of important Polish writings about patriotism in the Ciceronian sense of a compound of values and beliefs that prioritize the selfless commitment to the public good over the pursuit of self-interest.[23] But the final decades of the eighteenth century were awash with literary and nonliterary works on the subject of patriotism. The intense, even obsessive attention given to the question of patriotic obligations reflected the idea, germane to the political philosophy of the Enlightenment, that virtue and active citizenship are preconditions for liberty in a republic, understood as a form of government by elected representatives.[24] Montesquieu maintained, and it was commonly believed, that citizens of a republic must have the requisite virtue for ruling themselves and that civic virtue—the selfless dedication to the common good—in particular is essential to the health of a republican state.[25]

The new prominence given in Polish writings to the question of patriotism was also the consequence of a specific set of political circumstances in Poland-Lithuania. That is to say, alarmist concerns about a dangerous waning of civic virtue and a distinctively *political* public spirit, attempts to define the "true" patriot, and efforts to develop a new and effective language of patriotism intensified after a complex of hazardous policies, wayward plots, and political losses, as well as the schemes of neighboring powers, had brought unwelcome foreign influence into the state. For example, in an untitled essay published in the *Monitor* on 6 December 1769, Józef Epifani Minasowicz pins the label *false patriots* to those who serve their country ardently but imprudently and, in doing so, imperil it.[26] True patriotism, he suggests, requires prudent action. Public opinion immediately recognized that the essay was a veiled critique of the Confederacy of Bar, a revolt launched in the previous year in defense of the Catholic faith and nobility rights against both Russian hegemony and Stanisław August who was perceived as Catherine II's puppet. The publication of Minasowicz's essay provoked a rash of pamphlet literature on whether Bar confederates were indeed false patriots.

In the political rhetoric of the Polish Revolution, the distinction between "true" and "false" patriots played a major role again, but the basis for this distinction became broader, more complex, and somewhat opaque. The most apparent and substantive element of the new discourse of "true" patriotism was the endorsement of (or the opposition to): Stanisław August's policy of caution and moderation toward Russia, the independence of Parliament from the pro-Russian royal court, the abolition of a Russian-backed government known as the Permanent Council (1775–89), the pursuit of an alliance with Prussia, the modernizing reform of the state, and the restoration of hereditary succession to the throne. Hugo Kołłątaj's pamphlet, entitled *What Is Happening to Our Unhappy Homeland? A Dispatch Devoted to Truth and the Future (Co się też to dzieje z nieszczęśliwą ojczyzną naszą? Wiadomość poświęcona prawdzie i przyszłości*, 1790), is a case in point. A leading advocate of constitutional reform, Kołłątaj attributes false patriotism to those who have insisted that the Permanent Council be disbanded and an alliance with Russia terminated, but have offered no constructive vision of how to build up the strength of the state. In contrast, he equates the virtuous patriot with the good citizen—the loyal, responsible member of society who diligently cultivates his native talents and lives up to his obligations toward his compatriots. This may sound like a depoliticized concept of "true" patriotism—patriotism as social responsibility and disinterested public service; the guiding principle in this type of patriotism seems to be a kind of philanthropy. In fact, Kołłątaj's virtuous patriot is a political pragmatist: he always acts in the best interests of his country, which in some instances has necessitated accepting a degree of dependence on Russia. What ultimately counts is the concrete work he has been able to do in order to revitalize the state, even though the myopic and the ungrateful vilify him for having pursued accommodation with Russia.[27]

Debates on "true" and "false" patriotism burst forth again during the insurrection fought under Kościuszko's command in 1794. In the words of Józef Szczepaniec, the need to define the "true" patriot became "one of the central problems of the insurrection."[28] Kazimierz Hoszkiewicz's pamphlet, *What Does It Mean to Be a True Patriot? (Co to jest być prawdziwym patriotą?*), published anonymously in the summer of 1794, provides an especially illuminating case in point. Hoszkiewicz argues that it is necessary to distinguish between outright traitors and pseudopatriots. The former have received, or will receive, their deserts; for the latter—timid, cowardly, or ambivalent men who withdraw into armchair politics—there is still hope if they get some well-deserved chiding and a lot of passionate consciousness-raising. Rather than endlessly vilify Russia and complain about its aggression, pseudopatriots would do well to learn some empowering lessons from sincere patriots: that there is a fundamental connection between true patriotism and the cultivation of virtue; that there is an equally fundamental connection between virtue and liberty; and that true patriotism requires commitment to liberty in the sense of both political sovereignty and social equality. Echoing the title of Montesquieu's *The Spirit of the Laws* and adapting some of its key ideas, Hoszkiewicz concludes that "the spirit of true patriotism . . . wants citizens to be free of social prejudice, . . . reasonable in making new laws, and respectful of these laws"; at the same time, it wants citizens to be "ardently devoted to the defense of their country's territorial integrity."[29]

While polemical writings on patriotism such as Minasowicz's essay or Kołłątaj's and Hoszkiewicz's pamphlets have since faded into oblivion, Ignacy Krasicki's "Hymn to the Love of Country" ("Hymn do miłości ojczyzny," 1774) has achieved the status of the paradigmatic poem of modern Polish patriotism.[30] Written shortly after Poland-Lithuania had been forced to cede parts of its territory to Austria, Prussia, and Russia in 1772, "Hymn" famously seeks to quicken the pulse of patriotic desire by sanctifying love of one's *patria* on earth. To this end, Krasicki appropriates Christianity's glorification of the celestial *patria* and the self-renunciation in the service of Christ the King for a quasi-religious exaltation of self-sacrifice for an earthly *patria*. "Hymn" circulated widely well into the twentieth century, serving as the "bible" of Polish patriotism and inspiring numerous works along the way. Most prominent among them is Adam Mickiewicz's darkly, even bitterly ironic (and controversial) poem, "To a Polish Mother" ("Do matki Polki," 1831), in which death for the terrestrial *patria* becomes equivalent to *pro Deo (Christo) mori* but without any hope for resurrection.[31]

Diminished by the annexations of 1772, the Polish-Lithuanian Commonwealth was carved up again in 1793 and in 1795 "on the grounds that [it] had become a stronghold of revolutionary sentiment."[32] As a result of the partitions, the Commonwealth ceased to exist altogether as a state. Many Poles reacted to its dissolution with what Juliusz Nowak-Dłużewski has called "a national hysteria"—an anxiety that the loss of statehood would lead to the erasure of what was perceived as a distinct Polish cultural identity.[33] After 1795, then, the nurturing of strong patriotic bonds, understood as intense emotional ties to Poland and its cultural heritage, came to be seen as crucial. Thus it is not very surprising that during the era of foreign rule (1795–1918) patriotic sentiments were grist for paintings and prints, for popular songs, and for literature and the stage.

Some writers set forth a series of rules, with "thou shalt nots" outnumbering "thou shalts." Others professed love and admiration for their native land, while giving their characters such sententious opinions as that the Commonwealth was torn to pieces because selfish interest trumped a concern for the public good. Still others depicted an idealized Poland, a nostalgic world of community, stability, and certainty, in order to compare it with an unbearable real Poland under foreign rule, a shadow of its former self. But the most seductive contributions to the cultivation of patriotic bonds were made by writers who rediscovered and often exaggerated the heroism of past ages and the exploits and glories of ancestors.[34] While evoking the sheer exhilaration of combat and danger, they elevated their characters into exemplars of national virtue. The last decades of the nineteenth century saw this particular engagement with the past blossom into a sort of national passion, thanks to Henryk Sienkiewicz's best-selling novels such as *The Deluge* (*Potop*, 1886) that celebrates Poland's military triumph over Swedish invaders in 1660. The works of Sienkiewicz and other, less famous authors of historical fiction reflect a conviction that the memorialization of the ancestors' heroic struggles is arguably the most important incentive to patriotism because it fosters collective pride. Moreover, works such as *The Deluge* provided readers smarting from the humiliating loss of their state with compensatory strategies. That is to say, such works invited readers to cherish supposedly quintessential Polish virtues—in particular, valor, high honor, and a fierce love of freedom that only death can silence—and to revere Poland as a bearer of supreme moral worth, indeed a country above comparison. While one might charitably view such assumptions about Polish superiority as an unfortunate side effect of living under foreign rule, or, less charitably, as narcissistic self-absorption, this flattering self-image has helped cement the most common, quasi-religious understanding of "true" patriotism as heroic self-sacrifice for Poland's independence, in accordance with Cicero's maxim, "*Patria mihi vita mea carior est*" (Fatherland is dearer to me than my life).[35]

As Barbara Hodgdon notes, however, "No cultural practice ever achieves absolute 'coercive power' but, rather, constitutes a site of continual struggle in which the production and framing of meaning are constantly open to negotiation and renegotiation, including critique and resistance."[36] Given the context I have just outlined, it is unavoidable, therefore, to ask: What happens in patriotic drama when the "legitimate" passion of patriotism meets the "illegitimate" energy of transgressive nonconformity because a patriot does something unexpected that challenges assumptions about gender- and class-coded identities and roles? This question is central to my investigation. And it leads me back to the expansion of the conceptual terrain of patriotism in Poland during the high Enlightenment. The Enlightenment legacy is still felt today every time Józef Wybicki's "A Patriotic Song" ("Piosenka patriotyczna"), better known as the Polish national anthem, is performed.[37] But a closer look at a rich yet relatively untapped archive of Polish Enlightenment drama yields results that hardly fit long-standing convictions about the patriotic discourse in eighteenth-century Poland. To illustrate this point, I want to turn briefly to a now-forgotten play that commanded sufficient public interest to go into two editions in the late 1780s.

As L. P. Hartley has famously observed, "The past is a foreign country: they do things differently there."[38] If the past is another country where they do things differently, we may well ask whether we are doubly abroad if we visit, say, Poland of the late eighteenth century. In 1788, Stanisław Kublicki announced in the preface to his drama *The Defense of Trembowla, or the Manly Courage of Chrzanowska* (*Obrona Trembowli, czyli Męstwo Chrzanowskiej*) that the play's purpose was to teach both sexes due equality. Writing in an era obsessed with the cult of great men, he reminded his readers that familiarity with eminent figures from the past and a bond of identification with them are the foundations of the patriotic ethos. He also pointed out that a number of great Poles who distinguished themselves in the past were women. Why, then, he asked, does the history of Poland remain a story of male heroic endeavor?

The boldness of Kublicki's question is stunning. To read his play against historical accounts of its eponymous protagonist, Zofia Chrzanowska, also known as Anna Dorota Chrzanowska, is to begin to understand just how radical his ideas were for his time and place. Kublicki's Chrzanowska emerges as the heroine of the hour, but her patriotism has a transgressive edge. Sashaying through the play like a breath of fresh air, she demonstrates that femininity is a fungible category rather than an unalterable essence, determined by biology. Kublicki's Chrzanowska is a woman who invents herself, not freely, not fantastically, in a void, but in a concrete historical situation: the Ottoman attack on the Polish-Lithuanian Commonwealth in 1675. Kublicki's woman, then, is realistically ambiguous, a sex-gender amphibian, subject both to natural laws and the human production of meaning.[39] Or, to put these points slightly differently, his play makes it clear that gender, be it femininity or masculinity, is neither an inherent quality nor a fixed set of behaviors; rather, both femininity and masculinity are contextually variable. This brief example—a play by one of the most active members of the Four-Year Parliament—suggests that misogynistic satires, long considered the epitome of the Polish Enlightenment writers' stance on women, were hardly the last word on the subject in eighteenth-century Poland. The archives of the Polish Enlightenment, an era long assumed to be magisterially Augustan and masculine, are full of surprises, and almost any point of entry can be chosen to find a path to a hidden symbolic world that over time has been splashily obscured by a few mainstream texts.[40]

III.

To develop the argument of this book, I take as my cast of characters a group of militant patriots who in their various ways are "guilty" of transgressive behavior that contravenes the social or customary norms of their time and place. They pour their energies into selfless service for the common good but insist that their adherence to the "proper" exercise of patriotism would mean, ironically, that they have abdicated their responsibility as patriots. While their compatriots are determined to keep social fences in good order, transgressive patriots follow their own script, bold but risky. Scornful of certain normative values and critical of discriminatory practices, of exclusions and marginalizations, they defy the expectations shaped by ideas about gender, class, and authority. Their transgressions hold out a promise of a more egalitarian, or at least more inclusive, Poland, but they also give rise to anxieties that the norm-breakers and boundary-trespassers are playing with fire. What makes their refusal to bend the knee to custom particularly alarming is the context in which it occurs: the national effort to defend their country against aggression from abroad. While apologists for the existing social order claim that transgressive activism, with its potential for civil strife and anarchy, is as threatening to the war effort as opposition to the war itself, the protagonists of this study seize the opportunity presented by war to resist their compatriots' passion for social boundaries and status hierarchies, even though such nonconformity may result in discord and dissension.

My cast of characters, then, might look like the nonconformists who figure prominently in John Stuart Mill's classic treatise, *On Liberty* (1859).

The latest threat to liberty, in Mill's view, is the tyranny of the majority—not the subjection of a people by the authorities, but the subjection of the individual by society itself. Nonconformists earn his respect and admiration precisely because they resist the societal pressure toward conformity and, in doing so, constitute a new type of liberty: freedom from the tyrannical authority of custom and public opinion. In contrast to Mill's nonconformists, however, the protagonists of this book set the stakes higher. They engage in a struggle against "the tyranny of opinion" and "the despotism of custom" at moments of national crisis.[41] To paraphrase a well-known passage in *On Liberty*, they might have said: precisely because the tyranny of opinion is such as to make transgression of social or customary norms a reproach, it is desirable, in order to break through that tyranny, that men and women involved in patriotic endeavor should be transgressive.[42]

This is an appropriate moment to introduce the protagonists of my book by name: Zofia Chrzanowska, Emilia Plater, Tadeusz Kościuszko, and the apocryphal Queen Wanda. Given that their patriotic credentials have assured them membership in the Polish pantheon of illustrious men and women, it must seem odd, if not extravagant or preposterous, to regard these exemplary patriots as transgressive dissenters. And considering that Kościuszko has emerged as the very image of absolute integrity, an austere and saintly figure, his hands clasping a sword and his face raised to heaven in prayer, any attempt to cast this "incredibly decent" man—a leader "who disdained to wage total war [and] who hanged neither traitor king, bishop nor magnate"—as a transgressor may seem to border on sacrilege.[43] The first point to be made in this context is that the lives of Wanda, Chrzanowska, Plater, and Kościuszko, like the lives of iconic patriot-heroes and patriot-heroines elsewhere, are storytelling gold; hence they have been an indispensable resource for inventing national genealogies, "unique" national virtues, and usable patriotic traditions. Teachers, writers, artists, and politicians have drawn heavily on this resource to satisfy "the impulse to moralize reality," to divert attention not only from negative aspects of the past but also from modern problems that are not totally dissociated from earlier difficulties and dilemmas, to create an illusion of national unity, to anchor a supposedly shared "thought-world," to protect collective memory against the pressure of challenges and alternatives, to buttress national self-esteem, and, of course, to give substance to the elusive concept of patriotism.[44] It is less widely recognized today (and this is my second point) that the reception of Wanda, Chrzanowska, Plater, and Kościuszko in Polish culture has not been unproblematic; this reception is made up of a long history of idealization and adulation and an equally long history of unease, derision, vilification, denial, and silencing. At various stages of their reception history, they were perceived as dangerous in several senses of the word—dangerous to the existing social order and its asymmetries of power relationships, to gender norms, to sexual morality—precisely because they rebelliously defied their compatriots' notion of gender- and class-coded identities and responsibilities.

The bulk of this book is structured around plays that mine a rich quarry of historical myths about Wanda, Chrzanowska, Plater, and Kościuszko. Following Paul K. Longmore's helpful distinction, I use the term *historical myth* "not in the colloquial sense of a fantastic and 'untrue' story, but in the technical sense of a story which combines factual and fictional elements to express a people's fundamental aspirations and convictions."[45] Put simply, historical myth—how people tell the story of their past—is a construction. For it to stand, it must have a certain narrative consistency and its own internal logic, as well as external reference points to which others can relate. And it must be communicable. Shaped by assumptions about which aspects of the past are worth saving, whose experiences are worth telling about, and what needs to be left out, historical myth offers insight into the thoughtways of those who choose to believe it even when it is shown to be less than an accurate representation of past reality. It would be reductive, then, to equate historical myth with error, a result of ignorance, misunderstanding, or imperfect memory. Let me offer a few examples, all directly related to the subject of this book.

If one were to deny that "Warsaw, growing explosively under a *roi-philosophe*, was the great clearing-house and factory of new ideas" in Enlightenment Poland, or to doubt that the National Theatre, established in 1765, played an important role in that intellectual ferment, that would be merely an error.[46] But to suggest that of all the theatres operating in eighteenth-century Poland only the National reclaimed the stage for the forces of enlightenment and developed innovative strategies in a battle for hearts and minds is a myth. This myth has been widely accepted because it satisfies the assumptions that private theatricals by provincial dilettantes insulated themselves from the burning political issues of the day and that theatres maintained at aristocratic residences were merely status symbols and bastions of escapist pleasures. What is more, this myth supports the presupposition that the provinces were necessarily stagnant and unenlightened, in contrast to the vibrant cultural scene in Warsaw under the enlightened patronage of Stanisław August.[47]

It would be another error if one were to claim that the National Theatre failed to attract a diversified audience, or that it never became a hub of social life in the capital, a place where magnates rubbed shoulders with city merchants, titled ladies with tradesmen, and princes with prostitutes. However, it is a myth to suggest that what went on at the National amounted to social revolution because it drew in a socially heterogeneous audience.[48] Although patricians and plebeians came to the National as much for social interaction and display as to see a show, and although the social mix was a large part of the National's attraction, its seating system was class-based; the socially encoded hierarchy of box, pit, and gallery drew the line at fraternization between classes. The appearance of public togetherness disguised a reality in which a duchess dismissed a dressmaker and a petty noble rarely conversed with the grandees of Warsaw high society.

It would be yet another error if one were to say that the Polish Revolution ignored political aspirations of the urban middle class. But it is an exercise in mythmaking to assert that the Law on Royal Towns, passed by Parliament on 18 April 1791 and later incorporated into the Constitution of 3 May 1791 as Article III, "Towns and Townspeople" ("Miasta i mieszczanie"), invested towns with the right of representation in Parliament. Widely disseminated by scholarly studies and popular commentaries on the origins of modern Polish democracy, this myth ignores the tripartite separation of powers—legislature, judiciary, and executive—conventionally derived from Locke and Montesquieu; it also overlooks the restructuring of the Polish-Lithuanian government after the Four-Year Parliament abolished the Permanent Council on 19 January 1789. By bypassing these essential details, the myth is able to claim that there were urban representatives in the Four-Year Parliament and that they were allowed to vote on issues concerning towns and commerce.[49] In truth, the law of 18 April 1791 did not extend parliamentary representation to towns. Instead, it admitted urban delegates to three committees with administrative and judicial responsibilities and empowered those delegates to vote on municipal and commercial matters there. In the legislature, however, they could only testify during parliamentary hearings, without the right to vote.[50]

If one were to argue that the insurrection of 1794 lacked a broad social base, that would again be an error. But attributing Kościuszko's dazzling victory over a far stronger Russian force in the battle of Racławice on 4 April 1794 solely to an audacious attack by a motley crew of peasant irregulars is a myth.[51] After the Racławice triumph, inflated reports that they took to their scythes and charged into battle spread like wildfire, buoying up the nation's morale. Since then, the glamorous tale of their patriotism and bravado has given rise to the Racławice myth that apotheosizes cross-class consensus and solidarity in the arduous struggle for Poland's freedom. Arguably the most durable and generative of all myths surrounding the movement for Polish independence and statehood, the Racławice myth conveniently blots out social inequalities, while shifting attention to the reassuring notion of national unity.

Likewise, it would be just an error if one were to insist that Polish women merely wept and waited while their men fought unjust regimes. Although expected to be docile and submissive, Polish women assumed many responsibilities in the struggle for national liberation—as fund-raisers, nurses, couriers, gunrunners, and soldiers. However, to claim that the fight against foreign oppression broke down the barrier between separate "spheres"—a public sphere for men and a private one for women—in Poland or to suggest that with equal danger came equal opportunity is a myth.[52] In truth, women in Poland, as elsewhere, lived in a society where the concept of gender difference was firmly established and gender inequality was the norm.[53] Yet the fantasy that Polish men and women were equal partners at a time when other societies shielded women from the hurly-burly of public life and marginalized them in the apolitical private sphere has taken deep root in Polish culture because it conveniently casts Polish women as foil to their (supposedly) benighted sisters in the West.[54] The seductive appeal of this fantasy has not been lost on Polish women. Recalling her coming of age in Poland during the 1970s, Eva Stachniak remarks, "Our mothers kept reminding us that Polish women were always heroic, reliable partners of their men.... Our role was sacred.... We felt powerful, worshiped, and we never looked behind the myths."[55]

IV.

The plays featuring my cast of characters—Wanda, Chrzanowska, Plater, and Kościuszko—abound with transgressions, although one person's transgression could be another's patriotic imperative. For a woman to refuse marriage, dress like a man, and fight in a military campaign; for a serf to abandon work on his master's farm and join an insurgency; for a nobleman to dress like a peasant and put weapons in peasants' hands—each of these acts is subversive of social boundaries and status hierarchies. The ways in which the plays engage with curious and unusual phenomena and respond to the strains and stresses unleashed by behavior outside the social norm provide rich insights into cultural anxieties of the past.

Challenges to the principles of social conformity and harmony; fear of the abandonment of hierarchy, discipline, propriety, and gender-specific (or class-specific) clothes; discord and dissension—these are powerful themes. I doubt if it overstates the case to say that even today some of the plays I discuss seem outlandish, or at least unusual. It is not particularly surprising, however, that rebellious peasants and townsfolk, unruly wives, manly women, unmanly men, and male and female cross-dressers should hold such strong appeal to writers who supplied the drama of patriotism. Transgression of the customary boundaries of gender and class was threatening to a social order founded on clear-cut distinctions and precipitous hierarchies yet immensely appealing as a topic of dramatic representation. Patriotic plays without a thrilling, even *risqué*, deviation from cookie-cutter plots and characters would be dull to read or watch; therefore, their potential for attracting a broad audience would be diminished. The plays themselves, however, are surrounded by questions.

What are we to make of the fact that two Enlightenment plays, both published in 1788, celebrate the fiercely patriotic Chrzanowska, but only one of them introduces the character of her young son? Does this particular play adopt Chrzanowska's child as a means of expressing an exemplary, or a cautionary, message? Does it attempt, in other words, to persuade a skeptical public that a mother could also be a soldier in the patriotic cause, or, rather, does it confirm one's worst fears about mothers abandoning their families?

What did it mean when in 1791 a member of Parliament, depicted in historiography as a reactionary conservative, lashed out at the Warsaw National Theatre for neglecting plays he had seen performed in household theatres in the provinces?[56] Why were such apparently minor theatricals integral to his polemic? To be sure, they celebrated the virility of strong-willed and rebellious women, and they did so at a time when voicing utter abhorrence and disgust at "those feminine-masculine bastards, those hermaphrodites" was not uncommon.[57] The vitriol of this statement takes us close to the heart of the matter. One would have thought, then, that the legislator whose career is believed to have been steeped in the murkiest shades of conservatism would attack those audacious theatricals as a breeding ground of dangerous ideas that threatened to disrupt the binary gender order. Instead, he was ready to draw his sword on their behalf. How was this possible? Was his conservatism laced with a dash of libertinism?

What transformed an awkward neoclassical tragedy about Wanda, composed in prosodically indifferent verse by a little-known woman writer, into a dazzling theatrical success in 1807? And how can we explain the fact that neither the author nor her publisher capitalized on this success, so that the play appeared in print only 120 years later?

How can we account for the fact that the final-act death scene in a play that opened in 1897 to vast popular acclaim does not include a call for a priest to administer the last rites to a patriotic heroine who has risked her life for Poland? And considering that a significant number of patriotic plays in the late nineteenth and early twentieth centuries showed more and more women stepping forward as patriots and even shouldering arms, would it be fair to assume that the conceptual terrain of patriotism was becoming feminist-oriented?

Behind such questions lie stories and counterstories, anchored in the specificity of historical time and cultural space and shaped by contestations over the meaning and practice of patriotism, but the plays never tell us everything we want to know, especially if we ask questions such as these: What was the truth of the matter? What really happened? Whose account should be believed? Even if one could find a definitive answer to these questions, this book concentrates on a different kind of question, for example: How can an analysis of the dramaturgical and rhetorical strategies of thematizing Chrzanowska's "unfeminine" trespassing onto male territory in the two plays of 1788 help us reassess, through a gender-sensitive lens, the inconsistencies and dissonances in the cultural ideals of the Polish Enlightenment?

To recapitulate, this book is neither a history of the other traditions of Polish drama and theatre nor a series of sketches about the literary depiction of the struggle for Polish independence and statehood. Instead, it examines a body of dramatic writing that engages with the problem of patriotism, and in particular with the paradox of patriotism conflated with transgression and the association of this paradox with attempts to foster a more inclusive conception of citizenship. Some of the writers whose plays I discuss worked in mahogany. Others worked in plain pine. Still others worked in plain pine and stained it mahogany; sometimes it is difficult to tell. I propose to take the plays out of the range of one-word answers, setting aside "Are they any good?" in favor of "What are they doing in propounding their arguments?" (to invoke Wittgenstein's aphorism).

A few caveats are in order. First, this book does not deal with the question of the Polish literary canon. I purposefully avoid the entire debate on what constitutes literature that meets canonic measures of greatness. Instead, I retrieve and analyze a vast and fascinating trove of material that lies outside the current canon. Second, it would be extremely naive to take the sheer volume of plays on patriotic themes at face value. Constant exhortations to patriotism may mark a disparity between ideal and reality, or at least an anxiety that patriotism is fragile and fleeting. Third, it goes almost without saying that authors expressed in their plays what they were willing and able to say about patriotism but not necessarily what they believed; calibrating their response to meet the needs of a particular occasion, some kept their doubts to themselves. Fourth, while I do not wish to call attention to the truism that this book regards Wanda, Chrzanowska, Plater, and Kościuszko primarily as characters in plays and that dramatic character is always a construct in a fictional discourse, it is perhaps necessary to note that an investigation of textual representations of patriotic activism is not the same as documentation of actual patriotic behaviors. But I share Katharine Eisaman Maus's argument in her study of Shakespeare that even blatantly mythologized representations can reveal more than documentary realism about conflicts of everyday life.[58]

Accordingly, I shall be looking at how plays engage with competing, sometimes clashing views of patriotic idea(l)s, principles, and concerns, what purposes their engagement serves at specific historical moments, and what interests might speak through their dramatic structures and rhetorical figures. Each chapter approaches these questions from a distinctive perspective that is meant to interact in a thought-provoking but nontotalizing manner with the angle of vision in other chapters.

I should make one more caveat before proceeding further. Patriotism has a history, or more precisely, histories. However, this book does not offer a history of patriotism in Poland, nor does it pretend to cover all possible conceptions and manifestations of patriotism in Polish culture since the Enlightenment. My project is more modest. In order to produce a single book whose chapters may inform or underpin arguments about a complex interaction between patriotism and transgression, I concentrate on plays featuring the character of a militant patriot whose activism is linked, in often startling or provocative ways, to rebutting certain normative values. Yet I do not wish to suggest that by excluding particular writers I have thought them less worthy of attention. Inevitably, readers will be able to list other authors—whether Maria Konopnicka or Eliza Orzeszkowa, Stanisław Brzozowski or Witold Gombrowicz—whose accommodation or quarrel with patriotism was important to their work. However, those authors did not write plays about patriot-heroes and patriot-heroines who twinned patriotic commitment with transgressive nonconformity.

This book forgoes a sweeping, floodlighting approach in favor of a few carefully angled shafts of illumination. Those seeking detailed discussion of theatre practice, popular culture, national mythology, Catholic hagiography, and censorship policies in Poland during the period covered here are likely to be disappointed. These are all important areas of research, but a comprehensive coverage of them is beyond the scope of this study. So is a full-scale reappraisal of the tangled story of the Polish Enlightenment, in all its complexity, paradox, achievement, and lost opportunity; there can be no doubt that a tremendous amount of work is still to be done on Polish Enlightenment culture. I hope, however, that the suggestive potency of my case studies may provoke further research, exemplification, and debate.

V.

This exploration of some of the many questions, not all answerable, that are posed by the problem of patriotism begins in the combustible atmosphere of the 1780s. Throughout the decade, feelings ran high over Russian incursions into Polish-Lithuanian affairs, over the widely resented Permanent Council, and over what was perceived as Stanisław August's slavish submission to Catherine II and her ambassadors in Warsaw. The political scene was intensely polarized, a war zone of camps, strategic alliances, skirmishes, and maneuvers of encirclement and exclusion. The print market was flooded with polemical pamphlets that to modern tastes seem scurrilously abusive propaganda against political adversaries. Vitriolic accusations and insinuations, excoriating denunciations, and retaliatory salvos were freely exchanged, and slanderous insults were hurled back and forth. As expressions of suspicion grew more frenzied and strident, and warnings against rulers more anxious and defiant, polemicists began to concentrate on two issues they regarded as both extremely urgent and closely interrelated: how the state should be governed and how to distinguish "true" patriotism from "mistaken" versions of it. In this war of words, drama and theatre were enlisted to help shape and mobilize public opinion. In the political culture of the 1780s and the early 1790s, however, few genres proved as contentious as the drama of patriotism.

In chapter 1, "Controversies over 'True' and 'False' Patriotism, 1786–91," I use what is arguably the most acrimonious controversy in Polish Enlightenment culture—a fractious dispute, with direct and far-reaching political ramifications, over Niemcewicz's *The Return of the Deputy*—as a case study that sets the scene for the subsequent chapters. First performed at the National Theatre on 15 January 1791, the play immediately became the target of a vehement protest in Parliament. Flaming with outrage, Jan Suchorzewski, a Kalisz MP, accused Niemcewicz and the National Theatre of endorsing and facilitating a turn toward royal despotism and arbitrary power in the Polish-Lithuanian Republic. His rhetoric was of "tyranny," "shackles," "yoke," and "dire straits." The production of *The Return of the Deputy*, he fumed, is positive proof that the rule of law has taken a backseat to monarchist designs to curtail citizens' rights and liberties.

In scholarship on the Polish Revolution, Suchorzewski has been tarred and feathered as a counterrevolutionary who sailed through the reforms of the high Enlightenment serenely unreformed. He is typically portrayed as a voice of the conservative consensus that emerged in opposition to legislative innovations to modernize Poland-Lithuania—a backwoods bigot, scornful of enlightened aspirations and puritanically hostile to theatre, a deluded reactionary tethered to aristocratic power-holders, or a furiously fanatical, even mentally unstable firebrand whose passions were stoked by paranoid anxieties. His speech, accordingly, is dismissed as a demagogic harangue, designed with unabashed viciousness to thwart the reformers' worthy efforts to save the state from scandalous anarchy, while the broader controversy over *The Return of the Deputy* is depicted as a clash of theatre devotees and antitheatre moralists against the backdrop of a Manichean struggle between the party of enlightened progress and the party of anti-Enlightenment reaction. Given all the vitriol thrown at Suchorzewski, it comes as a surprise to find that his speech reveals one of the most avid, perceptive, and sophisticated advocates of theatre in late eighteenth-century Poland, a passionate playgoer who, like Niemcewicz, firmly believed in the power of the stage to do good in society. To understand Suchorzewski's polemic more fully, then, it is necessary to consider some neglected questions. What could have led a (purportedly) reactionary legislator to trump *The Return of the Deputy* with the gender-bending plays he saw in provincial theatres: Kniaźnin's *The Spartan Mother* and Józef Wybicki's *The Polish Woman* (*Polka,* 1788)? What exactly made them at once so riveting and so seminal for him?

The first part of this chapter is devoted to unraveling the controversy over *The Return of the Deputy*—a dispute in which those on both sides claimed to be true patriots and regarded their adversaries as pseudopatriots on the Russian payroll. My approach is to situate Suchorzewski's protest not only in the context of political debates but also within eighteenth-century theories of acting and the eighteenth-century conception of the sympathetic imagination. I want to argue that his polemic, for all of its rhetorical vehemence, is a sensitive exposition of problems such as the near magical power ascribed to theatrical performance by the eighteenth-century cultural paradigm or, conversely, the potential waywardness of reception, inherent in the concept of the patriotic cultivation of the individual through aesthetic pleasure; his polemic is also a clear-sighted articulation of a series of propositions about stage practice, patriotic drama, and an ethic of spectatorship. The second part of the chapter attends to *The Spartan Mother* and *The Return of the Deputy* to uncover and analyze some of the neglected rhetorical labor of the Polish Enlightenment discourse about gender. I compare the plays' cultural investment in mothers and restore to view what is perhaps *the* distinctive hallmark of the patriotic agenda in these dramas: their resourceful engagement with the notion of allegedly natural gender identities and roles and, crucially, with ideas about gender relations.[59] In this chapter, then, I show that Suchorzewski's argument, backed up by his extensive theatre-going experience, casts in a more hybrid light the relationship of drama and theatre to political ideas and political action in late eighteenth-century Poland; I also develop a new interpretive framework for understanding how gender was inscribed in the meaning and practice of patriotism in Polish Enlightenment culture.

In chapter 2, "Poland Unmanned? Zofia Chrzanowska," I return to the neglected rhetoric of the Polish Enlightenment discourse about gender.

Here, my discussion centers on two 1788 plays about the patriot-heroine who distinguished herself during the Ottoman attack on the Commonwealth of Poland-Lithuania in 1675: Wybicki's *The Polish Woman* and Kublicki's *The Defense of Trembowla*. Written at a time when the male constituted the universal standard, and the female, viewed as primarily a sexual being, was construed as a sexual subset of the universal human, *The Polish Woman* and *The Defense of Trembowla* (like *The Spartan Mother* and *The Return of the Deputy*) belong to the broader Enlightenment debate about sexual difference, the sex-specific character traits of man and woman, the place and function of women in society, and the doctrine of sexual complementarity. In order to examine *The Polish Woman* and *The Defense of Trembowla* without losing sight of local particulars, I begin by contextualizing them within the fraught and increasingly toxic Polish politics of the 1780s, but my main concern is to investigate how and to what ends the two plays engage with the disconcerting question of gender transgression by a female patriot who is loyal and dutiful, yet dismissive of the strictures on women's behavior and scornful of the sex-determined split in the allocation of tasks to be performed by the man and the woman. She thus risks being stigmatized and denigrated (or ridiculed) as a descendant of the Amazons, that mythological tribe of "unnaturally" strong females existing outside male control.

The Polish Woman and *The Defense of Trembowla* present a puzzling surprise to the modern reader in that they are quite innovative in their approach to the problem of gendered dichotomies. Not only do they insist that "true" patriotism is not necessarily gendered masculine, and not only do they subvert the expected dynamics of male-female relations by challenging the social model of woman subordinated to and dependent on man, but they also contradict the prevailing view of women as complementary to men. Most crucially, both plays pivot on the idea that gender identities do not spring fully formed from the biological difference between the sexes—from the fact that some human beings produce semen and other human beings do not. In these plays, the sharp antithesis that unrealistic and coercive ideals of femininity and masculinity have drawn between men and women is shown to be untenable. Altogether it is an extraordinary vision, especially when compared with other contemporary views in Poland. What are we to make of this radical skepticism about the "natural" gender order? Are Wybicki and Kublicki, perhaps, Polish feminism's forgotten founding fathers in the attic?

In chapter 3, "Is There Transgression in This Text? Wanda, Queen of Poland," I consider the particularly heavy burden borne by Polish neoclassical tragedy as the genre responsible for reenvisioning the nation's past to counter a crisis of the collective identity and produce a strong sense of pride in distinctive Polishness during the decades immediately following the fall of Poland-Lithuania. In particular, I examine the complex and perplexing dynamics in Tekla Łubieńska's *Wanda, Queen of Poland* (*Wanda, królowa polska*, 1807) that represents the first thoroughgoing attempt in Polish literature to revise the inherited narrative about the apocryphal queen. According to legend, Wanda committed suicide to avoid compromising her (and her subjects') Polishness by marriage to Poland's enemy, a German prince. In Łubieńska's bold rewriting of the legend, not only is Wanda in love with the prince, but her subjects urge the queen to marry him in order to secure the stability of the young Polish state. As in the traditional story, however, Wanda takes her own life. This raises several questions: Why does Łubieńska's Wanda reject the institution of marriage? Why is she adamant in her refusal of the hereditary system of her realm? Why is she unconcerned about bearing heirs to the throne to ensure dynastic continuity? Why is death infinitely preferable to her, even though her suicide endangers the Polish kingdom? To address these questions, as well as the broader issue of the interaction between, on the one hand, the seemingly self-evident idea of patriotic allegiance and commitment and, on the other, the problem of gender, I discuss *Wanda, Queen of Poland* against another neoclassical tragedy, *Wanda* (1826), by Łubieńska's contemporary, Franciszek Wężyk.

Chapter 4, "No More Separate Spheres? Emilia Plater," is a riposte to the preceding two chapters. It extends my investigation of the tangled knots in the modern history of patriotism and gender by bringing into sharper focus what is arguably the most transgressive challenge to gender boundaries: female soldiering. To expand our understanding of the strategies used by patriotic drama to subvert (or support) binary oppositions that conceal hierarchies, I turn to plays about Plater, the most significant Amazonian heroine in Polish history, and about Plater-inspired female gender benders. The works considered here range from Wanda Brzeska's and Ludwik Stolarzewicz's one-act plays for women's schools to Zygmunt Nowakowski's *A Sprig of Rosemary* (*Gałązka rozmarynu*, 1938), ranked among the fifteen best dramas written in Polish.[60] Completed between the 1890s and the

1930s, the plays coincided with the women's rights movement and particularly the issue of suffrage. In this context, the pivotal question is: Do the plays capitalize on the Plater precedent to confront gender stereotypes and their constraining effect, to reevaluate rigid gender categories and disrupt a firmly established gender polarity, to envision a radical expansion of women's roles and activities, and possibly even to argue in support of the basic equality of men and women?

The starting point for my discussion is that the historical Plater, a young woman who took up arms to defend her country during the uprising of 1830, never got away with her gender insubordination—her soldiering, her male attire, her cropped hair. Since the 1830s, her shockingly transgressive disregard for gender norms has been the subject of scabrous tales, ridiculing her patriotic enthusiasm as a kind of displaced eroticism at best and at worst as a cover for promiscuity. In scholarship, commentators continue to harbor mixed feelings about Plater, voicing both a recurrent reservation about her patriotic motivation and a recurrent suspicion of her actual role in the uprising. Such responses demonstrate just how threatening Plater's gender-bending and, more broadly, women's "deviations" from their normative (i.e., noncombatant) patriotic script have been to the binary gender order with its equation of the front line, unflinching courage, and derring-do with masculinity, and support services with femininity. The idea of women in combat forces has been difficult to accept precisely because it draws attention to the constructed nature of masculinity and femininity. And yet it is not unusual for patriotic dramas to pay glowing tribute to Plater and Plater-inspired heroines. Would it be accurate to assume, then, that Plater-themed plays attempt to recruit the audience to new ideas and practices?

A surface reading suggests that the plays are deeply invested in the imbricated logic of gender-blind patriotic duty and the boundary-crossing militancy to which it leads in the teeth of challenges such as foreign invasion and domination. As a result, the plays support one of the fundamental ideas in Polish culture: the myth that the women's participation in the struggle for Poland's freedom involved a fairly unproblematic loosening of the gender order. A closer examination reveals that the issue is not so simple. As I show in this chapter, anxiety over gender transgression is seldom where one expects to find it. A woman abandoning her family and taking up arms, which would seem to be one of the worst transgressions of any kind, is not necessarily considered transgressive, especially when her military service is only a desperate last resort to repel an attack from abroad. Her zeal may convert her compatriots' anxiety into awed respect, and her soldierly or "masculine" qualities may be downplayed in favor of her "feminine" ability to sacrifice her private concerns, interests, and aspirations to the needs of her besieged homeland. By contrast, suspicion that a female combatant is a designing impostor and an aggressive interloper who refuses to stay in the zone of acceptability and instead invades the province of men to assert her own autonomy and agency mobilizes playwrights to deploy elaborate maneuvers in order to deal with this particular challenge to gender boundaries.

In chapter 5, "Apocalypse Now? Tadeusz Kościuszko," I move to an eclectic group of nineteenth-century plays about Poland's most widely celebrated patriot-hero to examine, from yet another perspective, ambivalences and anxieties clustered around the issue of "improper" patriotic activism. A veteran of the American Revolution, Kościuszko, along with Jeremy Bentham, James Madison, Thomas Paine, and George Washington, was among the eighteen eminent foreigners made honorary French citizens by the National Assembly of France in 1792 for their courage to defend liberty. Two years later, this cosmopolitan citizen of the world, as many of his contemporaries perceived him, assumed command of an insurrection to free Poland from foreign oversight. Since then, few men in Polish history have been more glorified than Kościuszko and few events more aggrandized than the battle at Racławice in which he defeated a superior enemy force. Exalted as an avatar of unassailable integrity and deeply felt patriotism, the cosmopolitan Kościuszko has metamorphosed into a hero who is believed to be echt Polish.

Unlike Plater's, Kościuszko's position in the Polish pantheon, along with his deposit account in the national memory, is secure rather than suspect. His biography serves as an instructive tale of patriotic excellence and moral strength, and his career in the American Revolution is a touchstone of Polish and Polish American pride. Kościuszko's admirers, for example, are apt to invoke Thomas Jefferson's opinion: "General Kosciusko [sic] . . . is as pure a son of liberty, as I have ever known, and of that liberty which is to go to all, and not to the few or the rich alone."[61] And few commentators doubt that his victory at Racławice, commonly attributed to the bravery of peasant forces, was a foundational event in the history of democracy in Poland. However, Kościuszko's celebrity status as the Polish national hero par excellence and his posthumous role as a *lieu de mémoire* (memory-place) obscure the fact that his achievements have been fiercely contested from the very beginning.⁶² In particular, his attempts to tackle social inequality proved more a liability than an asset to the Polish discourse of patriotism because many viewed his commitment to democratic principles, provocatively highlighted by his cross-cultural and cross-class transvestism, as an open invitation to revolutionary violence.⁶³

This chapter sets out to investigate how and to what ends the Polish discourse of patriotism has attempted, through the genre of drama, to come to terms with its most illustrious male transgressor. In my readings of plays, ranging from the first Polish drama about Kościuszko, *Kościuszko's First Love* (*Pierwsza miłość Kościuszki*, 1820), written by Konstanty Majeranowski, an impresario of Romanticism in Poland, to Anczyc's perennially popular *Kościuszko at Racławice*, I examine their dramaturgical and rhetorical labor to accommodate Kościuszko's transgression of social boundaries and status hierarchies into "true" patriotism. I argue that while the plays inevitably rework historical material to establish a sturdy template for the man-myth Kościuszko who could stand in for Poles in all their heterogeneity, they do not neutralize every radical element of Kościuszko's life story to make him a marble hero. On the contrary, they maintain the oppositional and libertarian dimensions of patriotism, locating "genuine" patriotic sentiments with the defense of rights rather than privileges. What these rights are, however, is a matter of dispute. Should the political imperative of Poland's independence come before the challenge of social justice? Should they be prioritized at all? Is this possible? It is tempting to conclude that with *Kościuszko at Racławice* Anczyc finally succeeded in appropriating Kościuszko for a seductively romanticized narrative about cross-class reconciliation and solidarity. It is tempting to conclude, moreover, that it took a writer of Stanisław Wyspiański's caliber to bring back to light, in *The Wedding* (*Wesele*, 1901), those aspects of the Kościuszko story that threatened to undermine the idealized narrative. These conclusions are generally correct, if we limit our purview to highbrow drama. The picture looks quite different, if middlebrow drama is taken into account. Accordingly, I end this chapter with a reading of Adam Bełcikowski's *The Warsaw Street-Seller* (*Przekupka warszawska*, 1897), one of the most successful (and most enigmatic) plays in pre-1918 Poland.

In chapter 6, "Controversies over 'True' and 'False' Patriotism, 1941–89," I return to the problem I raised in the first chapter: the entanglement of patriotic drama in culture wars at a time when patriotic allegiance becomes a major ideological battleground. Here, I use as my case studies three plays and a political pageant. Each of them takes up the question of patriotic sentiments, obligations, and commitments to address preoccupations in society at large with "true" patriotism and "faux" versions of it at a critical juncture of post-1939 Polish history. Pivotal to their dramaturgical and rhetorical projects is the patriotism/transgression nexus of the Kościuszko story.

I begin with a play by a writer who remains beyond the pale of Polish literary studies because she is commonly regarded as a traitor to her native soil, a henchwoman to Soviet oppressors, and an advocate of the subservience of literature to the class struggle: Wanda Wasilewska's *Bartosz Głowacki* (1941). When the Soviet Union invaded Poland's eastern borderlands in 1939 and Sovietization was imposed by terror on the local population, Wasilewska welcomed invaders as liberators. A strong believer in Soviet communism and a leading supplier of propaganda for the Soviet regime, she gained the trust of the authorities and personal access to Stalin and soon rose to a position of power and influence in Soviet officialdom. And yet, intriguingly, the dramaturgical and rhetorical strategies of the play about Głowacki, the foremost peasant soldier in Kościuszko's army, contradict her engagement in the Soviet propaganda campaign to promote the proletarian struggle for a revolutionary transformation of society. One would have thought that the last thing one would find in *Bartosz Głowacki* would be a certain skepticism about class-struggle sloganeering and, in particular, some cautious tiptoeing around the idea of fraternal internationalism, but one would be wrong. To make sense of this puzzling drama, first performed by a Polish theatre company in Soviet-occupied Lwów in 1941, I include a discussion of the actors' boldly inquisitive responses and audacious, even risky protests during the rehearsal process.

I then turn to Otwinowski's *Easter*, a play about the Warsaw ghetto uprising of 1943. First performed in 1946 in response to the postwar hostilities against Holocaust survivors and the persistence of anti-Jewish sentiment, *Easter* set off a firestorm. I argue that the controversy merits a closer investigation not only for its historical interest but also for its relevance to a more nuanced understanding of how patriotism becomes tangled in contradictions. I argue, moreover, that to arrive at a more comprehensive understanding of Otwinowski's distinctive contribution to postwar debates about patriotism and antisemitism, it is necessary to recover neglected subtexts of *Easter:* its oddly incongruous conflation of the Jewish uprising of 1943 with the Polish insurrection of 1794 and its baffling concern with the story of John à Lasco, a Polish-born Protestant theologian and a major figure in the history of Reformed, Presbyterian, and Puritan ecclesiologies, who became a minister in a Protestant church in London during the reign of Edward VI, son of Henry VIII.

I conclude chapter 6 with an analysis of two Kościuszko-themed events performed during the momentous 1988–89 season that saw an electoral triumph of Solidarity and the end of communist rule: the production of Bojarska's *The Polish Lesson,* arguably the most compelling drama about Kościuszko, and Wałęsa's Racławice extravaganza-cum-masquerade that played a role in determining what kind of Poland would emerge from the turmoil of the 1980s. The most obvious attraction of the play and the pageant is an attempt to reclaim the man-myth Kościuszko as a viable patriotic ideal, even though he seemed to have become a passé figure, irrelevant to the political struggle of the 1980s. It is my argument, however, that while the play and the pageant draw on the Kościuszko story that has been central to the discourse of patriotism in modern Polish culture, they invite audiences to consider afresh the allegiances and political visions that patriotism has been enlisted to defend and support. In particular, I argue that the iconoclastic *Polish Lesson,* never published and now forgotten, shows Bojarska to be one of the relatively few Polish playwrights who have attempted to extend the range of how patriotism is understood by their contemporaries.

These are the chapters, the ideas, and the archives (in the double sense of the term *archive*) that constitute this volume. Moving beyond a conventional study of dramatic literature, this book turns to plays and other materials to ask larger questions about cultural practice, including disputes over class and gender boundaries and controversies over patriotic attachments and obligations. What concerns me here in particular is a fascinating and occasionally outrageous body of writing that belongs to what I have called the other traditions of Polish drama and theatre. It would be inaccurate to say that no one has opened the pages of these plays to find out what they have to offer. It is true, however, that they have typically been dismissed as irrelevant to the history of Polish culture. At best, they have been reduced to texts of merely antiquarian interest. I am unrepentant in believing that the attempt to gain acquaintance with the less familiar traditions of Polish drama and theatre is an undertaking of great interest to cultural studies. One reason is simply that, as I hope to illustrate, this body of work is so rich and full of surprises that it complicates some long-standing and widely held assumptions about Polish culture. A further reason is that by continuing to disregard little-known materials, we risk that our understanding of the past will be impoverished and distorted. As always, much depends on what we think cultural history should be for, and on what we want it to do.

Part of my project in what follows, then, is to recover previously lost or otherwise ignored works by writers such as Łubieńska, Otwinowski, and Bojarska, to consider their vision of the perceptions, attitudes, interests, concerns, expectations, sensitivities, and escapist fantasies of the public, and to examine the ways in which these works grapple with cultural ambiguities, inconsistencies, and contradictions within historically specific epistemologies. But my underlying concern is to allow the voices of the past to rant and rave and to whisper and beckon. Sometimes the cacophony is excessive, but at other times the silence is intolerable. I want to capture and calibrate both historical noise and historical silence. In doing so, I hope to provide fresh insights into currents of cultural dissent that have been largely untouched by critical and theoretical methods and thus remain insufficiently understood. Surrendering this textual territory to the forces of cultural amnesia allows them far too easy a victory.

1   Controversies over "True" and "False" Patriotism, 1786–91

I.

ONE COLD MORNING IN February 1793, Warsaw residents rose from their beds to find that someone or several someones had posted a curious playbill on their buildings during the night. The playbill announced a thrilling attraction—part musical entertainment, part ballet, part blood-curdling spectacle:

> Benefit of Mr. Szczęsny Potocki!
> Next Friday
> Will be performed a comedy never seen since 1775!
> By permission of Her Majesty Targowica Confederacy,
> The Russian, Prussian, and Austrian companies
> Are proud to present
> An original comedy in three acts entitled
> THE PARTITION OF POLAND.
> Written by W. Frederick.
> A trio,
> FREEDOM, EQUALITY, INDEPENDENCE,
> Will be sung before act 1.
> Act 2 will feature a duetto,
> MORE DISCORD THAN CONCORD,

> To which will be added
> A ballet between acts 2 and 3, entitled
> SCHOOL FOR MADMEN,
> With solo dancing by Mr. Suchorzewski,
> Accompanied by cannon fire.
> Brilliant illumination consisting of towns and villages ablaze.[1]

This bill of fare for a fine evening's entertainment provides a remarkable example of political satire in late eighteenth-century Poland, much of it genuinely fascinating and exhilarating even today. The squib does not spare the neighbors of the Polish-Lithuanian Commonwealth who recently negotiated a new partition of its territory, but a principal target of the playbill's sarcasm and scorn is Stanisław Szczęsny Potocki, a wealthy aristocrat who maneuvered Poland-Lithuania into catastrophe. In the spring of 1792, Szczęsny Potocki met in St. Petersburg with a group of Poles. Some of them were magnates, others came from the lesser gentry, but all of them were outraged at the reformist legislation of the Revolutionary Parliament in Warsaw.[2] It was their hope that Catherine II would help them abolish the Polish reforms and in particular the Constitution of 3 May 1791 that made the revamping of the Commonwealth's system of government possible. The Constitution, they claimed, was not only a usurpation that destroyed liberty in their country but also a threat to all of Europe because it enshrined "the fatal example set in Paris."[3]

Catherine II concurred. On 27 April 1792, while still in St. Petersburg, Szczęsny Potocki and his colleagues signed a Russian-approved Act of Confederacy, postdated to 14 May and ostensibly drawn up in the town of Targowica; hence their plot has come to be known as the Targowica Confederacy.[4] In the morning of 18 May, a Russian ambassador in Warsaw made public an official statement by Catherine II. In it, she announced that she dispatched her troops to the Commonwealth on "a friendly mission," to help the true sons of the Polish soil—sincere patriots "burning with a pure and noble desire to save their homeland"—to protect the country against "the illicit power in Warsaw."[5] Later that day, two Russian armies, totaling 98,000 men, entered Poland-Lithuania. By late May, a full-scale war was under way. King Stanisław August, who over the past year "effectively became the head of the majority political party, unofficially known as the 'patriots,'" now found it increasingly difficult to weigh principle against expediency.⁶ Torn between conflicting emotions and interests, he bent to Catherine II's demand that he order a cease-fire and accede to the Targowica Confederacy.⁷ When the guns fell silent on 24 July, the triumphant leaders of the Confederacy assumed control of the country.

In coordinating the Targowica conspiracy, Szczęsny Potocki played a dangerous game that always had the potential to backfire. And, in fact, it did. The Targowica leaders soon found that Russian aid to dismantle the Polish reforms was bought for a very high price indeed. In the Act of Confederacy of 27 April, they bartered the sovereignty of the Commonwealth for the restoration of the pre-1788 status quo under Russian protection, but they insisted on preserving the territorial integrity of the state. Thus it came to them as a shock to learn that Catherine II had secretly initiated the second partition of Poland-Lithuania. And although Austria held back, King Frederick William II of Prussia welcomed the opportunity to expand his territory. On 16 January 1793, Prussian troops marched into the Commonwealth. Seven days later, Prussia and Russia signed the treaty of the second partition.⁸

The playbill that the residents of Warsaw saw on that bitter February day in 1793 singles out three individuals from the dozens of political actors involved in the larger "theatre" of the Targowica plot and the second partition. Two of them—"W. Frederick" (i.e., Frederick William II) and Szczęsny Potocki—are familiar figures to those interested in Central European history of the period. But who was Jan Suchorzewski, and what did he do to compel the attention of the anonymous author or authors of the scathing squib? Why was his involvement in the Targowica conspiracy considered so singularly offensive that the author (or authors) chose to point an accusing finger at him rather than, say, Franciszek Ksawery Branicki, Catherine II's son-in-law and one of the architects of the Targowica Confederacy, or Szymon Kossakowski, another top figure in the Targowica leadership and a longtime agent of the Russian court who took money from Russia to subsidize his high living? Why did Suchorzewski come in for so much mockery and contempt?

To address these and other questions, this chapter focuses on a brief but congested period, perhaps the most baffling and controversial moment in the cultural history of eighteenth-century Poland, between the closing of the *Monitor*, a leading popularizer of Enlightenment ideas, on 31 December 1785, and Suchorzewski's speech to Parliament on 18 January 1791 to demand action against what he perceived as a flagrant miscarriage of the National

Theatre's mission as a public institution and a scandalous misuse of its resources to facilitate a turn toward tyranny in the Polish-Lithuanian Republic.[9] The dramatis personae in this chapter are Suchorzewski, the protagonist; Julian Ursyn Niemcewicz, his antagonist; and behind them, Franciszek Dionizy Kniaźnin, the author of a play Suchorzewski saw in the provinces.

My project here is in part to unravel a controversy over Niemcewicz's *The Return of the Deputy*, an acrimonious dispute in which those on both sides claimed to be true patriots and viewed their opponents as false patriots—malcontents, demagogues, office-seekers, or paid Russian agents. The play at the center of this dispute scarcely seems capable of becoming such a contentious text since it draws on the staples of patriotic literature, chief among them the contrast between generous love of country and egregious self-interest, the damage caused to the country by disunity and disloyalty, and the summons to the present generation to show themselves worthy of their patriotic ancestors. And yet this drama, masquerading under an innocuous title, *The Son's Homecoming* (*Powrót syna do domu*), exploded with the force of a land mine on the political scene when it premiered at the National Theatre on 15 January 1791.[10] Three days later, in a speech delivered in his forthright style (or with a hysterical fury, as his critics would have us believe), Suchorzewski told Parliament that the National Theatre was a front for secret intrigues and shady dealings to impede liberty in Poland-Lithuania.

I first gather what seems most pertinent from the historical record, reconstruct Suchorzewski's argumentation, and relate it to the major political debates of the period (sections II and III). My point is not only to provide a backdrop for the following sections but also to place Suchorzewski's speech in its original context in order to understand better his objections. I then suggest an analytical approach to open up new perspectives on his polemic (section IV). To flesh out my analysis, I take a fresh look at a play that Suchorzewski adduced as his main counterexample: Kniaźnin's *The Spartan Mother* (section V). I conclude with a new reading of *The Return of the Deputy*, widely regarded as the pivotal, and indeed paradigmatic, drama of the Polish Enlightenment (section VI). However, the key question here is not whether one of the plays is better than the other, but what the plays and their reception can tell us about the expectations and anxieties surrounding patriotism, the gender order, and the agency of drama and theatre at the time of their original productions.

In scholarship, Suchorzewski, a member of the Four-Year Parliament, has been passed over in silence or scorn. To some, he has been a grotesque figure, a man full of puff and pomposity, a vain, posturing sort who took on a ridiculous cast when he tried to play the role of an honest and dedicated patriot for which he was ill suited. His political ideas were embarrassingly premodern, his blowsy histrionics in Parliament appalling, his undentable self-assurance in his unique ability to serve his country preposterous.[11] Others have cast him as a villain in a morality play entitled *The Spirit of Enlightenment against the Spirit of Obscurantist Reaction.*[12] In it, he has been called many names, in ascending order of dangerousness: humorless, voluble, shrill, blatantly publicity-seeking, thin-skinned, given to intemperate rants, prone to "hysterical outbursts," "psychologically unbalanced," obsessively suspicious, driven by delusions of persecution, fervently doctrinal, furiously fanatical, vengeful, corrupt, devious, and, worst of all, congenitally evil.[13] Disdainful of what they see as his inferior intellect, aversion to new ideas, and gruff, provincial manners, commentators have pigeonholed Suchorzewski as a reactionary from the rural backwater who detested theatre as well as enlightened aspirations; therefore he responded with unmitigated outrage to the worthy efforts of the National Theatre, a stock company under the talented leadership of the actor-playwright Wojciech Bogusławski, to maximize public support for the modernization of the state. Commentators have concluded that Suchorzewski's polemic, motivated by treasonable political schemes, antitheatrical prejudice, and personal pique, is a peculiarly malicious and virulent example of partisan rhetoric embroiled in a struggle for power. According to this logic, the incident of 18 January 1791 must be seen as a dangerous filibuster by the modernizing reformers' most implacable opponent who was determined at all costs to spread some toxic publicity in order to block their legislative initiatives. In short, Suchorzewski's protest has been said to epitomize deplorable factionalism and ideological intransigence that threatened to turn the Four-Year Parliament into a theatre of empty gestures, while his tenacious refusal to appreciate the sophisticated marvels of the National Theatre has been interpreted as a symptom of his obtuseness, insensitivity, or aesthetic mulishness.

Discussions of Suchorzewski's parliamentary career are so suggestive that it is not difficult to feel confident that backward people had no right to stand in the way of progress. But it would be disingenuous not to acknowledge some complications. Admittedly, Suchorzewski's speech of 18 January 1791 seems to echo the antitheatrical argument of Rousseau's *Letter to M. d'Alembert* (*Lettre à M. d'Alembert*, 1758): dramatic representation is limited to the established pleasures of an audience; therefore, it imprisons us in the chains of our depravity by indulging our vanity. At the same time, however, Suchorzewski's speech is marked from beginning to end by a fascination with the experience of acting, which suggests his deep and passionate involvement with theatre. His account is also notable for illustrating the argument with references to theatrical productions outside Warsaw; besides invoking Kniaźnin's *The Spartan Mother*, he considers Józef Wybicki's *The Polish Woman*. Moreover, his polemic, while strongly rooted in a political struggle, reveals a keen interest in new theories of acting and presents a serious engagement with central problems of theatre production and cultural reception, ranging from the act of signifying dramatic character to an ethic of spectatorship. However, his extensive theatre-going experience, his enchantment with the magic of theatre, and his pro-theatre arguments have gone entirely unremarked in scholarly commentary.

While Suchorzewski is all too easily depicted in scholarship as retrogressive and censorious, and his protest on 18 January 1791 is reduced to his partisanship on behalf of the conservative opposition to enlightened progress, I suggest that such an approach underestimates the breadth of his interests and erudition. I want to move away from cartoonish accounts of what happened in Parliament on that day and to argue that Suchorzewski's speech deserves to be read closely from the first sentence to the last. I submit that the incident of 18 January 1791 is an exceedingly interesting one, complicating as it does some of the most cherished assumptions about the public sphere of Enlightenment Poland and the role of drama and theatre in that sphere. Furthermore, I submit that the dispute over *The Return of the Deputy* was not only a battle between political factions to determine whose vision of Poland would prevail and by what means, but that it was also a controversy over competing concepts of "true" patriotism and over what could be considered an ethical and effective method for cultivating patriotic sentiments through plays and theatrical performances. I hope to show that Suchorzewski's richly layered speech reflects on the role of theatre—any theatre—in creating and manipulating the public and asks, provocatively, whether the very idea of the public might not be undermined by the harnessing of theatre to the demands of political agendas. Thus, his speech provides rich material for a study of the ever-fragile connections between politics, including political philosophy, and theatre and drama at a critical point in history.

To recapitulate, this chapter opens a window on the turbulent world of Polish culture and politics in the closing decades of the eighteenth century. It begins in Parliament three days after the premiere of *The Return of the Deputy* at the Warsaw National Theatre, detours through the realm of political ideas, agendas, and dissensions, spills over into the area of competing truths in scholarship on Enlightenment Poland, makes a stop at a household theatre in Puławy, about seventy miles south of Warsaw, to consider Kniaźnin's experiment in questioning the ideology of sexual character or a sex-specific, quintessential nature of man and woman, and returns to Niemcewicz's now-classic play to examine its discourse about gender. Along the way, it explores the "shadow" side of the enlightened world of Niemcewicz and the National Theatre, grapples with the ambivalent cultural investment in mothers, resists the temptation to apply anachronistic standards to an eighteenth-century political culture, and raises questions about the criteria of "credible report" and "objective interpretation" and perhaps also about the progress of the Enlightenment in Poland. The centerpiece of this chapter is a story that embroiled the center and the periphery, the mainstream and the marginal, engaging both the National Theatre and what we might now regard as the alternative theatre. It is a story that linked concerns of playwrights and politicians, local worthies and central magistrates, professional actors and those outside the theatrical profession, as well as the intersecting spheres of men and women. In attempting to unravel this convoluted story, I hope to recapture a world we have forgotten and to recover aspects of it we never knew.

II.

The story starts simply enough on Tuesday, 18 January 1791, with a speech to Parliament on the subject of the National Theatre and its production of Niemcewicz's *The Return of the Deputy*. At first glance, the play does not seem controversial. The cast features familiar character types: the bigoted conservative (who also happens to be a tyrannical and miserly father), the enlightened *raisonneur*, the prudent matron, the handsome gentleman, the seemingly naive country girl, the fashion-obsessed society lady, and the sleek and chic rake who is always dressed to kill. The action turns on comedy's staple, the courtship plot. Walery, an up-and-coming member of the Four-Year Parliament, takes advantage of an extended recess to visit his parents, Mr. and Mrs. Justice, at their country estate where he hopes to see Teresa, the daughter of their neighbor, Mr. Windbag. Walery and Teresa are in love, but Mr. Windbag, his eyes glittering with gold, favors the foppish Mr. Charming, who seems to be rich enough to forgo Teresa's dowry. When Mr. Charming turns out to be a bird of passage who will not be snared in a marriage unless it comes with a decent dowry, Mr. Windbag withdraws his opposition to Teresa's marriage to Walery.

But *The Return of the Deputy* is not just another comedy on the courtship theme. Niemcewicz sets the formulaic plot against an incisive exploration of contemporary reality, making sure that the Justices' house is always abuzz with politics. The Justices are keenly aware that Stanisław August's Saxon predecessors on the Polish throne had guided the country into a state of political torpor; during the reign of Stanisław August, a weakened Commonwealth was forced to submit to the indignities of the first partition. Niemcewicz's characters now live in a truncated state dominated by hostile powers, against whom prudence, industriousness, and a ready wit seem to be the best defense. Although illicit hegemony has triumphed, Walery and his colleagues, all reformist members of Parliament, do not wait for the day when the dice will be shaken differently. When Russia gets involved in a war with Turkey and the internal affairs of Poland-Lithuania move down on Catherine II's list of priorities, they seize opportunities and overcome obstacles to assert the rights and status of Parliament and to initiate far-reaching reforms in order to pull the Commonwealth out of backwardness, stagnation, and decay.

Although the play confronts the earnest issues of the time, it is marked by an air of measured calm, which explains much of its enduring appeal. There is no sense of desperation, but a steady confidence in the power of good arguments, from the people with the best ones. The main reason for the decline of the Commonwealth, Mr. Justice argues, is that the common good has been lost in the pursuit of private interest. Accordingly, he sermonizes against the demoralizing pathologies of the old political system, epitomized by feudal loyalties, baronial jurisdictions, and parliaments subject to the veto of a single member.[14] He enthusiastically endorses the modernizers' proposals to restore hereditary succession to the throne, to strengthen the executive, and to replace the *liberum veto* with majority voting.[15] There is no doubt in his mind that comprehensive modernization, which also includes a move toward a wider diffusion of civil liberties, is the only path to reclaim the sovereignty of the Commonwealth.

In contrast, Mr. Windbag is the epitome of brutal self-interest and dyed-in-the-wool cynicism. A beneficiary of royal patronage, he holds a lucrative crown property and serves as a regional official. In his view, everything depends on patronage, rank, and wealth; little depends on merit; virtually nothing depends on selfless service for the public good. While Mr. Justice makes an eloquent case for an urgent need to eradicate the pathologies that have been rotting the Commonwealth's institutions from within, Mr. Windbag insists that the parliamentary reform movement constitutes a serious threat to the state. While Mr. Justice argues that the source of all the evils now afflicting the political system of Poland-Lithuania can be traced to one single monster, the *liberum veto*, Mr. Windbag retorts that the *liberum veto* is the cornerstone of liberty. While Mr. Justice asserts that the underpinnings of good government are justice and enlightenment, Mr. Windbag takes thuggish pride in his well-honed skills in cheating his social inferiors. No possible amount of evidence and argument can ever make him believe that any other way is better than his own, or that the course he has pursued could be in the least modified. Rustic in inclination, antiquarian in mind-set, with a somnambulant faith in the political system of Old Poland, he remains trapped in a cobwebbed time warp.

The lesson of *The Return of the Deputy* is clear: reforms to transform an obsolete, fossilized system of government into a modern polity are long overdue. In this play, then, patriotism seems to refer, on the one hand, to a rejection of a political system that has functioned according to vested interests, where advancement has been due to patronage and not to merit, where public accountability has been wholly forgotten, and the politician has ruled the public rather than representing it, and, on the other, to a vigorous assertion of the status and rights of Parliament and the ethical imperative of civic responsibility, public usefulness, and prudent action. Given that the positive characters' confidence in the ultimate triumph of the Enlightenment never wavers, the comedy leaves the audience with an exhilarating sense that the Commonwealth is being buffeted by an accelerating current of constructive change, even though some segments of society remain in deep freeze.

By odd coincidence, *The Return of the Deputy* opened at the National Theatre two days before Stanisław August's fifty-ninth birthday on Monday, 17 January. Was the scheduling of the opening night for Saturday, 15 January, more than coincidental? Was the opening night perhaps intended as a birthday fete cum political rally to publicize the king's recent decision to mend his fences with the antiroyalist opposition in Parliament and to endorse its reformist agenda? We will never know for sure. But we do know that the National Theatre's production of *The Return of the Deputy* took Warsaw by storm.

To envision the spectacle-spectator dynamics at the performances of *The Return of the Deputy* in January 1791, it is helpful to distinguish the play's theatrical environment from the standard working conditions of modern theatre such as a darkened auditorium in which spectators are allowed privacy during the show. Until the early nineteenth century, playhouses were lit by candles and later by oil lamps; by the 1820s and 1830s, candles and oil lamps were replaced by gas lighting. Although ingenious devices were invented to make it possible to adjust the lighting on the stage, it was not easy to turn off house lights and then to bring them back, even after the technology of gas illumination was introduced. As a result, it was customary to keep the auditorium fully lit throughout the evening. But spectators liked it that way because they went to the theatre as much to be seen as to see. The undarkened auditorium also enabled them to interact with one another at will, especially when their favorite player or character was absent from the stage. Whenever he or she was on the stage, however, they often compensated by being massively enthusiastic, clamoring for particular monologues or songs and attacking—sometimes with words and sometimes with missiles—those actors who refused to comply with their requests. Put simply, the eighteenth-century playhouse was a tumultuous place. To restrain the disruptive behavior of audiences, it was not unusual for theatre managers to post two grenadiers on either side of the stage. Even so, plays commenced with difficulty and were regularly interrupted. Spectators' interventions—their riotous displays of approbation and censure—were features endemic to stage performances, frequently altering their shape and duration. Energetic and uninhibited participants rather than mere onlookers, audiences were thus as much a part of a performance as the actors on the stage; the mandates of self-control in public began to change audience behavior only in the second half of the nineteenth century.

It is not particularly surprising, then, that the spectators watching *The Return of the Deputy* at the National Theatre in 1791 were boisterous rather than decorous. Eighteenth-century performances were, to repeat, rowdy and often chaotic affairs. And yet there was something unusual about the raucous praise for *The Return of the Deputy* during the first two performances. On 15 and 16 January, ovations began before the curtain went up, and they quickly shifted into high gear.[16] Euphoric cheers and long rounds of applause repeatedly interrupted the monologues of the play's positive characters. The spectators were especially eager to applaud and encore the lines that extol the wisdom, civic virtue, and tireless dedication of the reformers in Parliament, give credit to the king's leadership, and stress the miraculous hand of Providence. Watching *The Return of the Deputy* on 15 and 16 January, then, was less like attending a play and more like attending a rally. The fact that on those nights the spectators warmed up to the play even before the curtain rose suggests that the house was packed with a friendly audience and that its enthusiasm may have been prearranged.[17]

Three days after *The Return of the Deputy* opened, Parliament met for a deliberation of a tangled mass of fiscal and legal issues, raised by a recent audit of the Treasury Commission.[18] The assembly hall in Warsaw's royal castle was a buzz of noise and a stir of movement. At 10 o'clock, the taciturn and conflict-averse Speaker of Parliament, Stanisław Małachowski, called the session to order. The proceedings barely had time to begin when one of the MPs seized the first available opportunity to take the floor, insisting that there was a matter of great importance he wanted to divulge. He was Jan Suchorzewski, a well-to-do nobleman from the Wielkopolska region in western Poland.[19]

Suchorzewski made his first appearance on the political scene in 1786, when he was elected to Parliament from the province of Gniezno. His political ascent gained momentum two years later, when he won an election to represent the province of Kalisz in what would become the Four-Year Parliament. He brought to bear political nous, a prodigious memory, a lucid legal mind, a formidable work ethic, grinding attention to detail, a gift for piercing veils of illusions, and an exceptional knack for lightning one-liners and stinging repartee. He was anxious to serve a republic whose survival he knew to be at stake, and it was his outspoken and uncompromising devotion to it that made him for many years a prominent figure in Parliament. A man of unforced bonhomie in whom a peculiar angry sensitivity and irritability toward those he regarded as his country's enemies vied with a philosophy of civility and moderation, he became known as an unsparing critic of national self-delusions garnished with patriotic jargon, a scourge of officeholders who were on the Russian payroll, and a consummate parliamentarian, committed to no party or faction. He cultivated his identity as a political independent with polemical gusto. In 1789, for example, he did not hesitate to stand up to a Warsaw publisher antipathetic to Enlightenment ideas, Stefan Łuskina, and to challenge his royal patent that enabled him to establish a growing stranglehold on the newspaper press in Poland. Concerned that the coverage of parliamentary proceedings in Łuskina's *Gazeta Warszawska* was tendentious and unreliable, he successfully piloted through Parliament his own proposal for an independent biweekly publication to brief the public on the actions of the legislature; this in effect broke the newspaper monopoly that Łuskina had wangled from Stanisław August in 1773. Suchorzewski was especially withering in his criticism of enrichments from public office and straightforward thefts from the public purse, but it was a policy of accommodation toward Russia that he denounced with the greatest vehemence. In his thundering philippics, he warned against the dangers of Russia's expansionism, supported tougher measures such as a ban on the sale of grain to the Russian military, pleaded for a strong army to defend the Commonwealth, and even pressed for war with Russia. Well endowed with a sense of mission, of important work to be done, he was certainly capable of excess when the issue at stake ignited his internal fires. Indefatigable and undaunted, he made some of his most electrifying speeches when the temperature in the assembly hall fell below freezing and the Speaker of Parliament had to sign documents with a pencil because ink in inkwells turned into solid ice.[20]

Suchorzewski's speeches and, more broadly, his mastery of the *ars rhetorica* or the art of rhetoric won him recognition in Poland-Lithuania as one of the best orators of the age, on a par with Stanisław August.[21] He was well aware that to be properly a skilled orator is to be equipped for battle, powerfully armored and protected. If an orator is to have any prospect of winning the war of words and thus of gaining victory for his side of the argument, he must learn to wield the weapons of oratory. The figures and tropes of speech provide him with perhaps the most important means of attaining the ultimate goal of the oratorical arts: that of persuading his listeners not merely, or even primarily, by the force of argument, but rather by exploiting the persuasive resources inherent in language itself. To arm and equip himself with the figures and tropes of speech is automatically to increase the emotional power, and hence the effectiveness, of his utterances; conversely, even the most honorable speeches are liable to miscarry if an orator remains content to present them in a pallid style. Every inch a skilled rhetorician, Suchorzewski conveyed his arguments in a manner at once graceful and flamboyant, erudite and down-to-earth. Eloquent and vivid phrases, periods proceeding through balanced or parallel structures, and clauses moving to carefully controlled rhythms, as well as an idiosyncratic mix of sophisticated urbanity and earthy humor—these are some of the hallmarks of his characteristic style. Suchorzewski's oratorical skills also included a penchant for parliamentary theatrics. He welcomed situations of heightened tension because he recognized that the outrage and conflict stirred by audacious, even provocative gestures were more clarifying and enabling to the skillful politician than ostensible harmony.

In two words, Suchorzewski mattered. A highly dedicated legislator with impressive rhetorical gifts at his command, an orator who relished attention and flourished in the limelight, he was a leading actor (and I mean this not as a judgment on his sincerity but as a statement about his public activism) on the stage of Polish politics in the late 1780s and early 1790s.

On 18 January, Suchorzewski started out with some alarming news. Violent crime, he reported, is on the rise in Wielkopolska, but the Military Commission, chosen by and accountable directly to Parliament, is slow to protect citizens against acts of banditry. As soon as he raised the temperature significantly, Suchorzewski began training his verbal artillery on the National Theatre. One could hear the rounds clicking into his chambers and the salvo being aimed at Krasiński Square, the theatre's location at the time.

At the National Theatre, Suchorzewski charged, ticket prices were going through the roof, while the repertoire was going downhill. To press the point, he castigated a 1774 law that enabled Parliament to turn the National Theatre over to a privately owned theatrical monopoly. Suchorzewski did not name the person holding the monopoly, but it was understood that he meant Stanisław August's chamberlain, Franciszek Ryx. Implying that Ryx won an exclusive and lucrative privilege to license theatrical entertainments because he was a protégé of the king, Suchorzewski sneered: "Nowhere in Europe is theatre more expensive than in Warsaw."[22] According to Suchorzewski, in other words, the scandalous state of affairs at the National Theatre was not just some random aberration but a consequence of a system in which the National, by definition a public theatre par excellence, was not democratically accountable. When several legislators protested that Suchorzewski's allegations were unrelated to the issue on the floor, he fired back that one way to replenish the public purse would be to abolish the theatre monopoly in Warsaw.[23]

Permanent public theatres, a relatively recent innovation in Poland, were targeted by some moralists as a key source of morally inappropriate pleasure and a dangerous incentive toward vice.[24] Such theatres were thought to offer a repertoire that ridiculed virtue and rewarded debauchery; in doing so, it inflamed the senses, awakened illicit desires, and promoted lustfulness. One would have thought, then, that Suchorzewski was concerned about the National Theatre's complicity in encouraging indecent liberties, condoning illicit sex, and corrupting sexual virtue, but one would be wrong. From his perspective, the problem with the National Theatre was its disservice to the cause of liberty, not its disservice to sexual morality.

To make his position absolutely clear, Suchorzewski offered the following overview of his credentials as a dutiful and loyal citizen:

> The essential guiding principle of my entire life has been love for king and homeland. It is this love that has compelled me—today and in the past—to speak the truth to my king and my homeland. I have never gone around advertising, over and over again, my praise for the king . . . , but neither have I belonged to secret and malevolent parties seeking to shake down the throne or pestering the king and his family for political and material favors. I have never called the king a "Muscovite" or published venomous squibs urging the overthrow of the throne. In my love and devotion to king and homeland, I have never wavered, and will never waver. When our republic was in dire straits, I urged the king and my fellow citizens to throw off the yoke of foreign oppression. Those weren't empty words; I put my life and property at my country's disposal to help shake off the alien yoke. . . . I have learned that it becomes a true republican to be steady and determined in his devotion to his homeland, regardless of the most frightening and overpowering violence that might lurk around the corner. I am determined to tell the truth, even though I might be threatened with violence and death. . . . When the good of my homeland is at stake, when the liberty of each of my fellow citizens is at stake, I will gladly accept ostracism, a cup of poison, or the most degrading death.[25]

In order to gain a hearing for his side and to undermine his opponents at the same time, Suchorzewski then spoke with enthusiasm about certain aspects of Niemcewicz's play. He praised the exhortations to extend civic rights to burghers, whom he called "fellow citizens [*wspól-obywatele*]," and to end the exploitation of serfs.[26] He also seconded the professions of admiration for the French people and their struggle for liberty.[27] What he could not tolerate, however, was the use of the National Theatre to vilify with impunity the fundamental principles according to which the Polish-Lithuanian Republic was constituted and governed. From his standpoint, the production of *The Return of the Deputy* demonstrated that the men at the National Theatre were willing to sacrifice that most valuable of possessions, liberty—that is, the collective freedom of citizens to rule themselves—on the altar of tyranny.

Suchorzewski was appalled. The key issue for him was the reformers' proposal to replace elective kingship with a hereditary, and thus well-nigh monarchical, throne. From their perspective, the Commonwealth's lack of dynastic continuity was a colossal piece of political folly because it prevented the king from effective leadership and offered exquisite opportunities for internal chaos and foreign interference during interregnums. But Suchorzewski saw serious problems in the idea of abolishing the elected throne. He built his argument around the all-importance of the rule of law, the cornerstone of self-government and liberty. In essence, he argued that tyranny begins with contempt for the rule of law.[28] Niemcewicz's drama, his argument continued, gives cause for alarm precisely because it agitates against the legal safeguards protecting the political system of the Commonwealth and supports an imposition of major constraints on the prerogatives of the nobility, foremost among them the right to elect the king. If the laws and constitutions of a republic can be shaken to their very base, the rights of the citizens will be only a scattered wreck, and the citizens themselves will be forced to submit to the lash of an insolent domination by arbitrary power. The real threat to a republic comes, then, not from foreign attack but from plays such as *The Return of Deputy* and their political side effects. While contemporary moralists claimed that public theatres opened a floodgate for immoral desires and corrupting sensual pleasures, Suchorzewski was convinced that one particular public theatre—the Warsaw National Theatre—became the gateway to illicit intellectual pleasures and through them to risky constitutional experiments. To make matters worse, much worse, he contended, a National Theatre that takes advantage of a monopolistic arrangement to present an assault on the rule of law as diverting comedy is a national tragedy.

Suchorzewski reserved much of his strongest criticism for the men and women in the Parliament's public galleries, who eagerly embraced the most recent production at the National Theatre:

> At a time when our country was being partitioned, when senators and deputies were forcibly removed from this assembly hall, when soldiers wielding firearms were letting some deputies in and pushing others away, when our rights and freedoms were brutally trampled, why didn't the Warsaw theatre enjoin citizens to resist the brutalities, to defend our homeland, to revive the manly courage [męstwo] of the Poles of old? Why didn't the Warsaw theatre put on plays such as *The Motherland and Her Only Son* or *Kazanowska*? No, such plays weren't allowed on the Warsaw stage. Not only that. After I came back from Puławy, where I saw *The Spartan Mother*, the Warsaw public laughed and made fun of me: "How are you doing, Spartan hero? Did you rout Russians and put them out to sea?"
>
> My colleagues, who are here, can testify to what happened when *The Motherland and Her Only Son*, a play that enjoins citizens to defend our homeland, was performed in Wielkopolska, at Mrs. Dąmbska's and in the home of Mrs. Gorzeńska and her family. As soon as this play opened, officials arrived from Warsaw to make sure that we weren't starting a revolution. Needless to say, *The Motherland and Her Only Son* was not revived at the Warsaw theatre. But today, when a play extols the shackles of despotism enshrined in hereditary succession, . . . the Warsaw theatre erupts in applause: "Bravo, author!"
>
> Plays that enjoin citizens to defend our homeland were not allowed at the Warsaw theatre. Even preachers weren't allowed to say from their pulpits: "Rescue your homeland." . . . A Capuchin friar, who was a preacher in Warsaw, gave a sermon, crying out for the defense of our homeland, but he couldn't finish his sermon because he was arrested and taken away. . . . Now I turn to you, my audience. You shouted "Bravo, author!" [at the performances of *The Return of the Deputy*]. Why weren't you just as eager to stand up for that Capuchin friar and shout "Bravo, preacher!"?[29]

In other words, Suchorzewski accused Warsaw theatregoers of a leaky memory, snobbish attitudes, tendentious judgment, and an opportunistic bent, if not duplicity and craven servility. He also reminded them that the patriotism to which they think they are responding is something they have not felt and do not really share. At the same time, he expanded on his earlier point about the pernicious effects of placing the public institution of the National Theatre in the hands of a private monopolist. To Suchorzewski, the fact that *The Return of the Deputy* was performed at the National Theatre, while other plays, also relevant to Poland-Lithuania's political circumstances, were barred from it, was telling evidence that a threat of royal despotism and arbitrary power was very real.[30] For all the debates in Parliament, the king's drive toward tyranny was readable from his willingness to manipulate the theatre licensing monopoly, held by his protégé, in order to exert control over the political views voiced onstage. Suchorzewski also revealed that the center paid close attention to private theatricals in the provinces and that it evinced a strong suspicion of plays that were performed outside its oversight, which only confirmed, in his opinion, that the center's contest for control over theatrical representation was a contest for control over political representation.

The assembly hall had no great acoustic virtues, but Suchorzewski's powerful voice reached every corner. Rising to a crescendo, he spoke with perhaps even more passionate intensity, even more dramatic force than before. He saw no point in beating about the bush. In essence, he was saying: This is a sovereign state; liberty depends in no small degree on watching vigilantly for symptoms of institutional hypocrisy that involves a disparity between the publicly avowed purposes of an institution and its actual performance of function; one such symptom is the National Theatre's production of a play that is in effect an assault on liberty and an incitement to lawlessness; this should not be tolerated with no consequence or sanction because it is respect for the rule of law that holds together the order on which self-government rests. Accordingly, he called for a judicial inquiry to investigate the case. In particular, Niemcewicz ought to be interrogated about his complicity in turning the National Theatre into a piece of political machinery to agitate against the legal foundations of the state, chief among them elective kingship, "confirmed by the king's oath and reaffirmed by the instructions from the regional assemblies," and the municipal police ought to be questioned about why they failed to intervene when the stage was being used to revile and deride the rule of law.[31] Suchorzewski also made a motion that the instructions the members of Parliament received from their regional assemblies be read out to remind everyone that the electorate overwhelmingly supported retaining the elected throne.[32]

Suchorzewski spoke for a long time, but we do not know how long.[33] Although his words are available to us in parliamentary records and a published pamphlet, it is impossible to capture Suchorzewski's speech as delivered because his style of presentation was often spontaneous and alive to the rhetorical potential of the immediate situation. If the parliamentary transcripts offer a guide, he must have spoken with dramatic flair and burning intensity, expressing himself in a manner at once dignified and trenchant, respectful and confrontational. What we do know is that his speech was responsible for a raucous disruption in Parliament. All contemporary accounts note that the assembly hall was loud with noise that at times drowned out his words. Many of the legislators, infuriated by his breach of parliamentary protocol, heckled and jeered. Others prodded Małachowski to intervene and return the proceedings to the order of the day. Stanisław Sołtan complained: "The rules forbid us from digressing from the agenda, and yet we introduce theatrical roles in Parliament."[34] Niemcewicz remained silent, but he rose and took a bow every time Suchorzewski mentioned his name. The spectators had a field day, reacting with patronizing smiles and outright guffaws. In the noisy commotion, Małachowski did try several times to dam Suchorzewski's torrent of words, but Suchorzewski, skilled in the rough and tumble of debate, was unstoppable. He pressed on, braving the laughter and the heckles and ignoring attempts to have him ruled out of order. However, no one offered to second the motions he put before the assembly. The debate returned to the subject of the Treasury Commission, arousing strong emotions again—this time over the use of public funds to finance the 1787 purchase of a palace for a Russian ambassador to Warsaw. As the session drew to a close, Suchorzewski rose to repeat his earlier motions. Again, no one seconded them, and no vote was taken.

III.

To say that in January 1791 Parliament was riven by fundamental differences in ideologies, allegiances, and desiderata, as was much of the country during this overheated revolutionary winter, would be an understatement. But the incident on 18 January 1791 was neither the first nor the last time that a member of Parliament violated the protocol. And yet "a duel between Suchorzewski and Niemcewicz" was widely quoted and discussed by their contemporaries, as if they did not quite know what to make of it.[35] Given that the political scene was deeply polarized, it would have been easy to welcome Suchorzewski's speech as a sensationalist but justified exposé of political machinations to use the public stage for factional advantage or, alternatively, to castigate his polemic as an inflammatory smear campaign. Instead, public opinion concluded that this gifted and likable man made a fool of himself.[36] This suggests that his outrage against the misuse of the National Theatre was rationalized as an irrational outburst: he got some things wrong, and there was no need to pretend that he got them right, but this bout of bumptiousness should not detract from his overall record.

In historiography on the Four-Year Parliament, however, Suchorzewski's speech, one of the strongest statements against the restoration of hereditary succession in Poland-Lithuania, has earned him unconditional condemnation. It is standard practice to describe him as hostile to enlightened ideas and adamantly opposed to modernization, as a bully and a believer in censorship—in short, as a man beyond the appeal of reason and logic, unable to appreciate objective fact or truth, but inflated with self-importance and holding forth in the posture of oratorical bombast. While the modernizers were bearing the torch of Enlightenment and pressing for reforms to rescue the state from anarchy, this conspiracy theorist attributed hidden and malevolent powers to them and attempted to whip up a demagogic firestorm against their legislative initiatives. In his hands, a conjunction of gargantuan ambition, an arrogant assumption of expertise, bullnecked obstinacy, and the love of the limelight with paranoid delusions and finger-wagging fanaticism, all intensified by an extraordinary gift for chicanery and self-dramatization, became a deadly weapon to destroy the Commonwealth. There were patriots and waverers. There were backward zealots. And then there was Suchorzewski, the most fanatical and ruthless of the zealots. In a version of the incident of 18 January 1791, popularized by nineteenth- and twentieth-century historiography, then, the story of Suchorzewski's protest is a warning about the dangers of reactionary politics dressed up as patriotic conviction. Tarred and feathered as a devious and untrustworthy public official and a conniving traitor, he occupies a top-ranking position in "Poland's historical demonology."[37]

Given the range of available evidence, it is not particularly difficult to establish a coherent account of the events that led Suchorzewski to aim his fire at the National Theatre. But when one sits down to analyze the incident, one becomes aware that the very naming of the protagonists declares allegiance.

On the one hand, to call Niemcewicz enlightened is to align oneself with commentators who have done their narrative best to exaggerate

Poland-Lithuania's backwardness in order to justify their claim that the eventual victory of the reformers—the Constitution of 3 May 1791—represented a remarkable leap forward. For those commentators, the Constitution was an unequivocal triumph of reason, civic virtue, genuine patriotism, and progress, even though it had an uncertain legitimacy. At a rump session of Parliament on 3 May, a constitutional bill was pushed through by means of a coup that involved military muscle-flexing and other intimidating tactics, a suspension of normal parliamentary procedure, the use of fabricated evidence, and a resolution criminalizing both criticism of and opposition to the Constitution as sedition and treason.[38] Intriguingly, the Parliament's observation galleries were packed that day with spectators of both sexes and every social rank who cheered the constitutional bill even before the session began and the bill was read out. This suggests that the enthusiasm of the spectators in Parliament on 3 May, like the enthusiasm of the audiences at the National Theatre on 15 and 16 January, was not necessarily spontaneous and disinterested.

On the other hand, to call Suchorzewski reactionary is to overlook his own legislative initiatives to strengthen the Commonwealth by modernizing its form of government. For example, on 4 January 1791, or just two weeks before his vigorous and, to many, rebarbative polemic against *The Return of the Deputy*, he repeatedly (and unsuccessfully) insisted that Parliament consider his proposal, tabled since 8 October 1790, to repeal the *liberum veto*. He also, it will be remembered, authored a bill to remove many barriers between blue blood and commoner. His commitment to modernizing reforms and democratic principles placed him on the progressive wing of Parliament, far away from those sectors of the parliamentary opposition that opted for the status quo.

There is no doubt that hereditary succession was a hot-button issue in the Four-Year Parliament. But to see the dispute over the hereditary throne principally as a conflict between forward-looking forces and the bastions of blinkered political conservatism is to ignore Suchorzewski's distinctive arguments. The debate in Parliament on 30 August 1790 may serve as an especially illuminating case in point. On that day, Niemcewicz proposed a referendum to canvass the regional assemblies about restoring the hereditary transmission of the crown. He argued that dynastic continuity would steady the ship of state because it would eliminate destructive interregnums that laid the country open to every foreign predator. This was the point of view that infuriated Suchorzewski. Despite his vehement and, at times, high-flown rhetoric, however, he took great care to spell out the blind spots in Niemcewicz's proposal. He astutely pointed out that Niemcewicz presented the disadvantages of elective kingship but said nothing about the risks involved in hereditary succession. To Suchorzewski, the right to elect the king best guaranteed individual liberty; the loss of this right, along with the threat of royal despotism and arbitrary power, was too heavy a price to pay for Niemcewicz's utilitarian calculus. He rejected any schemes that would undermine liberty by conditions of domination and dependence and reduce free-born people to servitude. Carried away by the force of his own rhetoric, he told Parliament: "I don't hesitate to tell you that I don't want Poland to exist, I don't want to be Polish, if being Polish were to equal being a slave."[39]

Certainly, there are ways of bringing Suchorzewski's protest against *The Return of the Deputy* under rhetorical control. But does it unlock the story of his remonstration to resort to name-calling, to make gossipy personal insinuations, or to pour withering scorn on his claim that he was no less a patriot than those who disagreed with him? Does it unlock the story to brand him "the foremost demagogue in Parliament" who ranted and railed, "a puppet" of reactionary magnates, or "a pawn" of a Russian ambassador?[40] Does it unlock the story to lump him in with "careerists and cardsharps" who hunted public office with avidity, to reduce his terms in Parliament to a loud-mouthed and sharp-elbowed jostle for personal gain, to brush him off as "a blathering parliamentarian" who was "generally disregarded" by his contemporaries, or to ridicule him as a deluded "zealot" who sniffed the taint of tyranny in every nook and cranny?[41] Given this kind of rhetorical control, Suchorzewski, at his most reputable, is a gullible provincial, afflicted by a self-destructive fondness for gambling at the Russian ambassador's palace, a willing dupe of aristocratic power-holders who buttered him up shamelessly and used him as a tool for ensuring Russian dominance, a presumptuous carpetbagger who strayed into some murky waters and played his hand amazingly badly in the politics of the period, or a sneering, relentless opportunist, fizzing with gleeful cunning. At his least reputable, he is evil incarnate—an inveterate cynic lacking any moral core, a devious political schemer, a well-disguised fraudster, and an out-and-out renegade. Suborned by Catherine II's ambassador with discreet gratuities, this Russian hireling wrapped himself in a cloak of prim respectability, prettified his speeches with words like "virtue" and "commonweal," and feigned a scrupulous respect for the law in order to undermine reform efforts. But none of this gets to the bottom of the story, or his insistence that he really did care about patriotism and liberty.

Here it is necessary to confront a classic problem in writing about the past: an acute case of hindsight. Knowing the end—Suchorzewski's involvement in the treasonable Targowica plot—one might see many previous episodes as converging toward it. The omens are easy to pick out. Suchorzewski's remonstration in Parliament on 3 May 1791 is particularly conspicuous. To obstruct the passage of the constitutional bill, he threw himself to the floor, urging the king and the legislators to protect liberty.[42] Then, he grabbed his six-year-old son and raised him up in the air, pledging to kill the child right there, in Parliament, to spare him life under intolerable tyranny.[43] Reading backward from Suchorzewski's involvement in the Targowica conspiracy as well as his histrionics on 3 May, one finds it very tempting indeed to dismiss his polemic of 18 January 1791 as shrill partisan demagoguery and to conclude that his overheated patriotism was camouflage for treasonous schemes.

That said, there is no getting away from the fact that Suchorzewski joined the plot that opened a fateful gateway for a conquest of his country. By most measures, his political swerve leaves him open to charges of treason. His motivation, however, remains a puzzle. Was he not a tireless defender of the Commonwealth's sovereignty? Did he not stand up in Parliament against hegemonist encroachments from abroad? Did he not protest against Russian interference in Poland-Lithuania's internal affairs? Did he not author the Law on Royal Towns, and was not this legislation an attempt to bind different communities together in a common effort to save the state? Had the Internet been in existence then, Antoni Siarczyński who transcribed the proceedings of the Four-Year Parliament would have been sure to delete Suchorzewski's speech on royal towns within a year. For in the spring of 1792, he joined Szczęsny Potocki and other Poles in St. Petersburg and enlisted under the banner of the Targowica Confederacy. How does one account for this complete U-turn? Why did a political independent known for his unyielding commitment to principle, a man who rejected the Machiavellian ethics of dirty hands, align himself with those who believed that the only way to save Poland-Lithuania was by Russian intervention?[44] Why did a deeply dutiful patriot who was bursting to raise an army sufficiently strong to protect his country get involved in a conspiracy that facilitated its conquest?[45]

It should be said in fairness that by the spring of 1793 Suchorzewski broke with the Confederacy and moved a force of about three thousand cavalrymen under his command to Moldova (Moldavia).[46] But it is not easy to hypothesize why this unbending anti-Russian polemicist, a legislator who repeatedly made hawkish calls for action against Russia, took part in a Russian-backed plot in the first place. Did his concern for the public interest mingle with some unruly, even anarchic impulses? Did his moralistic outrage trump his clear-sightedness and experience? Was he, perhaps, far too principled to be a good strategist? To what extent did he act out of frustration, anger, or self-interest and to what extent out of self-deception or honest miscalculation, in pursuit of some higher political goals? Because of the gaps in the record of his life, attempting a judicious and impartial assessment of Suchorzewski is a demanding task. Roman Kaleta, who has cast a cold eye over his political career and examined its progress more closely than anyone else, suspends his inquiry by stating that Suchorzewski was a curiously amphibious figure whose life, strangely divided, had an almost tragic cadence.[47]

Whatever reason or complex of reasons was driving Suchorzewski's decision to join the Targowica conspiracy (and this is an issue to which I will return), the satirical cruelty, directed at him in the playbill with which I began this chapter, suggests that his change of orientation was felt especially acutely precisely because it appeared to have nothing in common with his previous record. One might cavil at an actorish tendency to overegg his judgments, but it was his passionate concern for his country more than anything else that made Suchorzewski's reputation as a leading member of the Four-Year Parliament. He was widely regarded as a sensible and honest man of deep convictions, a forthright spokesman for an unchanging set of high-minded principles, and an exemplary citizen whose patriotism was no mere rhetorical flourish; his role as a de facto supporter of foreign invasion was all the more shocking for that. There were, after all, other noblemen who also took part in the Targowica plot, but none of them were respected and admired members of Parliament, and that made all the difference. Suchorzewski's involvement in the conspiracy condemned him in the eyes of his contemporaries. By 1793, public opinion came to view him as a monstrous aberration. In the following year, after Warsaw was liberated from Russian control during the Kościuszko insurrection, he was charged with treasonous collaboration with Russia and tried in absentia by a military tribunal. He was sentenced to death and hanged in effigy on 29 September 1794.

The shadow that Suchorzewski's political choices have cast over his reputation has occluded many aspects of his career, and his infamy as a political villain has encouraged scholars to disregard the contradictions and complications of the speech of 18 January 1791, the best-known of his parliamentary orations. It is not my intention to argue that Suchorzewski should be exonerated from his involvement in the Targowica plot. Rather, I submit that to dismiss him as an unscrupulous cynic, a venal deal-maker, and an outright traitor is to deny the complexities of the political culture of eighteenth-century Poland. Furthermore, I submit that we might better understand Suchorzewski's speech by examining his rhetorical labor to expose what he perceived as the National Theatre's complicity in an attempt to institute a tyrannical regime in the Polish-Lithuanian Republic. According to a long-standing interpretation, this rhetorical labor revealed reactionary strains in Suchorzewski's vision of liberty. It is necessary, then, to take a closer look at how he understood liberty and tyranny.

I begin by considering Suchorzewski's liberty-or-death statement that I quoted earlier: "When the good of my homeland is at stake, when the liberty of each of my fellow citizens is at stake, I will gladly accept ostracism, a cup of poison, or the most degrading death." Here Suchorzewski projects a specific public persona: a man who for his terrestrial *patria* and the liberty of its citizens will not shun the darkness of death. It would be easy to label this self-presentation as histrionic bluster or pretentious, tail-chasing froth, to deride the excesses of Suchorzewski's oratory, and to draw readers into a scornful alliance against his (presumed) general benightedness. Read in the context of the period's libertarian discourse, however, the unflinching determination of Suchorzewski's statement resonates differently. Its rhetoric suggests that he chose to bolster the legitimacy of his argument by modeling his public self-display on what Bernard Bailyn has called "a 'Catonic' image, central to the political theory of the time": a potent compound of oppositional politics and an ethic of self-sacrifice in the cause of liberty.[48] In particular, the rhetoric of Suchorzewski's declaration that he cares more about the good of his country than about his own life appears to resonate with the same lines in Joseph Addison's *Cato* (1713) that, according to some accounts, inspired Patrick Henry's "Liberty or

Death" speech on the eve of the American Revolution.⁴⁹ Addressing the Virginia Convention in Richmond on 23 March 1775, Henry purportedly ended his stirring oration with the words "Give me liberty or give me death!," a close paraphrase of Cato's lines in Addison's drama, one of the most popular plays on the eighteenth-century stage.⁵⁰

There is no evidence that Suchorzewski was familiar with Addison's play, although he might have been.⁵¹ Given that selective readings of Roman history were a staple of Polish school curricula, however, it is highly likely that Suchorzewski knew the story of Addison's protagonist, a classic hero of liberty: Marcus Porcius Cato (95–46 BCE), also known as Cato the Younger or Cato of Utica.⁵² A long-term critic of Julius Caesar's political ambitions, Cato associated himself with the ideals of the Roman republic so closely that he chose to kill himself rather than accept life under Caesar's tyranny. Cato's death came to be invested with intense political and philosophical resonance, and his name "was to become a metonymy for *libertas*," a term "understood particularly in the sense of freedom from domination."⁵³ By the eighteenth century, the ideological assumptions of what may be called Catonism consisted of three overlapping beliefs: that liberty is the highest good, for which no sacrifice is pointless; that the most important calling a person can follow is service to his or her country; and that the good citizen's proper stance toward those in power is to remain vigilant because they might use their authority to further their own ends rather than the commonweal. In other words, Catonism involves more than the inseparability of liberty and civic virtue or the belief in *libertas* as an absolute value, as a cause worth dying for; it requires the good citizen to keep in mind that power perpetually threatens liberty and to watch vigilantly for danger signals of designs against it. As Reed Browning points out, "The notion that eternal vigilance constitutes the price of liberty is thoroughly Catonic, but in the formulation that would have won widest assent in the early eighteenth century it would have been expanded to specify that eternal vigilance was both the stance of the patriot and the price of liberty."⁵⁴

By now, it is evident that it would be reductive to read Suchorzewski's speech as a simple advocacy of the liberty-or-death imperative. Whether or not Addison's protagonist became a favorite model for Suchorzewski to craft an effective public persona for himself, he shaped his patriotic stance to the pattern not merely of Cato, but of Catonism. Or, to put the same point somewhat differently, he assumed the identity of a Catonic patriot: a man involved in oppositional politics who commits himself to public service to defend liberty and is prepared to give his life for it; moreover, he harbors distrust and suspicion of those in power, even when they profess goodwill. His distrust and suspicion pivot on his understanding of liberty as being always endangered by those who are driven by a lust for lawless authority and who connive to augment their power, to make it independent of the people from whom they derived it and for whose sake they had received it. In contrast, the Catonic patriot insists that he never places himself above the law and that he can be neither bought nor influenced. He always remembers that the people entrusted him with power to serve them rather than himself. Thus, it is his obligation to remain constantly vigilant for attempts to circumscribe liberty and to make sure that tyrants-in-the-making, ambitious for themselves, be exposed and ousted from office. Read within this Catonic framework, Suchorzewski's decision, however odious, to join the Targowica plot becomes easier to understand. As Browning reminds us, moderation is not a viable option in Catonism; therefore "the Catonic spirit, defensive in origin and nature, cannot endure over a long period of time without being regularly fueled by external threats to deeply held principles. Thus, to account for the power of Catonism one must identify an event that would have aroused . . . the most deep-seated . . . fears—an event that portended the destruction of all that [was] valued."[55] For Suchorzewski, that event was the abolition, by the Constitution of 3 May 1791, of the right to elect the king.

There is more, however, to Suchorzewski's conviction that liberty was in peril. Perhaps the most fruitful strategy, or one branch of it, is to posit a double set of negotiations, a nested epistemology, involving patriotism and liberty. At one level, we are faced with Suchorzewski's stance as a Catonic patriot, manifested in his inexhaustible commitment to constant vigilance to expose the threat of tyranny and preserve liberty—the stance that I have just discussed. But at another level, we are confronted with two contending concepts of liberty. While critical attention has focused on the relation between Suchorzewski's speech of 18 January 1791 and the conservative nobility's opposition to modernizing reforms, I want to argue that his polemic hardly makes sense without an understanding of the two concepts of liberty. One of these concepts, called Roman-republican (or neo-Roman), was inherited from the pre-Enlightenment past. The other concept, derived from the ideology of limited monarchy and strongly influenced by a landmark of

Enlightenment thought, Montesquieu's *The Spirit of the Laws*, was primarily the invention of the eighteenth century.

Let me begin by briefly presenting the concept of liberty propounded by limited monarchists; it is this concept that Suchorzewski found unacceptable. The limited monarchists

> defined civil liberty as the security provided to the individual citizen by the law, and warned against the gathering of the legislative, executive and judicial powers in the same hands. In Polish conditions that meant strengthening the effectiveness of all three powers, and protecting the executive, consigned to the monarch, from the interference of the legislature. The monarchy could be kept within bounds, as in England, by the power of parliament over the purse-strings. Only a proper executive power could protect the weak from violent oppression by the strong. Without that security, the liberty experienced by an individual citizen was purely theoretical.[56]

Of the Polish Enlightenment writers and thinkers, it was Wybicki, a political theorist of startling originality as well as a playwright and a poet, who, in his *Political Thoughts on Civil Freedom* (*Myśli polityczne o wolności cywilnej*, 1775–76), conceptualized most fully "the thesis of a strengthened monarchy as the guarantor of civil liberty;" Józef Pawlikowski, in his *Political Thoughts for Poland* (*Myśli polityczne dla Polski*, 1789), became the most energetic exponent of this thesis.[57] Given foreign encroachments and depredations during much of the eighteenth century, the concept of liberty that is limited in the public sphere by state authority personified by the monarch found adherents among some Polish nobles. They began "to appreciate the need to balance national sovereignty against individual liberty"; that is, they "reluctantly and belatedly conceded the need to sacrifice some of their individual liberties and privileges in order to recover and uphold the collective freedom—or sovereignty—of the Polish nation."[58]

For the supporters of the Roman-republican theory of liberty, Suchorzewski among them, the idea that only a strengthened monarchy was the guarantor of liberty was precisely the crux of the problem. According to the republican concept of liberty, which originated in classical antiquity, "Human freedom is subverted not merely by acts of interference, but also and more fundamentally by the existence of arbitrary power. . . . It is not sufficient, in other words, to enjoy our civic rights and liberties as a matter of fact; if we are to count as free-men, it is necessary to enjoy them in a particular way. We must never hold them merely by the grace or goodwill of anyone else; we must always hold them independently of anyone's arbitrary power to take them away from us."[59] Or, to put it another way, liberty can be lost even in the absence of actual interference. The very presence of arbitrary power, however permissively or even benignly it may be exercised, creates conditions of domination and dependence and thus reduces free men to servitude. As Władysław Smoleński points out, this concept of liberty was espoused not only by Polish Roman-republicans, but also by a number of advocates of constitutional reform who would have been shocked to hear themselves described as republican in their political allegiances and linked with their opponents such as Benedykt Hulewicz, Albin Kazimierz Skórkowski, and Suchorzewski.[60]

Taking the Roman-republican theory of liberty into account helps explain why for Suchorzewski the enemies of liberty were to be found closer to home. He understood the Commonwealth as a political body that thrived on liberty, defined as the sum of privileges and constitutions, immunities and rights accumulated over centuries and confirmed by elected monarchs in cooperation with representative, parliamentary institutions. As a result, he deeply distrusted the idea that it was necessary to sacrifice some aspects of liberty in order to protect liberty. He was convinced that every attempt to limit liberty could be the first step toward despotism. Accordingly, he opposed any schemes that would expand the royal prerogative and strengthen the monarch's power; in particular, he inveighed against proposed extensions of executive influence under royal direction, which he found not only offensive, but also dangerous. His concern was that kings—each being, so to speak, a one-man institution—found it difficult to separate their institutional and personal interests. To Suchorzewski, then, the arrangement whereby the king is the chief executive officer in the state, responsible for protecting the security of the state and the liberty of its citizens, was a contradiction in terms.

The two concepts of liberty clashed fatefully on 3 May 1791. When a group of politicians sprang a constitutional bill on the legislature, the Roman-republicans interpreted the proposed constitutional reform as a fundamental assault on liberty in Poland-Lithuania. As such, the reform was, from their vantage point, "synonymous with an invasion from abroad."[61] Accordingly, they viewed the defense of liberty as being equal to the defense of homeland. Moreover, they argued that it was justifiable to seek foreign military aid in order to protect liberty. As Anna Grześkowiak-Krwawicz remarks, it would be simplistic to view this argument merely as an outlandish propaganda ploy used by the Targowica Confederacy to legitimate its treasonous disregard for state security.[62] To the Roman-republicans, the argument in support of foreign military intervention followed logically from their fundamental doctrine that "the cause of protecting liberty takes precedence over the cause of strengthening the state."[63] To ignore this argumentation is to risk applying anachronistic standards of public morality and patriotic discourse to the political culture of the eighteenth century.

IV.

I have begun this chapter with a narrative of the events that took place on that one day in Parliament not only to reconstruct Suchorzewski's argumentation but also to set the basis for discussing the difficulties and limits encountered in creating such a narrative. Certainly, the writing of my narrative about Suchorzewski's protest has required a rejection of demonization. In the preceding discussion, I have proposed a far more complex, enigmatic, and challenging Suchorzewski than the conventional figure presented in historiography. So far, I have given most attention to locating the discursive sources of his political stance or what has traditionally (and reductively) been described as his obscurantism and fanatical zeal. I now turn to his views on performance practice, dramatic representation, and an ethic of spectatorship and bring his preoccupation with theatre into conversation with the other features of the argument he made on 18 January 1791.

As noted earlier, Suchorzewski's targets are many: frozen hearts, patriotic cant, the politics of theatrical representation, control mechanisms to regulate stage productions in order to undermine the rule of law and to impede liberty, violation of the principles on which freedom rests, and a threat of royal despotism and arbitrary power. Correspondingly, those who have written on the incident of 18 January 1791 have been eager to claim that his protest was a sally in a campaign that pitted ardent supporters of theatre against antitheatre moralists within the larger context of partisan politics and factional feuding. Commentators have been somewhat surprised at the strength of his conviction that *The Return of the*

Deputy represented a fall into bad theatre, but they have attributed this conviction to his conservative politics, his closed mind, and his aesthetic underdevelopment. For example, Marian Brandys portrays him as a loud and blustering ignoramus from the hinterlands who had a tin ear for the instructive pleasures of literature and theatre.[64] In sum, commentators have taken Suchorzewski's polemic as yet more proof of the tenacious backwardness and invincible ignorance of the provincial gentry. However, it would be facile to construe his anxious misgivings about the National Theatre as evidence of his implacable, even puritanical, animosity toward theatre and to conclude that he joined forces with those eighteenth-century moral philosophers who denounced theatre on the grounds that it was morally tainted and injurious. The color has faded from much of his polemic, but what still shines out is the stunning self-assurance of the legislator who took the provinces for the center of the theatrical scene in late eighteenth-century Poland. Unconcerned by the views of those who looked down on provincial culture, he repeatedly invoked the performances he admired in household theatres outside Warsaw. The story of his theatre-going experience, along with his engagement with problems of theatre production and cultural reception, is the superbly dramatic centerpiece of his speech.

It is exhilarating to read Suchorzewski on the subject of provincial theatricals precisely because his speech comes across as a testimony by a passionate playgoer for whom theatre was a matter of wholehearted devotion rather than merely a piece of political machinery. I suggest that if certain critical principles are followed, it is possible to arrive at a more complex understanding of his argument about theatre. One principle is to move beyond the straightforward story of his distaste for, and his censure of, the National Theatre and to restore to view the powerful current of pro-theatre feelings in his speech, however awkwardly or elliptically these feelings are expressed. Second, there is much to gain by adopting his perspective from the margins or peripheries. One of the advantages of peripheries, after all, is that they are potentially privileged sites from which to look at the center and to examine what it has excluded. Third, to appreciate the full significance of his argument about theatre, we must recover its neglected historical context—the plays he saw outside the capital—and investigate why such apparently minor productions exerted a powerful hold on him. I submit that his speech is perceptive and illuminating, not least on the relationship of performance practices to political ideas and political action (including patriotic activism) in late eighteenth-century Poland.

While he excoriated the National Theatre and its production of *The Return of the Deputy*, Suchorzewski also furnished counterexamples, all of them amateur at-home theatricals: Kniaźnin's *The Spartan Mother*, staged at Adam Kazimierz Czartoryski and Izabela Czartoryska's country estate in Puławy; and Wybicki's *The Polish Woman*, performed under different titles in the Wielkopolska region.[65] By his own account, Suchorzewski saw *The Polish Woman* at least twice, at the homes of Helena Dąmbska and Ludwika Gorzeńska; he also attended a performance of *The Spartan Mother* at Puławy. He was so impressed with these household productions that he used them as counterevidence to develop his argument about theatre. It is only reasonable, then, to consider the plays against which he measured *The Return of the Deputy*, even though critical commentaries on the controversy over Niemcewicz's drama either ignore Suchorzewski's counterexamples or reduce them to political ammunition.[66] Accordingly, I discuss *The Spartan Mother* in section V of this chapter and *The Polish Woman* in chapter 2.

Here I concentrate on Suchorzewski's concern with the complex dynamics of theatre production and cultural reception. I do not claim that his perceptions and comments add up to a coherent and unified program or theory. However, the following questions are his ongoing preoccupations: How are theatrical enactments shaped to make an appeal and to elicit response? How can they ethically and effectively be put to good use in society? How can theatre not only present patriotic models by means of dramatic spectacle but also inspire patriotism that would not be a transitory emotion, lasting no longer than the illusion that produced it? But considering that passionately patriotic preachers failed to move and persuade their fellow citizens to follow an honorable course of action, how can we be positively certain that the feeling solicited by theatrical representation is an accurate barometer of sustained patriotic energy and commitment? Given the difficulty of depending on patriotic sermons for patriotic consciousness-raising and mobilization, is it ever possible to bridge or at least narrow the divide between theoretical or contemplative patriotism and patriotic action through theatre? Rather than regard Suchorzewski's protest as a histrionic spectacle of the conservative imagination, in other words, I propose to argue that his speech goes to the heart of some of the most sensitive dilemmas and irresolutions in Polish Enlightenment culture. This will seem to be an ambitious claim perhaps, but it is one that I think a careful reading of his argument bears out.

It goes almost without saying that Suchorzewski's polemic derives much of its rhetorical force from his antithesis between, on the one hand, the state of the National Theatre, gravely in need of reform, and, on the other, the vibrant theatrical scene in the provinces. It is less evident that his polemic owes its passionate intensity more directly to his understanding of theatre as a powerful shaping force. His speech, far from being an expression of antitheatrical prejudice, demonstrates time and again his fascination with the capacity of theatre to empower audiences by offering "provocations to thought and patterns for action."[67] His unflagging enthusiasm for the apparently minor provincial productions that were viewed by the suspicious officials in Warsaw as a hotbed of dangerous ideas is a flip side of his vehement censure of *The Return of the Deputy* on the grounds that it poses a serious danger to the public interest by sanctioning monarchist designs to deprive citizens of their fundamental rights. His anxiety over Niemcewicz's play, his outrage against the National Theatre, his determination to sabotage what he saw as the National's complicity in an attempt to impose "the shackles of despotism" on the Polish-Lithuanian Republic, and his cherishing of the alternative theatre as an oppositional voice reveal his strong belief in the efficacy of dramatic representation. What is always ignored in accounts of the controversy over *The Return of the Deputy,* moreover, is the fact that he shared this belief with Niemcewicz. To be sure, Suchorzewski argued that citizens cannot feel secure as long as Niemcewicz's play holds the boards, while Niemcewicz hoped that his public-spirited satire would have a salutary effect. But negative or positive, their focus remained on the social and political ramifications of theatre and drama. In subscribing to the idea that the stage can have a vital role in society, both men participated in the broader dialogue regarding theatre's responsibilities that took place during the Enlightenment. Enlightenment intellectuals viewed theatre as a force capable of socializing the public into certain value orientations and modes of behavior; the moral cultivation of the individual through stage performances, in turn, was seen as a means for regulating social relations. This idea is most famously exemplified by Richard Steele's emphasis (in the *Tatler*) on the use of theatre for the purposes of molding people into solid citizens: "There is no Human Invention so aptly calculated for the forming [of] a Free-born People as that of a Theatre."[68] Likewise, William Dunlap, known as the father of American drama, regarded theatre as a "powerful engine," capable of transforming society.[69]

However, there is something else going on in Suchorzewski's speech, which my argument has not accounted for. This something else can be given voice through the question: Can theatre make us better? For both Suchorzewski and Niemcewicz, as for many other Enlightenment thinkers and writers, it was a question expecting the answer "Yes!" As I have suggested, both of them were convinced that theatre was uniquely suited to engage audiences and to open the way to their improvement. Belief in human beings' ability to perfect themselves and their society, along with confidence in the capacity of theatre to serve as a public school of virtue—these are familiar themes of the Enlightenment. But what would it mean, exactly, to be made better by watching plays? It is here that Suchorzewski's and Niemcewicz's views diverge. While neither of them imagined the playhouse as a refuge from political debate, the experience obtainable from watching plays, along with the process of obtaining this experience, meant something entirely different to each of them. In the remainder of this section, I consider their views on the reception process that takes place in the playhouse and on the implications of this process for the drama of patriotism.

To Niemcewicz, as *The Return of the Deputy* makes it clear, theatre has an obvious appeal to both imagination and reason. But the play, overflowing with instructive monologues and rational argumentation, serves as a reminder that without the reasoning faculty we can never expect our feelings systematically to motivate us to the course of action required by political and social progress. In *The Return of the Deputy*, emotion unaided by reason is regarded as ruinous to men and women. Accordingly, the play calls for the liberation that only rational inquiry and patient reasoning can provide. To Suchorzewski, this is precisely the problem. His choice of counterexamples—plays in which the cult of reason is cut down to size and the passions safeguard virtue rather than corrupt it—suggests that he rejected the overinvestment in the rationalist imperatives of the epoch or the claims that feelings are merely reason's buttress. He thus implicitly drew on the Humean idea that reason is too slow to motivate us to action; hence the passions must provide this driving force.[70]

One way to view the controversy over *The Return of the Deputy*, then, is to approach it as a dispute between "emotionalists" and "antiemotionalists." This dispute concerns not only the playwright's construction of characters on the page but also the actor's art in performance. Accordingly, Suchorzewski's speech can be read as a contribution to a debate about the role of feeling and intuition versus craft and technique in acting—a debate that has been taken up by many theatrical theorists and practitioners. As Denise S. Sechelski points out, "This basic theoretical split (does an actor learn, and thus feign, the gestures of emotion? or does he somehow produce some natural feeling that then leads to natural histrionic expression?) is a crucial one in acting theory."[71] In the eighteenth century, there was much discussion of these questions. In *The Paradox of the Actor* (*Paradoxe sur le comédien*), written in the 1770s and 1780s, Denis Diderot challenges the assumption that "it takes feeling to portray feeling."[72] He argues that the intensity of feeling can sustain only a few scenes; as an objective of performance, however, intense emotion necessarily results in a reductive or superficial enactment. For Diderot, acting should be "the work of a cool head, of a profound judgement, of an exquisite taste, of a painful course of study, of long experience and of an uncommon tenacity of memory."[73] He defines a great actor as an imitator, the antithesis of the man of sensibility: "I want him to have a great deal of judgement; I require in that man a cold and tranquil spectator. I therefore I demand in him penetration and no sensibility, the art of imitating everything, or, what amounts to the same thing, an equal aptitude for all sorts of characters and roles."[74] To counter the emphasis on feeling that leads actors astray, then, Diderot advocates an acting method based on close observation, reflection, and technical competence, or what Graham Ley aptly calls "the cold science of passion."[75]

Sechelski, among others, has called attention to rival theories of acting in the eighteenth century.[76] Juxtaposed to Diderot's *Paradox* are the writings of Aaron Hill (especially *The Art of Acting* [1746]), for example. Whereas Diderot presents "the most notable defense of the distant, double-natured actor," Hill, in Sechelski's summary, "claims for the actor the potential to identify genuinely with the character's emotions," and he delineates "a scheme for representing the passions" that entails the communication of emotion "from the actor's body to the body of the audience. The emotion produced from the association of feelings in the body can be transmitted to the spectators, whose imaginations should instigate a chain reaction similar to that occurring in the actor; thus, they will naturally feel the same emotions being realized and presented by the player on stage."[77] According to Hill, in other words, it is possible for actor and audience to become connected through "'natural' representation," that is, through performance by players who are able to display a sincerity of feeling or to "show appropriate physical signs of emotion..., even though their performance practice depend[s] on a highly stylized notion of expression."[78] The "natural" representation allows for a sympathetic performance in which the feelings of the audience are "sparked and subsequently engaged in those emotions displayed by the actor."[79]

Regardless of whether he was familiar with eighteenth-century theories of acting, Suchorzewski's speech reveals a perceptive "emotionalist" whose theatregoing experience, conflated with his preoccupation with "fake" and "real" patriotism, generates provocative and crucial questions: How can feelings become actualized on the stage? How can actors get beyond superficial signs of patriotic affection? How can the imitative character of the art of theatre be diminished or at least obscured? How can dramatic spectacle connect actor and audience through the patriotic sentiments of the characters the actors play? How can patriotic emotions and sympathies aroused by dramatic spectacle energize an active patriotic purpose, rather than sustain patriotic cant?

No issue in Suchorzewski's speech throws these questions into sharper relief than that of the Warsaw theatregoers and their frozen hearts. One of the most striking rhetorical stratagems of his argument is his extended but seemingly gratuitous excursus on the Warsaw society's scornfully dismissive, even hostile reactions to patriotic sermons. Admittedly, this rhetorical stratagem is part of his overall assault on the Warsaw public. However, I want to draw attention to the rhetorical operation itself. It is clear that Suchorzewski wants to avoid jumping to conclusions; therefore, he is intent on searching out a faculty of response in spectators by comparing their reactions to different kinds of performance, which include but by no means are limited to dramatic representations performed by actors on the stage. It is at this juncture that he brings patriotic sermons into discussion. In considering the Warsaw audience's responses both inside and outside the playhouse, he finds that they are consistent in their antipathy to the concept of patriotism as battlefield heroism in defense of one's homeland. Furthermore, by juxtaposing reactions of metropolitan and provincial audiences outside as well as inside the theatre, he implicitly asks why some people are ready to risk their lives for their country, while others shrug their shoulders.

At this point, it would be tempting to conclude that, in Suchorzewski's view, it is primarily in the provinces that one finds virtuous hearts, while the Warsaw spectators' inability to be inspired by patriotic sermons or to evince interest in plays such as *The Spartan Mother* and *The Polish Woman* is indicative of a catastrophic unbalancing of their affective connections. In other words, Suchorzewski seems to have judged that the production of *The Return of the Deputy* at the National Theatre was addressed to spectators whose reason is far more accessible than their emotions. Accordingly, it would be easy to dismiss his unflattering views about the Warsaw audience as rhetorical hyperbole by a self-serving politician representing a provincial constituency. The issue, however, is more complex. While it is evident that provincial audiences, presumably less blasé, or more emotional, and therefore more responsive to the affective impact of dramatic representation, serve as foil to Suchorzewski's Warsaw spectators, it is important to keep in view his key points: fostering an independent-minded, critical, and imaginative citizenry is essential to the health of a republic; however, one faction in Parliament has seized the public stage to promulgate its own agenda and to exercise undue influence on citizens through a production of *The Return of the Deputy*. From Suchorzewski's standpoint, while the play ostensibly makes an eloquent case for liberation through rational deliberation, its appeals to the sovereignty of reason have been used to control and dominate rather than to foster the ability to be shocked by a wrong use of power, whoever its agents happen to be. The massive enthusiasm of the Warsaw public for this play only shows how easily spectators can be taken in by the smooth deceptions of its political rhetoric and how quickly they can digest Niemcewicz's poison.

But what of the actors who performed this poison? Suchorzewski's rebuke of the Warsaw playgoers for their willingness to abdicate their spectatorial authority as free moral agents and to absorb uncritically what they saw on the stage, along with his strong criticism of both Niemcewicz's drama and the theatre licensing monopoly held by the king's political appointee, may obscure the fact that he does not spare the cast: "My charge is that the author has reviled and derided the right to elect the king, . . . and that the actors have reiterated that the author has extolled the shackles of despotism enshrined in hereditary succession."[80] This part of his speech makes it clear that Suchorzewski shared with contemporary theorists such as Diderot and Hill the seriousness about the art of the actor, but he found the actors performing at the National Theatre to be merely mouthpieces of Niemcewicz's overinvestment in rationalist protocols. In other words, the very nature of the dramatic vehicle they represented informed their performance practices, that is, their particular interpretations of character. We know that some of the National Theatre's leading actors, such as Bogusławski, used a more naturalistic style of acting that began to replace the older, "classical" or declamatory, mode. As Sechelski notes, however, "Modes of acting change, but change gradually."[81] Practitioners of the declamatory style were still on the boards at the National Theatre in the 1790s, clashing with players who embraced the newer principles of the actor's method.[82] From Suchorzewski's perspective, the overall effect of the acting in *The Return of the Deputy* was that the cast was in thrall to this rationalist text; therefore, all they could offer the public was, at best, exposure to superficial signs of patriotic sentiments. To Suchorzewski, moreover, the actors' unswerving loyalty to the text worked to reinforce the top-down approach that characterized the entire production: it separated stage practitioner from audience and curtailed the promise of participation that is central to every spectacle. As Marie-Hélène Huet has observed, "To appeal to an audience is to appeal to this possibility of a spectator-actor exchange, and an audience that does not achieve this exchange, this cycle, this transformation, is a mutilated audience—or, one might say, an alienated one."[83]

Before proceeding to an examination of Suchorzewski's concept of the actor-spectator dynamics that would be empowering rather than alienating, it may be useful to recapitulate the main points he has been making about drama and theatre practice. Essentially, he has been arguing that *The Return of the Deputy* is a Johnny-come-lately in the patriotic repertoire and that the play and its production at the National Theatre offer patriotism's false, theatrical counterfeit. To be sure, the play and the production advocate political and social reforms, some of which he finds acceptable. However, the play has been cleared for performance by a powerful theatre-licensing monopoly with the express intent of manipulating the public to win its support for a partisan agenda. The production, then, amounts to coercion and extortion, which in turn elicit opportunistic acquiescence. To compound the problem, the play relies heavily on rationalist protocols, thus making it difficult, if not impossible, for the actors to get beyond superficial signs of patriotic feelings. To compound the problem even further, both the play and the production obscure the fundamental fact that the first partition of Poland-Lithuania has yet to be undone; therefore, the republic is not free to explore and define its own interests unfettered and uncluttered by other considerations. And foremost among those considerations is a concern for political sovereignty that has been so blatantly violated. The danger Suchorzewski perceives in the kind of theatre proposed by Niemcewicz is not only that its proreform euphoria distracts attention from harsh international reality and thus desensitizes the spectators to the actual calamity, foreign control of Poland-Lithuania, but also that it encourages indifference to the imperative of self-sacrificing heroism for their homeland. As a result, the spectators' enthusiasm for the theatrical artifice of *The Return of the Deputy* is sterile: it will not generate patriotic sacrifice. In short, the pathway to patriotism is heavily barricaded at the National Theatre.

With these points, Suchorzewski paves the way for the central argument of his discourse on theatre: the opportunities offered by household theatricals. To him, they are the fulcrum for envisioning the relationship between dramatic representation and the cultivation of affective patriotism as a political ideal, one that holds out patriotic activism both as a civic duty and as the highest calling through which the citizen's full potential as a political being is realized. To begin with, he appears to be well aware of the problem with what Garry Wills, in his reading of George Washington through the Enlightenment conception of political heroism, has identified as "the 'spectator' approach to moral motivation" in the eighteenth century.[84] This approach, Wills argues, "led to a rather crudely didactic philosophy of art, to a belief that one could instill virtue simply by depicting it. This made artists seek out heroes, to dramatize their virtue, to foster patriotism by allegorical display and public spectacles."[85] To Suchorzewski, "the 'spectator' approach" to patriotic motivation constitutes a perversion of patriotic ethos precisely because it casts audience members as passive and uncritical recipients of what they see on the stage. The central question for Suchorzewski, then, is: How can theatre foster active patriotic culture, however imperfect aesthetically, over passive adulation and consumption of dramatic representations on patriotic themes?

As I have noted, Suchorzewski, in contrast to Niemcewicz, advocates dramatic writing that focuses on the constructive application of emotions to the environment by passionate individuals. However, he does not merely propose that a certain kind of dramatic representation, exemplified by the emotionally arousing plays he saw outside the capital, can serve as a better school of patriotic sentiments than the offerings by the National Theatre. Rather, he suggests that for theatre to serve as a crucible of active patriotic culture, it is necessary to reconceive the entire relationship between actors and audiences. While both Niemcewicz and the management of the National Theatre imagined the audience as a passive object of their didactic and propagandistic efforts, Suchorzewski insists that a theatrical performance should not merely tell the public what is patriotic; it should make spectators feel what it would be like to be patriotic. But to counter "the 'spectator' approach," it is not sufficient to restore the gaze of spectatorial authority and to shift the power dynamics in favor of the audience. This would still keep playgoers in their role as spectators. Consequently, he turns to specific household theatricals to articulate an ethic of spectatorship that in fact challenges the notion of spectatorship itself. That is to say, he suggests a theatre of patriotism that blurs distinctions between actor and spectator. To reduce the artificial aspect of the art of theatre, to foster the spectators' affective response, and to facilitate their identification with the characters' patriotic emotions, he supports at-home theatricals in which family and friends are involved as writers, composers, designers, stage crews, actors, and musicians. Without the transformation of an alienated audience into a participatory one, we can never expect our feelings to prompt political and social action. Direct participation in at-home productions, then, functions as a form of imaginative exercise that awakens the faculties from sloth. To put these points differently, Suchorzewski offers an idea that may seem to be a utopian fiction: the concept of participatory theatre as rehearsals for life. Obviously, he does not develop this idea in so many words. It remains, as it were, a sort of specter in his argument—shadowy, inchoate, more a potentiality than an easily recuperable presence.

V.

So where does one go from here? How does the historian of theatre and drama decide what questions to ask, what lines of inquiry to pursue? A further political contextualization might throw more light on the strains of the late 1780s and early 1790s. More work on the history of the Roman-republican theory of liberty might illuminate Suchorzewski's predicament in more exhaustive detail. Comparative reading of the history of treason might provide analogues for his decision to join the Targowica plot. A detailed local history might usefully locate his ideas about theatre within the mental and domestic environments of the Wielkopolska region. But given the paucity of evidence, how can we, more than two hundred years later, account for the elusive yet tenacious hold that a woman's amateur at-home theatrical had on her contemporaries?

This seems to be an appropriate moment to return to Puławy, where Adam Kazimierz Czartoryski and Izabela Czartoryska maintained a thriving cultural center, a kind of an enlightened republic of arts and letters, and to revisit Kniaźnin's now barely remembered drama, *The Spartan Mother*, which Suchorzewski invoked as his chief counterexample. However, the point of my exploration is not simply to retrieve a neglected text. Rather, I want to approach it from a historicizing perspective that would allow a context-specific reinterpretation without reducing the play to the general circumstances of the period. One of my goals in what follows is to seek a fuller understanding of *The Spartan Mother* as a blueprint for what Margaret R. Hunt has called one of the "heavily politicized cultural interventions" into the key debates of its time and place.[86] But my principal aim is to examine Kniaźnin's dramaturgical and rhetorical procedures in order to begin to untangle a farrago of patriotic and gender discourses. Given that ancient Sparta, often known as Lacedaemon, has been famous not only for its men but also for its women, proverbially "the only ones who give birth to men," and considering, moreover, that influential accounts such as Plutarch's *Life of Lycurgus* have presented Spartan women as enjoying considerable freedoms that stood in contrast to the domesticity of Athenian women, it is unavoidable to ask: How and to what ends does Kniaźnin engage the heavily gendered idiom of the Spartan woman? Does his play, perhaps, open up potentially liberating perspectives that would facilitate a revision of binary gender distinctions?

For the play's historical setting, Kniaźnin has chosen, tellingly, the fourth century BCE when Sparta's power declined in the aftermath of the Peloponnesian War, rather than the period of Sparta's florescence in the sixth and fifth centuries. Although Sparta and its Peloponnesian allies won the war against Athens, the conflict left Sparta weakened and disoriented. The plot of *The Spartan Mother* revolves around the characters of Teona and her sons, Lycanor and Clyton.[87] It is set in motion by the decision of the city of Argos to enter the Theban war against Sparta. Until this moment, a modest force of Spartan soldiers under Lycanor's command has stood firm against the Theban attack. The Spartans' fitness, experience, and daring have more than matched the numerical superiority of the Theban army. Now, with the aid of a fresh supply of troops from Argos, the Thebans inflict heavy losses on the Spartans and come close to victory. Left with only a small kernel of his army, Lycanor decides that he should return to the city for reinforcements before he can risk another counterattack. But Teona assumes that he has fled from battle, and she reacts with anger and scorn to what she perceives as a degrading breach of the Spartan ethos. Because victory or death is the law at Sparta, Lycanor's behavior, she insists, taints with dishonor not only him but also his mother, since it suggests that she has failed to raise him to be a virtuous citizen who fights to the last in the defense of his country. She declares Lycanor a coward, unworthy of her, and appoints her younger son, Clyton, as his replacement. Shamed into Herculean heroism, Lycanor rejoins his soldiers in battle and mounts a new attack that ends in a spectacular victory for Sparta.

This bare summary hardly does justice to the emotional intensity of the play. Written in opposition to the excessive rationalism of the mainstream Enlightenment, it reflects the cult of sensibility in its eighteenth-century meaning that stresses the ability to be deeply affected by another person's sorrows and joys and that identifies the emotional will, rather than the dictates of reason, as the guide to virtuous action. The cult of sensibility was built around the idea that intense emotional responsiveness to the joys and distresses of one's fellows is the glue of society and the wellspring of benevolent action: without sensibility, we are stripped of both the feelings that tell us how to act and the motives that make virtuous action possible.[88] In the play, Kniaźnin weds the discourse of sensibility, with its emphasis on sympathy and benevolence, to the mystique of patriotic passion. None of his Spartan characters is a "cold" man or woman. Consumed by the feverish demands of love for *patria*, they refuse to view the defense of their homeland merely as a matter of conscientiously fulfilling their civic duty. To serve Sparta well, men and women must follow an emotional directive prompted by the pulse of freedom in their flaming hearts. The intensity of their affective attachment to Sparta, however, does not result in an impetuous torrent of patriotic rhetoric. Even at emotion-packed moments, Kniaźnin's characters speak in terse or truncated phrases, as if the blazing heat of their patriotic passion interfered with their verbal articulation. This is evident, for example, in an emotionally charged yet verbally austere exchange between Teona and her sons before the final battle:

> TEONA (to Lycanor): I love you, son, but I love Sparta more. . . . If you prove unworthy of Sparta, you're neither my son, nor a Spartan. What's your answer to this?
>
> LYCANOR: Mother, my heart has an answer for you, for Sparta, and for the whole world.
>
> TEONA (to Clyton): Do you feel this?
>
> CLYTON: I do, and I envy him![89]

Teona's choice of verbs in her question for Clyton is characteristic. Where one might expect to find the verb *hear*, she uses *feel* instead. Yet the terseness of this dialogue is precisely the technique for conveying heightened emotional intensity.

Archival evidence suggests that Kniaźnin wrote *The Spartan Mother* in close collaboration with Czartoryska, a gifted and versatile theatre artist—actress, director, and designer.[90] Wealthy, literate, cosmopolitan, and married to a cofounder of both the *Monitor* and the National Theatre, Czartoryska was at the frontier of cultural progress. Alive to new currents of thought and style, she shunned the rigors of French neoclassical conventions and experimented with hybrid, context-sensitive theatrical forms. At the same time, she refused to limit her household theatricals to "female," that is, private or domestic topics—the only matters with which women were thought to be sufficiently familiar. For Kniaźnin's new play, she proposed a political theme and shared her research about Sparta with him.[91] *The Spartan Mother*, with music by Wincenty Lessel, went into rehearsal in April 1786.[92] Czartoryska planned a production on a large scale, with a cast of fifty-nine, including a chorus.[93] She recruited performers from the ranks of the family, friends, and staff. Her sons, Adam Jerzy and Konstanty Adam, were cast as Lycanor and Clyton, respectively. She took the role of Teona. Niemcewicz, her husband's protégé and secretary, got a choral part. The opening night, on 15 June 1786, drew more than five hundred spectators. The guest of honor was Szczęsny Potocki, lionized as the model patriot of the day; his lavish gift of troops and cannons to strengthen the Commonwealth's army, along with the demand he voiced in the Parliament of 1784 that full sovereignty be restored to Poland-Lithuania, was still in everyone's memory. Although household theatricals were almost always occasional and deliberately ephemeral, *The Spartan Mother* had a run of several performances between 1786 and 1788. In mid-September 1791, the production was revived as part of festivities that accompanied a review of a Polish army. Since then, the play has not been performed again.

Although the theatrical life of *The Spartan Mother* was very short, its contemporary resonance was comparable to that of *The Return of the Deputy*. All historical accounts indicate that *The Spartan Mother* galvanized public interest, inspiring a breathless outpouring of comment.[94] The admiration of the first awestruck spectators at Puławy was unequivocal although expressed in a style that eschews concrete detail. They felt, however vaguely, that the production offered something else than rational understanding permits—a "strangely beautiful" spectacle in which aesthetic pleasure and patriotic passion were seductively confused.[95] The premiere of *The Spartan Mother* commanded sufficient interest to create a demand for manuscript copies of the script, which circulated throughout the country before it was published in 1787.[96] To be sure, some of the poems in praise of the play and the production—for example, Szczęsny Potocki's "To Princess Izabela Czartoryska" ("Do Księżny Izabeli Czartoryskiej") and Niemcewicz's "To Polish Women" ("Do Polek")—are dutifully obsequious puffs that were promptly showcased in the first edition of *The Spartan Mother*. But its suggestive and captivating rhetoric soon became part of the public discourse that set the stage for the Four-Year Parliament and shaped its debates; the play also served as a major discursive resource for politicians and political theorists such as Hugo Kołłątaj, Ignacy Potocki, and Stanisław Staszic.[97] Moreover, *The Spartan Mother* found a cultish following among other playwrights, prompting two spin-offs: Wybicki's *The Polish Woman* and Kublicki's *The Defense of Trembowla, or the Manly Courage of Chrzanowska*. Most important, the rhetoric of Kniaźnin's play lives on in Wybicki's 1797 poem, "The Song of the Polish Legions," which has since become Poland's national anthem. The poem's famous opening lines—"Poland has not perished as long as we are alive"—are remarkably close to Teona's kudos for Clyton's selfless devotion and stubborn courage: "We are still alive, and our country will not perish as long as such [public] spirit fires up every Spartan."[98] Put simply, although few if any Polish Enlightenment dramatists had a more confident indifference to Warsaw than Kniaźnin, his resolute provincialism did not hinder the resonant success of *The Spartan Mother*.

In scholarship, however, *The Spartan Mother* has received little attention.[99] Its marginalization suggests that the success of scholarly commentary centered on *The Return of the Deputy* as the classic, most eloquent statement in drama of the Four-Year Parliament's modernizing project unintentionally cuts off other avenues for analysis, foreclosing the possibility of seeing *The Spartan Mother* as the other pivotal play of the momentous period between 1786 and 1791, when an inflammable mix of righteousness and prudence, provocation and polish, reckless selflessness and flagrant self-promotion held sway in Polish politics. There is now a broad agreement among scholars that Kniaźnin's fame and excellence belong to the history of Polish poetry and that it is a mistake to suppose that his merits could also lie in his contribution to Polish drama and theatre. Augustyn Jendrysik's assessment of *The Spartan Mother* is particularly instructive. The play, he argues, is distinguished by an air of simplicity that is far from simple to achieve. The writing is nimble and lucid, the action unfolds gracefully, and the characters display "a rich range of subtle psychological reactions" without falling into tedious verbosity and self-indulgent, gushing sentimentalism.[100] Even so, *The Spartan Mother* is "an anemic text" that "has little artistic merit."[101] To prove his point, Jendrysik confidently, if not quite correctly, claims that by the time *The Return of the Deputy* opened at the National Theatre, *The Spartan Mother* was a faint memory.[102] In other words, Jendrysik's approach demonstrates an intriguing slippage of evaluative categories, which makes it possible to reduce a play rich in "subtle psychological reactions" to "an anemic text." Given this kind of interpretive control, it is not necessarily surprising that *The Spartan Mother* remains a politely overlooked embarrassment—a product of aristocratic patronage at Puławy, where passions were operatic and whims well-funded.

A different kind of interpretive control is exercised by commentators who confine the significance of *The Spartan Mother* to a political conflict between two powerful cousins, Czartoryski and Stanisław August.[103] In 1784, the Czartoryskis chose to withdraw from the vitriolic and scurrilous politics in Warsaw and moved their permanent residence to Puławy, where they established a major center of political and cultural patronage in deliberate opposition to the royal court. Puławy became a gathering place for men and women who shared the Czartoryskis' staunch conviction that the king, loyal to the Russian empress, should be viewed with suspicion. When *The Spartan Mother* went into rehearsal, the king continued his policy of accommodation toward Russia, while the Czartoryskis pursued an anti-Russian orientation, building up their following among the provincial gentry with a view to winning a majority in the Parliament that was to convene in October 1786. The production of Kniaźnin's drama was part of their campaign "to project Puławy as the true centre of genuine Polish patriotism . . . and republican tradition."[104] With this goal in mind, they took advantage of the vitality of a particular image of classical Sparta. Nowadays, Sparta tends to be considered a forerunner of the modern totalitarian state. But in the period stretching from Machiavelli to Rousseau, Sparta, the most stable of all ancient Greek republics, was often regarded as a well-constituted civic community, indeed a model for the constitution of liberty.[105] By adopting this image of Spartan antiquity into their patriotic discourse, the Czartoryskis sought to define by inversion the current state of affairs in Warsaw, to convince provincial nobles that they should look to Puławy for leadership, and to rally committed patriots to the banner of liberty. Accordingly, *The Spartan Mother* was first presented at a convention of the Czartoryskis' devotees, allies, and potential adherents in mid-June 1786.

In an audacious move, Alina Aleksandrowicz has turned away from the critical practice of treating *The Spartan Mother* as a minor composition caught up in the partisan politics of the mid-1780s, a work that merely provides an example of the way in which patriotism was tailored to fit the occasion. Without denying that the 1786 production of *The Spartan Mother* was a tool in the Czartoryskis' political campaign, she argues that the play is far richer and more original than previously acknowledged. While scholars have typically regarded it as stale political propaganda unworthy of sustained attention, she insists that, whatever others may have said to the contrary, *The Spartan Mother* merits serious recognition as a major innovative contribution to cultural history.

The argument in Aleksandrowicz's subtly revisionist reading is twofold. She reminds us that the Puławy of the later eighteenth century was not, in any limited sense, provincial. If anything, its remoteness from the capital encouraged intellectual and artistic independence and a willingness to experiment with new ideas. For Aleksandrowicz, a powerful case in point is *The Spartan Mother* because it helped foster a new, highly charged patriotic sensibility. There is, she argues, a line more traceable than is usually noticed from *The Spartan Mother* to the Polish Romantic ethos with its cult of self-sacrificial patriotic passion, uncompromising and uncontainable.[106] Moreover, Aleksandrowicz demonstrates that with *The Spartan Mother*

Kniaźnin initiated a long and arduous process of transforming habits of thought and expression about women in Polish literature. Drawing on her exhaustive survey of representations of female characters by Kniaźnin's predecessors and contemporaries, she shows that writers were either indifferent or antipathetic to unconventional role models for women.[107] Even Penthesilea, queen of the Amazons, proved problematic. Aleksandrowicz cites Szymon Szymonowic's 1618 tragedy, *Penthesilea*, in which the Amazons come to fight on the Trojan side in the war at Troy, and the queen meets her death at the hands of Achilles. Achilles then launches a moralistic diatribe over Penthesilea's body, asserting that "a warrior woman is truly a monstrosity" because she violates "the universal order" in which everyone has his or her proper place and social function; a woman's role is to be a mother and a homemaker.[108] Eighteenth-century authors continued the tradition of censuring women.[109] At a time when the views of Polish Enlightenment thinkers and writers about women could hardly be described as enlightened, Kniaźnin turned to the authority of ancient Sparta to counter his contemporaries' misogynistic opinions that shaped (and still shape) popular ideas about eighteenth-century Polish women.

In my reading of *The Spartan Mother*, I build on Aleksandrowicz's groundbreaking work to take up new questions about the play and to examine its overlooked components. The starting point for my discussion is Suchorzewski's unabashed admiration for the play. In *The Spartan Mother*, gender hierarchy is relaxed, and political authority feminized. Yet Suchorzewski did not mind. How so?, one may ask.

Any literary work that takes Sparta as its subject matter prompts the question: Which Sparta? The word *Spartan* in the title of Kniaźnin's play inescapably evokes the familiar characteristics attributed to Spartan citizens: austerity, physical prowess, endurance, military courage, and strict discipline. But Kniaźnin's Sparta is and is not Spartan. It is an exemplary state, the land of public spirit and political fortitude, the home of warrior heroes who were for centuries virtually unbeatable at war, but we hear nothing about the Spartans' frugal and austere way of life, their contempt of pleasure, or their innovative provision for girls' athletic training. The lacunae and inconsistencies in Kniaźnin's portrayal of Sparta are not surprising. "For over two and a half millennia," notes Elizabeth Rawson, "politicians and philosophers, in the light of their own needs and convictions, have regarded now one aspect and now another of Sparta as significant. From almost the dawn of Greek history enormous prestige surrounded her, and this was exploited to recommend the most disparate virtues and institutions."[110]

This process has been facilitated by the patchy nature of historical evidence. From the sixth century BCE onward, the Spartans we know have been constructed from Athenian sources and those influenced by them. As Rawson points out, "The bewilderingly contradictory attitudes taken to Sparta in post-classical times can only be understood when it is seen how contradictory the ancient sources are too."[111] To complicate matters still further, all the sources about Sparta are "strongly tinged with propaganda" because Sparta was perceived as the antithesis to Athens.[112] As a result, Sparta has lent itself easily to either idealization or denigration. For example: "An Athenian conservative, indignant at the faults obvious in his own democratic constitution, would naturally contrast them with what appeared to him the vastly superior and well-disciplined state of affairs in Sparta," but "the democratic citizen, who was fairly satisfied with his own government, would seek to find things in the Spartan constitution and economy which showed what a 'dreadful lot' the Spartans were!"[113] Sparta's admirers wanted to bring back its manly men and its strong control over the individual; its critics deplored Sparta's authoritarian culture and obstinate militarism. Those who wrote about Sparta and Athens were particularly eager to exaggerate differences between Spartan and Athenian women to make their own point. The philo-Lacedaemonian would declare that "Athenian women were mindless dolls, orientally secluded, and without knowledge of their husbands' affairs"; the philo-Athenian would claim that "Spartan women were over-sexed breeders of brutal soldiery" for the war machine.[114]

Kniaźnin's drama is part of a long tradition of the idealization of Sparta, a process that began in antiquity; in particular, Plutarch's *Life of Lycurgus* and *Sayings of Spartan Women* have played a major role in propagating the idealized Spartan legend. In the opening sentence of his preface to *The Spartan Mother*, Kniaźnin announces that his characters typify widely known Spartan characteristics: "This work of imagination ... shows ... how Spartans of both sexes breathed the air of ennobling freedom and how men and women of all ages were equally impelled to secure power and glory for their nation."[115] Then, apparently drawing on *Sayings of Spartan Women*, he builds his play around the classic formulation of the Spartan mother who sends her son off to battle, telling him to return with his shield or on it. Unsurprisingly, then, the lesson that Kniaźnin's Sparta has to teach is a compound of public spirit, patriotic devotion, and military courage. Like many other authors, including some ancient commentators, he strives to present Sparta in the best light possible in order to support a political cause. As I have already remarked, Kniaźnin's depiction of Spartan perfection proved very useful to the political designs of the Czartoryskis and their supporters, enabling them to draw an implicit parallel between themselves and public-minded Spartans and to advertise their determination to extirpate the "shameful indifference, softness, and servility" associated with the opportunistic politics of Warsaw.[116]

But Kniaźnin's Sparta has some peculiar features. It is, of course, not surprising that in this idealized account we hear nothing about Sparta as a land of strict government intervention where newborn infants were inspected by a public committee to determine whether they were fit to live. Nor is it surprising that a play celebrating the Spartan mother makes no mention of the limited role that Spartan women had in raising their sons: boys who reached the age of six were separated from their mothers and placed in military barracks with other males until they were thirty years old. And it would be unrealistic to expect that a decorous eighteenth-century play would feature buxom young women exercising in scanty tunics or dancing naked. That said, some aspects of Kniaźnin's construction of Sparta are indeed puzzling. One of them is the paucity of information about Teona's husband, who seems to have been killed in an earlier military campaign. Teona briefly invokes his heroic example as she sends Lycanor off to war. Handing him his father's shield, she reminds Lycanor: "Either with this or on this. Be brave . . . like your father. This shield is your sacred inheritance from your father."[117] But this is all we hear about him. Teona's refusal to dwell on the loss of her husband might be attributed to her fortitude and her dislike of unnecessary verbiage. It is harder to account for the fact that his name, unlike the names of other Spartan heroes, is never mentioned. Clearly, this nameless husband and father, however worthy of emulation, is not to detract attention from Teona.

Teona's widowhood serves yet another function. In her study of attitudes toward Sparta in the Western cultural tradition, Rawson argues that the classic formulation of the Spartan mother, strong-willed and outspoken, proved to be a problematic model for women in postclassical times. As she puts it, "Few men wanted to be saddled with a virago in the home."[118] It is thus hardly surprising that writers tended to soften the image of the Spartan mother by transforming a scourge who harangues her menfolk to remind them of their public obligations into a supremely virtuous and morally directive woman who gently inculcates civic virtue in her sons. Kniaźnin's approach is different. To be sure, his Teona is the quintessential Spartan mother of "with your shield or on it" fame. But she is not a domestic matron, quietly exerting her influence from the family hearth. Instead, Kniaźnin presents Teona as a furious enforcer of the Spartan ethos who rails at her son and wishes him dead because she would not tolerate what she perceives as his cowardliness. Admittedly, Teona also makes strategic use of inspirational maxims such as "the brave always win" and "courage, not multitude, wins," but even then the central issue is one of power and control rather than merely one of inspiration.[119] And if few men wanted to be married to a shrewd and domineering woman who awakens terror rather than tenderness in them, it seemed only logical to present a virago as a widow. That way the fraught issue of husband-wife relations, or the relation of the subordinate to the superior and vice versa, could be safely bypassed.

Kniaźnin's play, in other words, offers a story of how a woman, unaided by a man, has exercised her power with consummate skill and sometimes ruthless tactics to save her country. And in concentrating on the male character's crisis in patriotic identity, the play suggests that a strong female figure is indispensable as a patriotic mentor. This raises the question: Where do Teona's authority and power come from?

First, however, I want to consider other unconventional features of Kniaźnin's Sparta. Although Spartan matrons were known to flock to temples to thank the gods that their menfolk had died gloriously fighting for Sparta, here Teona's female friends and neighbors gather in a temple of Mars to entreat the god of war to spare the lives of their sons. It takes a long monologue by Teona to restore the women's fortitude. However, this haranguing overtness is reserved for her public appearances. In other scenes, conflicts within Teona over Lycanor's fate are evident enough, not only in her soliloquies, but also in her dialogues with her daughter, Telezylla. In a moment of despair, for example, she tells Telezylla: "You don't know what it means to be a mother."[120] The reason for Teona's distress is not only the purely personal concern that she might lose Lycanor, but also her obsessive worry that Lycanor might fail the Spartan ideal by returning alive but without his shield.

It must seem puzzling that Teona does not have unconditional faith in Lycanor's commitment to Sparta's freedom, even though she believes that he has inherited patriotic devotion and courage with her milk. To put it differently, she is convinced that the true Spartan identity must be in the blood and therefore is unchanging. She also reminds herself that she has given Lycanor exemplary upbringing, socializing him in the ethos of patriotic heroism. She concludes: "It's impossible that he could erase all this."[121] And yet she worries that he may turn out to be a coward after all. Teona's uncertainty lends psychological complexity to her character. It also thickens the atmosphere of suspense, since no one—not even his mother—can be sure how Lycanor will behave in battle. But perhaps most importantly, Teona's doubts encourage us to regard the whole idea/phenomenon of patriotism as elusive and unpredictable.

In yet another departure from the conventional view of Sparta, the Spartan mother is not the only woman who spurs Lycanor on to glory, nor is glory the only reward for his patriotic service. In Kniaźnin's play, men's patriotic motivation depends in large part on the seductive presence and the sexual availability of the young and unmarried Leucyppa. From her aria in act 1, in which she pledges a gift of her heart to the bravest of Spartan warriors, to her presentation of rose blossoms to the victorious Lycanor in the finale, she helps produce a secure knot of erotics and politics, erotic passion and national romance. One could criticize Kniaźnin for transposing the medieval conventions of courtly love and knightly heroism into the Spartan setting.[122] But one could also argue that Kniaźnin's anachronism makes it clear that the inspiration provided by the Spartan mother is not sufficient, and so it needs to be augmented by eroticizing men's patriotic motivation: the fairest woman becomes a trophy bride for the winner.

It is time now to return to the question of Teona's power and authority. At first glance, there seems to be no surer or richer source of Teona's empowerment than her motherhood. Established in her household as a mother, she has ceased to be an object of exchange. Motherhood has also allowed her to enter the community of women and participate in religious ceremonies. Moreover, her rise to power, if it may properly be called power, has been facilitated by the absence or inadequacies of male authority figures. One could argue, then, that Teona, impelled by single-minded patriotic devotion, merely transfers her leadership skills from the household to the state when the state is in danger.

And yet the issue is not quite as simple as it may appear. Kniaźnin's decision to write a play about a woman who wields political power appears to have been fraught with both doubt and anxiety. One of the first things to notice about his preface to *The Spartan Mother* is that he feels compelled to account for Teona's authority and power. The way he goes about this is revealing. He could have cited, for example, an exchange, recorded in Plutarch's *Sayings of Spartan Women,* between a woman visiting Sparta and Gorgo, the wife of Sparta's king, Leonidas. When the visitor asked Gorgo, "Why is it that you Spartans are the only women who can rule men?," Gorgo replied, "Because we are the only ones who give birth to men."[123] Instead, Kniaźnin justifies his particular construction of Teona by giving her an impeccable pedigree and elevated social status. His Teona has gained access to the all-pervasive authority of the Spartan ruling dynasty through her descent from a royal family that claimed Hercules as its founder. It is her identity as a blood relative of Hercules that empowers Teona to disregard the norms and conventions of femininity and to govern like a man. Or, to put this point another way, Teona's transgression of gender boundaries is legitimized by her genealogical connection to the iconic hero rather than by her motherhood.

Only one factor of the textual context (i.e., the preface to the play) remains inexplicit in Kniaźnin's otherwise very explicit explanation of Teona's status. If he found it necessary to justify his choice of a patriotic heroine who is as devoted to her country as her menfolk is, it is clear that he knew he was addressing an audience that was not prepared to accept an ordinary woman in a position of power and leadership.

VI.

I have been focusing in this chapter on how Suchorzewski's speech of 18 January 1791 disrupts conventional understandings of the Polish Enlightenment's concepts of liberty and patriotism and expands our framework for making sense of the relationship of theatre and drama to the polarized political culture of the late 1780s and early 1790s. In particular, I have been arguing that his polemic sheds fresh light on the efforts of the institution of theatre, private as well as public, to negotiate a position from which to exercise authority in fractious disputes over "true" patriotism and "mistaken" versions of it. Now I want to return to Niemcewicz's play that occasioned Suchorzewski's "fiery oration."[124]

One way to begin a discussion of *The Return of the Deputy* is to bring up Walerian Kalinka's pathbreaking research in the 1870s about the role of public opinion in Polish politics during the late eighteenth century.[125] Kalinka found "the tyranny of opinion" momentous for its bearing on the deliberations and negotiations in the Four-Year Parliament.[126] For example, the men and women who filled the public galleries in Parliament were outspoken and assertive; their vociferous and at times raucous involvement in the debates—by cheering, catcalling, heckling, hissing, and voice-voting along with the legislators—constituted a political theatre that did not merely agitate for reforms but also performed some effective interventions by exerting pressure on the skeptical, the lukewarm, or those who muddled through.[127] Drawing on Kalinka's research, Stanisław Kot goes so far as to assert that informal pressure groups and their splatter critiques "terrorized" the conservatives in Parliament; consequently, a number of them, seemingly too fettered by the instructions of their regional assemblies to make major changes, voted outside the ideological prescriptions of their constituents "in order to win the applause of the observers in the galleries, the welcoming reception in salons, and the popular recognition in the streets of Warsaw."[128]

There is only anecdotal evidence to support Kot's claim about the conservative legislators' appetite for celebrity, but it is clear that the modernizers did not underestimate the importance of maximizing their rhetorical opportunities and coordinating political with poetic pressure in preparation for a showdown. Niemcewicz's play, in which verse trots, skips, ambles, and sails on a tide of pungent wit, is a case in point. Elected to Parliament in 1788, this prolific poet put his shoulder to the modernizing wheel.[129] Ever a rapid writer, he composed *The Return of the Deputy* in a matter of three weeks.[130] Rather predictably, he chose the genre of satirical comedy. If laughter, as the classical theorists of rhetoric—Aristotle, Cicero, and Quintilian—argued, is almost invariably an expression of scorn or contempt and disdainful superiority, it is hardly surprising that he should have viewed laughter as such a potentially lethal weapon of political debate. For it follows that, if he can manage to expose the opponents of the reform movement as laughable, he can hope to bring them into contempt, thereby undermining and depreciating their arguments while augmenting his own case at their expense.

As I have noted earlier, the play is largely focused on the characters' debates about highly contentious topics, ranging from parliamentary reform to hereditary succession, then the most controversial issue in Polish politics. While Mr. Windbag gives Mr. Justice a run for his money, responding with objections, scornful jibes, and, at times, real indignation and real tears, Mr. Justice, the reformers' mouthpiece, is assigned the winning arguments: only a few years before, Poland-Lithuania seemed divided and ungovernable, with the spread of seditions and with parliaments blown off course by the *liberum veto*; now it is beginning to regain its power and prestige in Europe. As a satirist, Niemcewicz does not hesitate to coarsen the view of the period by creating the impression that the dispute is played out against the backdrop of a Manichean struggle between perfectly virtuous modernizers and irredeemably self-interested reactionaries. The agitational intent here is plain. The play identifies political pathologies and shows why it is imperative to push for the modernization of the state. To be sure, Niemcewicz mischievously cushions the controversial issues with funny and sexy clichés of the courtship plot. But the strong and explicit political statement, conveyed in a series of rhetorical maneuvers—praise for the return to good government following the anarchy of the Saxon era, a glowing tribute to the modernizers' wisdom and prudence, an unwearying polemic with those who are anxious to stop the clock, a flattering portrait of "citizens cheerfully pay[ing] their taxes"—unavoidably turns *The Return of the Deputy* into a form of lobbying for the modernizing project.[131] It is not surprising, then, that the play has been described as "a propagandistic pamphlet and a sharply worded rebuttal to the many treatises by defenders of royal elections."[132] As Jan Ij. van der Meer, among others, has concluded, "The love-intrigue serves merely as a pretext for a political theme."[133]

Yet not all is as it seems. There is no question that *The Return of the Deputy*, with its double message of political peril and pressing need for reform, was part of the effective publicity fostering a sense of the glorious dawn of Polish modernity. But it would be unfair to assume that Niemcewicz had no ambition beyond making propaganda for the modernizers. A playful, elusive writer, he is never quite what we expect him to be. His default creature is the red herring, that most slippery of fish.

It is only a slight exaggeration to say that *The Return of the Deputy* sounds like a creative adaptation of Kant's miniature essay, "An Answer to the Question: What Is Enlightenment?" ("Beantwortung der Frage: Was ist Aufklärung?," 1784). "For Kant," Roy Porter remarks, "Enlightenment was mankind's final coming of age, the emancipation of the human consciousness from an immature state of ignorance and error."[134] For Niemcewicz, Poland-Lithuania's coming of age through its participation in the Enlightenment project is made all the more urgent by political circumstance. Acutely aware of the need to face the vulnerabilities of the state, he offers the following comment in his preface to the play: "In a free country where every citizen participates in the public business of governance, it is necessary to correct not only the mores of private life but also opinions that are harmful to the whole country. It is of utmost importance to recognize that opinions, whether false or true, harmful or reasonable, will determine the fortune or misfortune of the [Polish-Lithuanian] Republic."[135] What makes this statement striking is not only the idea that the private sphere (i.e., "the mores of private life") is linked directly to the public realm but also the argument that the mental constructs (i.e., "opinions") held by individual citizens are no less decisive than actual actions in determining the future of a republican state. In other words, Niemcewicz defines *political* in a more personal and immediate way than was recognized by many of his contemporaries in Poland. Or, to put this point more strongly, *The Return of the Deputy* is a political drama, but like all good political dramas, it is also deeply personal.

Scholarship has long recognized that in *The Return of the Deputy* Niemcewicz has his eye on both public events and the minutiae of private life and that he calls attention to the fundamental connection between moral and political constitutions.[136] The play draws on the belief, widespread in the eighteenth century, that a steady commitment to virtue is indispensable to the preservation of a republic: its citizens not only need to act virtuously, but also to cultivate a certain kind of virtuous character. Selfish behavior by individuals can have only disastrous results for the well-being of a republic; conversely, liberty belongs only to a virtuous citizenry.[137] Sensitive to the implications of private matters for public affairs, Niemcewicz's positive characters are convinced that an improved type of family, cooperative and noncoercive rather than rigidly hierarchical and authoritarian, is best equipped to school citizens-to-be in the disinterested benevolence presumed to constitute the foundation of civic morality. In Mr. Windbag's vision, by contrast, neither families nor citizens can govern themselves; therefore, both ought to be bound by fear. The play implicitly likens Mr. Windbag to political tyrants, bent on subjecting their dependents. While his patriarchal domination, fueled by the mercenary belief that marriages should be contracted for interest rather than love, threatens to block his daughter's happy marriage, his political power as a predatory feudal lord, sovereign within his fief, presents the most immediate and obvious threat to the happiness of the Polish-Lithuanian Republic. It would be reasonable, then, to suppose that the juxtaposition of two variants of familial relationships, represented by the Justices and the Windbags, is but another rhetorical maneuver to make effective propaganda for political reform. In this perspective, the cooperative, harmonious, and unselfish family is an attractive metaphor deployed to represent the reformers' ideal of political relationships and to counter the political vice of disharmony. In short, the Justice family is a new Poland-Lithuania in miniature.

And yet there is more to *The Return of the Deputy* than the rather predictable conceptualization of family as the correlative of polity. Indeed, the premium that critical commentary has placed on the connections between the play and the political conflicts of the late 1780s obscures some of its other layers of meaning. For example, although it has been classified as a political comedy, *The Return of the Deputy* can be viewed as a moral parable in which virtue is pitted against vice, and men and women explore the possibilities for absolute and undeviating virtue on this side of the grave. Or it can be viewed as a story of attempted seduction and of potential victims of male arrogance, imperiousness, and design—with the caveat that the real subject of the play is not whether young girls should resist sexual temptations or how disastrous marriages come about, but what hope virtue has in a corrupt world. There are also other interpretive possibilities. Here, I propose to argue that the play's engagement with the problem of gender is no less important to its discursive domain than a scathing critique of dysfunctional political institutions.

During the eighteenth century, the general biblical prescription for family relationships continued to be taken more or less seriously in most quarters. Scripture taught that the primary social unit was the patriarchal family. Children were enjoined to give absolute obedience to their parents; woman, in accordance with St. Paul's teaching, was in her original nature weaker than man and therefore subordinate to him in all things. In the second half of the eighteenth century, however, marriage and family organization, the patriarchal household, and connections between family and polity began to provoke new questions, and the education of women became a matter of public concern. For example, in October 1762, the year when the Jesuits were expelled from France, Rousseau published *Emile,* his popular treatise on education, that stimulated interest in the subject of female education—often by those who disagreed with his treatment of the subject. Written at a time when gender expectations were changing and often contradictory, *The Return of the Deputy* was scanning the gender horizon. To expand our understanding of the play, then, I turn to its gender dynamics. The play's concern with paths to men's and women's happiness, the place and function of women in society, the experience of being female in a male-centered culture, patriarchal habits, predatory sexual attitudes, marriage and family life, intimacy between husband and wife, matrimonial misery, styles of parenting, experiments in more permissive child-rearing, the parent-child relationship, parental power and control, the schooling of men and women, and the benefits of an intellectually rigorous education for women—all these make this kind of reading inevitable. Admittedly, prior scholarship did consider gender issues in *The Return of the Deputy*—only to conclude that the prim erasure of sexual desire and the tendentious neglect of female agency are the play's fatal flaws.[138] I want to argue, on the contrary, that *The Return of the Deputy* has an identifiable antipatriarchal (though not necessarily feminist) agenda. If, on one level, *The Return of the Deputy* merely reflects the exclusion of women from the full rights of citizenship, I suggest that the play in fact pursues the opposite end by raising far-reaching questions about women's position in society and advancing ideas that will later prove integral to a movement toward women's political liberation.

I take as my starting point van der Meer's statistics about the distribution of lines among the major characters in the key scenes of act 1 (scenes 2 and 3). He has established that Mr. Windbag speaks 147 lines, and Mr. Justice, 150; in contrast, Mrs. Justice gets only 13 lines.[139] This leads him to conclude that although Mrs. Justice, the play's principal female character, "participates in the lengthy discussions with her husband and Gadulski [i.e., Mr. Windbag], her part is mostly confined to advising the men to drink their coffee before it gets cold and such remarks."[140] As a commentary about women's lives, in other words, the play falls into conservatism. It emphasizes women's traditional roles as wives, mothers, and homemakers, de-emphasizes their exclusion from the political sphere, shows no interest in female intellectualism, and remains silent on gender inequality. In stressing the play's antifeminist features, van der Meer also identifies the roots of the problem. Niemcewicz, van der Meer argues, could not bring himself to write differently on the subject of women, or he did not know how to, because he absorbed the severely misogynistic tradition of the Jesuit school drama that dominated the theatre scene in Poland for "hundreds of years."[141] This deeply ingrained Jesuit legacy is especially evident in the construction of the play's positive female characters. Each of them is a cultural marionette, in need of a puppeteer and ventriloquist to make her walk and talk. Mrs. Justice, deferential, mostly silent, and preoccupied with the daily routines of meals and social visits, is the epitome of this "female inertia."[142]

In van der Meer's view, then, *The Return of the Deputy* merely reiterates received ideas about the identities and obligations of the sexes. Men are destined for the turmoil and battle of public life; women, for the private and domestic sphere of family and children. In this play, accordingly, there are no women insinuating themselves into political circles and usurping the male role, no female interlopers intruding upon terrain from which they were, in both principle and practice, supposed to be excluded. This line of thinking about *The Return of the Deputy* is not without its logic. It is true that the play's definition of the woman's sphere is a limited one, that we see women only in domestic relationships, and that in the entire text we find no objection to the notion that women belong in the home, no demand for radical revisions of their status in society, and no argument for extending political rights to them. It is also true that the public realm in the play is exclusively the man's sphere of activity and that no character voices a concern that men claim "the Right . . . to govern Women, without their Consent" (to quote John Adams's hesitant admission about the young American republic).[143] One is tempted to agree with van der Meer that it is indeed the traditional perspective on women, with its emphasis on women's exclusively domestic roles and responsibilities, that reigns supreme in *The Return of the Deputy*. Although the play offers sharp criticism of the old political system and envisions drastic political change in Poland-Lithuania, what Niemcewicz says about women reinforces the gendered social order. This conservatism about women may well have served to make his political commentary more palatable. If Poland-Lithuania were to be changed into a modern polity, characterized by a new style of men's political behavior, as demonstrated by Mr. Justice and his son, it was surely reassuring to know that the women of that world would not change.

The play's engagement with the question of gender, however, is much more complicated than this, as I hope to show. In particular, to label Mrs.

Justice "passionless" or to write her off as "passive," "superficial," and "insignificant" is to provide unsatisfying, stereotypic answers about a character whose complexity is thereby ignored.¹⁴⁴ And considering the overwhelming propaganda in the late eighteenth century about homemaking as women's primary destiny, it is remarkable how little attention Niemcewicz devotes to the topic. Or, to put these points somewhat differently, the question of gender in *The Return of the Deputy* is only unproblematic and unambiguous if it is viewed in isolation from the gender norms of Niemcewicz's time and place.

Mrs. Justice's participation (or, according to van der Meer, her nonparticipation) in the largely political discussions is an issue to which I return later. First, I consider Mr. Justice and Mr. Windbag's intriguing digression from their debate over contentious political issues. In the middle of the dispute, they turn, rather incongruously, to the topic of female education (act 1, scene 3). The occasion for this abrupt shift is the arrival of Mrs. Windbag's note written in barely comprehensible Polish. One might expect that Mr. Justice and Mr. Windbag would receive the note, shrug their shoulders, and move on with their political polemics. Instead, they seize the opportunity to address the question of female education, and they do so with the same passion they have devoted to legislative initiatives and foreign alliances.

Mr. Justice opens this segment of the debate with a mini-lecture that could easily have been called "My Thoughts on Designing an Education for Girls." The lecture focuses on three related themes: how and what girls are taught, how and what they should be taught, and what is to be expected of them when they grow up. Thus, Mr. Justice's disquisition appears to draw on the Lockean environmentalist psychology of the Enlightenment: what people are is assumed to be dependent on how they are educated. Mr. Justice seems refreshingly aware of the limitations of girls' upbringing and education. At an early age, they are committed by their parents to French governesses who know little more than how to make hats. As a result, Polish women can converse in French and keep up with the latest styles, but it is all fashionable gloss to camouflage a lack of substance and self-discipline. The Polish-Lithuanian Republic, however, does not need fashion plates. If Poland-Lithuania is to remain Poland-Lithuania, the current education of girls must be reformed.

Given Mr. Justice's enthusiasm for the modernizing project, one would have thought that the rest of his mini-lecture would brim with explicitly fresh ideas—for example, advocating an improved or more intellectual curriculum for girls or perhaps even demanding equal education for both sexes—but this is not the case. Echoing Rousseau, Mr. Justice flatly declares that woman is meant for the delight and pleasure of man.[145] Accordingly, he would like girls to be trained in household skills so that they would make living comfortable for their future husbands. In assigning women to primarily nonintellectual pursuits, he extols the vocation of wife as an industrious and agreeable companion to a sensible man, indeed "a reward" for his "virtuous" service in the public sphere.[146] In short, he endorses an unashamedly gender-based education that relies on the patriarchal concept of womanhood, the ultimate aim of which is a respectable marriage.

The problem, as Mr. Justice sees it, is that parents now prepare their daughters for the marriage market by paying elaborate attention to external attractions and superficial accomplishments while neglecting domestic skills. In the marriage market, charm, flirtatiousness, and fluent French are at a premium; competence in the day-to-day tasks of household management is at a discount. To make matters worse, a new, Frenchified type of education fails to inculcate the private virtues that, Mr. Justice suggests, are the essential components of Polish womanhood: obedience, modesty in personal habits and dress, gentleness, sexual constancy, industriousness, and self-sacrifice. Instead, it encourages vanity, frivolity, and extravagance. As a result, girls grow into dangerously undisciplined women. Susceptible to the temptations of luxury, they squander money on impractical fashions, while boredom drives them to seek illicit pleasures.

In the entire play, the condemnation of the fashionable instruction in the social ornaments such as music and French is the only issue on which Mr. Justice and Mr. Windbag agree. Nevertheless, Mr. Windbag is quick to point out an inconsistency in his neighbor's argument: Mr. Justice supports a thorough modernization of the Commonwealth, yet he decries a new type of education, imported from Paris. Mr. Justice goes to some pains to answer this charge. It is not that education should become entirely independent of Paris; rather than imitate foreign models slavishly and indiscriminately, one should exercise good judgment and choose wisely. Mr. Justice further claims that both young men and young women are victimized by the glossy education *à la française,* but young women are more at risk. This is so, he suggests, because young women's minds are more impressionable, their characters more malleable than those of young men's. He concludes with a grim picture of the current state of Polish womanhood: skilled solely in the idle vanity of female ornamentation and lacking both strong morals and essential preparation for their domestic roles and responsibilities, Polish women waste their lives.[147]

Although Mr. Justice and Mr. Windbag dominate the debates about education and politics, there is yet another participant in these conversations: Mrs. Justice. It may be tempting to pay little attention to her because she gets just a handful of lines. In the debate about education, for example, she speaks a mere 6 lines, as opposed to Mr. Justice's 69 lines and Mr. Windbag's 37.[148] To van der Meer, this confirms that *The Return of the Deputy* is undermined by Niemcewicz's inability to portray women. I want to argue, on the contrary, that *The Return of the Deputy* makes countless forays beyond the boundaries normally imposed on women of Niemcewicz's era (even though these forays may not seem exceptional from our perspective today). In this boundary-crossing, Mrs. Justice plays a starring role.

At first sight, Mrs. Justice is as traditional a woman as it is possible to imagine. A devoted wife, a caring mother, and an expert household manager, she expresses her strong belief that husband and wife must be of one mind if harmony is to prevail at home.[149] Accordingly, she appears to have no identity apart from her husband's; her disposition, sentiments, beliefs, and interests seem to match his. So it comes as great surprise (to the reader or the spectator) that serious, fundamental disagreement does arise. When Mr. Justice vilifies Polish women on the grounds that they lack moral and practical qualifications for wifehood and motherhood because of their defective upbringing, mental inferiority, and weak wills, Mrs. Justice retorts:

> You're too harsh, my friend.
> There are women in our country
> Who know how to respect
> The sacred bonds of the conjugal union
> And who conscientiously fulfill
> The duties of wife and mother.[150]

From today's perspective, Mrs. Justice's riposte merely confirms that she is the epitome of domestic womanhood. Given the dramaturgical and rhetorical context, however, Mrs. Justice's riposte is stunning. While her husband argues that there are no serious, responsible women in Poland, she is not reduced to blushes and silence; on the contrary, she demonstrates that she has no truck with a "natural" feminine docility. When her husband questions the Polish women's ability to carry out their duties as wives and mothers, she does not hesitate to rebut his scornful generalizations or to expose his readiness to ignore her own domestic labor. In short, her riposte shatters the illusion that the play supports the principle of male authority and wifely submission; it even suggests that the model of the ever-obedient and self-effacing wife, her husband's docile and subservient vassal, is outdated.

What is more, the claim that Mrs. Justice is a "passive," "superficial," and "insignificant" character fails to take into account that she makes some vital interventions into the men's debates about public matters.[151] Admittedly, Mrs. Justice gets a modest number of lines, but her comments demonstrate both her informed interest in politics and her remarkable skills as a rhetorician. In other words, to focus on the number of lines allocated to her is to overlook that she deals with her antagonist, Mr. Windbag, less by arguing with him than by ridiculing his absurdities. To defeat him, she deploys the rhetorical figure of meiosis or ironical understatement, a device especially susceptible of being applied in a mocking way to belittle or undermine the arguments of one's opponents. This suggests that she is well aware of the importance of irony for anyone hoping to achieve victory in the war of words. This in turn implies that she is acquainted with the classical authorities on rhetoric. The Roman theorists of rhetoric, Cicero and Quintilian, regarded irony as the most effective of the mocking tropes. Their admirers, the rhetoricians of the later generations, agreed that irony, with its mocking inversion, represents the best means of producing a derisory effect and thereby discrediting one's opponent. In the debates between the Justices and Mr. Windbag, this half-educated feudal lord recognizes that he is no match for Mrs. Justice: "You always contradict me."[152] Here, the word *always* is a tribute to Mrs. Justice's rhetorical skills.

In the key scenes of act 1, then, Mrs. Justice emerges as an astute observer of the political scene and a well-informed commentator with a gift for ironic understatement. She is aware of the self-serving way in which a male-dominated culture has defined goodness for the female, but she is neither obsequious to men nor shy about countering the views she finds unreasonable and unacceptable. In short, *The Return of the Deputy* presents Mrs. Justice as an example of female learning, courage, and self-respect. Although enlightened rationality was associated with men, and the concept of nature was used to legitimate the notion that women were less capable than men of rational thought, the play does not regard the life of reason as a male preserve. Accordingly, it offers an improved image of woman as a rational individual, capable of absorbing and transmitting ideas and competent to discuss politics and other public issues: the dutiful wife and mother, the skillful household manager, and the intellectual woman can be found in the same person. To put these comments yet another way, the play demonstrates that biological sex provides no useful index of intelligence, rationality, and character. Although this point may seem obvious to modern audiences, it is a point rarely made by eighteenth-century Polish writers.

The positive assessment of Mrs. Justice seems to be undermined by the fact that she has embarrassed her husband by correcting him in front of his political adversary. And yet Mr. Justice does not take offense. He does not respond to his wife with irritation or disdain, nor does he brush her off with a patronizing comment that she talks about matters above her head. Instead, her riposte to his antifeminist diatribes prompts him to concede that his generalizations about the inadequacies of Polish women are unfair and unwarranted. Clearly, he does not feel that his authority has been impaired. His willingness to accept his wife's criticism, to learn from it, and to revise his line of argument accordingly, even in the presence of his political opponent, throws new light on their marriage. Their numerous departures from marital convention—in particular, a relaxation of hierarchy and a diffusion of authority in their relationship, an open-minded approach to disagreements between them, and acceptance of affection as the only proper basis of marriage—show that they are converts to a new type of marriage, known as the companionate marriage. As Dena Goodman notes, "The crusade for companionate marriage, or marriage based on the love and the free choice of the partners, was one of the central campaigns of the Enlightenment against tradition and patriarchal authority."[153] Although the companionate marriage was not fully egalitarian, the emphasis placed on mutual affection and esteem enabled new, more equalizing relations to develop between husband and wife, thus undercutting arguments in favor of strict wifely subjection and obedience.[154] The Justices' marriage is loving, friendly, respectful, trusting, and cooperative, in contrast to the Windbags' marital mismatch. Mr. Windbag believes that women are a commodity placed on the earth to fulfill men's financial needs; as a result, the Windbags' marriage is based on material gain and sexual anaesthesia for the husband and on an opportunity for the wife to indulge her expensive whims in order to escape her intolerable life, deprived of affection, friendship, companionship, and sex by her indifferent spouse.

So far, I have concentrated on Mr. and Mrs. Justice as husband and wife. Now I want to turn to their role as parents and foster parents. In addition to raising their three sons, the Justices have brought up Teresa, whose mother, Mr. Windbag's first wife, died when her daughter was a child. Dramaturgically, then, the play brings into sharp focus a complex of questions concerning parental roles and obligations, parent-child relations, and child-rearing attitudes and practices.[155]

That the greedy and thuggish Mr. Windbag tyrannizes his daughter and tries to cow her into silence need cause no great surprise. The Justices' idea of good parenting, by contrast, is noncoercive. Far from viewing children as creatures to be repressed, they recognize that youths possess minds of their own and are not always willing to conform to parental expectations of conduct. Their parent-child relationship is characterized by the substitution of suasion for domination, a decrease in parental power, an increase of children's autonomy, and the relaxation of parental control over the children's marriages. The children can marry whom they want, although to prevent a conflict-filled marriage, one must choose one's mate wisely. Moreover, the Justices do not regard strong emotional bonds between parents and children as an obstacle to good parenting. On the contrary, they view the proper combination of tenderness, indulgence, guidance, and friendly counsel as fundamental to enabling the children to grow into distinctive individuals and dedicated citizens. Unsurprisingly, Mr. Windbag is scandalized by such innovations. But the public careers of the Justices' sons as enlightened, dutiful, and empathetic citizens demonstrate that their mode of child-rearing has been successful.

The Justices' success as Teresa's foster parents seems more problematic. Commentators on *The Return of the Deputy* have balked at Niemcewicz's portrayal of Teresa as a timorous, bashful, self-effacing, and utterly pliable creature, always obedient to the will of others and always ready to serve and to please. On a first reading, it may indeed seem that the Justices have raised Teresa to conform to social convention, presumably because traits such as docility, deference, and obedience would make her welcome to the society in which she has to live. But to accept this impression is to miss the rebellious implications of Teresa's insistence that a woman should have the right to select her life partner. At a time when most marriages were still arranged, and it was eccentric to expect to marry for love, she refuses to accept the fate that her despotic and mercenary father and his second wife have decided for her: "They want me to marry this good-for-nothing scatterbrain. Ah! My disgust with him defeats my respect for the principle of filial obedience."[156] The dynamic here is antipatriarchal. It juxtaposes the independent child and the oppressive, unscrupulous parent who exercises coercive tyranny over her. It presents an alternative model to that of blind submission to parental dictates. It also suggests that the upbringing Teresa received in the Justices' home, instead of socializing her into acquiescence and submissiveness, has encouraged her independence and self-assertion. And since the idea that marriage might properly be based on free choice and mutual affection was new at the time, it is clear that the Justices' companionate marriage, happy and affectionate, only strengthens Teresa's loathing for marriages based on interest.

Given the play's emphasis on the ethic of selfless public service, there are still some questions about the Justices' child-rearing attitudes and practices that need to be addressed. On whom does Niemcewicz place the primary responsibility for raising enlightened and dedicated citizens-to-be? Does this responsibility fall more to fathers than to mothers because mothers (or any women) cannot be citizens?

Chastened by his wife during the debate about female education in act 1, scene 3, Mr. Justice abandons his gender stereotypes to give credit exclusively to women for instilling in their sons the public virtue necessary to sustain the republic.[157] By contrast, Walery pays a warm-hearted tribute solely to his father for having taught him from the earliest age "to love our homeland and to follow the path of virtue."[158] But it is Mrs. Justice who has the last word on this subject. In the play's penultimate scene (act 3, scene 6), she counters her husband's and son's encomiums with the argument that parental obligation is vested in both father and mother; therefore, it is their joint responsibility to raise and instruct the young in such a way that they can be "useful to their country."[159] Or, to put the same point somewhat differently, the civic virtue that buttresses the state depends on nurturance by both parents (and not just fathers) who are equally responsible for mentoring their children (and not just sons) and preparing them for the duties of citizenship. Although cultural discourse and practice have assigned a special association with the public sphere to men while denying this association to women on the grounds that they are morally encumbered by their supposedly excessive emotionality and dangerous lack of self-discipline, the play relegates the production and maintenance of public virtue to a new realm, one presided over by mothers and fathers, rather than exclusively by fathers. The inevitable corollary to Mrs. Justice's refutation of the sex-determined split in the allocation of parental responsibilities is that she does not believe women to be naturally endowed with a gift for rearing young children.[160] To be sure, in the world of the play some of women's duties, such as supervision of domestic servants and food preparation, are different from those of men. However, although it was written at a time when certain abilities, such as an aptitude for caring and nurturing, were assumed to flow effortlessly from women's nature, the play does not support such assumptions or the idea that gender identities are grounded in the biological difference between the sexes.

It will not be difficult to draw some preliminary conclusions. *The Return of the Deputy* combines old and new ideas of public virtue. It continues the idea of public virtue as civic glory, is mostly silent about the idea of public virtue as military courage, and opens the way for gender-neutral ideas about political activism by advancing an egalitarian approach to nurturing public virtue within the family. This necessitates two changes in societal attitudes toward women. One change involves the institution of marriage: the mere formulation of a demand for a new, more egalitarian style of parenting depends on a reassessment of, and a fundamental change in, power relations between the sexes. It is the companionate marriage that makes the development of less authoritarian and more cooperative relations between husbands and wives possible, which in turn enables them to take on undifferentiated parental roles. The other change involves radical improvements in the educational opportunities for women. Women with an advanced education would not only better fulfill their human potential, but they would also be better equipped to join their husbands in raising and mentoring citizens-to-be.

Mrs. Justice's contributions to the debates about politics and other public issues provide persuasive evidence that she has been educated beyond the level of most women at the time, even though girls' opportunities for intellectually rigorous schooling on a par with boys' were extremely limited.[161] In his portrayal of Mrs. Justice as a woman who has benefited from the upgrading of female education, Niemcewicz appears to be sympathetic to a feminist point of view. To the extent that women behave in less rational ways than men, he suggests, their conduct is the result of inadequate education, not natural incapacity. Seen from this perspective, the play's fundamental theme is the refusal to accept the axioms that nature has made women inferior to men and that women are incapable of education on an equal basis with men. Just as he rejects the idea that rationality and sound judgment are the exclusive domain of men, Niemcewicz also discards the notion of the sexes as polar opposites. Instead, he envisions men and women as rational equals. In addition, he emphasizes the public role of the mother-educator who helps raise virtuous citizens. In other words, while Niemcewicz does not go so far as to demand that women receive the full rights of citizenship, he makes it clear that women's capacity to reason makes them eligible for indirect political participation. Ironically, then, a pivotal political role is assigned to the least political residents of the republic. As Linda K. Kerber has argued in her study of the changing status of women during the Enlightenment, however, "The notion that mothers perform a political function is not silly; it represents the recognition that political socialization takes place at an early age, and that the patterns of authority experienced in families are important factors in the general political culture."[162]

That said, there is little doubt that a play presenting a more radical challenge to traditional gender roles would be more sympathetic to modern taste. If women are to claim a public role, according to *The Return of the Deputy*, it would have to be based in their domestic roles and responsibilities. Despite his advocacy of women's inclusion in the intellectual innovations of his day, in many ways Niemcewicz ends up affirming rather than challenging the traditional distinctions based on sex. From our vantage point today, then, Mrs. Justice is not quite a feminist heroine. To compound the problem, the play's formulation of a female political role is not fundamentally feminist because its primary aim is not to enhance the position of women. Instead, it reflects a shift to expediency. The success of the Polish-Lithuanian Republic depends in part on reconceptualizing women's child-rearing activities as public-oriented tasks; despite their formal exclusion from the political realm, women will have a share in it by training citizens-to-be.

While the play's emphasis on the importance of providing women with expanded educational opportunities is not to be slighted, the realignment of women with motherhood and the silence about their exclusion from institutional political life can be viewed as a betrayal both of women and of the Enlightenment itself. Moreover, considering that a substantive redefinition of the maternal role by intertwining it with the inculcation of public virtue limited the range of acceptable female pursuits and that, in the long run, the indirect political function of women generally supported conservative desires to keep them in the home, it is indeed tempting to conclude that *The Return of the Deputy* merely offered a particularly compelling argument to antifeminists who sought to justify the restriction of women to the ever-narrowing domestic sphere. Read within its immediate historical context, however, the play breaks with tradition. In the world of the play, women are entitled to extensive education on a par with men; they are also entitled, within the private and domestic sphere, to a new degree of authority and influence. Both of these entitlements would allow women to outgrow their conventional roles. Both, in the long run, would provide the legitimacy necessary for later, more successful, feminist agitation.

Although act 1 offers a glowing commentary on the reform initiatives in the Four-Year Parliament, the discussion of the most contentious issue—the restoration of the hereditary throne—is delayed until the third, and final, act. Act 3 also brings a resolution of the courtship plot. When Mr. Charming is exposed as a hunter of dowries, Mr. Windbag consents to the marriage of Teresa and Walery, but he does so on the condition that he will take control of his future grandsons' upbringing and education in order to mold them as he himself has been molded. While the characters await the outcome of a referendum about royal succession, then, Mr. Windbag raises the issue of succession within his family.

The fact that Mr. Windbag—a man who has no regard for the public good and who is beyond all hope of reformation—should be allowed to raise a new generation in his family is likely to be perceived by readers and spectators as something of a scandal. In the play, however, no one is alarmed when Mr. Windbag announces his plan to turn his future grandsons into clones of himself, so that they can act as a brake on progress. Instead, Walery assures Mr. Windbag that he and Teresa will do everything they can to earn his favor. If Walery means what he says, then the celebratory tone of the play's ending glosses over some knotty problems that bode ill for the future of Poland-Lithuania. Here, then, is the play's fundamental dilemma: How can virtue be exacted from the vicious? Mr. Justice's eloquent argumentation has not been able to damage Old Corruption that is far too unblushing, and too profitable to its beneficiaries, to crumble easily; the transfer of educational authority from the enlightened husband and wife to an unscrupulous feudal lord snared in the net of greed and ignorance will only help perpetuate Old Corruption's defects. In other words, although the play offers a number of plausible ways to encourage the good to be more so—chief among them, better education, benevolent reform, and female influence—its advocacy of virtue is powerless before persons who have no conscience. That is the lesson of the play's closing scene.

But what if Teresa and Walery have daughters as well as sons? Mr. Windbag, of course, is not interested in his future granddaughters because women cannot be citizens. Thus, Teresa and Walery will be free to raise their daughters in keeping with the new ideas about child-rearing, parent-child relations, gender roles, marriage, and the husband-wife bond. Ultimately, then, we are left with the suggestion that the play silently entrusts the arduous process of Poland-Lithuania's long-term modernization into the hands of enlightened women like Mr. Windbag's future granddaughters. In short, *The Return of the Deputy* is a political satire that is also informed, quietly but effectively, by a vision of a new and different society in which women would enjoy an expanded political agency.

VII.

During the rest of the 1790–91 season, *The Return of the Deputy* continued to play to sold-out houses. Together with Bogusławski's 1790 adaptation of Louis-Sébastien Mercier's *The Vinegar Seller's Cart* (*La Brouette du Vinaigrier*, 1775), it became a major source of box-office income for the National Theatre. There were also other monetary rewards. At curtain call during the third performance (on 20 January 1791), the fans of Karol Świerzawski, the National's leading actor, presented him with a purse of gold in appreciation of his virtuoso portrayal of Mr. Windbag.[163] The play returned to the stage the following season, attracting record numbers of spectators again. The director of the National Theatre, Bogusławski, promptly capitalized on the fact that the fame—or notoriety—of *The Return of the Deputy* just grew and grew. He dashed off a sequel, with an eye on the forthcoming anniversary celebrations to commemorate Stanisław August's election as king. Entitled *The Nation's Grateful Tribute* (*Dowód wdzięczności narodu*), the sequel opened at the National Theatre on 15 September 1791. The cast again featured Świerzawski as Mr. Windbag.

Like *The Return of the Deputy*, *The Nation's Grateful Tribute* takes place at the Justices' country estate. The time is early September 1791. The characters—a mix of some of Niemcewicz's protagonists and Bogusławski's own inventions—gather for a lavish fete both to eulogize Stanisław August for having spearheaded the modernization of the state and to celebrate a newly forged alliance between nobles and burghers, made possible by the Constitution of 3 May 1791. To most of the characters, the Constitution marks the advent of a renovated world of joy, peace, confidence, and prosperity. Predictably, the only dissenting voice is that of Mr. Windbag. In the opening scenes, he grumbles that the Constitution is an outburst of folly that has deprived noblemen like himself of their fundamental liberties, but he concedes that several constitutional provisions, including the restoration of hereditary succession, make sense. What he cannot tolerate, however, is the Constitution's challenge to the traditional social order: burghers are to enjoy some of the rights and privileges of the nobility, and serfs have won legal protection by the state. To Mr. Windbag, the very idea that the Constitution allows urban delegates to testify in Parliament is anathema. In short, this firm upholder of social hierarchy is concerned that the line that has served to divide nobles from commoners for centuries is beginning to fade. His instinctive contempt for the lower classes, combined with his anxiety that Poland-Lithuania could be fair game for explosive anarchy, tempers his enthusiasm both for constitutional reform and the Justices' fete.

And yet the fact that halfway through the play Mr. Windbag is impressed by the patriotic loyalty and devotion of a young officer, Mr. Upright, suggests that this overbearing and predatory feudal baron has lost some of his arrogance and cynicism since we first met him in *The Return of the Deputy*. In Niemcewicz's play, Mr. Justice expounds the virtues of courage, civic responsibility, and selfless dedication to one's country, but Mr. Windbag, always intent on protecting his interests, declares with disconcerting ease that foreign incursions on Poland-Lithuania are not without their benefits. In Bogusławski's sequel, by contrast, Mr. Windbag is so taken by Mr. Upright's rejection of an attractive offer to betray his country and join a Russian army that he immediately presents him with his best horses and an expensive, pearl-studded saddle. One would have never thought that the antipatriotic, self-seeking, and miserly Mr. Windbag would be capable of such patriotic effusions and lavish gift-giving, but Bogusławski's sequel makes the optimistic point that the unwonted sense of genuine freedom after 3 May 1791 has created a psychological environment in which even the most selfish, irresponsible, or corrupt are capable of metamorphosis.

The louche Frenchified fop, Mr. Charming, is another case in point. In Niemcewicz's play, he is an icy and calculating schemer, heartlessly indifferent to the fate of his country. In Bogusławski's sequel, the constitutional reform and an infectious surge of exultant patriotism in the wider society inspire Mr. Charming to abandon his foppish and self-indulgent lifestyle and to do his share of public service by enlisting in the national cavalry, a kind of gentry militia. He arrives at the Justices with his regiment to add splendor to the fete. The transformation of a fop into a cavalry officer and an ardent patriot triggers the second stage of Mr. Windbag's metamorphosis. He fits himself out in proper knightly attire, complete with a demi-armor and a sword inscribed with Horace's maxim, "*Dulce et decorum est pro patria mori*" (It is sweet and honorable to die for one's country). Thus outfitted, he joins Mr. Charming's troops in a show of martial skills and demonstrates that he is no novice to the military way of life. What initially looked like Mr. Windbag's miraculous metamorphosis from a provincial bully and an unscrupulous opportunist bent on personal gain into a patriotic citizen, then, is in fact a return to his earlier, youthful persona when he adopted Horace's classic maxim of patriotism and defended his country against invasions. Mr. Windbag completes his transformation when he hears Mr. Mouthful's stirring oration on liberty, patriotic activism, and social equality. Mr. Mouthful is a young artisan from a nearby town whom burghers have elected as their delegate to testify in Parliament. Earlier, Mr. Windbag derided the idea of sending urban delegates to Parliament because he assumed that working-class men were semiliterate and inarticulate. His assumptions are now proven wrong: Mr. Mouthful is educated and has a gift for public speaking. Mr. Windbag admits that he has learned a valuable lesson in the spirit of the Enlightenment: "A person from the lower classes can be a man of reason, too; it all depends on good education."[164]

The Nation's Grateful Tribute, then, is a story of noblemen awakening to their responsibility for promoting the public good. However, gender relations, so richly explored in *The Return of the Deputy*, receive little attention in Bogusławski's play. While *The Return of the Deputy* shows that an improved education for women is a key issue in the efforts to better their condition, the sequel is silent about the need to provide women with better educational opportunities. While *The Return of the Deputy* advocates change in women's social status and supports their indirect participation in public life, the sequel restores limitations on the spheres of activity open to women and relegates its only major female character, Mrs. Justice, to a mere supporting role. Furthermore, the sequel insists that while the male characters are capable of self-improvement, Mrs. Windbag is not. Although she does not appear in the play, we learn that she has moved to Warsaw where she plans to remain unless her husband satisfies her costly whims. It is clear that she still refuses to engage in useful pursuits; instead, she embraces the ideal of leisured femininity and engages in the leisure activities that she understands to be appropriate to her station and her sex. In short, *The Nation's Grateful Tribute* makes a great case for rationality and the importance of serious education, for social equality, and for the necessary and long overdue correction of error, but all of Bogusławski's female characters are excluded from this vision.

2 ||| Poland Unmanned?
Zofia Chrzanowska

I.

IN DECEMBER 1797, a veteran of the American Revolutionary War petitioned the US Congress for a pension. There was nothing particularly remarkable or unusual about the petition—except for the fact that the petitioner was a woman, Deborah Sampson Gannett. Fifteen years earlier, she had enlisted in the Continental Army disguised as a man, signed a receipt for a bounty of sixty pounds as "Robert Shurtlieff" (possibly "Robert Shurtliff"), and served undetected for over a year.[1] In applying for a pension, she found an enthusiastic advocate in Philip Freneau, known to his contemporaries as "the poet of the Revolution."[2] To support her petition, he wrote a poem, "On Deborah Gannet [sic]," and published it in the New York *Time-Piece* on 4 December 1797.

In the poem, Freneau presents Gannett as "a heroine in a bold career" who has distinguished herself by her passionate devotion to liberty, as well as her military drive, tactical acumen, and deeds of derring-do.[3] Her "generous toils" in the cause of American independence from Britain have been entirely selfless, but in her waning years she deserves at least some of the rewards that men have so long monopolized for themselves.[4] Intriguingly enough, Freneau depicts Gannett's "bold career" not as a curiosity or an anomaly, but rather as an illustration of a variety of female experience that would have been more widespread had not women been discouraged from undertaking activities usually reserved for men.

From the perspective of gender studies, however, perhaps the most intriguing aspect of Freneau's poem is the argument he makes in the final stanza. Freneau calls on his readers, including the members of Congress, to

> reflect—how many tender ties
> A woman must forego [sic]
> Ere to the field of war she flies
> To meet a savage foe—
> How many bars has nature plac'd,
> And custom many more
> That women never should be grac'd
> With honours won from war.
> All these she nobly overcame,
> . . . .
> Check'd not her military flame,
> But scorn'd a censuring age,
> And men that with contracted mind,
> All arrogant, condemn
> And make disgrace in woman kind
> What honour is in them.[5]

Freneau's argument is twofold. First, he insists that restrictive social or customary norms presented a far more formidable obstacle to Gannett's determination to fight in the war than her biological femaleness. Second, his references to "a censuring age" and "contracted mind[s]" make it clear that he regards notions of what constitutes "disgrace in woman kind" as time- and culture-specific rather than timeless and universal.

It would not be extravagant to say that Freneau's argument provides evidence of feminist thought long before any formal move was under way for the emancipation of women, indeed long before the word *feminism* itself came into use. Gannett's "bold career" provides him with an opportunity for explicit criticism of the binary gender system, underpinned by polarized preconceptions of what counts as appropriate male or female behavior. If women can perform as well as men, as the poem reminds us, it follows that the division into the spheres of activity open to men and those open to women is a questionable social convention. Freneau's argument, then, suggests that one should view with skepticism, if not suspicion, the idea that the biological difference between men and women legitimates the separate and dissimilar places in which they find themselves in the social order. His argument also suggests that gender, be it masculinity or femininity, is not a stable and fixed essence, determined biologically; rather, gender exists discursively within historical coordinates that are not immutable. In short, Freneau's argument drives a wedge into essentializing equivalences between sex and gender and thus anticipates the sex/gender distinction that has been so useful in feminist theory as a bulwark against biological determinism: while the division of the biological characteristics of sex is a fact of nature, the division of genders is a fact of social and cultural construction, open to negotiation.[6]

It may be difficult to believe that Freneau's poem was written in the eighteenth century. As I have argued in the introduction to this book, the Enlightenment saw a fundamental revolution in sexual science, impelled by an imperative to find uniform laws of nature and to establish the exact differentiation of sexual character. The Enlightenment science of sexuality designed and implemented new methods of measuring sexual difference to buttress the ideology of sexual character, with its vision of men and women not as equals but as complementary opposites, and to ground gender roles in the biological divergence between the sexes. Thus, the differences between masculinity and femininity came to be understood as a polar distinction rooted in, and justified by, biology. Considering that the deterministic link between sex and gender continued to shape the prescriptive guidelines for socially acceptable behavior for men and women well into the twentieth century, it is fair to say that the questions Freneau's poem raises about cultural practice with regard to gender are ahead of his time.

The same might be said about two Polish plays that were first published nine years before Freneau's poem appeared in a New York newspaper: Józef Wybicki's *The Polish Woman* and Stanisław Kublicki's *The Defense of Trembowla, or the Manly Courage of Chrzanowska*.[7] On the most obvious level, the plays can be read as unproblematic patriotic paeans, commemorating a victory in a military campaign against an Ottoman attack and celebrating an exceptional woman whose plucky intervention and "manly courage" (to cite Kublicki's subtitle) made the victory possible. However, in honoring an ordinary woman who "check'd not her military flame" (to quote Freneau's poem) and ventured into traditional male territory, both plays necessarily pose destabilizing alternatives to the prevailing conception of gender roles and identities at the time. In doing so, the plays (like Freneau's poem) put into question the essentialist frameworks that depend on the "naturalness" and fixity of gender categories. In short, the plays raise the issue of the fungibility of gender and extend this issue into the realm of citizenship and the patterns of inclusion and exclusion that shape membership in a citizenship community. As Barbara Hobson and Ruth Lister point out, "Historically, men as a group have been tied to citizenship through their soldiering, and thus always have been treated as having stronger claims for political and social citizenship" than women.[8] Within the gendered historical template of citizenship, women have been assigned the role of reproducers and civilizers, "responsible for bearing and rearing the next generation of citizens," yet women's claims to citizenship through mothering "have not had the same discursive power as those made on behalf of men who have 'served their country' in war."[9] In presenting Zofia Chrzanowska's radically different claim to citizenship through transgressive, gender-bending militancy, Wybicki's and Kublicki's plays appear to challenge established ways of thinking about patriotic activism and the practice of citizenship in relation to gender.

Was it just a coincidence that Wybicki and Kublicki chose to take up the story of Chrzanowska (ca. 1640–ca. 1700)—an audacious, unruly, even scandalous patriot-heroine who flouted normative femininity—in 1788? Why at this date rather than earlier or later?

It might be tempting to see *The Polish Woman* and *The Defense of Trembowla* as part of the vigorous polemics that accompanied the Four-Year Parliament. The modernizers, it will be remembered, pressed for a comprehensive package of reform legislation to put the state on a firm and even keel. To drum up public support for their cause, they used a double strategy. They "tried their best" to reassure the conservative, traditionalist sectors of the electorate that "what they were advocating was not at all removed from the spirit of the old *Rzeczpospolita* [i.e., the Republic of Poland-Lithuania]."[10] At the same time, they launched a campaign to secure a wide dissemination of their arguments for reform; their arsenal included newspapers, poems, plays, pamphlets, and single-page circulars and broadsides, that generation's equivalent of today's sound bites. However, the explosion of reformist debate skirted the subject of the status of women within society.[11]

This is not to say that women were excluded from participation in the public sphere. A very small number of women wielded influence and made their voices heard in a world where men, by their own account, were the proper custodians of knowledge and power. In particular, elite women engaged in informal lobbying and canvassing as *salonnières*, directed much of the raucous political theatre in Parliament, and served as unofficial diplomats. At least one elite woman, Countess Amelia Mniszech (1736–1772), and possibly also Princess Zofia Lubomirska (1718–1790) went beyond lobbying and drafted their own proposals to reform the political system of the Commonwealth.[12] But femaleness—or, more specifically, gender ideology, i.e., the network of significations that have traditionally delimited the category *woman*—disqualified women for parliamentary representation and political office. As elsewhere, it was taken for granted that manhood was a prerequisite for full citizenship or institutionalized political participation. Those women who gained public attention by engaging in the power play of high politics were vulnerable to scathing ridicule and vilification by commentators across the entire political spectrum.[13]

By recounting the story of the transgressive Chrzanowska at that moment, under those circumstances, what did Wybicki and Kublicki hope to gain? Their plays seem to convey a palpable sense of a thoroughly feminist pride in their own "heroine in a bold career." Could it be, then, that the plays were an attempt to contest unenlightened, even misogynistic views of Polish Enlightenment thinkers and writers about women? Could it be, in other words, that their colleagues' misogynistic writings—such as Ignacy Krasicki's satires on fashion-obsessed society ladies aping French styles—provided Wybicki and Kublicki with opportunities for the retaliatory defense of women? Or, rather, did Wybicki and Kublicki use the Chrzanowska story as a tool of political persuasion to shame their sluggish or skeptical male compatriots into "manly courage"? If so, was it meant to prod them to save the state by modernizing its system of governance? Or was it intended to sway public opinion toward an anti-Turkish alliance with Russia after Stanisław August had met with Catherine II in 1787 to offer Polish military assistance in Russia's war with the Ottoman Empire—an involvement that would have required Parliament to approve the alliance and impose heavy taxes to augment the Polish army?[14] Given rising Russophobia among the Polish nobility, however, isn't it more likely that Wybicki and Kublicki chose Turkey as a timely euphemism for Russia at a time when the Four-Year

Parliament began to dismantle the edifice of Russian hegemony in Poland-Lithuania and "anti-Russian gestures were the height of fashion"?[15]

Regardless of the authorial intent, of which we know little, it is reasonable to take as my starting point the fact that the story of Chrzanowska's transgressive patriotism enters Polish drama in the highly politicized context of the 1780s or, more specifically, in the context of anxieties about the future of the state and disputes over ways to rescue it from decline. At the same time, I suggest that the puzzle of gender in Wybicki's and Kublicki's plays deserves closer scrutiny.

II.

At the center of this chapter is a story of transgression that cuts to the heart of cultural practice during "a censuring age." It is a story about love and anger, decorum and effrontery, discipline and deception, and the dos and don'ts of "proper" patriotic conduct. Its components include invasion from abroad, flagging morale, conspiracy, concealed weapons, attempted murder, and attempted suicide. The story involves civilians and soldiers, gendered space, and one of the more striking cases of gender nonconformity recorded in Polish history. What makes this story significant, rather than merely interesting, is the cultural landscape it illuminates, the contours it reveals, and the opportunity it presents to examine responses to a violation of the socially prescribed norms of gender-appropriate behavior. If pushed hard enough, it may be made to expose social tensions and cultural accommodations at a time when it became the subject of Wybicki's and Kublicki's plays.

In this chapter, our window opens at Trembowla, a garrison town and a major fortress in a string of border posts in a volatile frontier region between the Polish-Lithuanian Commonwealth and the Ottoman Empire. The year is 1675. The two countries are at war with each other. In mid-August, Jan Samuel Chrzanowski, an experienced army officer who has distinguished himself in recent campaigns, is posted to Trembowla to take command of the fortress, but is ordered to bring only half of his regiment. On 21 September, a Turkish army, which vastly outnumbers a 300-strong Polish force, surrounds Trembowla. The Turkish commander-in-chief calls on Chrzanowski to surrender, promising to spare the garrison. Chrzanowski turns down the offer; the Turks attack. Although the fortress suffers heavy losses, Chrzanowski is determined to hold out. When the Turks make excavations to plant explosives underneath the fortress, however, some of his men lose heart. Chrzanowski's wife, Zofia Chrzanowska, gets wind of their secret plot to surrender and alerts her husband. He confronts the conspirators and threatens to have them executed for treason. To boost the morale of the decimated and exhausted troops and to help out with the defense, Chrzanowska takes up arms. She fights bravely at her husband's side and leads sorties from the fortress to harass the Turkish forces. Her fearlessness is rousing. And yet, according to some accounts, Chrzanowski begins to doubt whether the fortress, lacking adequate supplies, can sustain further resistance. Although the story of Chrzanowski's wavering may have been inserted in a later version of the events, all accounts agree that something about the defense sparks a furious protest from his wife. Brandishing two knives and shouting angry, abusive words, she threatens to kill Chrzanowski and to take her own life. According to one version of the incident, she also threatens to blow up the fortress. Her violent outburst proves exactly what the situation requires, and the garrison holds its own until Polish reinforcements arrive. After two weeks of siege, the Turkish commander sounds the retreat.[16]

The Trembowla incident, while interesting in and of itself, takes on added significance when considered alongside the ideas and practices that constituted the normative framework for conceptualizations of masculinity and femininity. Read in this light, the incident was outrageous on several counts. To begin with, Chrzanowska transgressed the matrimonial command of wifely subordination. Her patriotic passion, uncontrollable and uncontainable, overflowed the boundaries set by patriarchal authority and undermined the "proper" governance of women by men. Second, Chrzanowska's outrage flouted the widely accepted assumption that legitimate angry emotions, or proper anger, were the prerogative of the male. At Trembowla, Chrzanowska overstepped the line of propriety and acted with the angry authority of a man; that is to say, she demonstrated the assertiveness that was required of a self-respecting man but was frowned on in women. Third, Chrzanowska further defied gender boundaries by serving as a soldier rather than a mere morale-booster. In her day, and it was a long day, femininity was associated with frailty, timidity, and passivity, while the central quality of manhood was identified as the ability to act with firmness, decision, and fearlessness. As a result, the female was perceived as an inferior being, requiring ceaseless guidance and protection from men. Chrzanowska's exploits, however, called into question the common claim that submissiveness was characteristic of, or appropriate for, women. The woman at the center of the Trembowla incident, then, can be described as a radical risk-taker. She had to contend with a powerful gender order in which the divide between masculinity and femininity was fundamental to every aspect of life, yet she was able to trouble the dividing line and to confound normative ideas about how women should speak and behave.

To say that the story of the Trembowla siege does not lack a dramatic flair would be to make an understatement. In the late 1780s, this stirring episode caught the imagination of two writers and legislators who were involved in radical politics: Wybicki and Kublicki.[17] It is indeed one of the fascinating puzzles in the history of Polish drama that Chrzanowska was featured as the leading character in two plays at once. In choosing the Trembowla story, however, Wybicki and Kublicki walked a precarious tightrope. The incident at Trembowla—essentially, an inversion of expected gender roles and an affront to received ideas of masculinity and femininity—unavoidably brings up a familiar theme of the overmastering wife and the overmastered husband. The problem here is that this theme functioned in European literature as a comic trope, an integral part of risible topsy-turviness.[18] In reclaiming the story of the Trembowla siege for patriotic drama, then, it could have been tempting to place Chrzanowska at the margin rather than at the center of male activity, to shift the focus from her "military flame" to her morale-boosting role, or even to censure her impetuous trespassing onto male territory by showing that her outrage was disproportionate to her husband's offense. And yet Wybicki and Kublicki were uninterested in disciplining their gender-bending patriot-heroine. *The Polish Woman* and *The Defense of Trembowla* are particularly intriguing precisely because they unapologetically presented a patriotic model that stems from nonnormative behavior, and they did so at a time when the discourse of femininity continued to propagate the model of the docile, self-effacing, and obedient woman. In celebrating travesties of the rules of female conduct, both plays valorize violations of decorum, inversions of protocol, breaches of discipline, and even challenges to the gendered social order. What are we to make of all this? What *can* we make of the plays from a vanished world, a world before the deluge? Are they tips of lost icebergs? Do they alert us to a submerged feminist tradition in eighteenth-century Polish culture?

In prior scholarship, *The Polish Woman* and *The Defense of Trembowla* have received scant commentary, if at all. For example, Maria Bogucka, in her important study, *Women in Early Modern Polish Society, against the European Background*, brings up the story of Chrzanowska, but passes over Wybicki's and Kublicki's plays in silence. In discussing views of Polish Enlightenment writers about women, she highlights Franciszek Salezy Jezierski's article, "Women" ("Kobiety"), in his compendium, *A Few Terms, Alphabetically Arranged and Properly Explained* (*Niektóre wyrazy porządkiem abecadła zebrane i stosownymi do rzeczy uwagami objaśnione*), first published in 1791. She enthusiastically credits Jezierski, one of the leading radical writers of the Polish Enlightenment, with "open[ing] a new epoch" in the history of Polish attitudes toward women, and specifically with being "the first to challenge the old virtue of 'modesty proper to the fair sex,' that prevented women from appearing in the public forum."[19] How one interprets Jezierski's compendium, however, depends on what one includes in the discussion. Admittedly, Jezierski remarks that "woman . . . is of the same nature as man; nothing prevents her from exercising her will, her reason, and her power."[20] This observation may sound like a factual statement of gender equality, but Jezierski immediately points out that in reality there is a great deal to prevent women from asserting their will, reason, and power. Their opportunities, he argues, are seriously curtailed because women live in a world controlled by men and therefore are socialized into self-effacement, submissiveness, and obedience. For all his realistic assessment of the difficulties women have faced, however, Jezierski is eager to dichotomize character traits by sex and to make scornful generalizations about women. In an article entitled "Illness" ("Choroba"), he defines women as "the sex that is prone to laziness and vanity."[21] To illustrate this point, he contends that women like to pretend illness in order to attract attention and to solicit flattery. He expands on this argument in the other sections of the compendium, deploying the familiar repertoire of gender stereotypes that seek to prove women's inferiority and thus to bolster the traditional gender hierarchy. Time and again, he asserts that women are vain, deceitful, cunning, shallow, and incapable of sacrificing their creature comforts for higher, selfless purposes.[22] In short, Jezierski's book both dispels and reinforces conventional thinking about women. This combination of progressive and traditional discourses reflects the contradictions of the Enlightenment project with regard to gender. As a result,

Jezierski's compendium is useful to a discussion of gender in the Polish Enlightenment only in the sense that it can serve as a good corrective to generalizations about how "the theory of Enlightenment married harmoniously with the reality of everyday life in Poland."[23]

When *The Polish Woman* and *The Defense of Trembowla* are considered in scholarship, they are regarded as mere offshoots of Kniaźnin's *The Spartan Mother* and the Czartoryskis' campaign to define "true" patriotism in opposition to the "false" patriots in Warsaw—Stanisław August and his circle.[24] Such views, however, gloss over crucial differences between the three plays. Admittedly, Kublicki was elected to the Four-Year Parliament as the Czartoryskis' protégé. Moreover, *The Polish Woman* and *The Defense of Trembowla* are dedicated to Józefa Potocka, thus implicitly honoring her husband, Szczęsny Potocki, the Czartoryskis' model patriot in the 1780s and the addressee of Kniaźnin's dedication in *The Spartan Mother*. It is also true that Wybicki and Kublicki were familiar with *The Spartan Mother* and that all three plays share the same thematic template: a seemingly hopeless military situation is turned around thanks to what might be called female patriotic excess. However, *The Polish Woman* and *The Defense of Trembowla* imagine female patriotic excess in ways quite different from those used in *The Spartan Mother*. It is hardly necessary to say that Wybicki's and Kublicki's heroine is not another Teona.

Although scholars of the Polish Enlightenment have devoted much attention to the ways in which plays and performances sought to inculcate patriotic sentiments and civic obligations, the problem of gender is missing from these investigations, apart from rather predictable references to the supporting cast of wives, mothers, and daughters. In discussing *The Polish Woman*, for example, Roman Kaleta only briefly acknowledges Chrzanowska's courage and determination, while offering an extensive and insightful commentary on two of the male characters.[25] The problem with Kaleta's reading, of course, is that Wybicki's Chrzanowska is not relegated to a supporting role. In a critical aside, Kaleta appears to address this issue by noting that the attention lavished on Chrzanowska in *The Polish Woman* is a rhetorical ploy to convince the audience of "the advantages of an alliance between men and women who are inspired by a shared commitment to defend their homeland."[26] To expand on this idea, Kaleta turns to Wybicki's earlier plays. His paradigmatic example is *The Samnite Woman* (*Samnitka*, 1787) because, he argues, it shows that women have the power to transform their "husbands, sons, and lovers" into men of action.²⁷ How do they accomplish that great end? Kaleta sidelines the plot of *The Samnite Woman* to focus on a single sentence: "Women rule men's hearts and teach them how to act."²⁸ This maxim suggests that men are directionless, inadequate, and generally deficient—in short, unmanly; they need women to lead them into rectitude, to discipline them to be virtuous citizens, to lure them to the exercise of manly virtue. However, Kaleta does not delve into the disquieting implications of the line he has quoted from *The Samnite Woman*. Instead, he merges *The Samnite Woman* and *The Polish Woman* into a continuum because he finds that the maxim "Women rule men's hearts and teach them how to act" applies equally well to the characters in each play. But to accept Kaleta's conclusion is to overlook the fact that the plot of *The Samnite Woman* is antithetical to that of *The Polish Woman*. In contrast to *The Polish Woman*, *The Samnite Woman* emphasizes male domination and female subordination. Although some female characters in *The Samnite Woman* serve as facilitators of male patriotic passion and activism, they are primarily presented as angels of submission and sexual rewards: a man who distinguishes himself in battle gets the fairest woman.

Clearly, Wybicki's and Kublicki's plays are part of the *terrae incognitae* occupied by dramatic writings still awaiting rediscovery and close reading through a gender-sensitive lens. Lest it seem that I tendentiously smuggle modern ideas and theories into texts from the past, I offer that it was Kublicki's preface to *The Defense of Trembowla* that set alight my interest in the problem of gender during the closing decades of the eighteenth century in Poland.

The preface begins with two traditional ideas: a belief in the potency of examples and a conviction that history is the best training manual to wean the public from fruitless passions and to quicken the pulse of patriotic desire, especially when a national community is in crisis. Kublicki suggests that we do not learn patriotic devotion and civic responsibility from abstract formulations. Rather, we need certain emblematic presences with whom we could imaginatively identify. This role is best served by great individuals from the past who provide us with both instructive models and haunting second selves. It is through rehearsing in our minds the deeds of those great individuals that we may summon up the strength to imitate their virtuous conduct. So far, Kublicki's preface offers no surprises. The eighteenth century was a period obsessed with the idea of emulation—of putting representations of great men (and, on occasion, of great women) before the eyes of the population so vividly that their example would lead to widespread imitation.

Kublicki then introduces the metaphor of parent and child to describe a relationship between a national community and its pantheon of great men and women. Just as a child is inspired by both parents to become a responsible adult, a national community needs to foster strong bonds of identification with both male and female heroes in order to produce responsible citizens. This argument makes it clear that a national community inspired solely by great men or by great women is a dysfunctional family. In Kublicki's view, the Polish national community is such a dysfunctional family because it has accepted the arbitrary exclusion of great Polish women from public memory. Now that Poland is in crisis, historians and writers are eager to publicize inspirational models, but the great individuals whom they celebrate are invariably men. According to Kublicki, this exclusion of women from Polish historiography and literature is a prejudicial weakness that hampers the process of modeling patriotic behavior: "It's a pity that the deeds of our heroines do not command the attention of our talented authors. There are only brief references to them, scattered here and there in historical accounts, although they merit a separate presentation.... Writers, why are you reluctant to immortalize our heroines? ... You have talent; now gather up your courage to break the silence about their virtues, so that they can live on in the memory of future generations."[29]

Kublicki's appeal is a thoroughly radical proposition, demonstrating that he understood the need to challenge what nowadays is called a male-centered perspective in historiography and literature. Alert to the influence of women in history, he argues that Polish heroines have been doubly slighted: by historians who fail to accord them proper recognition and by writers who lack historical documentation to give them their due. Urging historians and writers to rise above the prejudices of their time and to rediscover the heroism of their female ancestors, Kublicki wants both to recover lost cultural resources and to pursue fresh lines of thinking and writing. He views his play on Chrzanowska as an attempt to blaze the trail and to encourage others to follow suit, so that they can correct the gender imbalance and thus heal the dysfunctional national community.

As I have noted earlier, it is tempting to reduce Wybicki's *The Polish Woman* and Kublicki's *The Defense of Trembowla* to an unproblematic celebration of an exceptional woman who made an invaluable contribution to a military campaign to defend her country. It is equally tempting to make much of the role exchange taking place between men and women in *The Polish Woman* and *The Defense of Trembowla* and to reduce these plays to a mere reversal of the usual male/female hierarchy. To avoid such temptations, I propose to explore an overlooked component of the plays: the paradox of patriotic loyalty and devotion conflated with gender insubordination. Accordingly, I want to consider *all* of their female characters and to examine how and to what ends the plays stake, protect, and cultivate their momentous investments in women. When women speak in these plays, in whose interests are they speaking?

III.

Featuring a Polish "heroine in a bold career," *The Polish Woman* and *The Defense of Trembowla* are strangely cryptic texts, at once revealing and opaque. While, on the one hand, they follow the familiar story about how a major success of a Polish army in the seventeenth century was mainly due to a woman's "manly courage," they also, on the other hand, graft onto the preexisting narrative several intriguing dramaturgical stratagems.

Both plays begin on an uplifting note: the numerical superiority of the Turkish troops is more than matched by the almost suicidal bravery of Chrzanowski and his men. They do not wait for the attackers to close in on Trembowla, but instead ride out of the fortress to counterattack. Victory seems to be within reach. In a sudden reversal, however, the Polish forces are pushed back to the fortress. The crux of each play is the enraged Chrzanowska's violent confrontation with her husband over the question of surrender. In Wybicki's *The Polish Woman*, she draws her sword on Chrzanowski. In Kublicki's *The Defense of Trembowla*, she wields two knives, as in the original story. In both plays, she not only browbeats her husband into persevering but also humiliates him by proclaiming herself the new commander of the fortress.

Before proceeding to analyze the plays, it is helpful to situate them in the context of the Enlightenment discourse of gender and its polarization of the sexes.[30] Although Enlightenment thinkers set a new intellectual agenda that began to pay unprecedented attention to the worth and the place of women in society, they also "separated women and men by the physical characteristics of sex and affirmed maleness as the universal standard, thus relegating women to a category of difference."[31] Enlightenment political theory only rarely contemplated the idea of women's political participation in civic society, and gender discourse continued to cast women as inferior in intellect to men, as weaker vessels that had to be both disciplined and protected. For example, in the longest of the four entries entitled "Femme" in the seventeen volumes of Denis Diderot and Jean Le Rond d'Alembert's *Encyclopédie* (1751–65), women are depicted as "weak, timid, shrewd, false, less capable of attention than men, vicious, vindictive, equivocable, cruel, curious, less capable of friendship with their own sex, living a continual lie called coquetry, vain, superficial, deceitful, inconstant, etc."[32] It was also believed—and the most distinguished and enlightened minds of the eighteenth century, such as Kant and Rousseau, shared this belief—that woman's destiny, unlike man's, is wholly defined by her biology; this gender dualism, itself the product of patriarchal history, presumed that "woman was closer to nature than man because of her physiological role in sex and motherhood."[33] The notion of a close relation of woman to nature was used, on the one hand, to celebrate women's supposedly natural aptitude for nurturing and caring and, on the other, to justify their exclusion from political rights. Because of their alleged closeness to nature, women were perceived as emotionally unstable, prone to irrational impulses, and incapable of impartial judgment. According to his logic, women should not participate in political assemblies or concern themselves with public matters because they do not have the mental or emotional capacity to do so.

Written at a time when Enlightenment discourse and practice privileged maleness, thus reinforcing the time-honored notions of female inferiority and the attendant restrictions on women's participation in the public sphere, *The Polish Woman* and *The Defense of Trembowla* break with the customary assumptions and perceptions that attributed certain qualities to women to keep them in their place. It is as if the siege of Trembowla became for Wybicki and Kublicki a shining opportunity to prove such assumptions and perceptions wrong. At the center of each play is a woman who demonstrates her quick intelligence and adamantine strength of will, her self-confidence and assertiveness, her public spirit and defiant courage in the face of a looming military disaster. She does not solicit protection by men; instead, she takes matters into her own hands. And whatever she does—whether it is challenging her husband's judgment or taking up arms and assuming command of the fortress—falls outside acceptable gender norms.

It would be unfair to Wybicki and Kublicki, however, to fail to notice that despite the many similarities between their plays each of them presents a somewhat different Chrzanowska. In *The Polish Woman,* Chrzanowska is an admirable woman whose patriotism and heroism are unquestionable. She even risks straining her credibility by asserting that Polish women are free of the failings that have been regarded elsewhere as an intrinsic part of the female nature. In *The Defense of Trembowla,* Chrzanowska is admirable, but not particularly pleasant or likable. She is forthright, brave, and determined, but she can also be meddlesome and condescending. No wonder both her husband and her sister-in-law, Dobrogniewa, resent her rebukes. To put these points more broadly, Kublicki's play has psychological nuance that Wybicki's drama often lacks.

These differences aside, both plays show a Chrzanowska who has only contempt for the notion that women are fit for nothing but trivial pursuits. She goes far beyond typical expectations and assumes a leading role in the male sphere of military action, risks danger, and wins glory in a heroic defense of a key outpost: Trembowla teeters on the edge of collapse only to be saved by Chrzanowska's fearlessly "unfeminine" behavior that transgresses the limits of the gendered status quo. It is the paradox of Trembowla, then, that the restoration of the patriotic ethos with its own set of codes, values, and norms is made possible by Chrzanowska's violation of the normative ideas about gender roles and identities.

This ostensible meaning of Wybicki's and Kublicki's plays is not without problems. *The Polish Woman* and *The Defense of Trembowla* present anxieties about the loss of political sovereignty in terms of concerns about the men's slide into effeminacy. In the world of both plays, men are supposed to be manly: honest, strong-minded, assertive, self-reliant, intrepid, valiant, protective of women and country. But they are not, with fateful consequences for Poland. They are often described as self-indulgent, luxury-loving, faint-hearted, panic-prone, sluggish, craven, untrustworthy, even treacherous. In short, Poland has declined because the common good has been neglected by men who have come to occupy the position designated female in traditional debates about gender identity. While Poland's vulnerability to attacks from abroad is blamed on the men's effeminacy, their remasculinization is associated with a threat of female patriotic excess, exemplified by Chrzanowska in her position as the self-appointed commander of the Trembowla fortress. This kind of heroine-worship is double-edged because it can be easily absorbed into the language of gender stereotypes, chief among them the stereotype of the wily or manipulative woman.

In other words, while Wybicki's and Kublicki's plays cede considerable power and authority to a female character who refuses to conform to conventional notions of gender, her power and authority come at a considerable price. For all their empowering potential, the plays may seem to be trapped in essentializing equivalences between sex and gender, after all. This suspicious reading appears to be borne out in some of Wybicki's and Kublicki's dramaturgical choices. For example, Kublicki introduces the character of the Chrzanowskis' son, Zbigniew. Why is it important for Kublicki to highlight Chrzanowska's motherhood? Could it be that her motherhood is meant to provide a counterbalance to her gender nonconformity by supporting more traditional options for women?

IV.

Although the title of Wybicki's play honors "the Polish woman" (presumably Chrzanowska, here renamed Kazanowska), it is a male character, Plichta, who often steals the show. A veteran of many military campaigns, Plichta is never stingy with his experience, his time, and especially his words. Throughout the play, he regularly launches into long monologues on the dangers overcome and the glories won in previous campaigns to defend country and freedom.

Plichta's dominant position is established in the opening scenes (act 1, scenes 1 and 2) in which he instructs his son, Bogumił, and a young officer, Zgłobicki, in civic virtue and patriotic morality. Blind and scarred, with a bullet embedded in his flesh, Plichta uses his disfigured body as both a memorial to heroic Polish struggles in the past and a visual aid to bolster his rhetoric of selfless and steadfast devotion to the public good. In short, Plichta comes across as a compelling model of manly patriotic passion. Scenes 4 and 5 offer a younger version of this model: a dashing lieutenant named Złotopolski who has just distinguished himself in a fierce skirmish outside the Trembowla fortress. Złotopolski acknowledges Plichta as his mentor; Plichta embraces Złotopolski as his disciple. Together, they stand as a powerful motivating example. However, these explicit constructions of male heroes as patriotic models ineluctably provoke the question: With exemplary male patriots like Plichta and Złotopolski, why does Wybicki's play need Chrzanowska at all?

It might be tempting to conclude that Chrzanowska's gender transgression is necessary to avert the surrender of Trembowla within the world of the play, but it is not sufficient to inspire patriotism among readers and spectators. For a sustained lesson in civic virtue and patriotic devotion, they must have Plichta's didactic monologues, fortified by displays of his scarred body and reaffirmed by Złotopolski's recent success. It could be argued, however, that it is the other way around. Plichta's speeches and demonstrations, while necessary, are not enough to move and persuade the audience because they merely follow a long-standing and therefore predictable convention of patriotic edification and stimulation. It is gender-bending women and their nonnormative, even transgressive, activism in the patriotic cause that can make readers and spectators, however indifferent or hostile, sit up and take notice. To test this idea, I turn to Wybicki's construction of female characters in this play, intriguingly entitled *The Polish Woman*.

Halfway through act 1, a terrified and disheveled young woman runs in. She is scarcely able to speak. She obsessively repeats a phrase about her parents who have been killed in a Turkish raid. Although she has managed to escape, she appears to have been raped. When pressed by Zgłobicki to reveal her identity, she introduces herself as a "Polish woman," and only later does she give out her last name, Koniecpolska.[34] There can be no doubt that the entire scene is deeply informed by Koniecpolska's traumatic experience. One would have thought, then, that her chilling account of wartime violence would prompt Zgłobicki to splutter with outrage and to show his empathy. Instead, he reacts with disgust. As he observes in a churlish aside, Koniecpolska presents a disagreeable, unfeminine sight. In other words, his notion of proper or normative femininity depends on women's sexual respectability; it follows that women who have been raped or threatened with rape are morally compromised. This way of thinking casts doubts on the integrity of a victim of rape. It is not coincidental, then, that Zgłobicki suspects Koniecpolska of having fabricated her story to enter the fortress and gather intelligence for the Turks.

From a dramaturgical perspective, the disturbing subplot of Koniecpolska's personal trauma, which delays Chrzanowska's first appearance until two scenes later, would seem to serve two related functions in the play: to bring an immediacy and urgency to the threat of predatory invaders and to strengthen the Polish men's resolve to rout them. However, Zgłobicki's reaction makes it brutally clear that the motivating value of Koniecpolska's trauma for the Polish troops is limited because she is regarded as automatically suspect. At this point in the dramatic action, moreover, the troops' morale needs no further boost because the mood at Trembowla is buoyant as a result of Złotopolski's successful expedition.

It is necessary, then, to take a different approach to the Koniecpolska subplot. Her self-presentation as a "Polish woman" springs a not-so-subtle imagistic surprise, suggesting that the play's title does not refer exclusively to Chrzanowska. The Koniecpolska subplot, moreover, creates a space within which the audience—readers and spectators alike—is reminded specifically about women's concerns and dilemmas. Koniecpolska's spoken lines tell contradictory stories, at once urging the Trembowla troops to avenge her and, within the same monologue, regretting that she must rely on their willingness to serve as her avengers. Frustrated with her powerlessness, she expresses the wish to escape womanhood entirely, or at least now and then, in order to take up arms and meet the enemy in battle. In doing so, she implicitly invokes the primary logic of manhood, which taught that, once slighted, a man must avenge that slight, if he is to be esteemed as a man. At the same time, she is the first character in Wybicki's play to wonder about a system of gender difference that disempowers women: "Why doesn't the weaker sex bear arms? Are women the weaker sex because of tender upbringing or because of nature?"[35] In posing these questions, she raises the issue of the relationship between gender and sex. Is it culture or nature that makes women unfit for military service? To put this in broader terms, is it culture or nature that determines women's lives?

Introduced very early in Wybicki's drama, the Koniecpolska subplot defines the strains and stresses of the play's local time and circumstance in explicitly gendered terms. In act 1, Koniecpolska raises questions about gender constructs; in act 2, gender constructs are subjected to intense scrutiny. Briefly, the context. Following up on Złotopolski's success, Chrzanowski leads a sally against the Turkish forces, while women, including Chrzanowska and Koniecpolska, anxiously wait inside the fortress. The news that Plichta brings to the women is devastating. The Polish troops have suffered many losses, and so Chrzanowski has ordered a retreat and initiated negotiations to surrender Trembowla. Suggesting that genuine courage always presupposes heedfulness because heedless courage is really recklessness, Plichta argues that a prudent and timely withdrawal can be a valuable military tactic, equal to victory. But Chrzanowska would have none of this. She insists that tactical withdrawal may be useful in theory, but in reality it is no more than cowardice. She contends, moreover, that the hasty retreat of the Polish forces under her husband's command has uncovered a larger problem, hidden beneath the deceptively attractive veneer of self-congratulatory patriotic enthusiasm: the evanescent nature of men's vaunted "manly courage [męstwo]."[36] Without mincing words, she attributes military failure to the effeminacy of Polish men who have become skilled in the art of submissiveness. As she emphatically points out, her husband is no exception. These are fighting words. It is no wonder that Plichta tries to mitigate Chrzanowska's anger: "Don't blame the commander so hastily."[37]

Although one may agree with Plichta that Chrzanowska is jumping to conclusions when she brands her husband and his men with the epithet "effeminate," her argument is not without its sterling logic.[38] From Chrzanowska's perspective, the situation in which men relegate women to supporting roles (such as embroidering a flag) and claim męstwo for themselves, yet ultimately let it slip away from them, offers a valuable warning about the pitfalls involved in generalizing about the capacity for męstwo as an inherent property of men. What Chrzanowska contests, in other words, is the concept of męstwo understood in ontological terms. This concept can be summed up as follows: because one is a man, one is capable of performing deeds of manly courage. She counters this essentialist notion with the idea that access to what is called manly courage should be determined not by sexual identity but by function: anyone willing and able to show męstwo while serving the public good can join. In short, męstwo should be viewed as a transgender category open to anyone, regardless of his or her biological sex. The other female characters, including Koniecpolska, agree. When Chrzanowska calls on them to take up arms and counterattack the Turkish forces, the women's response is prompt, unanimous, and enthusiastic. Act 2, then, is driven by a deliberate questioning and undoing of restrictive social or customary norms that have governed concepts of femininity and masculinity. What is perhaps most surprising about this gender disarray in act 2 is Plichta's lack of surprise. Since he is a living testimony to cultural tradition, one might expect him to insist on upholding the gender order. And yet he does not see Chrzanowska's gender-bending effrontery as inappropriate or unacceptable. When she enlists his help in arming her female battalion, he fully supports what amounts to a contestation of the gendering of identities and social roles.

Act 3 opens with Chrzanowski's meeting with his advisers. He presents his reason for negotiating surrender with the Turks: it is unrealistic to expect that a Polish army will come to his aid. What, then, constitutes better service to homeland: suicidal action or survival? This is Chrzanowski's dilemma, but one that he has resolved in favor of surrendering Trembowla. To continue the doomed defense would be a foolish action, an unnecessary loss of lives. Chrzanowski's considerations expose the negative value of the traditional idea that it is better to die in battle than surrender. To Chrzanowski, survival, not death, constitutes the meaningful self-sacrifice and patriotic service, and he is prepared to make some concessions to secure it. It is at this point in the deliberations that Chrzanowska enters, her sword drawn. Wybicki's version of the confrontation scene, far more elaborate than Kublicki's, takes up much of act 3 and involves all the characters. As a result, Chrzanowska confronts her husband publicly, hectoring and threatening him in front of his troops. And yet the entire episode emphasizes Chrzanowska's tactical acumen and leadership skills rather than her death threats. This is most evident in her ability to win support for her idea that victory is possible because the key to victory is more audacity, less analysis. But even her choice of a knightly sword instead of butcher knives shows how careful she is in crafting her self-presentation to gain authority in order to inspire others.

During the confrontation scene, Plichta launches yet another of his lengthy monologues on Polish military campaigns in the past. This time, Chrzanowska interrupts him curtly: "Be silent! We've heard enough of your examples."[39] From now on, Plichta will no longer treat the men and women of Trembowla to his orations. In the world of the play, then, the silencing of Plichta constitutes a radical break with the two traditions that he embodies: the tradition of patriotic activism that excluded women and the tradition of heavy-handed patriotic instruction. The two scenes that follow (act 3, scenes 4 and 5) are paradigmatic, a distillation of the play's interests, its methods, and its aims. Scene 4 shows Koniecpolska, armed with a musket, patrolling the battlements of the fortress at night. In scene 5, Koniecpolska and Chrzanowska prepare for a combat engagement with the enemy. Both scenes are emphatically manless to impress on the audience the image of women in arms, actively participating in the defense of Trembowla.

In Wybicki's *The Polish Woman*, then, the siege of Trembowla provides women with an opportunity to ungender such gender-specific categories as manly courage. Anyone, man or woman, can perform acts of manly courage. The distinction between masculinity and femininity proves to be a porous boundary.

V.

Kublicki's *The Defense of Trembowla* is at once less daring and subversive and more compelling than Wybicki's *The Polish Woman*.

On the one hand, Kublicki's play clears Chrzanowski's reputation by attributing the initiative to surrender Trembowla to some of his men. Moreover, Kublicki's version of the confrontation scene is short and confined to a small group of family members and trusted friends. As a result, Chrzanowski is spared public humiliation. And although his wife declares herself the new commander of the fortress, Chrzanowski asserts his masculine authority and prevents her from taking up arms. She argues that wartime patriotism is gender-blind; he insists that warfare is a man's job. Kublicki, then, presents Chrzanowski as a vocal and effective spokesman for the idea that even the dire and desperate circumstances at Trembowla do not justify a violation of gender rules. To put this point more broadly, Kublicki's Chrzanowski serves to reassure the audience that even if women attempt to pursue activities reserved for men, the traditional gender system will always prevail in the end.

On the other hand, the resistance of Kublicki's Chrzanowski to Chrzanowska's military service inescapably highlights the tension between female aspirations for autonomy and achievement and male response. In other words, although both *The Polish Woman* and *The Defense of Trembowla* acknowledge that gender does matter in the sense that the socially prescribed standards of masculinity and femininity impose restrictions on what women can and cannot do, Wybicki's play offers a seductive success story about an independent-minded and stout-hearted woman of undaunted will who acts as if those restrictions were not applicable to her, while Kublicki's drama, in contrast, concentrates on the pervasive disciplining power of the gender order.

This issue is introduced in Chrzanowska's very first monologue (act 1, scene 2): "We, women, are said to be easily frightened. Men think we are good only for petty intrigues. Such is the power of prejudice. Today, let's compete for the glory that manly courage [*męstwo*] brings. Let's prove the prejudice against our sex wrong."[40] In other words, the play opens with a Chrzanowska who is acutely aware of, and outspoken about, gender constructs that constrain women in a world controlled by men. She identifies the most recognizable clichés of femininity itself: timidity, feebleness, and trivial pursuits (as opposed to fortitude, courage, and public service). There is no doubt in her mind, however, that women have the capacity for *męstwo*. Accordingly, she calls on women to defend Trembowla. And yet the issue is not so simple. Chrzanowska does not merely urge women to take up arms in order to save Trembowla. Rather, she reminds women of the dynamics of the traditional gender system in which notions about their supposed inferiority serve to keep them in their place. She suggests that the particular circumstances at Trembowla are empowering because they lend legitimacy to women's gender-bending aspirations that otherwise might have been reviled, ridiculed, or belittled. In short, the women's participation in the defense of Trembowla is not only an action in the cause of Poland's freedom, but also an action in the cause of gender equality.

This is an appropriate moment to compare how each play imagines the relationship between Chrzanowska and the other female characters. In *The Polish Woman*, Chrzanowska always appears in the company of Koniecpolska and the female residents of Trembowla. They engage in joint projects, whether it is embroidering a flag or taking up arms. In the confrontation scene, moreover, Chrzanowska's female companions support her charges against her husband and his men. The insistent grouping of women together suggests female community and solidarity. It is not surprising, then, that Chrzanowska declares: "we, Polish women."[41] This female bonding extends to Polish women in the past. At the close of act 2, Wybicki's female characters concede that their military activism is transgressive, but they invoke the legitimizing precedent of their female ancestors who abandoned "the comforts of home for the hardships of the battlefield."[42] In *The Defense of Trembowla*, in contrast, the female cast consists only of Chrzanowska and her sister-in-law, Dobrogniewa. However, the rhetoric of Kublicki's Chrzanowska—her use of the phrases "we, women" and "our sex"—is far more inclusive than the category "we, Polish women." It demonstrates her awareness that she voices women's concerns that are transnational rather than specific to Polish culture.

While the discourse explicitly challenging the gender order is central to *The Defense of Trembowla,* it is not the only discourse that can be heard in the play. So far, I have considered the discourse of women's activism, with its focus on the opportunities that war offers to women to resist gender rules, to claim their place in the public sphere, and to make the gender order more equitable. The other discourse—the discourse of women's passivity—goes against the grain of Chrzanowska's gender project. Rather unexpectedly, however, it is Chrzanowska who uses both discourses. The discourse of women's passivity surfaces in her response to the relationship between Dobrogniewa and her fiancé, Lieutenant Haraburda. For all her feminist concerns, Chrzanowska argues that eroticization of patriotism is the route to more effective patriotic action on men's part. Accordingly, she urges Dobrogniewa to take advantage of her erotic domination over Haraburda and to push him into outdoing other men in battle. Such views, however, do not go unchallenged. In a strongly worded rebuttal to Chrzanowska, Dobrogniewa rejects the idea of linking patriotic stimulation to a frisson of sexuality and refuses to be reduced to a sexual commodity for patriotic consumption. A man's patriotic motivation, she insists, must come from his inner conviction. As this polemic shows, Chrzanowska's voice in Kublicki's play embodies contradiction, speaking to female interests *and* male interests, espousing both resistance *and* conservatism.

As I have mentioned, Kublicki introduces the character of the Chrzanowskis' son, Zbigniew. This seems to suggest the need to soften Chrzanowska's feminist concerns with her motherly devotion. But the fact that the cast includes yet another member of the Chrzanowski family—Chrzanowski's sister, Dobrogniewa—implies that the issue is more complex. To investigate this issue, it is helpful to consider Kublicki's version of the debate whether to surrender the fortress. While Chrzanowski is determined to fight to the last, some of his men want to capitulate in order to minimize civilian losses. Chrzanowski begins to lean toward their arguments. Like Wybicki's Chrzanowski, he comes to regard surrender as a lesser evil because he wants to save lives for Poland. Unlike Wybicki's Chrzanowski, however, he is more involved emotionally in the surrender question because the lives of as many as three members of his family, including his young son, are at stake. Even if they are captured by the Turks, life in captivity is better than loss of life. Not so from Chrzanowska's perspective. She puts an explicitly gendered twist on the surrender question, arguing that captivity is differently gendered for men and women. For women, it entails the unwelcome possibility that they will be forced into sex work. Her awareness of this possibility casts new light on the confrontation scene. That is to say, her angry outburst at her husband is triggered at least as much by her concern about a specific gender issue as by her patriotic passion to save Trembowla.

In Kublicki's play, as in Wybicki's, gender boundaries are being continually probed and tested. Women in these plays regard their wartime service as an opportunity to pursue risky, unconventional ways of personal development, most notably in the area of female self-realization and empowerment. Hence, according to this criterion, one might describe Kublicki and Wybicki as feminists. It is Kublicki's play, however, that demonstrates with intricate complexity the way dramatic fictions play with cultural and social definitions of man and woman, masculine and feminine. In *The Defense of Trembowla*, as I have argued, we find a series of crisscrossing patterns that interchange empowering and disempowering discourses. The play moves from a Chrzanowska who feels free to experiment with new gender roles to a Chrzanowska who finds that male authority still has the power to prevent her from resisting restrictive gender rules. The play also moves from a Chrzanowska who upholds the idea of the sexual commodification of women for patriotic gain to a Chrzanowska who is concerned about sexual violence against women.

VI.

Wybicki's *The Polish Woman* and Kublicki's *The Defense of Trembowla* take on a different meaning when gender becomes part of the analytical framework. Moreover, both plays demonstrate that it is possible to turn to Polish Enlightenment literature to investigate the concept of gender as a fluid category. In reading *The Polish Woman* and *The Defense of Trembowla*, I must admit to a thrill that comes from discovering that an awareness of gender as construction and performance existed in Polish drama more than two centuries ago.

That said, a question arises: How acceptable were the gender transgressions of *The Polish Woman* and *The Defense of Trembowla* from the perspective of Wybicki's and Kublicki's contemporaries? Although the archives offer no overt answer to this question, I find a possible answer readable to a considerable extent from the production history of the two plays. Although both *The Polish Woman* and *The Defense of Trembowla* were published in 1788 and reprinted in 1789, neither of them was staged in Warsaw at the time. In a 1789 letter, Wybicki mentions that a colleague threw himself into energetic campaigning to have *The Polish Woman* performed in the capital.[43] Those efforts failed, and the play had its premiere at Wybicki's country estate in Manieczki near Poznań in 1788, followed by performances in other household theatres in western Poland.[44] During the 1792 war with Russia, a selection of freedom-themed songs from *The Polish Woman* circulated as an anonymous broadside; two years later, one of those songs made a hit with Kościuszko's insurgents.[45] But the play opened in Warsaw only in 1807, after French and Polish troops had liberated the city from Prussian rule, and the National Theatre launched a series of fetes and dramatic representations in honor of Napoleon. As to Kublicki's *The Defense of Trembowla*, there is no evidence that it was ever performed.[46]

Admittedly, one could argue that the National Theatre was not interested in *The Polish Woman* and *The Defense of Trembowla* because both of them are quite modest artistically. However, other plays of limited artistic value did see the limelight at the National. One of them was Wybicki's *The Nobleman as Bourgeois* (*Szlachcic mieszczaninem*) that supports a struggle for urban franchise and celebrates an alliance of the gentry with the burgher class against the feudal order. First performed in 1791, it was to become one of the National's most successful productions. The version used at the opening night, however, was considered too awkward stylistically and too radical politically; therefore, Wybicki (possibly in consultation with Wojciech Bogusławski who—in the sketchy eighteenth-century sense of the word—directed plays at the National) improved his work by polishing the style and toning down or excising all the indelicacies that more conservative members of the audience could have found offensive.[47] In other words, the perceived imperfections of a dramatic text did not automatically preclude its theatrical production, and Bogusławski was willing to work with playwrights to revise their scripts. One need only compare the production history of *The Nobleman as Bourgeois* with that of *The Polish Woman* and *The Defense of Trembowla* to see that Chrzanowska's gender-bending proved too transgressive for the National Theatre at the time.

On 12 December 1789, the *Gazeta Warszawska* ran an advertisement for the second edition of *The Defense of Trembowla*. Clearly, there was a market for the play. At the same time, however, the advertisement includes an intriguing verbal slip. The title of Kublicki's drama is listed as *The Defense of Trembowla, or the Manly Courage of Chrzanowski* (*Obrona Trembowli, czyli Męstwo Chrzanowskiego*), thus preemptively overriding the play's gender transgression and enabling Chrzanowski to steal the limelight from his wife, after all.[48]

3 ⫶ Is There Transgression in This Text?
Wanda, Queen of Poland

I.

PATRIOTIC PLAYS ARE NOT an easy genre. They not only have to catch the imagination and excite the emotions of an audience—readers and spectators alike; they also have to demonstrate convincingly that the duty of all true patriots to serve their country (and, if need be, to die for it) is absolute and unqualified. Patriotic plays, then, have to sound authoritative while being attractively presented. If they are just authoritative, they sound flat, sententious, or mushy in their honesty. If they are just attractively presented, they appear sheepish, evasive, or frivolous, scarcely patriotic plays at all.

Is there a way out of this conundrum facing the genre of patriotic drama? At first glance, Laura Mulvey's and Sue-Ellen Case's classic studies of the spectatorial contract suggest a solution that might be applied to patriotic plays. Assessed in the light of what Mulvey identifies as "pleasure in looking [that] has been split between active/male and passive/female," patriotic plays seem to be most effective when they seduce the audience with an erotically charged experience of patriotic passion.[1] To put it differently, patriotic plays seem to work most effectively when they use sexual fantasies for patriotic gain. Accordingly, the cast of characters ought to include a young woman, both beautiful and vulnerable, who will serve as a fetishized object of male desire and thus will play the key role in eroticizing patriotic allegiance and devotion. One way to tell the provocative, shocking, even scandalous story of the genre of patriotic drama, then, would be to trace its allegories as they escalate in a spiral of erotics and politics, sexual fantasies and patriotic excitement. As I have already suggested, the seductive appeal of these allegories seems to depend on the positioning of a female character as an object of desire in order to rally men to the patriotic banner.

But a second glance suggests that the issue is not so simple as this brief outline may imply. Theorizing about patriotic drama along the lines suggested by Mulvey's and Case's work inevitably raises the question: Where does this theorizing leave female readers and spectators?

In this chapter, I propose to examine the implications of gender and sexuality as they bear on the construction of patriotic desire and identification in two plays that, on an initial reading, produce a secure knot of erotics and politics, erotic passion and patriotic romance. These plays are Tekla Łubieńska's *Wanda, Queen of Poland* and Franciszek Wężyk's *Wanda*. Both were written during the first quarter of the nineteenth century, at a time when it was not unusual for Polish authors to demand that "acting roles for women ought to represent loving and virtuous mothers and wives."[2] As patriotic dramas, *Wanda, Queen of Poland* and *Wanda* are especially intriguing because, on the one hand, they show the young and unmarried queen displaying the formidable skills that have won her a prominent place in the Polish pantheon. Exemplary as this construction of Wanda may be, both plays, on the other hand, unapologetically revise the received story.

Łubieńska's and Wężyk's plays draw on the immensely popular and endlessly suggestive myth of the virgin queen during the pre-Christian era who, as generations of Polish schoolchildren have memorized, "jumped to her death in the [Wisła] river rather than marry a German prince."[3] Steeped in the conventions of neoclassical tragedy, both plays have a complicated relation to this dramatic genre.

Wężyk began writing *Wanda* in 1803, encouraged by Józef Sygiert, his slightly older friend and a promising poet, who was working on his own tragedy about Wanda at the time.[4] Sygiert was never able to finish his play because of illness and untimely death, but Wężyk braved on, completing the first version of *Wanda* sometime before 1807. That version was never published, and its manuscript is now lost. A revised version appeared in print in 1826, but it was staged only in 1876.⁵ In contrast, Łubieńska's *Wanda, Queen of Poland* reached the stage within a year or so after it was completed. It opened at the National Theatre in Warsaw on 17 April 1807, in the exalted atmosphere of hope and possibility that surrounded recent Napoleonic campaigns. Two years earlier, Napoleon had launched his armies eastward, eventually crushing Austria and Prussia. By January 1807, he secured French control over western and central Poland, including Warsaw. The mood of the country was generally optimistic. Napoleon's career excited the imagination of many Poles. They were confident that a Franco-Polish alliance guaranteed a final victory and that Poland's independence was within sight. Like many of their compatriots, Łubieńska and her husband, Feliks Łubieński, threw in their lot with the French. As a result of the treaty of Tilsit in July 1807, Napoleon created the Duchy of Warsaw, a rump state carved out of the prepartition territory. Łubieński was appointed the Duchy's Minister of Justice. As Norman Davies puts it, "For a brief moment, it looked as if the Polish nation might regain control of its destiny."⁶

In this political context, *Wanda, Queen of Poland* appeared more timely than Łubieńska perhaps could have anticipated.⁷ The audience celebrating a recent liberation of Warsaw from Prussian rule must have responded with a bow of recognition to a paean, in the final act, to the godlike "Gaul" and his "miracle-working powers."⁸ Much of the production's appeal, moreover, undoubtedly derived from the crisp and quotable epigrams that bolstered national pride by paying lavish tribute to brave and freedom-loving Poles. "Poles never shy away from the hardships of war"; "The willingness to sacrifice themselves for the nation—that's what distinguishes Poles"; "Poles will fight to the last to defend their ancient liberties"—these are only some of the most prominent examples.⁹ It is highly probable that such lines were greeted with enthusiastic applause. One may go even further and suggest that the flattering epigrams might have provided an important incentive to patriotic behavior and that the performances of the play might have been used as a recruiting tool for a Polish army under Napoleon's aegis.

To imagine more fully the appeal of the production for the Warsaw audience in the spring of 1807, it is helpful to consider the dynamics of live performance. While responding to contemporary circumstance, the production inescapably drew on the fundamental theatrical paradox: a here-and-now that is not here and now. It thus offered a metatheatrical resurrection of Wanda's Kraków on Warsaw soil. This dualism of a here-and-now that is not here and now provided (to borrow John Loftis's observation about the cultural work of neoclassical tragedy) a particularly vivid "set of illustrations of political propositions, in which partisan assumptions were given the appearance of natural law."[10] Or, to put these points differently, the metatheatrical Kraków allowed for a vicarious return to an imaginary pristine state of the premodern era, while reminding the spectators in 1807 that their struggle to re- establish a Polish kingdom was not a form of national thanatophilia, but a natural extension of the ancestral virtues, such as loyalty, courage, and fortitude, that Wanda's ancient realm stood for.

Łubieńska is one of the relatively small number of women in early nineteenth-century Poland who were able to break through the social barriers that hindered female appearance in print and especially on the stage.[11] The thrust of *Wanda, Queen of Poland,* her best-known work, is to present Wanda as a woman in love. By concentrating on the queen's tragically unfulfilled love life, Łubieńska transforms an otherwise somewhat forbidding national icon into a dramatic character with whom audiences might have a closer emotional tie. However, there are at least two factors that could have conspired to keep *Wanda, Queen of Poland* in the shade. First, the play introduces a Polish-German romance in which Wanda, the exemplary patriotic heroine who epitomizes national resistance to Germany, falls in love with her German suitor, Rytygier (Rüdiger).[12] Second, from a strictly literary point of view, the writing is less than polished. It is not particularly surprising, then, that *Wanda, Queen of Poland* premiered at the National Theatre anonymously. But if Łubieńska feared exposing herself to the jeers that still, at the beginning of the nineteenth century, greeted women writers, she was proven wrong. The Warsaw production was so successful that the play was staged in Poznań in the same year. And yet Łubieńska was determined to keep her identity hidden. Given the play's remarkable success on the stage, one would have thought that publication, anonymous or not, would soon follow, but that was not the case. *Wanda, Queen of Poland* was allowed to linger in archives for more than one hundred years before it was published in 1927.[13] This neglect is puzzling. After all, Łubieńska's less successful play, the lackluster *Charlemagne and Witykind* (*Karol Wielki i Witykind*), performed at the National Theatre in December 1807, went into two editions (both anonymous) in the following year.

Wanda, Queen of Poland invites comparison with Wężyk's *Wanda* that also incorporates an inventive yet disconcerting love plot into the familiar story. With their unusual twists of dramatic plotting and their sheer visual vividness, both plays break out of the bounds of neoclassical tragedy; this undoubtedly accounts for much of their popularity with nineteenth-century audiences who shunned many other neoclassical tragedies as too rigid and declamatory. Both plays fueled patriotic enthusiasm; this, too, accounts for their popularity. That said, questions remain. What are we to make of the fact that *Wanda, Queen of Poland*, Łubieńska's striking theatrical debut, was not published at the time? And what exactly does Wanda, who is in love with her German suitor, teach the audience through her extravagant example? Given her importance to the construction of Polish patriotic discourse and the process of Polish national self-definition in the partition era, the very suggestion that it would be possible for Wanda to love a ruler of Germany, Poland's long-standing enemy, seems to be the most grotesque contradiction in terms.

In the nineteenth century, Łubieńska's *Wanda, Queen of Poland* and Wężyk's *Wanda* stood out as the most successful plays on the Wanda theme. Today, they stand out as mini-masterpieces of gender trouble that await decoding. Out of some thirty dramas about Wanda, I discuss those by Łubieńska and Wężyk because the process of her self-representation as the reigning monarch unfolds in them in explicitly gendered terms.[14] Their radical revision of the Wanda story invites, if not compels, a focus on how and to what ends they rewrite a larger patriotic script that Wanda has come to represent in Polish cultural mythology.

II.

Legend has it that Wanda was the daughter of King Krak who founded the city of Kraków. After Krak died, his two sons fought tenaciously against each other for the throne. The conflict escalated into a full-scale civil war that ended in the death of one son and the exile of the other. With no lawful male heir available, Wanda became queen. The young monarch of uncommon beauty attracted the attention of a German prince. He proposed to her, but she rebuffed him and took her own life. Among the main constitutive elements of the traditional narrative, then, are: the emergence of a kingdom and a dynasty; Wanda's reign as the female successor in a male dynastic system; her refusal to match with a foreign prince; and her suicide to avoid such a match.

Even this brief outline reveals puzzling contradictions. Why does Wanda insist on remaining a virgin? For a virgin queen—in fact, for any monarch, of either sex—in a system defined as hereditary monarchy, the top priority was to marry and produce a legitimate heir to succeed to the throne. To remain unmarried was to imperil the state by leaving the question of succession open. In Wanda's case, the political vulnerability of the young Polish state makes the succession question even more urgent. For a new and insecure dynasty on the eastern fringe of Europe, a marriage with a foreign prince would have been a tremendous prize. Why, then, is it important for Wanda to cultivate her virginity, rather than secure both a line of succession after herself and a powerful foreign alliance? And if marrying a foreign suitor is out of the question, why does she fail to consider Polish suitors? Why is she peculiarly willing to kill herself, even though her death would certainly destabilize the kingdom again?

To answer these questions we need a time machine. Meanwhile, a useful starting point for grappling with at least some of the questions is to read Łubieńska's *Wanda, Queen of Poland* and Wężyk's *Wanda*, but to read them against the grain. I first trace the rise of the Wanda myth and consider the particular urgency it attained in the Polish imagination during the nineteenth century. The key question, I suggest, is not whether Wanda really existed, but what the discourse in which she features can tell us about cultural attitudes and alarms in the past.

First recorded in Wincenty Kadłubek's *The Polish Chronicle* (*Chronica Polonorum*, written ca. 1223), the Wanda story has been around for more than seven hundred years.[15] At first glance, it has little to offer. The setting is pre-Christian Poland, misty and austere. The protagonist is a young woman who never marries and dies a virgin. Yet she seems, if in rather special terms, to be living happily ever after. When one starts looking for her, she is everywhere: gamboling through early modern chronicles and schoolbooks, celebrated in highbrow poems and popular songs. Over the course of centuries, moreover, she has taken on an air of reality that few historical figures can match.

No one seriously questioned the historicity of the Wanda story until Enlightenment writers and educators began to debunk it as a premodern hoax. For example, Krasicki's novel, *History* (*Historia*, 1779), submits the story to ruthless satirical parody: Krasicki's Wanda attracts no male attention, and she drowns in a boating accident caused by a drunk captain.[16] However, the revisionist efforts by Enlightenment luminaries, who mocked Wanda as an affront to historical fact and rationalist protocols, went largely unremarked. Shortly before clandestine political resistance burst into open rebellion, known as the Kościuszko insurrection, she was called back into service. The rousing finale of Wojciech Bogusławski's enormously popular music drama, *The Miracle, or Cracovians and Highlanders* (*Cud albo Krakowiaki i Górale*), which opened at the National Theatre on 1 March 1794, included the following song:

> Wanda didn't want to marry a German man,
> And she was laid to rest in our land.
> It's always better to be with your own kind
> than to get hooked up with a foreigner.[17]

The political innuendo of this musical number and others like it was not lost on the Polish audience or the Russian ambassador in Warsaw at the time. Wanda stood for Poland; her foreign suitor, for Russia. Four days after the opening night, the ambassador ordered the production canceled.

The Miracle was revived in Warsaw on 8 December 1806, inaugurating a series of performances and fetes to honor Napoleon and to celebrate the Franco-Polish alliance. Wiktor Brumer exaggerates only slightly when he claims that "a performance of *The Miracle* in December 1806 ushered in the Napoleonic era" in Poland.[18] Stage productions became a major occasion for demonstrations, in the presence of Napoleon or his generals, of the Polish commitment to the alliance with France in the war against Poland's enemies.[19] One of the most successful plays of the Napoleonic era in Poland was Łubieńska's *Wanda, Queen of Poland*. Although the Wanda story had spread steadily in Polish culture from its modest beginnings in shady corners of medieval mythmaking, it is at this point in the early nineteenth century that Wanda's rise to stardom was launched. By 1830, she was "the most favored female character" in Polish literature.[20]

Her spectacular career continued unabated throughout the rest of the nineteenth century, as evident in the work of painters such as Aleksander Lesser and Maksymilian A. Piotrowski and playwrights such as Adam Bełcikowski and Cyprian Kamil Norwid.

It is not particularly difficult to account for Wanda's phenomenal success in nineteenth-century Polish culture. When political circumstances denied Poles their claim for statehood, writers and artists turned to the past to provide evidence of the Polish people's distinct cultural roots. Intriguingly, many writers and artists reached back all the way to a pre-Christian past. Their portrayal of this remote past was shaped by the need to highlight a particular symbolic continuity with the present. During the era of foreign rule, in other words, the virginal queen of ancient Poland who sacrificed her life for her terrestrial *patria* was a godsend endowed with vast symbolic capital. She could be celebrated as an epitome of Polish innocence, baffled by foreign arrogance and duplicity, and a prototype of unswerving Polish devotion to the cause of freedom.[21] Her self-renouncing passion could be appropriated for paeans to moral virtue and linked with religious ideas, perhaps even (distantly, if not explicitly) with self-sacrifice for the celestial *patria*.[22] And an almost hypnotically patriotic tale of a Polish queen who rebuffs a German suitor was ideally suited for the efforts to blur the line between patriotism and chauvinism and to insist that the true love of Poland should entail, at the very least, distrust of other nations. In her various guises, Wanda became an indispensable part of the cultural mythology that informed the process of Polish national self-definition during the period of the partitions.

This context needs to be borne in mind when considering nineteenth-century dramas about Wanda. Emphasizing the ways in which her biological sex paradoxically enables her to speak on behalf of the nation, existing scholarship on the Wanda plays offers two primary arguments about the significance of her gender. First, it is contended that Wanda fits within the traditional trope of woman as a loving, self-sacrificing caretaker. Referring to plays by writers such as Łubieńska and Wężyk, Dobrochna Ratajczakowa observes that they create a new image of Wanda as "the handmaiden of the nation" and "a passive heroine who safeguards the status quo."[23] This Wanda represents the ancient Polish virtues of honesty, simplicity, and loyalty, and her authority emanates from her willing self-sacrifice for her people and their principles. Attributing such emphases to Łubieńska's

Wanda, Queen of Poland and Wężyk's *Wanda*, this argument is assumed rather than demonstrated. From the textual evidence of the plays, it is questionable. Łubieńska's and Wężyk's Wanda is anything but a passive woman who supports the existing social order. In summarizing the plot of Wężyk's drama, Ratajczakowa does in fact point out that pagan divinities reject Wanda's vow of chastity because it violates "woman's natural destiny."[24] Ratajczakowa, however, leaves the implications of her comment unexplored.

The second major argument about the significance of Wanda's gender, while it is to some extent more accurate than the first, remains in crucial ways incomplete. In *A History of Central European Women's Writing*, Ursula Phillips describes Łubieńska as "one of the first Polish writers to confront the national situation directly and prescribe appropriate patriotic behaviour."[25] Like Ratajczakowa, Phillips invokes the idea of selfless devotion to the Polish patriotic cause. Unlike Ratajczakowa, however, she casts Łubieńska as a trailblazer for Adam Mickiewicz, Poland's touchstone poet and playwright. She concludes that Łubieńska's dramatic writings "anticipate the attitude of extreme personal self-sacrifice embodied in Mickiewicz's best-known works and demonstrate that he was not original in its promulgation."[26] Phillips's entry on Łubieńska in *A History of Central European Women's Writing* makes my task easier: Łubieńska's inclusion in this compendium obviates the need to argue that she is indeed an important author. That said, Phillips's commentary overlooks the fact that the dilemmas facing Łubieńska's Wanda have little to do with what happens in Mickiewicz's male-centered *Forefathers' Eve* (*Dziady*, 1823–32) and *Konrad Wallenrod* (1828). Even the eponymous heroine of Mickiewicz's *Grażyna* (1823) is not a helpful example, since Grażyna is a married duchess who, on a single occasion, disguises herself as her husband and leads his troops to battle, although it is he who ultimately prevails over the enemy. While Mickiewicz's narrative focuses on Grażyna's appropriation of male privilege and prestige, Wanda in Łubieńska's play, as I will show, seeks to construct a position for herself outside the male-defined status quo.

It is with these polemical points that I resume my discussion of Łubieńska's *Wanda, Queen of Poland* and Wężyk's *Wanda*. Each play is an elaborate charade. To try to make sense of the mixed signals that these charades convey, it is necessary to broach and, I hope, elucidate several interrelated questions. Does Wanda's position as a legitimate heir in a divinely sanctioned dynasty render the gender paradigms, which designate women as inferior to men, inapplicable to her? Or, rather, does Wanda's biological sex raise doubts among her subjects about the compatibility of womanhood with political power? And if it does, how does Wanda function in the contested capacity of a female ruler? Does she disarm her subjects' insecurities about female rule and establish her authority by appropriating the traditionally male discourse of the king's two bodies—a discourse that assumes the superiority of abstract, symbolic systems to actual, embodied experience? Or, rather, does she ground her authority in the metaphor of virgin mother, picturing and presenting herself as a loving parent who invests her maternity in her political rather than in her natural body? In short, what are Wanda's methods of dealing with the problem of gender?

With regard to the love plot in these plays, previous studies cast Wanda as a tragic figure, torn between individual desire and communal loyalty. According to this interpretation, Wanda's inner conflict can be resolved only through her death. What earlier studies overlook, however, is that Wanda's suicide exposes the Polish state to danger, thus contradicting her passionate commitment to furthering the welfare of her people.[27] Moreover, prior scholarship disregards the fact that Wanda's subjects are not necessarily happy with her much-vaunted chastity. She remains resolutely unmarried in a society that expects her to do the proper thing: to marry and produce a child (preferably male) to ensure the succession.

While the secondary literature on Łubieńska's and Wężyk's dramas typically links Wanda's virginity to her refusal to marry a foreign prince, I submit that this interpretive approach misses the complications of Wanda's situation in the plays. The concept of virginity can be a perfect tool for deception and self-deception, for high-mindedness and for occluding more complex motives so completely that they seem scarcely to exist. I want to probe more deeply into the reasons why the virginal state is attractive to Wanda. It is my argument that the issue at the center of Łubieńska's and Wężyk's plays is not Wanda's rejection of a foreign suitor, but rather her rejection of marriage and motherhood. The plays' chief fascination inheres in their serial revelations of why marriage and motherhood do not provide a comfortable or comforting role in which the queen could cast herself and how she jockeys to position herself in the zone of gender disarray, while seeking to appease fears about female rule.

III.

The action of Łubieńska's *Wanda, Queen of Poland* and Wężyk's *Wanda* takes place in Kraków and its vicinity during the final days of Wanda's short reign. At first glance, it may seem that both plays are purveyors of unreal estate. They appear to create a reality free from the interference of the present: a separate, distant world, idealized and mesmerizing. As I have already suggested, however, each play is more equivocal than it might at first appear. Loftis's elegant summation of the incisive power of neoclassical tragedy to speak to the present applies with equal force to Łubieńska's and Wężyk's dramas: "Tragedy took as its ostensible subject the affairs of monarchs, nobles, and generals in remote times and places and avoided literal social comment; but the superficial distance from contemporary concerns notwithstanding, tragedy was in even closer touch with the currents of political thought than comedy."[28]

To begin with, Łubieńska and Wężyk are too resourceful and alert as writers to make either play yet another account of a Wanda who refuses Rytygier's courtship. In constructing the plot and the characters, they have made several crucial changes from the traditional story. Some of the changes are in the interest of dramatic economy and psychological complexity, and other changes help advance the argument and sharpen theatrical images. In this section, I briefly survey the major amendments.

First, instead of the "one-and-only" Wanda, the plays show a protean Wanda. In both works, she is a defiantly hands-on ruler, determined, ambitious, and clear-sighted. However, while Wężyk's Wanda develops a talent as an adroit political operator who can be disingenuous, even manipulative, Łubieńska's Wanda chooses cooperative queenship and governs by counsel or consent. And although both Wandas have a flair for the endearing public gesture, it is Wężyk's Wanda who has the qualities that great performers possess: magnetism, consummate technique, watchability, superb timing, chutzpah. She also has an ability to exercise fingertip control over the emotions of a large group of people gathered in one place to witness a single event—as in act 1 when she unexpectedly turns a public presentation of her suitors on its head by declaring her marriage to her people. She certainly can "work" an audience of thousands, holding them in thrall. By contrast, Łubieńska's Wanda is less worldly, more modest and unpretentious. Even so, Łubieńska's play has an original contribution to make to the Wanda story, and a far-reaching one at that.

Second, it is assumed to be out of the question that Wanda would decide to remain single. In Wężyk's play, the succession question preoccupies her councilors, who create an ongoing crisis for her authority by admonishing her, over and over, to marry and bear an heir. Łubieńska's play goes over the same ground, but with a lighter touch. As was inevitable with the accession of a young woman to the throne, the identity of Wanda's husband-to-be is viewed in both plays as the foremost question of the day. Neither play, however, rules out the possibility that Wanda could match with a foreign prince. In Łubieńska's play, a crucial element of the plot is the foreign ancestry of Wanda's father, the late Krak. He was elected king after he had won the respect and admiration of the Polish people for his fearless campaigns on their behalf. This sets an important precedent for adopting a foreign prince as Poland's ruler. In Wężyk's play, Wanda is courted by a bevy of eager suitors, both native and foreign. From a political point of view, however, marriage with a Polish nobleman has serious drawbacks. If she were to accept one of her warlords as husband, the others would feel aggrieved at having been passed over, and this might destabilize the state from within. If, on the other hand, she were to marry a foreign ruler who could take the young and politically vulnerable Polish state under his protection, this match would give the Krak dynasty international legitimacy and a potentially invaluable ally against Poland's enemies.

Third, each play is a love story. Putting a new twist on the familiar narrative, it shows a Wanda who is in love with Rytygier.

Fourth, there is much to admire about Rytygier. He is a courageous fighter and a constant lover. More remarkably, he insists that he does not lay claim to the Polish throne. Instead, he offers Wanda different options to persuade her to marry him. He suggests that she abdicate the Polish throne and share the reign of Germany with him. Alternatively, he proposes to give up the German throne and to move to Poland where he would be content to share her private life, but not her monarchical powers.

Yet the love story is not crowned with a happy ending. Even in these revisionist versions of the Wanda myth, the plot culminates in the queen's suicide. Łubieńska and Wężyk could have altered the conventional motif of Wanda's fatal leap into the Wisła, just as they reverse her indifference to, perhaps even loathing for, Rytygier. Why, then, do they fail to apply dramatic license to her suicide? After all, there is a venerable precedent for preserving her life. In Kadłubek's *The Polish Chronicle,* an immensely influential narrative that "shaped the Poles' historical and national consciousness for many centuries," it is Wanda's German suitor who kills himself when his troops mutiny against him and turn away from battle, while Wanda continues to reign for years to come.[29] Łubieńska and Wężyk, however, appear incapable of imagining a happier future for Wanda on this side of the grave.

To recapitulate briefly, Łubieńska's and Wężyk's Wanda has been able, by a twist of political circumstance (the exile of her surviving brother, which left room for her to assume the throne), to convert a liability (being a woman in a man's world) into an asset (political power). Although she comes to the throne after a period of immense upheaval in the kingdom, she takes to the role of the reigning monarch with panache. She is widely respected as the daughter of the beloved Krak and admired as an adept ruler in her own right. However, her subjects expect her to marry and produce an heir to succeed to the Polish throne. Nevertheless, remarkably, she remains adamantly negative about marrying, even though she loves Rytygier, and her marriage to a foreign prince could have strengthened her kingdom. Her decision defies logic and common sense. To compound the problem, she takes her own life. Her suicide is politically inopportune, if not a dreadful folly, since it exposes the young Polish state to the dangers of internal turmoil and foreign encroachment. The nagging question returns: Why do Łubieńska and Wężyk retain Wanda's suicide, although they take liberties with many other elements of the traditional story?

IV.

In the remainder of this chapter, I examine the tensions and ambiguities that define each play. I begin by considering Rytygier's practice of courtship. As I have argued, Rytygier has admirable traits. His courtship of Wanda, however, does not fit within the chivalric code of ethics and behavior: he arrives belligerently, leading his armed troops. (In Wężyk's play, the German troops not only set foot on the Polish territory but also pillage their way through the countryside.) Rytygier's rough wooing, a blustering show of his military might, amounts to an invasion of the kingdom of Poland. What are we to make of his affront to Wanda's honor? If he loves Wanda and hopes to marry her, why does he insult the queen and her subjects by contesting the sovereignty of her realm?

For the Germans in Łubieńska's play, Poland is a land of exotic savages. They are shocked by what they regard as Poland's barbarism: it is a kingdom where the people have deposed the rightful male heir in favor of a young woman. As Radbod, one of Rytygier's warlords, says with contempt, "Poles took the crown away from Wanda's brother and gave it to Wanda."[30] In the eyes of the Germans, a legitimate heir is always male. According to this logic, Poland is not a legitimate state. As a result, the Germans do not consider themselves bound by chivalric conventions when they deal with Poles.

Like Łubieńska's play, Wężyk's drama attributes the Germans' breach of chivalric conduct to their perception of Poland as "a savage land."[31] Here, the violation involves not only an invasion of Wanda's realm, but also subterfuge. Disguised as an envoy, Rytygier enters the royal castle in Kraków to charm Wanda with his attention and persuade her to marry him. After Władyboj, Wanda's senior adviser, exposes this ploy, Rytygier defends himself by compromising Wanda: he suggests that she has been complicit in his deception. An exclamation of shocked disbelief by Ullo, Rytygier's companion, is a good indication of how humiliating this situation is to Wanda. It is evident, then, that for the Germans Wanda's biological sex as the reigning monarch is an issue. Is it also an issue for her subjects? And if it is, how does Wanda manage (if she does) this crisis of her authority? Let me turn to Wężyk's *Wanda* first.

His play begins with a Wanda who has no interest in love and marriage and is unconcerned with the succession question. Or, to put it differently, his play begins with a Wanda who defies the conventional wisdom that regards marriage as the ultimate goal of a woman's life; she also resists the normalizing force of popular expectations within the prevailing hereditary system. As the action unfolds, however, she meets Rytygier and falls in love with him. An initial interpretation might conclude that Wężyk's drama demonstrates the power of love to transform Wanda from a transgressively unfeminine woman who aspires to be a political leader into a repentant woman who, by the play's end, comes to regret that she has dared to violate "the laws carved by the hand of the Almighty."[32] Less nobly put, Wanda thought she was above love, marriage, and motherhood, but she finds that she is not. To make up for her transgression—to erase the shameful stigma of arrogance—she takes her own life. It might be tempting to conclude, in other words, that Wężyk writes as a strict moralist to de-transgress Wanda's transgression of gender norms and to uphold the gender order.[33] But what happens if we try to move beyond such reductive conclusions?

In Wężyk's drama, it goes without saying that the queen should marry and transfer her duties from the state to the household. Wanda's reign has been conducive to stability and good order, yet her subjects are disaffected. They view her virgin queenship not as a positive experiment, but as the single gravest matter for the future of the realm of Poland. Their desired solution is for Wanda to resolve the succession question through marriage and motherhood. As Władyboj argues in the opening scene, Poland is a young state that "needs a pair of strong hands," preferably those of a prince from abroad through whom Poland could contract a foreign alliance.[34] As a result, Wanda's council insistently forces the question of marriage on her, against her will and contrary to her own policy of postponement. This suggests two things. First, as a woman, Wanda lacks full legitimacy in the eyes of her people, who would prefer a male ruler to be in charge. Second, her subjects oppose the queen's celibacy as unnatural and thus inferior to faithful married love. Despite Wanda's success as a reigning monarch, in other words, the notion of a female ruler, particularly a young and unmarried female ruler, provokes anxiety among her subjects.

Wanda agrees to comply with a resolution of her council that she marry. The showpiece of act 1 is a public ceremony at which the queen is to adjudicate between rival suitors, including Rytygier, and to choose her consort-to-be. In her speech, she disarmingly acknowledges her female weakness by presenting herself as a self-effacing servant to her people. When addressing her subjects, she declares: "I am a creation of your own hands."[35] She even makes an emphatic pledge to keep faith solely with them: "I choose my beloved people as my consort . . . and I offer my virginity to the immortal gods."[36] For all her rhetoric about obedience and devotion, the problem is, of course, that Wanda here explicitly refuses to behave like a humble and dutiful servant to her people. She does not merely choose to remain single, contrary to their expectations. Rather, she insists on legitimating her transgressive decision not to bow down to the collective will of her subjects (and to patriarchal practice), and she does so by inscribing her maidenhood in an official, religiously sanctioned cult of virginity, even though the pagan divinities reject her vow of celibacy.

This surprise move marks the end of all prospects of courtship and marriage, and thus has the political and structural effect of relieving Wanda from the necessity of contracting some single, uniquely preferential foreign alliance with a consort-to-be and his affines. Clearly, Wanda is a mistress of rhetoric, which enables her to appear both as sincerely humble and as a force to be reckoned with. On the one hand, she stresses her obedience to the collective will of her people, thus presenting a self reshaped to suit their expectations. On the other hand, she finds an effective way to fend off suitors who press for her hand and to extricate herself from the obligation to marry and bear children. On the surface, then, the play seems to be about Wanda's duplicity. But one could also argue that the rhetorical strain perceptible from beginning to end of Wężyk's play expresses the extreme strain of Wanda's position in patriarchal society. She is well aware of widespread insecurities about female rule. As a result, she is particularly concerned with her self-creation as a ruler in order to prove to her subjects that she is indeed worthy of the throne. She seeks, by whatever means available to her, to legitimize her commitment to public service—a commitment that her advisers are eager to take away from her and to hand over to her husband-to-be.

As I have already mentioned, Wanda's rhetorical technique to legitimize her dedication to public service involves appeasing fears about female rule by adhering to conventions that assert the inferiority of women, only to supersede these conventions by adopting the ethic of sexual chastity. It might be tempting to conclude, however, that through her insistence on remaining chaste she merely perpetuates the conventional trope of a "pure" woman, free from "base" corporeal desire. Yet the issue is not so simple. Given the pressures on Wanda to marry and produce an heir, her willful commitment to chastity is her strategy of self-determination. By rejecting marriage and the male superiority that it authorizes, she asserts control over her sexuality and thus refuses to be reduced to the functional role of preserving the male-defined status quo. In short, Wanda's commitment to virginity is her answer to the question of female empowerment.

Does Wężyk's Wanda seek to legitimize her dedication to public service by any other rhetorical techniques available to her as a female ruler, such as claiming the role of the political mother or appropriating the prestige of male kingship? The first part of this question is easy to answer. In a fierce debate that follows Wanda's unexpected announcement of her marriage to her people, the conservative Archpriest states his belief in women's unique nature, which he identifies—not untypically for the times—with the realm of family and domesticity. Women have the power of love and reproduction; men have political power. Women can use their influence as mothers to inculcate in their sons such values as civic virtue, and this is the path that the Archpriest expects Wanda to follow. None of this interests Wanda. She responds to the Archpriest by saying that she can compensate for the crucial deficit in virgin queenship by becoming the mother of Poland's destiny. This is the only time when she uses the trope of virgin mother as a salient aspect of her self-presentation. Her answer is brief and almost offhand. It lacks the emotional intensity of her earlier response to the Archpriest, which I will discuss momentarily. In invoking the trope of virgin mother, then, Wanda merely uses a rhetorical ploy to satisfy the Archpriest.

The answer to the second part of my question is more complex. Let me do this in slow motion. By her own choice, Wanda holds a public presentation of her suitors in act 1—a sort of a masculine beauty contest where she would select her bridegroom—at the burial mound of King Krak. By choosing this particular location, in other words, she relies on the cult of her father to remind her audience that she is a legitimate successor in a divinely sanctioned dynasty. In the debate with the Archpriest that follows the presentation scene, however, she no longer grounds her authority in her metaphysical and political position as the legitimate heir in a dynasty. Her rhetoric of self-legitimation is markedly different from the standard rhetorical technique that was used, among others, by Elizabeth I, the best-known of all virgin queens. The standard technique involves disarming anxieties about female rule by acknowledging one's own femininity and then erasing it by appropriating the prestige of male kingship. Elizabeth I used this rhetoric in 1566 when comparing herself with her father: "As for my own part, I care not for death, for all men are mortal; and though I be a woman, yet I have as good courage answerable to my place as ever my father had."[37] Still more famously, she is supposed to have told the troops assembled at Tilbury in 1588 in the face of the Spanish Armada: "I know I have the body but of a weak and feeble woman, but I have the heart and stomach of a king and of a king of England too."[38]

Wanda, by contrast, refrains from drawing on the traditional discourse of the king's two bodies. She does not say that she has the heart of a king, although she has the body of a weak and feeble woman. Nor does she present herself as an exceptional woman whose royal status and unique capabilities make her inimitable. Rather, she articulates a consciousness of herself as an exceptional woman whose identity has changed. Her ascension to the throne has triggered, for her, chain reactions of transformation. She used to be a timid woman; now she is a daring warrior. To avoid a possible misunderstanding, I want to make this point clearly: the transformation is not transsexual, from woman to man, but transgender, from queen to warrior. As a sign of her new identity, Wanda always wears a sword. Moreover, while Elizabeth I almost certainly was not, as tradition would have it, clad in armor when she allegedly made her belligerent address to the troops at Tilbury, Wanda dons armor cap-à-pie, charges into battle with an upraised sword, and fights Rytygier and his men, thus proving her new identity.

The issue here, then, is not the abstract notion of the king's two bodies, but rather Wanda's actual experience that tests the boundaries between sex and gender and that challenges an essentialist view of gender identity. One of the most breathtaking accomplishments of Wężyk's play is to show that Wanda's gender identity is something chosen and assumed rather than biologically determined. In more general terms, the concept of gender identity represented by Wanda is a situational construct, or something adopted by individuals in specific social contexts in response to particular pressures or challenges, and therefore liable to change.

To her warlords and advisers, however, Wanda is merely a woman in a man's world. For all their paeans to her, they treat Wanda as if she were a lower being in need of direction, protection, and control. The scene in which Władyboj discovers Rytygier's secret visit to Wanda's castle is a powerful reminder that she occupies a vulnerable position as a female ruler. Putting more trust in Rytygier's word than in Wanda's, Władyboj condemns her in a demeaning rebuke for having been involved in secret dealings with Rytygier. Władyboj's reaction, a mixture of offended hubris and moralistic outrage, makes it clear what is at issue here. He assumes that Wanda has done something on her own, bypassing the authority of the council over which he presides. Consequently, he overreacts because he is deeply resentful of what he perceives to be yet another attempt by Wanda to assert her autonomy in the teeth of the council's efforts to subject her to its will and to make her a mere figurehead.

Always plucky, resourceful, and outspoken, Wanda begins to realize that she is fighting a losing battle. As the play draws to a close, she sees no option beyond suicide. She makes two attempts to take her life, succeeding at the second try.[39] While Polish cultural mythology has commemorated Wanda's death as a heroic act of patriotic self-sacrifice, in Wężyk's drama her suicide is an outcome consistent with her intolerable predicament as an ambitious woman trapped in patriarchal society.

V.

While Wężyk's play begins with a Wanda who has not met Rytygier yet, Łubieńska's drama begins with a Wanda who met Rytygier five years earlier. Their love blossomed, and they became engaged. Then Wanda inherited her father's throne, and she has since focused on the business of statecraft. It is notable that she began her reign with the highly independent thought that taking the conventional route of marrying and bearing heirs to the throne would not necessarily guarantee her security and that of the realm. Rytygier's unexpected arrival in Poland to claim her hand creates a psychological dilemma for Wanda. She still loves him, but she realizes that she is no longer the person who entered into an agreement to marry him. She is another woman, older, more mature. Moreover, Rytygier's insistence that the queen respect the agreement or he will make war against her country creates a political dilemma for Wanda, who, as a reigning monarch, is unshakably committed to promoting the welfare of her people. Rytygier's extravagant, threatening ultimatum puts Wanda in an untenable situation. She cannot reactivate her earlier, private self and marry him; at the same time, she wants to avoid fatal military entanglements. The issue, however, is even more complex.

Wężyk's focus is on the sometimes brutal sexism of Wanda's Poland and on its repressive impact on her. Łubieńska's focus, in contrast, is on Wanda's triumphant success as a ruler. While Wanda's subjects in Wężyk's play agree that the female sex is incompatible with the political domain, Wanda's subjects in Łubieńska's drama are confident that the queen is a worthy successor to her father's reign. She inherited formidable problems along with her crown; as a result of a civil war between her pugnacious brothers, the kingdom was weak and divided. But her remarkable political acumen, clemency, and tact, along with her commitment to govern by consensus rather than will, have set Poland on a new trajectory. Accordingly, she refrains in her public rhetoric from identifying with the role of virginal mother, which would have cast her subjects as her dependents. Instead, she views them as partners, always seeking out their opinion and advice. In short, Łubieńska's play invites us to conclude that Wanda's tenure on the Polish throne does constitute a successful experiment.

A closer look at Wanda's rhetoric of self-presentation, however, reveals that the issue is not so simple. In act 1, the dialogue between Wanda and Starża, the most loyal of her councilors, culminates in the queen's pronouncement: "It's not enough to have the crown. I want to be worthy of it. I will prove that Poles have made the right choice."[40] Such statements reveal that Wanda experiences her success as queen with ambivalence. Her insecurity suggests that she fears, rightly or wrongly, that her rule, or specifically her rejection of marriage and motherhood, might, after all, fuel public discontent. What techniques does she use to disarm her own insecurity and to reaffirm her right to rule?

In act 1, when she declares she will go to war with Rytygier rather than marry him, Wanda compares herself (not unlike Elizabeth I in her 1566 speech) with her father: "I will not stay at the palace, waiting for reports from the battlefield. Poles as well as Poland's enemies will know that Wanda has inherited her father's manly courage."[41] By act 4, however, there is an explicit change in the queen's rhetoric of self-legitimation. When Rytygier accuses Wanda of being fickle and reproaches her for breaking their engagement, she curtly responds: "Before, I was Krak's daughter; now I am queen."[42] Thus, she no longer inscribes herself in the prestige of male heroism and kingship. Instead, she asserts the independence and agency that her queenship allows. Why, then, does she find herself ultimately pushed to the edge? Although this question must remain suspended here, it will be broached later.

This is an appropriate moment at which to return to the question of constructing desire and identification in patriotic drama. To begin to address this issue, I want to examine how Wężyk's and Łubieńska's dramas cue the audience's perception and interpretation. In Wężyk's play, we can look at Wanda through the admiring eyes of two of her suitors: Rytygier and Skarbimir, a Polish warlord who ultimately proves his love for her with his own life while trying to rescue her from the Wisła. Seen through Rytygier's and Skarbimir's eyes, Wanda is a woman who excites love and desire. She is beautiful, sweet, and charming; therefore, she is worthy of the highest sacrifice, even the sacrifice of life. Ullo, Rytygier's companion, begs to differ. Seen through Ullo's eyes, Wanda's paradoxical conflation of "womanly beauty and manly courage" is repulsive.[43] He repeatedly laments her violation of what he considers women's natural destiny: marriage and family. Her masculine temperament and ambition belie her bodily form, suggesting that she is somehow deficient in the qualities that most become a woman. Thus, where Rytygier and Skarbimir see godlike perfection, Ullo sees a deformity. Wanda's deliberate breaking of the rules of respectable, "feminine" behavior has engendered an oddity, a freak, or a monster.

Łubieńska also highlights the male gaze, but in the process she insists on a Wanda who sees with explicitly gendered eyes. In the closing scene of act 2, rather incongruously for a neoclassical tragedy, Łubieńska inserts Wanda's detailed account of a dream. Scholars agree that the dream vision is a deliberate infraction of generic boundaries—a proto-Romantic element disrupting the play's neoclassical structure. However, the implications of this ostensibly gratuitous monologue have remained unexamined. In the dream, Wanda is lost in the woods. Suddenly she finds herself on the edge of a precipice and peers timidly into it. When she turns around, she notices Rytygier standing nearby. Leaning nonchalantly against a rock, he watches her in silent derision. Moments later, he chastises her for being fearful, but offers to lead her away to a safe place. Wanda, however, refuses to follow him. There are two other men who also watch Wanda. One of them is the blood-covered ghost of her oldest brother who was murdered by his sibling. He beckons to Wanda, offering his protection, but she remains still. The third man is a young stranger who rushes toward Rytygier and pushes him into the ravine. At this point, Wanda wakes up.

Wanda's quietly chilling account reveals the mind of a woman who is disoriented and frightened, but understandably so, given the precariousness of her situation as a ruler facing the prospect of a war. She is surrounded by men who position her as subservient to their gaze. They offer help, but they appear either predatory or threatening. She is aware of her vulnerability as a single woman, yet her refusal to follow Rytygier and her murdered brother makes it clear that she does not want to be "saved" either by marriage or by the male model of kingship, competitive and violent. This in turn implies that marriage, according to Wanda, is all too often a trap. So long as the institution of marriage perpetuates inequality, women had better beware of flattery and look to themselves, not to men, for hope of a better life.

This brings me to the other female characters in Łubieńska's play. While the cast of Wężyk's drama has no women apart from Wanda, Łubieńska's play introduces Warka, Wanda's lady-in-waiting. (There is also a group of anonymous women, presumably other ladies-in-waiting, but they remain silent.) Warka moves to center stage in the closing scenes of act 4, when her husband, a warlord named Wisław, sets off for a war with Rytygier. Here, on the one hand, Wisław invokes the example of Wanda's "manly courage" as an empowering inspiration for Polish troops.[44] On the other hand, Warka serves as a counterweight to Wanda through her own acceptance of the role of the passive and submissive woman. Thus, she represents the model of a patriotic wife who sends her husband off to war and patiently waits for his return.

Not surprisingly, the farewell scene, although peripheral to the main action, caught the attention of audiences and reviewers when Łubieńska's play was first performed in 1807.[45] They praised the relevance of this scene to the experience of many Polish women at a time when their fathers, husbands, and sons were enlisting in a Polish army under Napoleon's auspices. But this praise also suggests a sigh of relief that the play, despite Wanda's challenge to gender norms, reestablishes a sturdy template for women's normative behavior: men act, women wait.

Wanda, of course, has other ideas. As I have argued, Łubieńska's play highlights the queen's success as a ruler, yet she is not allowed to live on. It is as if the stock of available templates wanted Wanda to conform at last, whatever license she seems to have been given. Or, rather, she conforms enough to preserve the traditional plot that requires her suicide, but she also hints at a zone of transgressive independence that cannot be absorbed by available gender conventions.

VI.

In Polish cultural mythology, Wanda is still an iconic figure: radiant, pure, and two-dimensional. This image is so suggestive that it is tempting to assume that Wanda-themed plays, beginning with Łubieńska's *Wanda, Queen of Poland*, stage her patriotic perfection; therefore, they are fairly light on drama.[46] An alternative view, which I have argued in this chapter, is that two of the Wanda plays—Łubieńska's *Wanda, Queen of Poland* and Wężyk's

Wanda—offer, unsettlingly, a very different Wanda: a troublesome queen who is a radical risk-taker. In both plays, Wanda's attempt to break out of the social constraints that shape women's lives in a male-centered culture provides rich material for high drama.

There is no evidence to suggest that the counter-Wanda who defies social and cultural conventions surrounding sexual difference was met with mockery or hostile puzzlement, that Łubieńska's and Wężyk's plays were the source of a scandal, or that critics excoriated some scenes for being in questionable taste. And yet Łubieńska's drama was published more than a hundred years after it was first performed, and Wężyk's text, reworked into an opera libretto and renamed *Wanda, Daughter of Krak* (*Wanda, córka Krakusa*), was staged only in 1876. Moreover, contemporaneous accounts of the 1807 production of Łubieńska's play are remarkable in their silence about the dream vision in act 2. Was the scene toned down or razored out? Did audiences see a sanitized version of Łubieńska's text? This is a mystery, since we seem to have no evidence. Further evidence may still come to light. Given the idealization of patriotic women in Polish cultural mythology in the nineteenth century, however, it is not unreasonable to conjecture that the reason for delaying the publication of Łubieńska's *Wanda, Queen of Poland* and the production of Wężyk's *Wanda*, and for the silence about the dream vision as well, was the sensitive issue of Wanda's gender transgression, particularly in the context of patriotic drama. Wanda is, quite literally, a dangerous woman—dangerous to the existing social order.

Poised on the border between neoclassicism and Romanticism, Łubieńska's *Wanda, Queen of Poland* and Wężyk's *Wanda* emerge as more complex and provocative, indeed more disturbing, than one might have initially acknowledged. Their uncompromising critique of the binary gender system sets the plays apart in early nineteenth-century Polish culture. This is one aspect of the plays that still has an edge. As playwrights, both Łubieńska and Wężyk display a lot of conventional tricks, but they are also juggling with knives.

4 ∥ No More Separate Spheres?
Emilia Plater

I.

ALONG WITH ŁUBIEŃSKA's and Wężyk's Wanda (as well as such canonical literary characters as Britomart in Edmund Spenser's *The Faerie Queene* or Clorinda in Torquato Tasso's *Jerusalem Delivered*), Emilia Plater (1806–1831) appears to fit comfortably within a long "line of noble women warriors, virtuous viragos all, magnanimous, brave, and chaste."[1] The standard story of her achievement is as clear as it is reassuring. A young woman from a far-flung corner of Europe is unflinchingly defiant in the face of foreign occupation of her homeland. Single-minded and determined, she takes up arms, fights with great distinction, and lays down her life for her country's freedom. Plater's self-sacrificing patriotism has earned her a place alongside male heroes such as Kościuszko in the annals of the Polish struggle for independence and statehood; it has also won her recognition in Poland's National Symbolic. The best-known of Poland's patriot-heroines, she has come to represent unswerving commitment, even at the deliberate cost of one's life, to the cause of national liberation.

The cult of Plater, however, has obscured the full extent of the implications of her brief public career.[2] Plater's contemporaries strongly believed that men and women possess certain innate, though different, abilities and character traits; therefore, each sex has necessarily different duties to perform.

According to the traditional moral economy of gendered sacrifice and suffering in wartime, men fight, and women provide support services. In a society that had a place for women only within a narrow range of options, Plater was an unusual figure. Her choice of patriotic toil, which entailed abandoning the woman's "proper" sphere and joining combat forces, violated the boundaries and hierarchies defined by the discrete classifications of gender identity. In disrupting gender binaries and engaging in the type of patriotic activism from which women were excluded, she was willing to give up a socially authorized mode of female existence in favor of living a life *as if* women were truly equal to men. Her *as-ifness* put her in a position of double revolt: against foreign oppression of her country and against the binary gender order.

After an uprising against Russian domination broke out in 1830, Plater was eager to do more than patriotic women were expected to do. She reportedly seized the initiative in a moment of crisis and designed an ambitious plan for a bold attack to capture a Russian fortress at Dyneburg (Dvinsk), but a citizens' committee in Wilno (Vilnius) rebuffed her. Undaunted by "the ignorant presumption of the men" on the committee, she refused to bend the knee to custom.[3] She cut off her hair, put on men's clothes, and rode off to join the uprising. According to some accounts, she brought with her a force of seven hundred male volunteers, mostly local villagers. Her commanders marveled at the oddity of her conduct and urged her to go home, but she stood firm.

What Plater said of her contemporary, a militant Greek patriot-heroine, could easily have been applied to her: "Men, in the course of their duty, can but challenge death. Bouboulina goes beyond—she braves public opinion besides."[4] Like Mill's nonconformists, Plater demonstrated the courage to stand her ground as a woman who broke through "the tyranny of opinion" and "the despotism of custom."[5] Regardless of whether she was able to raise a regiment entirely on her own or was in command of the troops in any official capacity,[6] the choices she made—refusing to defer to male authority, discarding the external signs of her gender identity (i.e., long hair and female clothing), taking up arms, and claiming a position for herself within the male bastion of the military—represent a compound violation of a firmly established gender polarity.

It should not be particularly surprising, then, that the reception of Plater in Polish culture has been intensely ambivalent. Commentators typically admire her patriotism and distrust her contestation of gender norms. Brave and resourceful as she may have been, her gender nonconformity has raised the touchy issue of sexual morality.[7] In nineteenth-century accounts, suspicion that her patriotic passion was a sublimated form of more carnal enthusiasm, or even a cover for sexual adventures, is common. Some accounts present her as a flirt who provoked sexual attentions.[8] Others suggest that she joined the uprising to snare a lover or a husband.[9] Even her relatives were susceptible to this association of women's gender insubordination with sexual libertinism. In her family, she was remembered as "an eccentric grandaunt" who deviated from the decorum of her sex and imposed herself on male insurgents, hindering their actions and making them cringe with embarrassment.[10] If a woman deviated from her prescribed occupations, in other words, her femininity was jeopardized, and femininity as a social construct was inseparable from respectability. Plater's gender-bending activism also aroused a different kind of anxiety, one that was anchored in a perception that a female interloper, intruding on a strictly male province of military affairs and holding her own there, must somehow be masculine. The fact that Plater's male companions-in-arms defeminized her by addressing her as "Mr. Plater" suggests that at least some of them perceived her, not as a woman dressed as a man, but as a woman whose female sexual identity was suspect.[11] To most commentators, Plater's sexual identity is never really in doubt, but her gender identity floats somewhere between imperfect femininity and surrogate masculinity. Their accounts, in the nineteenth century and well into the twentieth, have accordingly attempted to diminish Plater's patriotic motivation by arguing that her military service was a way to compensate for her physical defects, private frustrations, and failures in feminine roles and to escape an unhappy domestic situation that included a troubled relationship with her father, who had been separated from his wife and was about to marry another woman.[12]

Whatever her intentions (and we have no reason to suspect that Plater was anything but sincere about her own commitment to the patriotic cause), it is clear that commentators have found Plater's ambiguously gendered persona and her "eccentric" or "unwomanly" activism disconcerting; some have even frowned on her maverick exploits. Since women were expected to follow a gender-appropriate patriotic script, a gender-bending woman structurally defied its tenets, whatever her morality. This point is underlined by the commentators' readiness to accept slanderous gossip circulating about Plater with no other proof than the fact that she was already inherently suspect because of her choice of career. Her soldiering has posed a threat to conceptualizations of femininity and masculinity and, more broadly, to fundamental cultural distinctions and hierarchies that shape and buttress the patriarchal social order. Recurrent speculations about Plater's flirtatious streak, sexual adventures, emotional privation, and poor marriage prospects are a good indication of the intensity of the anxieties she has provoked about the stability of the binary gender order with its investment in hierarchy, discipline, and propriety; these anxieties in turn have activated defensive efforts to bolster up a threatened worldview.[13]

Plater's soldiering also raises a different issue. There can be little doubt that this embattled but strong and assertive woman who overcame enormous adversity—a patriot who deliberately decided to flout public opinion, challenge stereotypes, and break with polarized gender roles based on the dichotomy of front line and home front, fighting men and supportive women—acquired the necessary experience to qualify as a feminist heroine. As one of the women who learned, often subversively, to assert themselves despite their oppression and who thus gained and imparted an important sense of their power, she fulfills a demand for images of "self-reliant, independent, strong, courageous" women with whom female readers could identify.[14] And yet it is difficult to get around the fact that a call for such empowering role models is not unproblematic. It is open to debate whether literary works in which female characters are cast as victims of discrimination and oppression offer nothing constructive in terms of feminist critical discourse. Regardless of authorial intention, the depiction of women's discrimination and oppression may serve to expose, not perpetuate, patriarchal practices. It may also help readers reflect on themselves, their relationships, and their society. It may even prompt readers to make decisions based on antipatriarchal values, even as they acknowledge the limits imposed on their autonomy and their choices.[15]

With these caveats in mind, I take up the question of Plater's double revolt to consider how and to what ends her gender-bending activism was imagined, modeled, and adapted in dramatic writing. Although her biography was widely publicized through Adam Mickiewicz's poem "The Death of the Colonel" ("Śmierć Pułkownika," 1833), as well as through Lydia Maria Child's *Brief History of the Condition of Women in Various Ages and Nations* (1835) and Margaret Fuller's *Woman in the Nineteenth Century* (1845), to mention only the best-known works, Plater made her first appearance in Polish drama only in 1895. As a dramatic character, she was soon be eclipsed by her numerous avatars—fictional heroines who turn to her for inspiration. The emergence of plays about Plater and Plater-inspired heroines coincided with intensified public disputes over women's access to higher education and over their right to vote. This chapter, then, is an attempt to bring Plater-themed plays and their nexus of patriotic commitment and gender nonconformity into historical focus, which will also involve an excursion into biographies of Plater, as well as a brief discussion of the ways in which she has been depicted in poetry. My interest in particular lies in exploring the range of significances attached to the figure of Plater or a Plater-inspired heroine in dramatic writing and what these significances can tell us about cultural change, especially about change in the discourse of gender equality. Given that a considerable number of patriotic plays invokes Plater's example, would it be accurate to say that by the early twentieth century the concept of gender in Polish culture became flexible enough to enable playwrights to envision a radical expansion of women's social roles?

II.

In North America, Plater lives on in a groundbreaking work by a pioneer feminist writer: Fuller's *Woman in the Nineteenth Century,* an expansion of her controversial 1843 essay, *The Great Lawsuit.* In *Woman in the Nineteenth Century,* Fuller assembles potted presentations of what we would now call role models: heroines of the past offered as assurance that women could indeed be people of accomplishment. She insists that the achievements of these remarkable women be recognized and that a new generation of women be urged to make them patterns for their own life choices. In "Countess Colonel Plater," she finds a helper in her campaign against patriarchal habits and misogynistic attitudes and enlists her support to advance the demand that hitherto male professions be opened to women:

> But if you ask me what offices they may fill; I reply—any. I do not care what case you put; let them be sea-captains, if you will. I do not doubt there are women well fitted for such an office, and, if so, I should be glad to see them in it, as to welcome the maid of Saragossa, or the maid of Missolonghi, or the Suliote heroine, or Emily Plater.
>
> I think women need, especially at this juncture, a much greater range of occupation than they have, to rouse their latent powers.[16]

To the chagrin of many American readers who were not ready to accept her Polish helper, Fuller defiantly declares: "Plater is the figure I want for my frontispiece."[17] Of all the women discussed in *Woman in the Nineteenth Century*, it was indeed Plater who proved most controversial. As Fuller put it, "The newspaper editors . . . are more indignant at my praise of Emily than at any of my other sins."[18]

The controversy over Plater did not prevent Fuller from extending her admiration to other Polish women. It is evident that she delighted in the surprising degree of freedom they allegedly possessed and in the range of possibilities supposedly open to them. In a pointed challenge to her compatriots' belief that Americans, above all others, are a free people, she contended that Polish women in practice enjoyed more liberty than their American counterparts. Reporting from Europe for the *New-York Daily Tribune* in 1848, she deliberately noted that Polish women were "women indeed—not children, servants or playthings."[19] Such well-meaning enthusiasm for Polish women has inevitably bolstered Polish and Polish American pride.[20] It has also helped obscure the everyday reality of women's lives in nineteenth-century Poland.

Mary Wollstonecraft, another pivotal figure in the rise of feminism, would not have shared Fuller's admiration for Plater. Unlike Fuller, Wollstonecraft, a revolutionary republican who loathed aristocratic women, did not approve of heroines. Great women get short shrift in *A Vindication of the Rights of Woman*: "I shall not lay any great stress on the example of a few women who, from having received a masculine education, have acquired courage and resolution . . . Sappho, Eloisa, Mrs. Macaulay, the Empress of Russia, Madame d'Eon, etc. These, and many more, may be reckoned exceptions; and, are not all heroes, as well as heroines, exceptions to general rules? I wish to see women neither heroines nor brutes; but reasonable creatures."[21] When Wollstonecraft denounced heroines in 1790, it was on the grounds that praise for the exceptional woman whose talents and genius set her apart from the other members of her sex was no substitute for respect for women in general. What was the exceptional woman an exception to, after all, but the frustrated, degraded condition of the majority? As long as most women were second-class citizens, the high-achieving woman would inevitably remain an oddity, a freak, and thus extremely vulnerable. As long as gender rules survived, in other words, such heroines would always have a whiff of the ghetto. To Wollstonecraft, ordinary women, "neither heroines nor brutes; but reasonable creatures," with no shaky pedestals to negotiate, are a firmer foundation for feminist hopes.

In Polish culture, Plater has been enshrined on a pedestal that seems stable rather than shaky. Its foundations were laid by her contemporaries, who contributed exalted accounts of this "true Polish woman"—of her patriotic devotion, remarkable force of character, resourcefulness, organizational skills, supreme courage, and self-sacrificing heroism—to newspapers published in Warsaw, Poznań, and Berlin during the uprising.[22] After the fall of the insurgency and Plater's death, the project of building a monument to Plater was continued in earnest by her compatriots who found refuge in France—men such as Mickiewicz, Michał (Michel) Pietkiewicz, Cezary Plater, Władysław Plater, and Józef (Joseph) Straszewicz. In their publications, they sought both to popularize the image of Poland as hero and martyr in a just and noble struggle for freedom and to reinforce the fears and prejudices about Russia widely held in Europe at that time.[23] With this goal in mind, they nudged the "true Polish woman" into the cultural limelight and turned her life to exemplary account. Cast as a symbol of heroic resistance against Russian despotism and praised as peerless among women, Plater rose from provincial obscurity to European prominence. In Poland, however, it is Mickiewicz's poem "The Death of the Colonel" that has secured her immortality.[24] Placed in the custody of his poetic imagination and talent, her story has become part of the common stock of Polish knowledge.

"The Death of the Colonel" owes much of its immense popularity to its captivating, even mesmerizing form, reminiscent of folk ballads. The poem's rhythm, with its almost liturgical repetitions, can feel like a snare, something one cannot escape from, a spell, a seduction. In the poem, Mickiewicz pays a tribute to Plater's heroism by promoting her from captain to colonel. At the same time, however, he removes her from the realm of action and immobilizes her on her deathbed.[25] He de-transgresses her gender transgression even further by emphasizing her piety. We as readers are thus led to believe that this "virgin-hero" (an appellation that gestures to the precedent of the Maid of Orleans) did not act on her own but was called to carry on the cause of freedom with a mandate from heaven.[26] And although in his later work Mickiewicz would highlight Plater's aristocratic pedigree, here, through a magic sleight of hand, he makes her a heroine of the common people.[27] Mickiewicz's Plater dies in a humble cottage, and her deathbed is a patriotic throne toward which grief-stricken villagers and peasant veterans of the Kościuszko insurrection press through wide open doors. With this poem, Mickiewicz has ushered Plater into the timeless realm of myth where the story of her life is that of her death. The messy contingencies of gender insubordination, the poem seems to suggest, would compromise—indeed, diminish—Plater's status as a patriotic icon; therefore, she is more useful dead than alive.

Given that Plater has been elevated to the full majesty of a national heroine, it is rather surprising to find that she is not among the well-documented figures of history. The main source of information about her, Straszewicz's *Émilie Plater, sa Vie et sa Mort*, is adulatory and filled with imaginative flourishes. Straszewicz casts a mantle of righteousness over Plater by placing her life story within the legitimizing framework of the Wanda myth twinned with the nationalist idea of Polish exceptionalism:

> In Poland, female education is deemed of more serious importance than in other countries. Females learn that they are children of Poland before they learn that they are women. Their education is eminently patriotic, and perhaps more national than that bestowed upon the men. Their understandings are formed with a view to future usefulness to their country.
>
> If we trace back our history to its source, we shall find a Wanda sacrificing her life for the country. Though perhaps a fabulous personage, yet she has been to our Polish heroines the model of their adoption, and they scrupulously follow her example. . . .
>
> In Poland, courage is the delight of women, and devotedness to the state is as common among them as it is rare among other nations.[28]

As in the Wanda myth (and in Mickiewicz's poem), however, it is the heroine's death, rather than her activism, that serves as the measure of her patriotic excellence. The historical Plater died after a long illness in the rural home of a gentry family on 23 December 1831, more than three months after the uprising had been crushed. But for Straszewicz, there could be no finer way to die than in battle for Poland's freedom. The very idea of survival appears to taint a hero's (or heroine's) life with insincerity. To accommodate Plater's inopportune illness within his mythologizing project, he links her death to the fall of Warsaw on 8 September 1831. A true lover of *patria*, Straszewicz's Plater dies from a broken heart when she hears that Warsaw fell into Russian hands.[29] Straszewicz, then, constructs a perfect heroic life, propelled by a moralizing purpose and a propagandistic mission. Plater is to be seen as the native daughter of a freedom-loving people who fought bravely against invaders but were overwhelmed by the forces of tyranny. Moreover, the image of Polish heroism pitted against Russian aggression and brutality is to be deeply imprinted on the consciousness of Straszewicz's contemporaries in the West in order to stir powerful emotions and to mobilize opposition to Russian actions in Poland.

Straszewicz's unalloyed paean to Plater established a foundation for some of the enduring myths about her. Plater's subsequent biographers relied heavily on his narrative, although their interpretations of her character and activism were governed by their own presuppositions and ideological agendas. I want to take three examples—the biographical accounts by Felicja Boberska, Bolesław Limanowski, and Kazimierz Żurawski—to explore how the meaning of Plater was constructed under different political circumstances: in 1880 (at the height of the Positivist movement that aspired to shape public opinion in support of political moderation and grassroots reform and that, accordingly, insisted on keeping a phantasmagoria of the martyred Poland, Christ-like in its heroic self-sacrifice, out of patriotic discourse) and in 1911 (during the turbulent period between the revolution of 1905 and the outbreak of World War I).[30] The key question, I want to suggest, is not which of the accounts is closest to historical fact, but what these accounts reveal about attitudes to gender nonconformity and, specifically, female soldiering, arguably the most alarming of all gender transgressions.

When Limanowski and Żurawski bring Plater's fainting spells and riding mishaps into the foreground, the reader might conclude that they take deliberate steps to soften her Amazonian image. Their emphasis on Plater's frailty and fatigue, in other words, might be seen as a strategy of upholding what she has threatened: essentialist definitions of gender identity that have served to keep women in their inferior position.[31] Plater is not to be a figure who would lead to a loosening of gender divisions; therefore, the biographers reinforce the traditional notion that women are unfit to withstand the physical strains of warfare. But Limanowski's and Żurawski's accounts could well be interpreted in exactly the opposite light. It would be reasonable to assume that they write with considerable realism and frankness about the weariness of constant campaigning. It is important to them to say how hard it is to be a soldier, to work the body constantly, and to risk it in battle. One could even argue that they use Plater's frailty and fatigue inversely to elevate her status: the hardships, pains, discomforts, and perils she suffered make her remarkable achievement all the more extraordinary.

Limanowski and Żurawski cite Plater's comment about Bouboulina. They concede that Plater's male colleagues did not make her feel welcome. But the reader's suspicion returns that both authors do in fact uphold presuppositions about gender roles and identities. When Limanowski and Żurawski are silent about why Plater came back empty-handed from her trip to Wilno, they seem reluctant to recognize the extent of resistance that she encountered even before she joined the uprising. And when they attribute the plan to attack the Dyneburg fortress solely to Plater's cousins, it is evident that they are unwilling to acknowledge her resourcefulness, competence, and self-confidence.[32] Admittedly, the paucity of factual information about Plater makes her an elusive subject for biography. Given the gaps in the records of her life, however, it is impossible to tell whether it was Plater or her cousins who came up with the idea to capture the fortress. And yet Limanowski and Żurawski choose to credit her cousins with the plan.

Is a biography by a woman more sensitive to the feminist content of the Plater story? In contrast to Limanowski and Żurawski, Boberska moves Plater from an auxiliary role to a position of leadership. For example, she repeats after Straszewicz that Plater was the sole author of the plan to seize the fortress at Dyneburg, but the citizens' committee in Wilno excluded her from its deliberations because she was a woman. At the same time, however, Boberska makes a significant effort to "feminize" Plater's behavior.[33] Boberska's tone remains ambivalent throughout the narrative, performing a complicated balancing act that juxtaposes celebration of Plater's intrepid patriotism and unease about her gender nonconformity. She modulates her tribute to Plater so insistently that she ends in a quite different key: Plater and the other female soldiers who fought in the uprising went against "the womanly nature," therefore they cannot be considered "models worthy of emulation."[34] According to Boberska, it is philanthropists and educators such as Klaudyna Potocka, Emilia Sczaniecka, and Klementyna Tańska Hoffmanowa who are "the ideal female laborers in the national vineyard."[35] The readiness to revise or suppress certain aspects of Plater's biography and to censure her on the grounds that she was not like Potocka, Sczaniecka, or Hoffmanowa confirms that her soldiering was perceived as a disturbing challenge to the boundaries of gender.

Writing less than twenty years after yet another Polish attempt, in 1863, to rise against foreign domination ended in defeat, Boberska nevertheless finds a way to counsel how Plater's heroism on the national scene can be translated into private, even intimate, and domestic terms. Having emphatically rejected Plater's soldiering as a viable patriotic model for Polish women, she reminds her audience that Plater, like Queen Wanda, proudly refused a marriage proposal from a foreign suitor on the grounds that he was an enemy of Poland: being Polish, she would not demean herself to marry such a man. In other words, although Plater denied her "womanly nature" by taking up arms, she redeemed herself by refusing to compromise her Polishness. The Plater who rebuffed her Russian suitor with the words "I am a Polish woman" becomes useful to the post-1863 project of peaceful resistance to the punitive denationalization efforts of the Russian government in the aftermath of the Polish revolt.[36] She is to empower Polish women so that they can confidently serve the national mission from their homes, as custodians of Polishness who preserve and instill a sense of obligation to the nation and its future at a time when political independence remains out of reach.

Boberska's concern with maintaining gender difference and safeguarding "proper" gender roles for Polish women within the patriotic project is reminiscent of the agenda that was formulated and propagated by the *Bluszcz* (*Ivy*), an enormously popular weekly magazine.[37] Launched by Maria Ilnicka in 1865, it was expressly addressed to women. After the uprising of 1863 had shattered the family lives of many women and forced them to seek employment outside the home, the *Bluszcz* attempted to draw those women back to the domestic sphere. To this end, it idealized women's domestic roles and glorified the values of traditional womanhood—motherhood and homemaking. At the same time, however, the *Bluszcz* was careful not to valorize the domestic and the private at the expense of, or in opposition to, any notion of the community or collective life. Rather, it encouraged its female readers to promote patriotic values through children's education. Thus "women's traditional work was acquiring characteristics of a public, patriotic, and heroic act."[38]

Three decades later, Żurawski finds, interestingly, that Plater is no longer a familiar figure. His observation suggests that her gender-bending activism became a mirage by the early twentieth century. Żurawski's immediate goal, then, is to restore Plater to a prominent position in the Polish cultural memory. Like Boberska, moreover, he mines the Plater story for patriotic edification. Unlike Boberska, however, he does not address his account primarily to a female audience. According to Żurawski, "all

Polish men and women" can be imbued—via Plater—with the same spirit of patriotism.[39]

Something else is at issue too. Żurawski speaks of an acute need for a patriotic icon that would help build community and consensus. His insistent emphasis on the need to bind social classes together reveals how he perceives post-1905 Poland: it is a country hampered by alarming social tensions and political factionalism. The Plater he has recovered from cultural oblivion, then, is recruited as a spokeswoman for the conservative ideology of cross-class solidarity. He imagines a Poland in which upper and lower classes, through their shared appreciation of Plater's selfless and passionate devotion to the common good, could learn to get along. Żurawski's Plater is thus a benevolent guardian of peace in the national household, a custodian of harmonious relationships within the traditional boundaries of social status. In short, Żurawski judges it desirable, in the interests of social harmony and reconciliation, to nourish a collective illusion, presided over by a Plater with a maternal overlay.

Limanowski's account presents another kind of problem. To emphasize Plater's identification with the common people, he serialized an early version of his work in a Lwów newspaper, *Dziennik Literacki,* under the assumed identity of a peasant, Janko Płakań. But the issue for Limanowski is not the conservative postulate of social solidarity. His preface to the 1911 edition makes it clear that he writes from the ideological position of a Polish socialist who believes that the struggle for Poland's independence must be bound with a social revolution.[40] As I have argued, however, Limanowski's reconstruction of the Plater story does not advance the idea of gender equality that stands behind Plater's transgression. In fact, his perspective is often hostile to the feminist implications of her activism. In his account, as in Boberska's and Żurawski's, Plater's uncrushable yearning is to be free—as a Pole, not as a woman.

III.

In the biographies of Plater, as I have argued, interpretive strategies clash on issues large and small, as writers shape her life story along the lines of their choosing. It is inevitable to ask: If she is a suitably versatile emblem for a host of causes, how and to what ends is the Plater story constructed in drama? Although this question must remain suspended here, I will take it up later. First, I want to examine in more detail the process of Plater's posthumous elevation to the Polish pantheon, even though she has been the object of suspicion, resentment, and hostility because she defied what seemed to be the natural destiny of the female sex.

The axis of the Plater story is one of the central events of modern Polish history: the fall of the Polish-Lithuanian Commonwealth in 1795. To prevent denationalization under foreign rule, women stepped into the breach as defenders of culture, preserving the Polish language, customs, and traditions. They also assumed many responsibilities in the struggle for national independence. They raised funds, supplied food and clothing, smuggled weapons, provided medical assistance, and served as military couriers. Some volunteered for combat. Women who joined the resistance movement in their different ways came from every class in society: titled ladies, housewives, house servants, laundry workers, seamstresses, teachers, artists, and farmers. Some were married with children, others unmarried or widowed, and some were mere schoolgirls.[41] The extent of their engagement in the independence movement has led to one of the fundamental claims in the mythology of Polish exceptionalism: a claim that Polish women have had a unique standing in modern history. While elsewhere gender ideologies imposed separate spheres, dividing societies into the masculine/public and feminine/private domains, the fall of Poland precipitated the rise of Polish women by compelling them to serve a public cause—the cause of Polish independence. Mickiewicz drew on this claim when, on 17 June 1842, he proudly told his audience at the Collège de France in Paris:

> The Polish woman does not excite her nerves by reading romances. She is not a delicate nymph, a passionate Italian, or a witty queen of salons. She is a daughter devoted to her father, a wife ready to follow her husband into the fire. . . .]
>
> Such is the inevitable path of humanity: to acquire a certain right, one first needs to make a sacrifice. It is in this manner that the woman in Poland secures her emancipation. In Poland, she has greater freedom than anywhere else . . . . Women will achieve importance in society not by debating about their rights or by proclaiming delusive theories, but by acts of sacrifice.
>
> In Poland, the woman takes part in conspiracies along with her husband and her brothers. She risks her life to bring help to prisoners. She is sometimes tried as a traitor to the state and exiled to Siberia. Several upper-class women have been punished [for their patriotic activism] with flogging in public squares.

These courageous women don't hesitate to mount a horse and to lead troops to battle. The name of Countess Plater is well known. . . .

    I repeat: the vast issue of the emancipation of women is significantly more advanced in Poland than in any other country.[42]

Undeniably, Mickiewicz makes a compelling argument to demonstrate that Poland is a place where women matter. But his argument, as the historian Wiktoria Śliwowska points out, relies on poetic hyperbole and brisk generalizations that should be viewed with a skeptical eye because they cavalierly overlook critical historical details: "In all three partitions, life went on as usual," and it was only "a narrow group" of women that engaged in oppositional activities.[43] Moreover, Mickiewicz maneuvers skillfully on the sensitive issue of women's rights. Admittedly, the struggle for Poland's independence did offer Polish women an opportunity to assume larger roles and new authority. In Mickiewicz's argument, however, Polish women's gender-bending is justifiable and ennobling only because it is done in a good cause: for Poland's liberation from foreign rule, not for gender equality. His argument thus rests on a paradox: Polish women secure their emancipation only by subordinating their own interests, aspirations, and desires to the needs of the nation and by aligning their convention-breaking acts of personal heroism solely with the project of national liberation. Women outside Poland, he sternly warns, waste their time by debating the issue of women's rights. His admonition sounds like a lecture by an overbearing uncle to a disobedient niece. In his effort to make the point clear, he makes it repeatedly: the basis of women's rights is a sense of self-sacrificing duty to one's country, not an empty sense of entitlement.

    By now, it may seem that Plater's gender transgression, even when explicitly resisted (as in Boberska's account), was justified as a necessary expedient at a time of grave national emergency and absorbed into patriotic discourse. And yet, as I have argued, her gender-bending activism continued to be contested. For many, it was hard to accept the idea of female soldiership because they regarded it as a violation of the role of women in society. The irksome questions return: How was Plater's cultural canonization possible if public opinion in Poland has been resistant to women's participation in armed combat?[44] How did she secure a place for herself in the Polish pantheon, while her female companions-in-arms, such as Wilhelmina Kasprowicz, Maria Prószyńska, Maria Raszanowicz, and Antonina Tomaszewska, have faded from view? After all, Plater made her initial appearance in Polish literature—in Konstanty Gaszyński's "A Poem on the Occasion of Miss Emilia Plater and Miss Maria Raszanowicz's Enlistment for the Insurgency" ("Wiersz z okoliczności wejścia w szeregi walczących panien Emilii Platerówny i Marii Raszanowiczówny"), written during the uprising, in the summer of 1831—as Raszanowicz's equal. The historical Raszanowicz was Plater's aide-de-camp, but in the poem they share command of the troops.

As I have mentioned earlier, Plater owes her posthumous career in no small degree to her compatriots in France who transformed her into a European celebrity. In their publications, her life was rescued from provincial obscurity and shaped into an exemplary biography to corroborate with vivid detail their efforts to remind Western public opinion of the Polish uprising and its brutal suppression by Russia, to maximize sympathy for the conquered Poles, and to drum up popular support for the cause of Polish independence. To understand the puzzle of Plater's posthumous fame more fully, however, it is necessary to consider the broader context in which her compatriots set out to construct the story of her life. The key components of the larger context are the deep anxieties throughout Western Europe about the rapid growth and military power of Russia, Tsar Nicholas I's opposition to the July 1830 Revolution in France, the widespread belief among the French that the outbreak of the Polish uprising prevented Russia's military intervention to suppress the July Revolution, and the rise of French Russophobia, combined, intriguingly, with the cult of Joan of Arc.[45]

Although Straszewicz, in *Émilie Plater, sa Vie et sa Mort,* invokes the precedent of Queen Wanda to develop a legitimizing framework for Plater, he recognized that his French readers needed a more familiar frame of reference. To recast the unfamiliar (and therefore easy to ignore) in familiar terms, he capitalized on the French cult of the Maid of Orleans and presented Plater as "the Joan d'Arc of Poland."[46] Admittedly, Straszewicz's Plater, unlike her French predecessor, does not claim heavenly inspiration. She is not a vessel chosen by God who carries her through great temptations and trials to her exemplary eminence. Like Joan, however, she believes herself destined to go to the aid of her country. Like Joan, she meets with rejection and scorn, but follows her innermost convictions.[47] Like Joan, she assumes a masculine role and responds with unwavering courage and integrity to what she deems to be her mission at a time of political crisis and uncertainty. To strengthen the analogy between Plater and Joan, Straszewicz uses scenes from Joan's biography as templates for his version of the Plater story. For example, Plater's rousing speech to inspire her troops echoes the urgency of Joan's mission at the court of Charles VII.[48]

At a time when the European public thought Nicholas I the incarnation of cruel despotism, and almost every Russian action on the continent was interpreted as constituting part of a reactionary and aggressive plan of imperial expansion, French writers picked up the connection between Plater and Joan. According to Justin Maurice, for example, Joan sent Plater to defend *"la liberté sainte"* and to crush *"l'ignoble barbarie"* of Russia.[49] Pierre Simon Ballanche went so far as to depict *"la vierge polonaise"* as *"autre Jeanne d'Arc,"* or the Maid's double, who saved Western civilization from Russian tyranny.[50] In each case, the Plater story reinforced the model biography of the French heroine as an ardent champion of freedom, while imbuing it with new resonance: their empowering sisterhood sounded a warning against the threat of Russia's despotism and rampant expansionism.

The conflation of the cult of Joan of Arc with acute Russophobia helped launch Plater's rise to stardom in nineteenth-century Europe; it also helped enhance her reputation in Polish eyes and smooth her passage into national hagiography.[51] That said, a vexed question remains about Plater's female companions-in-arms. They, too, had the precedent of the Maid behind them, but their activism has fallen into oblivion. What Kasprowicz, Prószynska, Raszanowicz, and Tomaszewska did not have, however, was Plater's high social status. They came from the impoverished gentry; she was a countess descended from one of the oldest and most distinguished aristocratic families in Lithuania. Her lineage has not prevented some commentators from circulating preposterous rumors and outlandish tales about her, but it has made her sacrifice seem larger: she gave up the worldly comforts of an aristocratic lifestyle to undertake the pains and privations of warfare in order to free her country from the Russian yoke. Tellingly, Mickiewicz, who in his 1833 poem had wrought a metamorphosis of Plater from an elite woman into a heroine of the common people, ten years later performed another metamorphosis, this time from a sturdy folk heroine into a frail countess.

IV.

Plater's legacy in Polish literature consists of Wacław Gąsiorowski's novel *Emilia Plater* (1910), several poems, and a handful of plays.[52] While the novel and the poems have been a sporadic subject of scholarly discussion, the dramatic works have not received sustained attention.[53] Here, I consider all the available plays that mine Plater's life story.[54] To contextualize them, I examine the Plater-themed plays against two groups of dramas in which Plater does not appear as a character, but her example is invoked in spoken lines and stage directions. The first group acknowledges women's aspirations to military service in the patriotic cause but draws a line between combatant and noncombatant options. In the second group, female characters cross this line, insisting that womanhood and soldiership are compatible.

In all three groups of plays, the women's determination to take up arms and defend their country against the enemy may be seen as the ultimate expression of their patriotism. But their struggle to claim a viable position for themselves within the military, historically an exclusive domain of men, may also be seen in broader terms, as an attempt to expand a range of socially acceptable roles for women and thus as a push for gender equality. In Stefan Kiedrzyński's *Engaged on a Battlefield* (*Zaręczyny pod kulami*, 1938), for example, the Lieutenant, a self-appointed custodian of gender norms, urges the heroine to abandon her plan to volunteer for combat in the Polish-Soviet War of 1920 and instead to choose an option that has society's stamp of approval: "There's a lot of other work that women can do. That work is just as important."[55] Jadwiga, however, has other ideas. Would it be accurate, then, to assume that plays in which female characters overturn the long-standing social prohibition on women's service in combat forces support the idea of gender equality? As usual, no simple answer will suffice.

First, I turn to plays featuring the would-be woman soldier. To say that this character is ubiquitous in patriotic drama is to state the obvious. Her frequent appearance seems to suggest that playwrights have found her to be a particularly attractive figure, rich in dramaturgical possibilities. Here, this large group of plays is exemplified by Witold Bunikiewicz's *The Uhlan Songs* (*Piosnki ułańskie*, 1919), Bronisław Bakal's *The Battle of Łowczówek* (*Bitwa pod Łowczówkiem*, 1938), Zygmunt Nowakowski's *A Sprig of*

Rosemary (*Gałązka rozmarynu*, 1938), and Zygmunt Reis's *Love of a Rifleman* (*Strzelecka miłość*, 1933), all of which take place during World War I. It also includes two one-act plays set in the interwar period: Ludwik Stolarzewicz's *Girlfriends* (*W gronie dziewcząt*, ca. 1935) and *We, Women, Will Also Take Up Arms* (*I my dziewczęta wojować będziemy*, ca.1935). Written for women's schools, each boasts an all-female cast.

In *The Uhlan Songs*, a veteran of the 1863 uprising goes so far as to suggest that women's contribution to the patriotic project should not be confined to their more traditional, supportive roles. He is proud of his wife, who did not hesitate to fire on Russians soldiers to protect her family during the uprising. But his granddaughters laugh at his idea of drafting women to help the war effort in 1916. While *The Uhlan Songs* refuses to grapple with the contentious issue of female soldiering, *The Battle of Łowczówek* and *A Sprig of Rosemary* accept the challenge only to use the comic stage device of see-through transvestism.

In *The Battle of Łowczówek*, Jagna, a young peasant woman, puts on her father's clothes and runs away from home to volunteer for Józef Piłsudski's Polish Legions. To justify her gender-bending, she invokes the precedent of Plater's celebrated heroism: "Emilia Plater could serve in the army, and so can I!"[56] She disappears from the world of the play, marching off "in a funny way" because her oversized trousers are slipping off her hips.[57] We are left with a titillating image of a female clown in drag who at any moment may lose her pants. It is obvious that this broad farcical effect aims to discredit the would-be woman soldier and her trespassing onto male territory. She is an impostor not meant to be taken seriously.

After Jagna has left, her father declares: "If they take her on, I'll sign up as well. I can't be too old yet. They must take me on!"[58] It may seem, then, that Jagna's role in the play goes beyond providing comic relief mixed with sexual innuendo. Before we as readers or spectators congratulate Jagna for spurring her father to action, however, it is helpful to wait for the conclusion of his monologue. Jagna's grandfather, we find out, fought in the 1863 uprising. "Nothing came out of it," her father says, "but maybe this time—who knows?"[59] While Jagna has been inspired by Plater's example, he follows in his father's footsteps. Each gender, in other words, has its own model of patriotic behavior, and the two models must be kept separate—and unequal. The authority of the male model remains intact, while the Plater model is not allowed to legitimize Jagna's aspirations to military service.

The opening scene of *A Sprig of Rosemary*, one of the most popular patriotic plays on the Polish stage, also uses cross-gender masquerade, but adopts a different strategy of keeping women in their place. The action takes place in August 1914 outside the Polish Legions' recruitment office in Kraków. An unnamed young woman disguised as a man runs out of the office. She wanted to enlist, but balked at the codes of male behavior that require potential recruits to undress in public. Sobbing and stomping her feet, she gives vent to her frustration. A nurse named Sława intervenes and dispatches the would-be woman soldier to parental jurisdiction. This brief incident, soon overshadowed by the wartime pageantry that fills the action of *A Sprig of Rosemary*, may appear insignificant. But its strategic placement at the very beginning of the play suggests that something important is at issue. The scene allows female readers and spectators to test the limits of the permissible only to warn them against the unconventional aspirations that the young woman has entertained. Whether a woman can perform military duties becomes irrelevant beside an insidious appeal to the female readers' and spectators' sense of respectability. No respectable woman, the scene makes it clear, would want to subject herself to the humiliation of undressing in front of a male crowd.

At the same time, *A Sprig of Rosemary* carefully avoids antagonizing men and women. The male characters are spared any direct involvement in the incident with the young woman who has attempted to overstep gender boundaries. Moreover, their comments convey amazement and admiration rather than censure: "What? A girl! Bravo! An Amazon! Emilia Plater! That's incredible!"[60] The task of controlling the young woman falls to another woman, one whose occupation, by traditional standards, is more appropriate to the female sex. Sława restores the male prerogative by returning the young woman to silence and invisibility. She performs the task with aplomb, earning the men's praise. They are quick to note that she was charming even as she shouted at the young woman. Later, Sława is rewarded with marriage to the play's hero. The young woman, by contrast, vanishes after the opening scene, and we know nothing more about her. She does not even have a name to be left behind, while the nurse bears the telling name of Sława, or glorious fame.

Although *The Battle of Łowczówek* and *A Sprig of Rosemary* do not ignore women's patriotic desire, they successfully eliminate the nonnormative aspirations that threaten gender distinctions. An occasional impostor is promptly removed from the dramatic action, while "true" female patriots take up nursing. Reis's *Love of a Rifleman,* in contrast, seems to take women's unconventional aspirations far more seriously. The play's heroine, Zosia, comes from a family that disapproves of women's military service, but she refuses to follow a ready-made social script and insists on making her own choices. She rebuffs an unwanted suitor, flees her confining home life, and joins the Polish Legions. Appointed a courier, she seizes the opportunity to show her mettle. Under barrages of fire, she smuggles to safety Polish deserters from a Russian army. One of the men she rescues at the risk of her life is her future husband. When the war is over, she accepts his marriage proposal and withdraws into the domestic sphere.

By now, it is evident that *Love of a Rifleman* sends mixed signals. Zosia is allowed only a noncombatant role, yet war gives her the chance to prove her capacity for martial daring and to win the recognition that would have been inconceivable in peacetime. Her heroic exploits are celebrated, but her "unfeminine" conduct capitulates to conventional gender roles. She must forsake the independence of the single life for a woman's true calling: wifehood and motherhood. It would be tempting, if a little glib, to conclude that *Love of a Rifleman* is, simply enough, a tale of patriotic passion in the service of a marriage plot. That is, Zosia's exemplary performance as a courier has no real impact on the course of the dramatic action other than securing her a husband. But the play's mixed signals complicate this conclusion. Given Zosia's role as a courier rather than a combat soldier, the patriotic effort in the play involves only a slight relaxation of the gender order, yet even this modest loosening becomes so threatening to gender norms that it begins to look like gender ambiguity or indeterminacy. But then Zosia is a woman who has repeatedly asserted her autonomy and agency. She has resisted the gender disciplining of her family, spurned a well-to-do suitor, and run away from home. As a result, Reis takes pains to allay suspicion about Zosia's gender (and possibly sexual) identity. Her bubbly rebelliousness and energetic nonconformity in the first two acts are tempered and directed into more acceptable (and marriageable) channels in the third. To stabilize her gender, in other words, Reis locks Zosia within the unambiguous heterosexual respectability of wife and mother.

It is unavoidable to ask: How are women's breaches of gender-appropriate patriotic activism represented in plays addressed specifically to women? Stolarzewicz's *Girlfriends* and *We, Women, Will Also Take Up Arms* provide particularly interesting cases in point. The most striking aspect of the two plays is the emphatic refusal, from beginning to end, to depict young female patriots as women of marble. *Girlfriends* is filled with laughter, song, and dance. *We, Women, Will Also Take Up Arms* opens with a waltz and ends with a lively debate whether to go to the movies or to throw a party. To an audience accustomed to a different kind of patriotic drama, these plays may come as a surprise.

For Halka in *Girlfriends*, the direct source of patriotic inspiration is her late father. A Ciceronian patriot, he always put his country first. On his deathbed, he passed on to his daughter a remarkable imperative that makes the courage of willing self-sacrifice for homeland gender-blind: "Remember, when you grow up, you, too, must be a Polish soldier. Polish women owe their lives to their country."[61] Halka's girlfriends concur: "Your father was right. We won't abandon our homeland in its patriotic hour!"[62] Swept up by patriotic enthusiasm, they rapturously invoke the empowering example of Polish women who took up arms in the patriotic cause. Put another way, they shift the locus of patriotic inspiration from the legacy of Halka's father to that of transgressive women patriots. Halka's mother attempts to restore the gender order by reminding Halka and her girlfriends that most women served as couriers rather than soldiers. Her words, however, fall on deaf ears.

In a sequel to *Girlfriends*, entitled *We, Women, Will Also Take Up Arms*, we see a group of female students attending a meeting of the Women's Auxiliary Corps. The room is adorned with portraits of famous Polish women, including Plater.[63] Under the watchful eyes of their illustrious predecessors, the students take a patriotic pledge to serve the public good. Since their training program covers not only nursing but also military exercises and the use of arms, we may be tempted to assume that Stolarzewicz's play recommends a broader, more flexible range of career options for women than, say, *A Sprig of Rosemary* was willing to countenance. As the action unfolds, however, it becomes evident that Stolarzewicz's play, its defiant title notwithstanding, seeks to prove that women's chances of succeeding in combat forces are low because most women lack men's "natural" skills. Women can, however, succeed as nurses. While not denying them access to the military outright, in other words, the play discourages women from overstepping gender boundaries even before they actually attempt to enlist.

At first glance, the second group of plays belies Stolarzewicz's rhetorical maneuvers. In Antoni Stefan Ździebłowski's *A Heroine of the Uprising of 1863* (*Bohaterka z Powstania 1863 roku,* 1893) and Kiedrzyński's *Engaged on a Battlefield,* women join the military in wartime and distinguish themselves as soldiers. They seem to be saying: look what we can do if given the chance. Initially, then, it may appear that both plays support the gender-bending idea of women's service in the armed forces. To test this hypothesis, I turn first to Kiedrzyński's play.

Like Zosia in Reis's *Love of a Rifleman,* Jadwiga in Kiedrzyński's *Engaged on a Battlefield* comes from a family that frowns on the idea of women's military service. Unlike Zosia, however, she dutifully seeks parental permission to enlist. When the Polish-Soviet War of 1920 breaks out, she wins the support of her grandfather, a veteran of the 1863 uprising, who concedes that Polish women did take up arms in times of national need. She returns from the front wounded, but triumphant. The Lieutenant, who has initially dismissed her military aspirations, acknowledges that his troops owe their battlefield success in no small degree to Jadwiga's prowess and derring-do. By the end of the play, however, Kiedrzyński resorts to the marriage plot to rectify the gender order that has been destabilized by wartime necessity. Accordingly, Jadwiga abandons her nonnormative aspirations in order to assume the role of wife and mother. Like *Love of a Rifleman, Engaged on a Battlefield* refocuses the audience's attention on traditional social norms sanctified by (impending) marriage at the play's conclusion.

This kind of gender disciplining is conspicuously absent in Ździebłowski's *A Heroine of the Uprising of 1863,* even though the play thrives on sudden twists of action. When the eponymous heroine, a young peasant woman named Anusia, joins the campaign of 1863, a commanding officer assigns her a nurse's duties, but she wants to fight for Poland until the last. Impressed with Anusia's pluck, he eventually shares the command of the troops with her. After the suppression of the uprising, Anusia returns to civilian life, but the play dispenses with the conventional closure of marital engagement: a man she loves has committed suicide. Ździebłowski adds two final twists to his play. Anusia discovers that she is a countess with a vast fortune, but she gives up her inherited wealth because it has been tainted with corruption and social injustice. She wants to earn her living, while serving the public good. Recognizing that a large proportion of the rural population is illiterate, she finds a new patriotic mission: educating peasant children. The play thus reinvents the Plater-inspired insurgent as a Positivist heroine. The post-1863 Anusia aptly illustrates Norman Davies's point that "the typical Polish 'patriot' of the turn of the century was not the revolutionary with a revolver in his pocket, but the young lady of good family with a textbook under her shawl."[64] When Anusia exchanges the insurgent's rifle for the teacher's lectern, however, her heroic exploits in the uprising are not sidelined. Instead, they confer moral authority on her. That said, the play does not admit the possibility that an ordinary woman might rise to a position of authority solely through her personal merit. If there is to be a female authority figure, she must be, like Anusia, an upper-class woman.

The character of Plater appears in Janina Sedlaczek's *Rallying under a Woman's Banner (Pod sztandarem kobiety,* 1895), Władysław Winiarski's *Yet Another Grave (Mogiła więcej,* 1912), Wanda Brzeska's *Emilia Plater* (1927), Tadeusz Konczyński's *Emilia Plater* (ca. 1933), and Tadeusz Orsza Korpal's *Emilia Plater: The Young Women of 1831 (Emilia Plater: Panny w r. 1831,* 1937). Except for Brzeska's drama, these plays seek to avoid the controversial issue of Plater's gender transgression by drawing on the sturdy templates established by Straszewicz and Mickiewicz. In Sedlaczek's *Rallying under a Woman's Banner,* for example, the Plater story serves to validate the claim that Polish women are superior to "German, English, and French women" because they gladly put *patria* before pleasure.[65] This claim in turn serves to fuel national pride by affirming Poland's moral superiority to the West. In Winiarski's *Yet Another Grave,* as in Straszewicz's account, Plater is a broken-hearted lover of her country, unable to survive the capture of Warsaw by Russian troops. Moreover, Winiarski's Plater, like Mickiewicz's, is mourned by peasants who gather around her body. However, *Yet Another Grave* is the only play in which we see Plater on her deathbed. The other plays focus on a Plater who leads troops to battle. Ablaze with patriotic fervor, she is a commander whose fearlessness and passionate devotion to the cause of freedom inspire soldiers to follow her.

Although the plays in this group attempt to avoid the issue of gender transgression, they cannot escape it. The compelling image of Plater as a commander throwing herself into the thick of a battle inevitably forces into the open the problem of her gender nonconformity. At the same time, however, Plater's full signifying power is tamed through the terms that the other characters use to describe her. According to some characters, she bears "a hero's soul in a woman's body."[66] To others, she is "a pure angel" or even "the glorious virgin," an appellation that alludes to the Virgin Mary.[67] Or, as an old soldier says to Plater in Korpal's drama: "Your hand is white and feminine, but you are strong and holy."[68] Rather predictably, such adulation proves to be an inverted form of sexism, intent on keeping ordinary women in their place. For a young insurgent in *Yet Another Grave*, for example, Plater is an object of inspired exaltation, but when his fiancée offers to join the uprising, he curtly replies: "Women don't go to war!"[69] It is natural for the young insurgent to exclude Plater from the category *women* precisely because she has in effect been unsexed so as to be reappropriated into the patriarchal social order as a custodian of the realm of ideal(ized) womanhood. She is held up and revered as a paragon of patriotic excellence yet placed out of reach for other women, who are led to believe that they cannot hope even to approximate her perfection.

The only exception is Brzeska's *Emilia Plater*, or so it seems. Like Stolarzewicz's one-acts, it is intended for women's schools; therefore, it has an all-female cast. We see Plater in her ancestral manor on the eve of the uprising. Her women companions would like her to conform to the traditional standards of female behavior. Young women should be cheerful. Marriage is the purpose of the woman's life and the only route to her fulfillment. When the country is in danger, "all that a woman can do is to weep and pray."[70] Plater counters these categorizing notions with the destabilizing work of her "otherness."[71] She refuses to accept a system of gender difference, one in which roles are prescribed, acknowledged, and performed accordingly. Risking ostracism, she defends her decision to forsake marriage and motherhood and to enter the traditionally male realm of warfare. In a moment of patriotic ecstasy, she even yearns for a spiritual marriage to another woman—Poland. To Plater, only this union is empowering: "I believe in Poland; therefore I believe in myself!"[72]

Plater's breathtaking rhetoric makes her, one might say, a feminist heroine—strong, independent, and assertive, as well as deeply aware of her otherness that works to undo any stable code of identity. As a result, it is easy to overlook the implications of the play's chronology. Brzeska collapses different time frames in order to move the arrest of Plater's cousin, Michał, forward in time. The historical Michał Plater was arrested for attempting to commemorate the Constitution of 3 May 1791 in a Russian-controlled school and charged with anti-Russian activities in 1823; in the play, his arrest coincides with the outbreak of the 1830 uprising.[73] In this all-female drama, he is present only indirectly, through a story told by one of the characters, but his patriotic heroism inspires Emilia to translate her vague forebodings and longings into a determination to assume his mantle and take up arms. Ostensibly a tribute to her independent spirit, the play is in fact a paean to the inspiring patriotism of her male cousin.

V.

Emilia Plater: these five syllables are full of implications for the politics of gender and the rhetorics of ambivalence and anxiety in Polish culture. I began this chapter with an investigation of the Plater myth, but my primary purpose has been to examine the reactions that the emblematic figure for the disruption of gender binaries—the woman soldier—has generated in dramatic writing. I took as my starting point the proposition that we cannot make sense of the Plater-themed plays by considering them apart from the generalizing frame of gender conventions to which they responded; nor can we deny their capacity to say something different, not yet said by their contemporaries, even when they seem to repeat what other writers have already said. This exploration prompts the question: Do the Plater-themed plays meet the feminist call for works that would "provide *role-models,* instill a positive sense of feminine identity by portraying women who are 'self-actualizing, whose identities are not dependent on men'"?[74] As might be expected, there are different answers to this question.

Privileging the cause of national independence over personal fulfillment, Plater already seemed destined for a long sojourn in the public imagination. Indeed, the story of her vaunted heroism appears to carry considerable cultural authority. And yet the delimitations of this authority have been striking. What emerges from the Plater-themed plays with irreproachable clarity is new corroborating evidence that her public career has been accepted grudgingly rather than readily. She has been prized for the gift of passionate action taken against overwhelming odds, for the grace of holding nothing back in the struggle to restore Polish independence, but the feminist implications of her gender-bending heroism have been a stumbling block for writers. While it is true that national heroes are always vulnerable to the way their life stories are told and interpreted, Plater has been subjected to a peculiar and peculiarly intense process of revision and modification.

However, it would be too hasty to conclude that the transgressive content of the Plater story has disappeared under the edifying image of a national heroine. A closer examination of the plays about Plater and Plater-inspired women soldiers reveals that the Plater figure is caught in a complex web of discourses. In a number of the plays, the precedent of Plater's celebrated heroism is strategically deployed as part of the self-justification or self-empowerment by the female characters who seize opportunities to enter the military preserve that has historically excluded women. In challenging gender norms, they move nomadically between femininity and masculinity, thus implicitly calling into question or at least qualifying the idea that these gender categories are natural and unalterable. At the same time, however, writers use an array of dramaturgical and rhetorical stratagems to restrict Plater's empowering example and to safeguard the idea that social roles should be assigned by gender. In some plays, gender nonconformity in the patriotic cause is tacitly accepted but defused through the idealization of the patriot-heroine who is to be admired rather than imitated. Other plays channel the energy of the Plater-inspired characters into a host of ideological projects that are not necessarily emancipatory in terms of gender. In others still, conventional love plots serve to reposition the gender-bending heroines back into the domestic sphere. And, of course, there are also plays that mock, trivialize, and marginalize women's unconventional aspirations and activities. At best, the Plater-themed plays' response to the idea of the gender-bending woman patriot is "Yes, but." The "but" may refer to the exceptional woman whose perfection represents a standard impossible for ordinary women to meet. Or the "but" may take the form of the unspoken assumption that female soldiering can be allowed only as a desperate last resort at times of supreme danger to the national community; women, in other words, may in extreme circumstances defend their homes, their families, or the interests of their country. Women's soldiering is thus "niched" into the area of exceptional circumstances. In Ździebłowski's *A Heroine of the Uprising of 1863* and Brzeska's *Emilia Plater*, both of which dispense with love plots, the female protagonist's transgressive refusal to follow a gender-appropriate patriotic script does allow the authors to broach sensitive topics such as female autonomy and agency. But the attempt remains cautious. Suggesting at first the fluidity of gender boundaries, the two plays come close to authorizing gender equality, only to retreat into processes of circumscription.

Admittedly, it would be extremely naive to confuse drama with an equal opportunity pamphlet. It is revealing, however, that even Ździebłowski's and Brzeska's plays ultimately defend gender boundaries to reassure the audience that men and women have notably different characters, different modes of behavior, and different social roles. If playwrights are fascinated by the possibilities opened to them by the Plater figure and her gender transgression, they draw the line at what would be gender equality. Accordingly, they go to great lengths to make sure that acknowledgment of Plater's heroic stature and achievement is not transmuted into encouragement to question the dichotomous gender order or to restructure gender relations. Although the Plater-themed plays mark a radical departure from the stereotype of the woman as an inferior being, weak and helpless, it would be misleading to conclude that this body of dramatic writing, by courtesy of the strong and compelling female characters, was brought into line with the age of feminism.

5 ||| Apocalypse Now?
Tadeusz Kościuszko

I.

NOWADAYS TADEUSZ KOŚCIUSZKO (1746–1817) is not ordinarily seen as a transgressor of social or customary norms.[1] Identified with ideals of integrity and justice, resistance to oppressors, respect for individuals, freedom of thought and worship, and safety from persecution, he has pride of place over other patriot-heroes in the Polish pantheon. His image as a leader with unimpeachable moral and patriotic credentials is so firmly embedded in the cultural imagination that to regard "the incredibly decent Kościuszko" as a transgressor must seem, if not extravagantly absurd or bizarre, at least eccentric.[2]

Kościuszko, if the most influential accounts of his life are to be believed, was a paragon of manly perfection: an heir to the time-honored traditions of chivalry, an exemplary citizen who lived up to Montesquieu's comment that republics differ from other political systems because they can rely on the virtue of their citizenry, a stout-hearted patriot for whom the motto "*Nec aspera terrent*" (Hardships hold no fear) could easily have been coined (but it was not), a doughty fighter in liberty's defense, and a charismatic commander who inspired confidence and personal fascination that drew men to his banners.[3] The image of Kościuszko leading peasant recruits under heavy artillery fire in an audacious attack on Russian batteries in the battle of Racławice is said to encapsulate the idea that the insurrection of 1794 opened the door to democracy in Poland.[4] And then, of course, there is the unstoppable General Kościuszko who quickly made a name for himself in the American War of Independence, winning Thomas Jefferson's enthusiastic praise: "General Kosciusko [*sic*] . . . is as pure a son of liberty, as I have ever known."[5] But it is Franciszek Dionizy Kniaźnin, the author of *The Spartan Mother*, who paid Kościuszko the highest tribute. In one poem, he eulogized him as "the Americans' defender"; in another, he went so far as to identify him with "the Lamb."[6]

The Kościuszko story, in its most familiar form, tells of a man who started with very little. As a younger son of a minor and impoverished nobleman, he should have had, at best, a respectable career among the gentry of his native Brześć Litewski (Brest Litovsk) region. But he set out, very successfully, to climb the ladder of military achievement and reached the heights of fame on both sides of the Atlantic. According to tradition, his main strengths lay in his sterling character and generosity of spirit. Guided by his virtues, he put sovereignty over vassalage, an upright life over the bended knee. In 1776, he crossed the Atlantic to assist American patriot rebels in their struggle to free themselves from British imperial control. In 1792, his spectacular action to repel Russian forces in the battle of Dubienka launched his overnight rise to national stardom. And when the supreme test came in 1794, he performed his patriotic duty with the courage, steadfastness, and fortitude that have been engraved in Polish memory ever since. On 24 March, he was sworn in as the commander-in-chief of an insurgency to undo the partitions of 1772 and 1793 and reclaim Poland-Lithuania's sovereignty. On 4 April, he galvanized Poland by routing a Russian army at Racławice, even though the enemy force possessed advantages in manpower, equipment, and supplies. It was his finest hour. After the battle, reports of the derring-do of his peasant soldiers flooded the country, boosting the national morale. During the summer, he led a successful defense against a massive siege of Warsaw by the joint armies of Prussia and Russia. In the early fall, he was confident enough to risk battle against a Russian army, but the resulting clash at Maciejowice on 10 October was a disaster for the Poles. In a boggy valley along the Wisła, he suffered a devastating defeat and was taken prisoner. At that point, according to the glossy story, the insurrection lost momentum, as if only his charismatic leadership had catalyzed the nation's will to resist.

Kościuszko's reputation is also dependent, to an unusual extent, on what he refused to do as a public figure. In 1792, he resigned his officer's commission and sought refuge abroad, rather than submit to the dictatorial powers of the leaders of the Targowica Confederacy. In 1796, after he was released from a Russian prison, he opted for emigration to North America rather than retirement in Europe. In 1799, he turned down a French offer to take command of Polish legions that were to be organized under the direct auspices of France in the Netherlands, the Rhine region, and Switzerland. In 1806, he rejected Napoleon's offer to lead a Polish army against Prussia. While Napoleon's troops marched across Europe, he cultivated his rose garden in a village outside Paris. After Napoleon's downfall, he withdrew to a provincial Swiss town and spent his winter years in obscurity.

No other Polish patriot-hero has such impeccable and wide-ranging credentials as Kościuszko. At the level of symbolism, his heroism or, more precisely, his *virtus* is intrinsically a good story, full of far-reaching resonance.[7] For example, his involvement in the emancipatory struggles of a country that was not his own—his eight-year service in the American revolutionary forces—may be invoked to demonstrate his commendable commitment to liberty that supersedes nationalist agendas; it may even be taken to exemplify the Enlightenment cosmopolitan ideal of the citizen of the world. But it is his activism in 1794 that has made Kościuszko such an eminently suitable hero in Polish cultural mythology. As some of the darker episodes of the 1794 insurrection, such as summary hangings of paid Russian agents in Wilno and Warsaw, have been sidelined or ignored and Racławice, a battle of relatively minor significance, magnified into a major military triumph, four themes have emerged as the core elements of the Kościuszko myth: his spotless motive, free from selfish and self-indulgent ambition or lust for power; his charismatic leadership and, in particular, his special rapport with peasant troops; his peasant recruits' show of patriotic devotion and battlefield valor at Racławice; and the Racławice-inspired conception that cross-class consensus and solidarity are the key to eventual victory in the struggle for Polish independence and statehood.

Posthumously, the man-myth Kościuszko would find himself drawn into the politics of a broader nineteenth-century process of nation building and cast as a patriot-hero with Poland in his bones, indeed the most Polish of Poland's national heroes, the epitome of allegedly quintessential Polish virtues: honor, love of liberty, defiant courage, boundless generosity, and "that most engaging quality of his nation, what we may term the Polish sweetness," which "never degenerate[s] into softness."[8] Although the biography of the historical Kościuszko defies a utopian desire for an unproblematic narrative of national glory, Kościuszko troped as a performer of immaculate Polishness has been a godsend to those who seek to imagine the twists and turns of modern Polish history as something other than a series of losses. The romanticized version of his life story has proved to be richly generative, inspiring ideas that still constitute modern Polish national identity.[9] Considering that the first name of the eponymous protagonist of the Polish national epic, Adam Mickiewicz's *Pan Tadeusz* (1834), is a tribute to Kościuszko, it would be difficult to find a more powerful demonstration of the way in which the Kościuszko myth is ingrained in the Polish collective consciousness.

The sheer scale and persistence of the Polish cult of Kościuszko make it an intensely interesting subject for research in itself, but his cultural authority has not been confined to the Polish context. Hailed as a heroic campaigner for liberty as a supranational cause, he became an iconic figure in the cultural imagination of the period that has conventionally been called an international Age of Revolution. In a famous session on 26 August 1792, the National Assembly of France awarded him, along with seventeen other foreign nationals, the rights of French citizenship. As Damian Walford Davies shows, moreover, Kościuszko's determination to resist tyranny served as "a monitory, educative model in the political consciousness" of writers such as Samuel Taylor Coleridge, Leigh Hunt, John Keats, John Thelwall, and William Wordsworth.[10] Like a classic hero of liberty, Marcus Porcius Cato, he was adopted as "an inspiring symbol of 'honest patriotism' defeated by imperial tyranny."[11]

For all the differences in specific biographical detail, the parallel between Cato and Kościuszko is illuminating. James William Johnson's summation of the reasons for the usefulness of Cato as a patriotic model in England of the early eighteenth century also applies to the rise of Kościuszko as a preeminent patriotic icon in Polish culture: "The details of his life were well enough known to make him a practical model for daily life as well as critical situations, for private as well as public behavior. His life presented such a diversity of activities that he could be used as a constantly manipulable symbol with shifting emphases and allusive values."[12] And if we substitute Kościuszko's North America and Western Europe for Cato's Rome, the remainder of Johnson's commentary is pertinent as well: "Cato had the additional advantage of being a figure that men from many walks of life could identify with themselves.... He came from an agricultural family background but his extended residence in Rome and his participation in its civic affairs made him urbane as well as rural.... In short, he was a model whose appeal to the segments of the ... populace was astonishingly wide-ranging."[13]

The story of Cato's unflinching commitment to the cause of liberty became the subject of one of the most successful plays on the eighteenth-century stage, Joseph Addison's *Cato*, first performed in London in 1713. I was intrigued by the immense popularity and widespread political influence of this seemingly stiff neoclassical tragedy both in Britain and North America.[14] I was also intrigued by the fact that Addison's contemporaries took exception to the love scenes that constitute almost half of his drama.[15] As a result, the play was later revised. In the new version, published in 1764, all the female roles were eliminated, and lines from the love scenes were incorporated into verbal exchanges between male characters. Attributed to one Joseph Reeve, the alternative version, rather predictably, is entitled *Cato without the Love Scenes*.[16] I concluded—a little reluctantly because Kościuszko is one of those heroes who are "at risk of being hyped to death"[17]—that I should take a closer look at how the man-myth Kościuszko has fared in dramatic writing. Twentieth-century plays, along with a political pageant, are the subject of the next chapter. Here, I turn to nineteenth-century dramas to explore how and to what ends they grapple with the disquieting problem of Kościuszko's conflation of patriotic devotion and transgressive nonconformity.

On first sight, Kościuszko's credentials are unassailable. What, then, constitutes his transgression?

One way to begin to address this question would be by noting that Kościuszko, like Enlightenment *philosophes*, sought to turn the liberty of reason to libertarian political ends. A passionate opponent of slavery, he was preoccupied with issues that still resonate politically: social justice, individual rights, equal opportunity. In 1794, at a time when Poland was a playground of the partitioning powers, he blurred his contemporaries' distinctions between patriotism and transgression by making a statement that defiantly challenged deeply ingrained status hierarchies: "I will not fight for the nobility alone. I want freedom for the whole nation and only for this will I risk my life."[18] To Kościuszko, in other words, the insurrection of 1794 was as much about the need for social change as about the restoration of an independent Poland.[19] And he actually transgressed the social boundaries of his time and place when he launched a giant recruiting drive both to fill the ranks of his regular army and to supplement his field forces with local militias. Although many nobles were nervous about arming serfs, however good the cause, Kościuszko's recruiting drive encompassed able-bodied men from all social groups. His mobilization of a nation-in-arms constituted a radical break with military practices, as well as with social norms, in eighteenth-century Poland.[20]

After the victory at Racławice, Kościuszko put on a homespun peasant coat (*sukmana*) to honor his peasant troops and to cement their loyalty. It was a legendary gesture. At a time when clothing defined a person's social identity and thus served as a means to control and sustain the social order, Kościuszko dressed across class lines to identify with those at the lowest level of social hierarchy. What is more, his proclamation, issued in the encampment at Połaniec on 7 May 1794, brought a clear commitment to agrarian reform.[21] It temporarily reduced the unpaid labor services (the corvée) that serfs were required to perform for their masters, and it granted serfs the right to leave their villages. Those serfs who enlisted in Kościuszko's army were released from the corvée for the duration of the uprising.

It is now a common assertion in scholarship that the Kościuszko insurrection was the fulcrum of modern Polish history: a new, democratic Poland was emerging from the chrysalis of the old. This is an attractive argument. The obvious question it raises, however, is this: Can a grant of temporary exemptions to peasants stand in for the rights of citizenship? Viewed in this way, Kościuszko's once offensive radicalism appears as a cautiously conservative maneuver. It was not always like that. The conflagration of the French Revolution cast a long shadow on Kościuszko's commitment to social change.[22] Often branded as a Jacobin and a freethinker, he was rumored to be an acolyte of the French revolutionists whose promise of progress threatened to take humankind down a road filled with terror, anarchy, and despair. This dangerous disciple of the devotees of the guillotine, the story continued, was intent on stirring up the masses to acts of violence in order to undermine the foundations of social order. Bolstered by an upsurge of a conservative reaction against the radicalism of the French Revolution, this view of his advocacy of peasants' rights and, more broadly, democratic principles as intolerably threatening to the status quo was further reinforced by a violent outburst of social anger that engulfed much of the Austrian partition in 1846. While Austrian officials looked on, bands of Polish peasants went on the rampage and killed Polish nobles with impunity.[23] After four weeks of unbridled violence, the jacquerie left a horrifying trail of butchered bodies and looted manors. In the alarmist imagination of the post-1846 period, Kościuszko appeared to many as a rabble-rouser or "a madman who instigated a revolt of the proletariat" (to quote Adam Asnyk's 1890 satirical poem).[24] Asnyk, of course, exaggerated, but his phrase encapsulated the anxiety surrounding Kościuszko's radical image. After 1846 (and, again, after 1848, the Year of Revolutions on the Continent and in Ireland and the date of the largest Chartist demonstration in London), Kościuszko's mythmakers were thus in a difficult bind: How to rally Polish peasants for the cause of Poland's independence without endorsing the idea of a social revolution?

Kościuszko's transgression of social boundaries and status hierarchies also has a very personal, indeed intimate, dimension. Sometime before he left for North America in 1776, possibly even before he went to France on a scholarship in 1769, Kościuszko met and developed some form of relationship with Ludwika Sosnowska, daughter of Józef Sosnowski, a wealthy, well-connected, and ruthlessly ambitious lord. Quite what the nature of Kościuszko's relationship (if it may properly be called a relationship) was with Sosnowska—whether it was platonic, sexual, romantic, or more simply a meeting of like minds—is hard to gauge. Very little documentation has survived, and the available evidence is inconclusive. Although Kościuszko always kept his inner life sealed off from scrutiny, his biographers have nonetheless transformed the pair into icons of romantic love, arguing that Sosnowska's despotic and mercenary father cast a cold eye on her impecunious suitor from the lesser gentry and arranged for her to marry Count Józef Lubomirski instead.[25] According to some vague reports, Kościuszko and Sosnowska attempted to run off, but the elopement was cut short by house servants. Like almost everything we "know" of the relationship between Kościuszko and Sosnowska, this story cannot be verified. Given the lack of reliable evidence, unequivocal answers are not a realistic prospect. Kościuszko might have fallen in love with Sosnowska, or he might have contemplated the stealing of the heiress as a means of improving his fortunes.[26] He might have turned to Stanisław August to plead for "support in his amorous endeavor," or he might not have.[27] The elopement might have happened, or it might not have.[28] However, a growing body of biographical studies claims that Kościuszko's failed love affair was to have a formative influence on his life because it drove him out of Poland and led him to enlist in the American revolutionary forces.[29] In going off to America and joining the patriot rebels, in other words, he was motivated not only by high principles but also by a deep sentimental wound.

At the same time, however, the biographers' insistence on Kościuszko's lifelong love of Sosnowska suggests a certain nervousness about the national hero who never married but had a strong appeal to younger men. One of them was Julian Ursyn Niemcewicz, the author of *The Return of the Deputy*, and his aide-de-camp in the campaign of 1794. They formed a close attachment whose exact character remains a puzzle. According to Jan Dihm, Niemcewicz's anguished display of grief at the Maciejowice battlefield betrays that "the aide-de-camp was head-over-heels in love [*zakochany bez pamięci*] with his commander-in-chief."[30] When he saw Kościuszko, badly wounded and apparently dead, Niemcewicz, by his own account, flung himself on Kościuszko's bloodied, seminaked body and covered it with kisses and tears.[31] After both of them were released from a Russian prison in 1796, Niemcewicz, at Kościuszko's request, accompanied him to North America. The relationship, whatever it was, was only intensified for Niemcewicz by Kościuszko's sudden and surreptitious return to Europe on a secret political mission in 1798. Left behind in America, Niemcewicz behaved like a jilted lover, heartbroken, disoriented, and obsessed by the images of the man he loves. This seems to suggest that their close relationship was a way perhaps of enjoying a strong homoerotic frisson. Whether or not the relationship ever took a physical turn, we will never know for sure. But in the biographies of Kościuszko, the story of his romantic devotion to Sosnowska conveniently serves both to justify his intriguing (not to say mystifying) refusal of marriage to another woman and to obscure the issue of homoerotic fascination, thus protecting him from what was perceived as the deepest cut in a man's reputation—suspicion that he was sexually attracted to young men. In short, the story of Kościuszko's secret romance with Sosnowska serves to reassert his heterosexuality and to exorcise the specter of same-sex desire. Kościuszko can be safely returned to his all-male world where he substitutes the love of country for would-be pleasures of the flesh.

It goes without saying that transgressive heroes must be tamed before they can be celebrated. Accordingly, Kościuszko's life story has been adapted to fit the demands of patriotic instruction and exhortation. But even if his mythmakers were biased and self-serving, shouldn't they be allowed to take their inevitable (yet often illuminating) wrong turns? This is precisely the point of my exploration. That is to say, it is easy enough to argue that the Kościuszko of myth bears only a passing resemblance to the living man. However, my line of investigation is different. I am interested less in searching for the "true" Kościuszko under the mantle placed on his shoulders by enthusiastic mythmakers, than in examining the process of revision and modification that Kościuszko has undergone in the course of his posthumous career, as different tellers put his biography to different uses at different moments in history. He was an individual in history and real time, but he is also the protagonist of a famous story in the timeless dimension of myth, and the way the story has come to be told tells yet another story, one about concepts of patriotism.

What Albert Furtwangler has written about Washington could also be said of Kościuszko: the image of Kościuszko in the cultural imagination may never be completely free of a perception of him as a hero fixed irrevocably at the center of a tableau or a series of tableaux.[32] For Washington, Furtwangler cites paintings by John Trumbull. For Kościuszko, a comparable set of paintings consists of Jan Matejko's *Kościuszko at Racławice* (*Kościuszko pod Racławicami*, 1888) and the enormous 360-degree panorama *Racławice* (1894), a joint project by a group of artists led by Wojciech Kossak and Jan Styka. There is little doubt that the key themes of the Kościuszko myth—his inspirational leadership, the derring-do of his peasant troops, and the imperative of cross-class solidarity in the cause of Polish independence—have been most influentially realized by the two canvasses precisely because they have been seen by millions of people. With these paintings, Matejko, Kossak, and Styka could justifiably feel that they burned the Kościuszko myth into the consciousness of their compatriots.

However, both paintings came late in the nineteenth century, after a representational canon for Kościuszko—an assembly of preferred narratives and talismanic images—had been established. In shaping and reshaping this canon, drama played a major role. In the early 1820s, Konstanty Majeranowski caught the public imagination with *Kościuszko's First Love* and *Kościuszko on the Seine* (*Kościuszko nad Sekwaną*, 1821); in 1880, Ludwik Władysław Anczyc struck gold with *Kościuszko at Racławice*. The intensity of enthusiasm that these plays aroused makes it clear that Majeranowski and Anczyc found particularly attractive and persuasive templates for imagining Kościuszko.[33] Yet studies of the man-myth Kościuszko give only perfunctory attention to dramatic writing on the grounds that the Kościuszko-themed plays are artistically inferior to the acknowledged masterworks of Polish drama.[34] As a result, the significance of this archive as a cultural, and not just a literary, phenomenon remains poorly understood, even though it offers revealing insights into the contests over Kościuszko's conflicting legacies and, more broadly, into disputes over "true" and "false" patriotism in the nineteenth century.[35]

Out of some twenty nineteenth-century plays on the Kościuszko theme, I have selected five for close textual analysis.[36] Taken together, they represent a diversity of dramaturgical and rhetorical strategies and of the attitudes expressed. I begin with Majeranowski's *Kościuszko's First Love* that constitutes the first major step toward securing Kościuszko for the National Symbolic. I then consider Józef Ignacy Kraszewski's *The Governor's Equal* (*Równy wojewodzie*, 1866) that inaugurates the post-Majeranowski series of the Kościuszko plays. I move on to compare two 1880 dramas: Bogusława Mańkowska's *Tadeusz Kościuszko; or, Four Scenes from the Life of the Hero* (*Tadeusz Kościuszko, czyli cztery chwile życia tego bohatera*) and Anczyc's *Kościuszko at Racławice*. I conclude by examining Adam Bełcikowski's *The Warsaw Street-Seller*, a seemingly conventional play that opens up an unconventional perspective on the Kościuszko myth.

II.

First performed in Kraków in 1820, Majeranowski's *Kościuszko's First Love* seems to cancel Kościuszko's transgression, political as well as sexual, in order to present a romanticized interpretation of his decision to join the American Revolution.[37] The year is 1775. Kościuszko falls in love with Julia, daughter of the Count. She reciprocates his feelings, but a treacherous Polish king concocts an intrigue that convinces the Count that Kościuszko plans to elope with Julia, even though the young officer is too much a man of honor to contemplate such a disgraceful act. The enraged Count orders Kościuszko arrested and imprisoned for life. The scheme fails, and Kościuszko sets off for North America. Just before his departure, he plunges into a prophetic monologue, unveiling his country's future. He foresees a heroic struggle of the national community to save Poland and credits peasant troops with exceptional courage. He caps the monologue with a puzzling homage to Tsar Alexander I, "the angel of the North," who will ultimately restore the Polish state.[38]

The anti-aristocratic thrust of *Kościuszko's First Love* is obvious. Anarchy reigns supreme, if it is possible for a magnate to imprison a man deemed undesirable as his daughter's suitor. Launched by the Count with the king's approval, the unlawful attempt to arrest Kościuszko becomes a metonymy of the lawlessness that has undermined the stability of the state and made it vulnerable to attacks from abroad. Is Kościuszko's paean to the Russian emperor, then, the flip side of the play's denunciation of the arrogance, dishonesty, and peacockry of the Polish aristocracy? I will return to this issue.

We may well expect to see Kościuszko as a determined patriot who wants to make his mark on history. Beginning with the opening scene, however, we see a lachrymose nebbish.[39] At the same time, rather incongruously, the characters recognize Kościuszko's leadership qualities and hint that he is singled out for glory in the political sphere. These two constructions of Kościuszko are so radically different that we may wonder whether we have the same man in mind. The Kościuszko we see lacks the drive, ruthlessness, boundless self-confidence, sangfroid, tenacity, and stamina needed to make it to the top. What is more, the play seems to offer no clue as to how the distraught lover will be transformed into an effective leader and a maker of history. What are we to make of the play's jump cuts and double focus?

While Kościuszko is hampered by self-doubt, uncertainty, and apprehension, Julia radiates confidence and strength. She confesses her love to Kościuszko, initiates a conversation about their future, and urges Kościuszko to go abroad to escape the wrath of her tyrannical father. In short, Julia is "masculinized," Kościuszko, "feminized." As difficult as it may be for many to imagine a "feminized" Kościuszko, it is even more surprising to see him indulging in nigh-Rousseauian sensibility: he bursts into tears at the sight of a homeless old serf whom he then saves from destitution. It would be easy to conclude that the play engages in a sentimental de-heroization of Kościuszko. But in fact Majeranowski is saying, or his play is saying, something rather more complicated. In stark contrast to macho, ruthless men such as the Count or a squire who has dismissed the old serf, Majeranowski's Kościuszko does not participate, even vicariously, in the victimization of others. Instead, he assumes the female roles of emotionally sensitive being and caretaker. His "feminine" tenderheartedness and uncontrollable tears may be perceived as a flaw, but they are nonetheless valorized as a manifestation of the finest masculinity. The play thus stakes a claim that proper heroes are those who can outwoman women, so to speak. To shape history properly, they must claim their place in the world through their capacity for empathy rather than will to power.[40] Paradoxically, then, refusing to be macho becomes a sign of strength. To put these points more broadly, Majeranowski's play reveals that the discourse of sensibility that arose around the middle of the eighteenth century, largely under Rousseau's influence, was, in 1820, still ennobling and not necessarily incompatible with masculinity.

As I have mentioned, it is Julia who proposes that Kościuszko seek refuge abroad. At first, he counters her advice with an argument that it does not become a man of honor to flee. Accordingly, he resolves to wait for the Count's henchmen. However, the manager of the Count's estate, Trzembosz, revokes his pledge of obedience to the Count and drives out the troops that have arrived to capture Kościuszko. Trzembosz explains that he has disobeyed the Count for two interrelated reasons: in the name of "the sacred rights of man" and on behalf of besieged Poland that only Kościuszko can save.[41] Kościuszko is shocked and outraged—not by the Count's scheme, but by Trzembosz's refusal to carry it out. To Kościuszko, such conduct cannot be reconciled with the rule of law. Trzembosz argues that it can. He invokes the bond of reciprocal rights and responsibilities between masters and servants. Just as servants are bound to obey their masters, so are masters bound to protect those who serve them. When masters fail to respect this system of mutually acknowledged obligations, servants must take action to protect their rights. In short, Trzembosz gives Kościuszko an introductory lesson in civil disobedience.

In arguing in support of the people's right to resist the abuse of power by the sovereign, is Trzembosz suggesting that Poland is on the brink of a social revolution? Not necessarily. One of the complicating issues in *Kościuszko's First Love* is the convergence of Polish patriotism and Russophile enthusiasm, evident in Kościuszko's prophetic monologue. Since this convergence did not seem to trouble Majeranowski's contemporaries, who flocked to see the play, it is unavoidable to ask: How was it possible for them to reconcile the play's pro-Russian, loyalist stance with the cultural memory of Kościuszko as a commander of an insurgency against Russian occupation?

Part of the answer is that in the period immediately after the peace settlements concluded by the victorious powers of the anti-Napoleonic alliance at the Congress of Vienna in 1815, pro-Russian sentiments were quite common among Poles. However, it would be misleading to draw facile, moralistic conclusions and to reduce the post-1815 wave of Russophile enthusiasm to servile opportunism. To arrive at a fuller picture, it is necessary to note that, on the one hand, the Polish aspirations for independence had just been dashed with Napoleon's defeat and that, on the other, Tsar Alexander I seemed to offer sound guarantees for Poland's political autonomy and constitutional liberties.[42] At the Congress of Vienna, he was instrumental in preserving, though in a somewhat reduced form, the Duchy of Warsaw. Renamed the Kingdom of Poland and placed under the protection of the tsar, it retained the *Code Napoléon* as its system of law and enjoyed a measure of constitutional autonomy that set it apart from the rest of the Russian empire. Two years later, Alexander supported a proposal that Kościuszko's remains be transported from Switzerland and buried in Kraków. Kościuszko thus joined the community of the illustrious dead dwelling in the royal crypt of the Wawel Cathedral. Poles who lined up to deliver memorial eulogies at Kościuszko's funeral gave short shrift to the failed insurrection of 1794, but paid a lavish tribute to the tsar, newly enthroned as the Kingdom of Poland's ruling monarch.

Yet another way to make sense of the puzzling nexus of Polish patriotism and Russophile enthusiasm in *Kościuszko's First Love* is to recognize that Trzembosz's argument about the reciprocal bond of duty between master and man may be understood as a warning to the tsar, should he fail to respect the agreement that bound him and his Polish subjects as a result of the settlements of 1815. Read thus, *Kościuszko's First Love* anticipates the moral economy of plays written and performed during the uprising of 1830. In Stanisław Bratkowski's *The Warsaw Student* (*Akademik warszawski*, 1831), for example, the characters lament the proliferation of lawlessness in the Kingdom of Poland. Alexander has granted Poles a constitution only to turn it into "a plaything of despotism."[43] Since the tsar has broken his contract with the Poles and no longer acts according to the mutual obligations and responsibilities linking ruler and ruled, the latter, Bratkowski's characters argue, are justified in revolting against Russia in order to restore the rule of law.

III.

In the three decades prior to the uprising of 1863, public commemorations of the national past drew largely on the symbolic capital of the 1830 revolt, thus deflecting attention from the insurrection of 1794.[44] When the man-myth

Kościuszko resurfaced in drama in 1866, Poland had once more suffered a humiliating defeat at Russia's hands. Determined to suppress any revival of Polish demands for political independence, Russian authorities instituted a series of punitive and repressive measures, ranging from confiscations of landed property to a policy of Russification (e.g., restrictions on the use of the Polish language in public schools). At a time when Poland was exhausted by war and postwar repressions, a group of young men and women countered the depressive national mood with a vigorous advocacy of options available to Polish society under foreign rule. Those men and women called themselves Positivists.

The Positivists—writers and thinkers—argued that it was time to make "a decisive break with the tradition of armed risings" that bled the country white and to treat hopes for a speedy liberation as no more than "fairy tales about the enchanted princess who is soon to awaken from her death-like sleep."[45] Rather than pursue unrealistic political aims, the Positivists' argument continued, Poles ought to break free from the vicious circle of pointless sacrifice and heroic failure. At what many regard as the most vulnerable moment in nineteenth-century Polish history, the Positivists thought themselves capable of inspiring their compatriots with a robust vision of how to make their country a substantially better place to live and, in the process, how to transform Poland from a home of lost causes into a self-confident, progressive, can-do part of Europe. Recognizing that political independence remained out of reach, they strategically unfurled a banner of modernization. Poles would do well to embrace compromise and work within the confines of a repressive political system in order to give Poland economic muscle by spreading literacy, promoting agricultural improvement, industry, and commerce, breaking down social barriers, and expanding equal opportunity. Needed now were educators, agricultural reformers, and founding fathers of commerce and industry, not freedom fighters. Stressing gradual change as progress, the Positivists held up an ideal of self-improvement based on hard work.[46] For the Positivists, then, patriotic sentiments were to be cultivated under the aegis of Political Acquiescence, Prudence, Moderation, Social Concord and Cooperation, Peace, Industriousness, Incremental Change, Stability, and Prosperity. The responsibility of the arts was to aid this project.

Less than three years after the bloody fiasco of the 1863 uprising, Kraszewski recovered the man-myth Kościuszko for his play, *The Governor's Equal*.

It was Kościuszko's first appearance as a dramatic character since Majeranowski's *Kościuszko on the Seine*, a sequel to *Kościuszko's First Love*, had opened in 1821.[47] The action of *The Governor's Equal* takes place after Kościuszko's return from America in 1784 when he has yet to make his mark on Polish history. He obtains a general's commission and is charged with reorganizing a Polish army. The play shows him only briefly, at a moment when he is asked to provide a character reference for a young aristocrat, Bronisław, who has joined the military to break with his rakish lifestyle and make a fresh start.

Kraszewski's Kościuszko is a self-made man who has overcome the handicaps of social prejudice to rise to prominence through singular achievement. He has learned to rely heavily on himself—on his ambition, talent, stamina, and relentless work ethic—to compensate for his modest social background. In short, Kraszewski presents a Kościuszko who counters the privileges of birth and rank with a meritocratic model of upward mobility. This Kościuszko, then, seems well qualified to challenge the inherited social order. Indeed, his transgressive potential can be traced in the textual rifts that suggest harsh criticism of Poland's social structure. For example, he still chafes at the thought of the humiliation he has suffered at the hands of his aristocratic superiors. To test his transgressive potential, however, it is helpful to examine the implications of his costume.

On his Polish uniform, Kościuszko wears the eagle emblem of the American Society of the Cincinnati.[48] Founded in 1783, the society was a fraternal order open only to former Revolutionary War officers and their direct male descendants. Since Washington was regarded as the quintessential modern Cincinnatus, or a patriot farmer who leaves his life of rural peace and contentment to serve his country at a moment of crisis but sheathes his sword and returns to the peaceful pursuit of agriculture at the first opportunity after the crisis is over, it was quite natural for the officers to select him as the society's first president and to adopt an anonymous maxim, "*Omnia relinquit servare rempublicam*" (He relinquishes everything to serve the republic), as its motto. Rather obviously, Kraszewski uses the society's emblem to cast Kościuszko as another modern Cincinnatus, but one whose supreme test has yet to come. In playing on the Cincinnatus theme, however, Kraszewski seems untroubled by the fact that the society was an institutionalized expression of social inequality. By excluding common soldiers and making its membership hereditary, the organization "was an avowedly elitist enterprise designed to sustain the aristocratic ethos of superior virtue that officers in the Continental army had been harboring since Valley Forge."⁴⁹ The society's membership rules and the aristocratic aura surrounding it gave rise to widespread criticism that the organization was a threat to the very values the American Revolution claimed to stand for. For example, Jefferson compared the society to a cancer growing in the heart of the new republic and argued that "a single fibre left of this institution will provide an hereditary aristocracy which will change the form of our governments from the best to the worst in the world."⁵⁰ And newspapers hinted that Washington, as a member of the society, betrayed the republican principles enshrined in the American Constitution. As the public outcry against the society escalated, Washington became ambivalent about serving as its president and insisted that its charter be revised. When several state chapters of the society refused to change their policies, he stopped wearing its emblem and boycotted its convention in 1787.⁵¹ Unlike those who attacked the society as a symbol of European aristocratic values and attitudes, however, Kraszewski's Kościuszko sees no conflict between his democratic convictions (exemplified by the concept of success through merit) and his membership in the society. This in turn plants a seed of doubt about his willingness to challenge social boundaries and status hierarchies.

This conclusion is borne out by the main plot that focuses on the young aristocrat, Bronisław. Under Kościuszko's tutelage, Bronisław makes up for his rakish misdeeds by distinguishing himself in a military campaign. By the play's end, however, the Polish army suffers defeat, and a Russian ambassador in Warsaw takes control of Poland. Wounded in battle, Bronisław decides to retire from the military and to settle with his wife-to-be in "the countryside where one can find peace and quiet, away from the world and the people."⁵² One would have thought that Kościuszko would fire up his protégé with new enthusiasm for his country's drive for political sovereignty, but that is not the case. While other Polish plays on the struggle for national independence visualize, usually through an emotional farewell scene with a woman pleading and wailing, the male character's split commitment and the pull of domesticity which he knows he must overcome, here an unwavering commitment to the private sphere is Bronisław's ultimate destiny. It is helpful to remember, however, that in 1866, when the play was first performed, his return to civilian life closely corresponded to the Positivists' depoliticizing admonitions.⁵³ At the same time, there is nothing in the text to suggest that Bronisław, now cast in the role of the gentleman farmer, might be interested in the Positivists' modernizing reforms. Battlefield heroism cedes its place to contented domesticity, the simple pleasures of rural life, and proper morality that has been instilled in Bronisław by his mentor. For a play featuring Kościuszko, this is a remarkably minimalist program.

Kraszewski's drama continued to be performed as late as 1907 but, rather predictably, never became an effective means of conquering hearts and imaginations. In 1880, two new plays about Kościuszko burst onto the cultural scene and captured public attention: Mańkowska's *Tadeusz Kościuszko* and Anczyc's *Kościuszko at Racławice*.[54] Each of them is an eloquent riposte to the Positivist concepts of patriotism.

Mańkowska's play traces the relationship between Kościuszko and Ludwika Sosnowska from the first stirrings of passion through their parting to a spiritual partnership. The opening act presents the familiar scene: Józef Sosnowski is scandalized that his daughter wants to marry her social inferior. Interestingly, Mańkowska moves Kościuszko's courtship of Sosnowska to 1787, after he has returned from America. This shift enables her to expand the repertoire of Sosnowski's objections to Kościuszko as Ludwika's suitor. At issue here are not only Kościuszko's income and social status, but also his political ideas and commitments. In Sosnowski's contemptuous shorthand, a man who has fought for such "foolishness" as American liberty is "a Jacobin," unworthy of his daughter.[55] In contrast, Count Lubomirski, who also contends for Ludwika's hand, meets with Sosnowski's enthusiastic approval. The remaining two acts show the by now famous commander who has sublimated his love for Ludwika into the driving force of his heroics during the insurrection of 1794. In the epilogue, Ludwika visits Kościuszko in Switzerland, bringing her two sons with her. The play ends on an uplifting note, as the boys pay a tribute to Kościuszko and pledge to continue his patriotic project. Thus, the plot comes full circle: Ludwika's sons draw inspiration from the man whom she has inspired.

Like Majeranowski's *Kościuszko's First Love*, then, Mańkowska's *Tadeusz Kościuszko* highlights the potential of love as a powerful motivator to strive toward noble and generous action for the public good. However, Mańkowska departs in three important ways from Majeranowski's template. First, she reverses his characterization of Ludwika and Kościuszko. Here, it is Ludwika who is the wilting lover, while Kościuszko remains strong under pressure. Second, she introduces the transgressive episode of elopement, re-coded as abduction. Kościuszko urges Ludwika to defy parental authority and to run away with him, but she averts her gaze and evades his pleas. The more he presses on, the more she wavers. At the end, she nearly faints, withdrawing into a state of canceled agency. It is at this moment that he takes her away. Third, Mańkowska refuses to depict Ludwika's father as an unequivocally negative character. Narrow-minded, domineering, and given to uttering crude diatribes, Sosnowski is nonetheless a fearless patriot who has served his country well, defending it against attacks by foreign powers. The handsome Count Lubomirski is also spared a negative characterization. His courage and presence of mind save Sosnowski's life during a hunting accident.

The elopement is promptly discovered, and Ludwika is returned to her father. From now on, traditional gender norms prevail. Ludwika dutifully marries Lubomirski at her father's insistence and becomes an exemplary mother who instills patriotic sentiments in her children. When she hears of an impending insurrection, she follows Kościuszko like a guardian angel. In Kraków, she stands to the side while he is sworn in as the commander-in-chief of the insurgency. At Racławice, she assists with the wounded. In short, she fits the traditional concepts of woman as the wife and mother, the muse, and the helpmate of man.

And yet I cannot leave this interpretation without asking why Mańkowska includes Ludwika in the Kraków and Racławice scenes at all. Why not simply omit her, when to do otherwise is to court danger? The point at issue is not simply that Ludwika nurses her ardor for Kościuszko, but, rather, that we never see her at home, tending the flame of domesticity. Instead, we repeatedly see her traveling across Poland and, eventually, to Switzerland. The highly charged, profusely metaphoric image of Ludwika on the road compels us to reconsider the initial interpretation. For all its support of the dominant presumptions of patriarchal culture about gender roles and identities, the play (perhaps against the author's better judgment) complicates traditional understandings of the gender system. As the action unfolds, it becomes evident that a powerfully suggestive crossing over is at work in the text. Although the actual elopement has failed, the transgressive intensity of forbidden desire is the key by which Ludwika's subversive potential is unlocked. She refuses her connection to the domestic sphere, choosing instead the provisionality and instability that are troped by the "in-between" metaphor of travel. In undomesticating Ludwika, in other words, the play introduces noise into the patriarchal script and its restrictive categories.

IV.

Mańkowska's *Tadeusz Kościuszko* invites us to conclude that the male protagonist's transgression of sexual norms has succeeded, after all. That is to say, Kościuszko the lover ultimately empowers the wavering, wilting Ludwika. Does Kościuszko the leader empower peasants? To address this question, I want to examine Mańkowska's play against Anczyc's *Kościuszko at Racławice*. Unlike Mańkowska, Anczyc dispenses with Kościuszko's private life. Both plays, however, hinge on a key point of agreement. They ignore his military failures in the 1794 insurrection and instead highlight the victory at Racławice, attributing it to the bravery of his peasant recruits. In doing so, however, the plays recognize that the peasants' activism could be a double-edged sword.

Once again, Mańkowska's play inserts some unexpected twists into the well-known story. As I have mentioned, the historical Kościuszko put on a peasant coat to salute his peasant soldiers after the battle of Racławice. In the play, however, his cross-class transvestism dates back to the Polish-Russian war of 1792 and continues until his old age when he wears a long jacket resembling a homespun *sukmana*. Mańkowska's Kościuszko, in other words, knows that clothes can be seen as a lingua franca, even if the dialects differ from place to place, a language necessary for announcing a public identity and establishing social bonds. Through the language of class-specific clothing, the play attributes to Kościuszko a long-standing bond with peasants, one that predates the insurrection of 1794 and continues during his years abroad. It is thus easy to think of Mańkowska's Kościuszko as a son of the soil, rather than merely a commander with the manners of a democrat who risked humiliation by dressing down at a time when clothes—the external signs of identity and status—were taken to be the measure of a person. What does his "peasantness" signify?

In the scene of patriotic oath-taking in Kraków in act 2, peasants have no voice of their own. To pledge their allegiance to Kościuszko as the commander-in-chief of the insurrection, they merely follow a script prepared by upper-class men. As soon as the ceremony is over, they quietly disperse to make room for their social superiors. In Mańkowska's play, then, peasants appear as one undifferentiated, sheep-like mass that poses no threat to the existing social order. In linking Kościuszko with the docile, nonthreatening villagers, his peasant coat serves to dispel charges, such as those voiced by Sosnowski in act 1, that he is a formidably disruptive, even dangerous, radical who prefers the lessons of Voltaire and American rebels to the Decalogue. In other words, although Kościuszko's coat is a garment that crosses class boundaries, the play's particular construction of the peasant community strips his cross-dressing of its transgressive potential.

Kościuszko administers the patriotic oath under a banner of Jan III Sobieski, a seventeenth-century soldier-king. In the epilogue, Sobieski is invoked again, this time through a Turkish sword that was part of his trophy in a military campaign for the relief of Vienna in 1683. When the Grand Vizier Kara Mustafa led 80,000 Ottoman troops and janissaries to the gates of Vienna, Sobieski took command of the combined armies of Central Europe and defeated the Ottomans in one of the most decisive battles of the seventeenth century. After the battle, he sent the sword, reputed to be Kara Mustafa's, to Pope Innocent XI as a votive offering for a Marian shrine in Loretto. In 1797, the sword was removed from the sanctuary and stripped of its precious stones. In the following year, Polish troops affiliated with Napoleon's army recovered Sobieski's sword and, having declared that only Kościuszko was worthy of it, presented it to him.[56] Mańkowska draws on these historical facts to frame the epilogue of her play. Kościuszko presses Sobieski's sword to his chest, his eyes looking up; Ludwika's sons kiss Kościuszko's own swords as if they were holy relics. The epilogue thus serves as a quasi-ritualistic act of incorporating the two young aristocrats into a patriotic brotherhood and initiating them into the mystique of Polish military glory, exemplified by Sobieski and Kościuszko. The scene brings the play to a halt for a ponderous, if hopeful, moment. Accordingly, the stage lights create the effect of the rising sun.

But where does this leave Kościuszko's peasant recruits? Their initiation into the patriotic project, it will be remembered, takes place under Sobieski's banner. But why Sobieski? What are the implications of the connection that the play seeks to establish between Kościuszko's peasant troops and Sobieski? Admittedly, the battle of Vienna is often numbered among the most important battles of the Western world. In Mańkowska's play, however, Sobieski is not only a military commander who broke the siege of a major European city, but also, and more importantly, a defender of Catholic Christendom who rescued it from the Ottomans before the gates of the capital of the Holy Roman Empire and who proclaimed that his victory should be credited to the intercession of Mary. Within this particular frame of reference, the play gives the story of Kościuszko's peasant soldiers a characteristic moralizing twist: they take up arms to defend the Catholic faith against Russian and German "heretics."[57] Clearly, the text performs extraordinary maneuvers to assuage anxieties that the peasants' activism might get out of hand and turn into revolutionary terror. These maneuvers may suggest that in the patriotic drama of the 1880s it was still prudent to evade the controversial issue of the political empowerment of peasants.

In contrast to Mańkowska's *Tadeusz Kościuszko*, however, Anczyc's *Kościuszko at Racławice* plays with fire. Although it is a truism of Polish studies that Anczyc claims Kościuszko as an apologist for cross-class reconciliation and solidarity,[58] I submit that it would be misleading to read *Kościuszko at Racławice* as a univocal work. If it really were a univocal text, a text of one counsel and a single truth, it would have had far less appeal than it did over many decades, under different historical circumstances, for diverse audiences. Anczyc was a playwright of great skill and resource, well aware that it would be naive to take readers and spectators, even like-minded readers and spectators, for granted. In what follows, I want to explore those aspects of the play's dramatic and rhetorical structure that prompt us to question our assumptions and perceptions.

The play begins on 24 March 1794, with Kościuszko's arrival in Kraków to assume a position as de facto head of a provisional government. Act 1 closes with a brief but memorable image of Kościuszko pledging before troops and townspeople to use the authority vested in him solely "for defending our homeland, for restoring our self-rule, and for preserving our liberty."[59] From the second act on, the action moves to the countryside, and the focus shifts from Kościuszko to the other characters. The plot thickens as drunken Russian soldiers loot a rural home and attempt to rape a young noblewoman, while a Jewish supporter of Kościuszko sets fire to a barn to summon Polish troops to her rescue. The play builds up to the battle at Racławice and the famous charge by peasant recruits led by Wojciech Bartosz. In recognition of Bartosz's exceptional courage in battle, Kościuszko not only promotes him to the rank of ensign, but also elevates him into the nobility and assigns him a new name, Głowacki.[60] As this brief outline makes it clear, the play enables some of the iconic images of the Kościuszko insurrection to come to life. At the same time, however, it marks them with curious accents. It is these accents that will interest me here.

When Kościuszko arrives to take command of the uprising, a surge of patriotic exultation sweeps through Polish society. And yet most peasants and nobles are unmoved by his call to arms. Peasants are unwilling to submerge their social and economic differences with the upper classes in the common cause. Nobles are skeptical of anti-Russian resistance, hostile to a mobilization of the masses, and offended by the extravagant idea of fraternization with peasant troops. Some nobles even suspect that the uprising is a cover for revolutionary terror. As the Squire puts it, "Kościuszko begins his insurrection by inciting serfs against their masters."[61]

Initially, then, *Kościuszko at Racławice* refuses to idealize patriotic behavior. Instead of enlisting the symbolic power of the man-myth Kościuszko to cater to simplistic expectations about what a patriotic drama for a broad audience should be like, the play demonstrates Anczyc's gift for looking beneath social surfaces to reveal indifference, doubt, calculating opportunism, various strands of catastrophic expectation, and populist fires burning on resentment. Instead of silencing critical voices, instead of glossing over dissent, the play admits a sense of disruption that involves a confrontation of conflicting ideological positions and a clash of values and interests. To put these points differently, Anczyc looks for ways to escape from the cloying cult of sentimental selflessness that characterized patriotic moralism in the nineteenth century.[62] This is arguably the most compelling aspect of his play, one that has gone unnoticed in critical commentary.

Moreover, Anczyc's drama is the first Kościuszko-themed play to mention Kościuszko's 1794 offer to peasants: a temporary exemption from the corvée for those who enlist in his army. Anczyc's insertion of this information is so striking that it may overshadow a significant detail: the offer fails to move peasants. Even Kościuszko's attempt to play on their religious feelings—that is, his mention of a successful defense of the Marian sanctuary at Częstochowa against Swedish Protestants in 1655 in order to cast the insurrection of 1794 as a war in defense of the Catholic faith—does not persuade them. The double motivator, economic as well as religious, simply does not work. In act 3, therefore, we see a different approach to the mobilization of peasants. A village poet performs a song that fires their hearts, while softening their distrust of the gentry.[63] The song testifies to the power of art to turn indifferent masses into eager freedom fighters. Before, peasants shrugged their shoulders; now they enthusiastically respond to Głowacki's call to arms.

Having a peasant leader incite other peasants to armed resistance, however, was an explosive idea that could make many readers and spectators uneasy, particularly at a time when the bloodbath of 1846 still loomed large in the collective memory. Accordingly, the earlier version of the play skirts the issue.[64] The revised text, by contrast, recognizes the peasants' potential for uncontrollable violence; therefore it provides, in act 3, a spatial configuration carefully designed to put readers and spectators at ease. The setting is dominated by a village church. Peasant recruits enter under a banner featuring the patrons of Poland (the Black Madonna of Częstochowa and Saint Stanisław) and proceed to the church to attend mass. The door is thrown open to reveal a brightly lit altar inside. The recruits fall to their knees and are blessed by a priest. The scene thus makes it clear that the Catholic Church sanctions and sanctifies the peasants' mission in the cause of Polish independence, but it also seeks to control the scope of their activism.

The threat of revolution, however, keeps coming back. It is difficult to resist a conclusion that the play's recurrent references to the radical excesses in revolutionary France in fact trope the massacre of the Polish gentry during the peasant uprising of 1846. In act 4, at the vulnerable moment of prebattle nervousness, two radical members of the Kraków city council use revolutionary rhetoric to win peasant recruits to their side:

> DZIANOTTY: Before, the gentry allowed Poland to perish; now, peasants and townspeople will liberate Poland....
>
> SZTUMMER: We can do without the gentry. We must follow the example of the French. Long live the people![65]

Dzianotty and Sztummer propose to better Kościuszko's offer to peasants. He has promised them a temporary exemption from the corvée; Dzianotty and Sztummer announce a land reform after Poland is liberated. Predictably, this enrages the landowners who have enlisted in Kościuszko's army. The newly forged national solidarity is on the brink of collapse; the anti-Russian insurrection threatens to spill into a civil war.

In the play's key monologue, Głowacki rejects Dzianotty and Sztummer's revolutionary overtures: "This is not France. We're not after the land of our landlords because that would go against the Tenth Commandment. . . . If we stand united—gentry, peasants, townspeople—Poland will be free."[66] Głowacki's scorn for revolutionary propaganda is framed in rhetorical terms that appear irresistible because they make room for the flattering notion of Polish exceptionalism. That is to say, the class threat is buried under the cultural threat posed by foreign models, and the cultural threat is used to highlight the superiority of Polishness over the aggressive, treacherous, and materialistic stance of the rest of Europe.

Anczyc's play ends with a joyous finale that offers a reassuring metaphor of a nation united in a common cause. Nobles, peasants, and townspeople gather together, basking in their triumph. The threat of revolution has been contained; peasants have stood bravely in defense of the same flag that the gentry and burghers have been fighting for. The high point of the finale is Kościuszko's ennoblement of Głowacki. Głowacki uses this occasion to applaud Kościuszko for offering peasants an opportunity to be active agents in the shaping of their country's destiny. In other words, the finale refuses to lock social inequalities within an idealized sphere of patriotic solidarity. Instead, it celebrates the porousness of social boundaries and the freedom to cross them. Dramaturgically, then, the finale deploys a classic form of dramatic emplotment that affirms regeneration through the creation of a new, redeemed community. The particular success of the finale is to speak at once to multiple implied audiences—urban and rural, upper- and working-class, conservative and progressive—and to argue to those audiences for a mode of civic identity that includes rather than excludes, that creates rather than denies community.

The spatial arrangement of act 5, however, suggests a more ambivalent logic. In act 3, it will be remembered, peasants stepped forward to enlist in Kościuszko's army under the watchful eye of the Catholic Church. In act 5, it is an old-fashioned gentry house, built on a slight elevation, that serves as the focal point, with a village visible in the distance. In other words, although the play sometimes seems to valorize the "down" rather than the "up" of Polish society, the final act spatializes a set of relations that reinforces the traditional social hierarchy and steers groups with lower status toward an attitude of deference to their social superiors. To put these points another way, the play closes with the evocation of a national community as a hierarchical, extended, and inclusive family, albeit a family with a difference. Earlier, the family was represented as querulous and ineffectual. Now, in order to create a new Poland and to protect the national body against infection from abroad, it is necessary to gather peasants and nonpeasants in a collective identity precisely through the act of not quarreling over that identity.

Anczyc, of course, was not unique in glamorizing what may be called benevolent paternalism. What is most remarkable about his play, however, is that it has managed, against all odds, to amass cultural capital that was still viable in 1989. The play does so by creating an appealing illusion of an inclusive and pluralist culture, while activating a biological metaphor, in which nations are seen as bodies vulnerable to life-threatening contagion such as "the Parisian plague."[67]

V.

Written over the course of more than half a century, the plays discussed so far might seem, on a first reading, to sidestep the thorny issue of transgression twinned with patriotism. Such a conclusion, however, would be premature.

Admittedly, each of the plays subjects Kościuszko to a process of revision and modification to suit its overall scheme in the service of mythmaking. In Majeranowski's *Kościuszko's First Love* and Mańkowska's *Tadeusz Kościuszko*, he is an emotionally wounded lover whose psychic traumas fuel his heroics. Additionally, Majeranowski's Kościuszko is a man with a heightened capacity to feel pity (which in the eighteenth century had none of the patronizing inflection it has today) and to act in accordance with the fellow-feeling thereby aroused, while Mańkowska's Kościuszko is a faithful son of the Church of Rome who leads his troops against the enemies of Catholicism. Kraszewski's *The Governor's Equal* continues the project of imagining Kościuszko as an exemplar of moral goodness, casting him as a high-minded sage who mentors an aristocratic rake in proper morality. And in Anczyc's *Kościuszko at Racławice*, Kościuszko heals traumatic cuts in Polish society and facilitates cross-class reconciliation, social accord, and national unity. In these plays, the tendency to oversimplify, romanticize, or idealize has its inevitable corollary, that is, a tendency to leave unexplored those aspects of Kościuszko's life that might complicate the glittering story of his heroism. Accordingly, failure and particularly the lost battle of Maciejowice are not allowed to intrude on the Kościuszko myth. Even in the prophetic vision in *Kościuszko's First Love*, in which Kościuszko collapses a quarter-century of Polish history, from the Constitution of 3 May 1791 to the establishment of the Kingdom of Poland at the Congress of Vienna in 1815, there is no mention of defeat, and the loss of statehood in 1795 is only implied.

And yet the cultural picture that emerges from these plays is full of ambivalence and contradiction. That is to say, their idealization of Kościuszko is bound up with an awareness of (or, perhaps, a fascination with) the disruptive potential of his example, threatening to violate boundaries and distinctions, and in particular to topple the hierarchies of gender, status, and authority. Read carefully, the plays both construct the Kościuszko myth and challenge, however subtly or implicitly, their own mythmaking in the course of creating the myth. For example, the compassionate sensibility and emotional intensity of Majeranowski's Kościuszko are disconcertingly "feminine" rather than conventionally "manly," and Kraszewski's Kościuszko does not consider the reformed rake's "unmanly" withdrawal from the public sphere into rural domesticity to be a betrayal of those who have fought for Poland's freedom. Their Kościuszko, in other words, does not fit the gender stereotypes underlying the concept of the martial hero.

Given the phenomenal popularity of *Kościuszko at Racławice*, an instant best-seller with staying power, it is tempting to conclude that Anczyc had the last word on the meaning of Kościuszko in the nineteenth century. He took the darkly suspicious idea of the empowerment of peasants and reworked it into a winning formula to contain the radical potential of Kościuszko's activism. The play seems to overflow with democratic, egalitarian sentiments; in fact, these sentiments are a facade concealing benevolent paternalism. *Kościuszko at Racławice* sealed Kościuszko's transformation from a "Jacobin" and a suspect champion of peasant rights to a potent symbol of integrative, cross-class patriotism, assuring him a posthumous triumph more durable than any of his military victories. By the time of World War II, *Kościuszko at Racławice* became the most frequently performed play in the Polish language.

It is also tempting to conclude that it was Stanisław Wyspiański's *The Wedding*, a masterpiece of modern Polish drama first produced in 1901, that

Apocalypse Now? Tadeusz Kościuszko | 219

brought back to light the buried anxieties, repressed traumas, and hidden "shadow" themes of the Kościuszko myth. To complicate such conclusions, I want to bring middlebrow drama into discussion. While not a celebrated masterwork like *The Wedding*, *The Warsaw Street-Seller*, a 1897 play by Wyspiański's contemporary, Adam Bełcikowski, offers its own revisionist approach to the Kościuszko myth.

Set in the summer of 1794, *The Warsaw Street-Seller* presents one of Kościuszko's main claims to fame: his successful defense of Warsaw against a siege by Prussian and Russian forces. However, the fundamental conflict that drives the dramatic action is between patriots and traitors, rather than between Poles and non-Poles. While Kościuszko leads the defense of the city, a group of Polish aristocrats suspects that he might be a Jacobin in disguise. Anxious to prevent a replay of the French Revolution on Polish soil, they conspire to collaborate with the enemy. Warsaw totters on the brink of disaster, but the eponymous street-seller named Magda volunteers to sneak into the Prussian encampment to gather intelligence for Kościuszko. Thanks to her courage, ingenuity, and perseverance, the aristocrats' treasonous plot is exposed, and Kościuszko is able to mount a surprise counterattack against the foreign troops, forcing them to abandon the siege.[68]

Admittedly, *The Warsaw Street-Seller* resorts now and then to melodramatic devices and effects. There are machinations of a highly placed villain, a confession scene set against a thunderstorm, and a last-minute restitution. Although one might dismiss Bełcikowski's play out of hand as banal and therefore unworthy of full-scale consideration, I must admit that his spirited handling of plot and character mostly has given me pleasure. Mostly, with one exception. This exception startled me, first by its oddity, then by its possible implications. The cause of my bewilderment was the play's closing scene. After Magda returns from her mission to the Prussian camp, several Polish soldiers begin to suspect her of being an enemy agent. Scorned and ostracized, she is driven to a willful suicide. She runs across a demarcation line and is shot by the retreating Prussians. Brought back to the Polish camp, she dies in full view, surrounded by Kościuszko's troops, but there is no call for a priest to administer the last sacraments. I wanted to pull out and reweave that loose thread, and many others like it in this priestless drama.

The enormous popularity of *The Warsaw Street-Seller* in the decades surrounding the beginning of the twentieth century suggests that the play may be read as a successful investment in a consciousness-raising mission to foster patriotism and national pride.⁶⁹ However, reading Bełcikowski's drama solely as a vehicle of patriotic consciousness-raising depends on a highly selective—indeed schematic—understanding of the text. One way to begin to unravel the complexities of this deceptively simple play would be to examine its frequent recourse to sexualized language. For example, Prussian soldiers speak of Warsaw as if it were a woman to be subdued and raped. I want to begin, however, by focusing on Bełcikowski's construction of the play's protagonist.

As in Anczyc's *Kościuszko at Racławice*, Kościuszko's presence merely frames the action. Here, we see a busy commander and military engineer who has designed fortifications that wrap around the city. He appears only twice, allowing the other characters to claim center stage. As in many other plays on the 1794 insurrection, such as Michał Bałucki's *Kiliński* (1893) or, again, Anczyc's *Kościuszko at Racławice*, the main character is a lower-class person who is initiated into patriotic heroism. This in itself, then, is neither striking nor novel. However, Bełcikowski's protagonist is a woman. In foregrounding Magda, he recovers the lower-class woman who has been obscured by accounts of the participation of upper-class women such as Plater in the struggle for Polish independence and statehood. Even the title is revealing. Rather than highlighting, say, Magda's courage, it stresses her unglamorous occupation.⁷⁰

This shift of focus from a hero with high name recognition to a heroine identified only as Magda invites a consideration of the dynamics of gender in the play. As Małgorzata Czyszkowska-Peschler points out, the attention of Bełcikowski's contemporaries "was necessarily monopolized by the imperative of national survival to the point where [they] had little patience with new social currents, let alone being ready to recognize in women's emancipation a legitimate social development whose time had come."⁷¹ By contrast, Bełcikowski finds ways to incorporate "new social currents" into his play. Its female protagonist is an emblem of the modernizing trends in gender structures. She earns her own living, and so she does not depend on a man for economic survival. Her autonomy is further underscored by the fact that she has no family and is not attached to any particular man. Young, single, and self-supporting, she is determined to find her own way in male-centered society. In short, Bełcikowski's seemingly modest play stands out as one of the most unqualified celebrations of female autonomy and agency to be found in nineteenth-century Polish drama. It is thus unavoidable to ask: Does *The Warsaw Street-Seller* offer a potent example of female autonomy and agency to support the idea of women's emancipation? And given that the play attributes Kościuszko's victory to Magda's heroism, does female incursion into male history-making become a stepping-stone to formulate a wider, more inclusive concept of citizenship?

To address these questions, it is helpful to begin at the beginning. Although clearly intended for a broad audience, *The Warsaw Street-Seller* lacks a love plot. Moreover, Magda has never been in love, and she does not envision marriage as the ultimate goal of women's lives. And yet, on a deeper level, a love plot does emerge. In act 1, scene 3, Kościuszko's soldiers, eager to find out whether she is sexually available, quiz Magda about her amorous pursuits. In a snappy repartee that makes the soldiers laugh nervously, she names the insurrection leaders, including Kościuszko, as her lovers. It is possible to venture a feminist analysis, presenting Magda as a strategist who uses verbal inventiveness as a means of empowerment and retaliation. Against a world of male sexual predators and investigators, she deploys the powerful weapon of words. Her stories give her authority and protection. It is she who frames the narrative, she who shapes her public presentation, she, if you like, who midwifes her own text. A crucial component of her text is the troping of patriotic devotion as erotic passion. Two scenes later, however, it becomes evident that this trope is not merely a rhetorical device to deflect unwanted sexual attentions. In offering to aid Kościuszko's liberationist project, Magda makes it clear that she wants to prove her love for Poland.

Yet even at this deeper level, matters are not so simple. To be sure, the language of patriotism is so heavily eroticized that patriotic devotion would seem to be indistinguishable from erotic desire. The patriot remains bound to *patria* by love rather than, say, mere loyalty. Whenever patriotic duty is invoked, we are more likely than not to find it phrased as *love of country*. And given that the grammatical gender imputes metaphorical femaleness to countries, desire for Britannia, Germania, Italia, or Polonia (to use Latinized terms), figured as desire for a woman, is a familiar trope in patriotic discourse. Considering this eroticized investment in patriotic desire, it is reasonable to ask: What happens when the patriot who desires Poland is a woman? The intrusion of female patriotic desire seems to render the normative arrangement problematic and in need of correction. How does Bełcikowski's play deal with this dilemma? Does it throw male and female patriotic desire into a single melting pot?

First, I want to take another look at Bełcikowski's construction of the heroine. Instead of an idealized female figure, he has chosen a matter-of-factly gritty woman with entrepreneurial skills and a gift for fiery repartee. In contrast to an icon of apotheosized patriotic womanhood such as Plater, Magda provides an accessible point of entry for us as readers and spectators into the world of the play. We enter the military zone with her when she brings food to soldiers, and so, with her and through her eyes, we experience the men's space. Hers is the gaze we are invited to follow. The effect of her act of looking inside the Prussian camp is, of course, Kościuszko's victory. To be sure, some soldiers on both sides of the fire line see Magda as an eroticized object of desire. But the play knows better. Far from offering a stereotypical character of the dewy ingenue, it presents a woman who defies objectification and asserts her agency.

This is an appropriate point at which to examine Magda's first encounter with Kościuszko. In act 1, scene 6, only moments after they meet, Kościuszko reveals to Magda his uncertainty about the outcome of the siege. In his commentary on *The Warsaw Street-Seller*, Wiktor Hahn thinks it "rather implausible" that Bełcikowski's Kościuszko confides in a woman whom he hardly knows.[72] Approaching the play from another perspective, however, one finds that Bełcikowski "feminizes" Kościuszko, although this feminization means something quite different from the feminization in Majeranowski's *Kościuszko's First Love*. Here, Kościuszko is "feminized" merely in the sense that he is shown to be a modest and approachable man, famous for the sweetness of his temperament. Thus, when a young woman asks him about the defense of Warsaw, he is not embarrassed to confide in her.

The openness with which Kościuszko speaks with Magda suggests a certain gender equality. This suggestion, however, is subverted by the fact that Kościuszko's tent becomes a site of the conventional association of women with domesticity. Kościuszko is cast as the benevolent father who comes home after a hard day's work, and Magda is cast as the dutiful daughter who performs tasks that contemporary audiences would have understood to be women's work.[73] She offers food to the hungry Kościuszko, makes coffee, and tends the fire. In short, she provides the comforts of home to the male hero. This point is made even more explicit when she refuses payment for the food. It is difficult to resist the impression that we are in the realm of conventional domestic drama where the gendered division of labor is scrupulously observed.

I want to complicate this conclusion. What, I would ask again, are we to make of Kościuszko's "unmanly" confession to Magda? One could argue that Kościuszko turns to her for the reassurances that others cannot provide. That is to say, he is drawn to her precisely because she offers a perfect screen on which he can project his anxiety about the outcome of the siege. As an outsider to what is fundamentally male territory, she is an ideal repository for projections of his inner conflicts. He wants her to mirror his desires: for more soldiers, for military intelligence, for a victory. He is so preoccupied with an urgent need for reinforcements that at one point he says, "Magda, I can see that I would have had one more brave soldier under my command, if you had been a man."[74] As Magda rustles about, in other words, he subjects her to his masculinized gaze, but his act of looking turns her into a potential soldier, fit for a rifle, rather than into an object of erotic desire. In short, his comment reveals his special gift of intuition: he knows a real soldier when he sees one. The only problem is Magda's biological sex or, to be more precise, the dynamic between her biological sex and the socially and culturally constructed gender.

Earlier, Magda considered herself devoted to the cause of Poland's independence, but she expressed her devotion more in sentiment than in action. She was content that her work as a supplier of food provided sustenance to Kościuszko and his troops. Now she weighs her work against the military project of male patriots and is embarrassed about the insignificance of her contribution. Under Kościuszko's discerning eye, she regrets that men and women are posited in separate and distinct categories even when Poland is in need: "I've often thought these days: God, why am I not a man? I'm sure I'd be good for something. But what can I do? I am who I am, and I can't change that."[75] To be a man is to serve Poland properly. To be a woman is, at best, to perform auxiliary services. Even in times of war, a woman can be only a woman, never a soldier. Although Magda experiences the "unfeminine" urge to fight for homeland, she respects the gender boundary. Barred from military service, she volunteers as a spy.

For many of Bełcikowski's contemporaries, the notion of women doing men's work created enormous anxiety, as the plays on the Plater theme make clear. Magda, of course, is not doing men's work. She is not a soldier like Plater. Instead, she is doing what women have always been said to do: she turns to weapons traditionally labeled feminine—artifice and deception. Granted, her motivations are noble, for she is driven solely by patriotic desire. What is more, Kościuszko sanctions the deception. And yet Magda is not allowed to live on. Why?

The answer seems obvious. Magda's subterfuge, though necessary, threatens to destabilize the moral geography of "true" patriotism precisely because it violates the chivalric ethos that shuns treachery. Despite all the legitimizing strategies, the world of the play cannot accommodate deception even for a good cause. To compound the problem, Magda's deception is not confined to her secret mission. Before she tricks the enemy, she deceives Kościuszko. During their first encounter, she resorts to a subtle rhetorical maneuver in order not to tell him that she has taken advantage of the war to make an extra profit by trading in the enemy camp. Because she withholds from Kościuszko this unflattering information about herself, she is already morally suspect when she volunteers to spy on the Prussian forces.

To reiterate the points I have been making, it is difficult to get around the fact that the play ultimately presents Magda as doubly threatening. She is threatening because she manipulates speech as women have always been said to do. She is also threatening because she manipulates speech as a female entrepreneur who is more concerned about profit than about politics. By conflating her duplicity with her greed, the play casts Magda as an embodiment of ethical chaos. Her suicidal leap across the demarcation line is necessary to restore the "natural" order of "true" patriotism.

For all its revisionist efforts, then, the play's regressive currents are easy to identify. A man achieves victory through female wiles. A woman's patriotic toil is accepted, but she is denied reentry into the patriotic community and put to death to erase her transgressive difference. In its closing moments, however, the play moves from the punitive to the redemptive. Just before Magda dies, Kościuszko publicly recognizes her patriotic heroism and presents her with a ring bearing the inscription "To my male defender—[signed] Poland."[76] Redeemed in a kind of deus ex machina, in other words, Magda metamorphoses from a despised spy to a celebrated defender of her country.

Once again, however, matters are not so simple. What occurs in the closing moments of the play needs closer attention. To begin with, although

Magda has refused to validate herself by a connection to a man, she is not allowed to die single. She must get married first. Presiding as a surrogate priest, Kościuszko marries Magda to Poland by placing the ring on her finger. But the wedding ceremony turns slyly, wryly "perverse." It cannot be aligned with, or safely contained by, heteronormative sexuality because Poland is gendered feminine. During the ceremony, Magda is assigned a masculine identity (the "male defender") and cast as Poland's male consort. To put it differently, Magda cannot resume her unambiguously "natural" female status even at the moment of her death. She is a woman whom Kościuszko objectified as a man who then served the liberationist project as a woman who is ultimately being rewarded as a man. In a startling twist, then, the marriage between Poland and her "male defender" seems to confirm what the play has suggested all along: that Magda, a strong and compelling figure, is a "masculine" woman.

By now, it is clear that *The Warsaw Street-Seller* is far more interesting than its now stereotyped reputation allows. Written at a time when the women's movement was gaining momentum, the play carries contradictory mixed messages. It begins with a self-supporting Magda who brings a smart-mouth, defiant sensibility to gender relations and emphatically asserts her autonomy. It is thus possible to see her as fighting against the constraints of gender roles that have been imposed on women. The play then shows a plucky Magda who takes on a dangerous mission in the national liberation movement; in doing so, she offers proof that women are capable of sharing a highly valued political sentiment, patriotism, and able to act effectively on it. In this sense, the play is a paean to women's self-assertion, resourcefulness, and courage. At the same time, however, the play confirms the dominant assumptions of patriarchal culture about women. Magda fits the clichéd image of a treacherous woman who deceives men, while her emotional outburst, which leads to her death, looks like uncontrollable excess or a frightening unleashing of impulse that has long been associated with women. The play does not deny the women's contribution to the liberationist project, but it defuses the dangerous suggestion that they may be men's equal partners in this project.

And yet the conceptual framework offered by the idea of female (dis)empowerment does not encompass the full range of interpretive possibilities in *The Warsaw Street-Seller*, as I have attempted to show. The play engages patriotic discourse in resistant, oppositional ways that refuse us as readers and spectators the comfort of the traditional understanding of gender as a fixed and unchanging essence, embedded in sexual difference. Accordingly, the play enacts an eroticized devotion to *patria* that almost provocatively cannot be subsumed under heteronormative sexuality. In doing so, it breaks down predictable codes and demands new possibilities, positionalities, and transformations. To put these points another way, *The Warsaw Street-Seller* works to unmask the instability of the categories that are presumed to define femininity and masculinity. It reveals, in its own way, that a sexed human being is more than sex and gender and that the experience of being of one sex or another is shaped by unpredictable intersections of biology, social and cultural convention, historical circumstance, personal motivations and desires, and individual choice.[77]

6 ⋅ Controversies over "True" and "False" Patriotism, 1941–89

I.

THE KOŚCIUSZKO MYTH, on even cursory inspection, turns out to depend on many misleading surface effects. Did Kościuszko really attempt to mend a broken heart by going to North America? Did he throw himself into the American Revolution to ease the pain over his failed courtship of Sosnowska? Wasn't he involved in a homoerotic friendship with Niemcewicz? Did he actually distinguish himself as a consummate strategist in the battle of Dubienka in 1792? Didn't he seriously miscalculate his chances of winning the battle of Maciejowice in 1794 and then allow the blame for the catastrophic defeat to be shifted to one of his generals, Adam Poniński? Didn't he boast in a letter to Jefferson that he was *"seul veritable Polonais en Europe"* (the only true Pole in Europe), even though he had signed a Russian loyalty oath upon his release from prison?[1]

The puzzle, then, is how Kościuszko came to occupy the role of the national hero par excellence in Poland's imagined community. Although there were other military commanders and political leaders who struggled against all adversity to restore an independent Poland, it is Kościuszko who stands at the head of the Polish patriotic tradition as the quintessential national hero: a paradigmatic figure who symbolizes his people and their aspirations. Kościuszko's mesmerizing and tenacious hold on the popular imagination is readable, for example, from the results of a public opinion poll, conducted on a representative sample of Polish society in 1994. When asked to identify a Polish historical personage who bolsters their pride in Poland, most respondents chose Kościuszko over Józef Piłsudski, John Paul II, and Nicholas Copernicus.² If he had walked the Polish soil in 1994, Kościuszko certainly would have felt that he had not lived in vain.

In the preceding chapter, I discussed those aspects of Kościuszko's biography that have been readily appropriated for Poland's National Symbolic and celebrated in suitably triumphalist terms under the banner of collective pride. I also argued that in order to account for the place of Kościuszko in the Polish cultural imagination, it is vital to take drama into consideration. To be sure, the veneration of Kościuszko began in his lifetime, and the foundations for some of the enduring stories about him—about his dauntless spirit and military skills, about his innate goodness and unremitting probity, or about his rock-ribbed conviction that the purity of his motives must match the purity of the causes he would serve—were laid by those of his contemporaries who did not write plays. A cult of the valiant Kościuszko flowered as early as 1793 in poems, in copperplate prints, and in artifacts such as rings and snuffboxes that bore his likeness.³ The sheer number of Kościuszko's portraits—an estimated one hundred—that were drawn, engraved, or painted during his lifetime testifies to "the power and vigor of the Kościuszko myth at its inception"; by contrast, all the portraits of Kazimierz (Casimir) Pułaski that we know of were made many years after his death.⁴ In the preceding chapter, I did not contest that Kościuszko's life proved an inexhaustible source of inspiration for poets and painters, or that they turned his biography to exemplary account. But I argued that it is dramatic works such as Konstanty Majeranowski's *Kościuszko's First Love* and Władysław Ludwik Anczyc's *Kościuszko at Racławice* that were crucial players in the making of the Kościuszko myth during the nineteenth century. Aware of the Jacobin sympathies attributed to Kościuszko and mindful of the disruptive potential of his example, constantly threatening to violate social boundaries, distinctions, and hierarchies, a group of playwrights mobilized all their dramaturgical and rhetorical inventiveness in order to construct Kościuszko not simply as a passionate champion of liberty and a symbol of resistance to tyranny, but primarily as a paragon of virtue and an impresario of cross-class solidarity and national unity in a society riven by deeply entrenched inequalities.

As I searched in libraries and theatre archives for Kościuszko-themed plays from the twentieth century, I began to have the slightly eerie feeling that I did not choose Kościuszko; rather, Kościuszko chose me. That is to say, my decision to include twentieth-century dramas had a topicality I could hardly have expected. In September 1988, just weeks after communist officials initiated exploratory talks with Solidarity representatives about liberalizing measures that eventually (and rather unexpectedly) restored democracy in Poland, a compelling new play about Kościuszko, Anna Bojarska's *The Polish Lesson,* opened in Warsaw. Directed by Andrzej Wajda, it had a successful run at Warsaw's Powszechny Theatre in the fall and went on to be performed to great acclaim during Solidarity's campaign for election to Parliament in May 1989. Less than two months later, Anczyc's *Kościuszko at Racławice* was called back into service to celebrate Poland's return to democratic politics in the wake of Solidarity's landslide victory at the polls. It may well be that Polish theatres overemphasized Kościuszko during the 1988–89 season. If one considers, however, that the leader of Solidarity, Lech Wałęsa, staged a curious extravaganza-cum-masquerade on the Racławice battlefield during the election campaign in May 1989, it becomes easier to understand why sometimes it seemed as if Kościuszko alone brought communist rule to an end.

I could hardly have anticipated that Kościuszko would be enlisted to support a political struggle in the late 1980s. I was well aware, of course, that his 1818 interment in the Wawel Cathedral in Kraków, where monarchs had been crowned and buried for centuries, marked his cultural canonization, that his tomb became a shrine to which visitors came like pilgrims, and that his numerous commemorative monuments served as rallying points for different, often radically opposed, causes, as republicans and monarchists, progressives and conservatives, egalitarians and paternalists, democrats and antidemocrats, nationalists and internationalists, believers and freethinkers claimed possession of him. For example, his modesty and selflessness, which had been attributed to his (alleged) Jacobinism in 1794, were, after his enshrinement at Wawel, reinterpreted by Catholic commentators as evidence of his exemplary Christian virtue, sufficient to elevate him to the status of a secular saint. Some 130 years later, communist authorities recast him as a champion of working-class radicalism and a precursor of Soviet communism. However, his identity as a fighter for Poland's freedom from Russian domination became a sensitive issue for communist propagandists, as a controversy over the *Racławice* panorama makes it clear. First exhibited in Lwów in 1894 to commemorate the centennial of the Racławice battle, the painting has acquired enormous symbolic capital as "a monument to the Polish national spirit" and "a symbol of the nation's aspirations."[5] After World War II, citizens' committees repeatedly petitioned the communist government to have the panorama repaired and displayed, but the authorities, apparently determined to suppress the symbolism of Kościuszko leading his men against Russian troops, ignored the petitions. The panorama was made available for public viewing only in 1985.[6]

Although I was well aware of the seemingly unlimited ease with which it was possible to draw on the man-myth Kościuszko in multiple, and sometimes contradictory, ways or to shape and reshape him in order to suit the needs of sharply divergent causes, I thought that his political moment had passed a long time ago and that the story of his life functioned merely as a kind of bric-a-brac, useful only as the decor for celebrations of "the wonderfulness of us." I assumed that the best one could do was to offer incense at a much-frequented shrine. I was wrong. Kościuszko's survival skills are supreme: he is a master of metamorphosis. Even so, mysteries remain.

It is a truism that the authority of national heroes is never so strong as in their posthumous life. They maintain a tenacious, subterranean authority over mentalities, motivations, dispositions, and behavior. Moreover, as Wałęsa's extravaganza-cum-masquerade at Racławice reminded me, even a body well settled in its grave can be caught up in the politics of the living. But the dead, and the memories of the dead, are unpredictable. They can be integrative and reassuring, or they can be disruptive, unruly, agonistic. On this point, Bojarska's *The Polish Lesson* and Wajda's production of the play, as well as Wałęsa's pageant, are particularly instructive.

Performed during the last year of communist rule in Poland, *The Polish Lesson* and the Racławice pageant are the subject of sections IV and V, respectively, in this chapter. I begin, however, with two "scandalous" plays that were written during World War II (sections II and III). One of them, Wanda Wasilewska's *Bartosz Głowacki*, takes up the enigmatic story of the eponymous serf who distinguished himself under Kościuszko's command in the battle of Racławice. Written and premiered in Soviet-occupied Lwów in 1941, *Bartosz Głowacki* was revived in postwar Poland in 1946 as part of the communist-sponsored bicentennial of Kościuszko's birth. The year 1946 also saw the publication and premiere of Stefan Otwinowski's *Easter*, the first play in any language on the 1943 uprising in the Warsaw ghetto. Drafted within weeks after the ghetto resistance was crushed and the ghetto torched to ashes, it presents a puzzling conflation of the ghetto uprising and the Kościuszko insurrection, as it broaches the vexed question of Polish society's relations with the Jewish minority.

These four case studies—the plays by Wasilewska, Otwinowski, and Bojarska and Wałęsa's Racławice pageant—provide a series of lenses through which I consider contests over the meaning of patriotism and struggles between competing views of patriotic idea(l)s, principles, and concerns at pivotal points in post-1939 Polish history when patriotic allegiance, yet again, became a major battleground.

II.

As the first postwar season opened, the Juliusz Słowacki Theatre in Kraków made plans to celebrate the Kościuszko bicentennial with a revival of Anczyc's *Kościuszko at Racławice* in 1946.[7] The production, however, never materialized. Rather predictably, the communist authorities refused to endorse a play from the other side of the ideological divide. Consequently, the Juliusz Słowacki Theatre's contribution to the Kościuszko bicentennial was a production of a play without Kościuszko: Wasilewska's *Bartosz Głowacki*. It opened on 24 March 1946.

Critical commentaries on Wasilewska are generally patronizing, slipping at times into moral indignation, unmitigated contempt, and downright hostility. She is perceived as a writer who enjoyed an inflated literary reputation due to her political involvement in Soviet communism and her career as a well-connected power broker with personal access to Stalin. According to a widely accepted understanding, moreover, she was a traitor to the Polish cause—a reprehensible renegade who sold her country to the Soviets and contributed to Poland's disastrous political destiny in the aftermath of World War II.[8]

After Hitler's Germany and its Soviet ally invaded Poland in September 1939, Soviet authorities made eastern Polish borderlands into western Soviet republics. Wasilewska took up residence in Soviet-occupied Lwów where she threw herself into vigorous activism as an organizer and a propagandist for the communist regime. In her speeches and articles, she presented the Soviet Union as a moral republic that honors and protects the working class. Accordingly, she was unapologetic about the Soviet annexation of the Polish borderlands, insisting that it was a necessary act of international responsibility. For example, in a speech given on the first anniversary of the annexation, she contended that the Red Army liberated the oppressed masses in the borderlands from the imperial tyranny of the Polish ruling elite. The Soviet Union, she told her audience, was fighting for a better world by resisting imperialism and spreading freedom.[9] Three years later, she cofounded the Union of Polish Patriots, a collaborationist organization that backed Stalin's designs for Soviet rule over postwar Poland.

Written during Wasilewska's stay in Lwów, *Bartosz Głowacki* is an intriguing text. In her articles and speeches, this spokeswoman for communism and fraternal internationalism explicitly proclaimed the interests of all working-class people as indivisible.[10] Such a position typically implied a rejection of the language of patriotism. For example, in a Red Sunday School in Glasgow in 1917 children were taught: "Thou shalt not be a patriot for a patriot is an international blackleg."[11] And yet Wasilewska chose to write a play about Głowacki, an iconic hero of Polish patriotism. Is the play, then, Wasilewska's own version of the Red Sunday School's commandment, demonstrating her opposition to the rhetoric of patriotism? Or is the play, at best, her coup to steal some of the Polish patriotic clothes to facilitate the imposition of communist ideology?

Wasilewska's play draws on an apocryphal version of Głowacki's biography. The historical Głowacki fell in the battle of Szczekociny in June 1794, two months after his bold charge on Russian cannons at Racławice. According to some undocumented accounts, however, he survived. Leon Kruczkowski popularized the apocryphal story in his novel, *Kordian and the Boor* (*Kordian i cham*, 1932), which explores the heavy constraints that an unbridgeable social divide between the gentry and the peasantry imposed on the idea of patriotic solidarity in the struggle for Poland's independence. Although the novel pivots on the events immediately preceding the outbreak of the 1830 uprising, it includes a brief narrative about Głowacki, told by the character of Mr. Miranowski, a veteran of the 1794 insurrection. Mr. Miranowski insists that Głowacki lived through Szczekociny and continued to fight under Kościuszko's command. In recognition of Głowacki's stalwart conduct at Racławice, his landlord, Mr.

Szujski, emancipated him and granted him a piece of land. On his return from the military, however, Głowacki found that Mr. Szujski had changed his mind. When Głowacki protested, Mr. Szujski taught him a lesson by having him sequestered for conscription into an Austrian army. This apocryphal story about Głowacki's survival, protest, and punishment provides a general outline for the plot of Wasilewska's play, although, as I will show, she breaks in significant ways with the version recorded in Kruczkowski's novel.

Bartosz Głowacki premiered in Lwów under Soviet occupation. Directed by Władysław Krasnowiecki, it opened at the Polski Theatre, one of the city's two Polish-language theatres at the time, on 24 March 1941.[12] Tadeusz "Boy" Żeleński almost certainly exaggerated when, in an enthusiastic review of the opening night, he welcomed *Bartosz Głowacki* as a long-overdue sequel to Anczyc's *Kościuszko at Racławice*.[13] But present-day readers might find themselves in agreement with Żeleński's view that the play, although Wasilewska's first, has the craftsmanship of a far more seasoned playwright's efforts. Informed with a vivid theatrical imagination, the writing demonstrates her gift for the memorable scene and the engaging detail. In the epilogue, for example, a startling juxtaposition of Bartosz's traumatic testimony with a cheerful folk song about him creates a powerful effect, "both moving and nightmarish."[14]

While reading publicity materials published in Lwów's pro-Soviet Polish newspaper, the *Czerwony Sztandar,* however, it is difficult to resist the conclusion that *Bartosz Głowacki* was a mere vehicle for Wasilewska's propagandistic rhetoric. Contributors to the *Czerwony Sztandar* presented her text as a site where truth was summoned in the cause of denouncing manipulations by "Polish bourgeois historians" and setting the historical record aright.[15] For example, Krasnowiecki noted approvingly that Wasilewska took advantage of the artistic freedom available in the Soviet Union to debunk "one of the many myths that were officially propagated" in prewar Poland through "tendentious, reactionary" publications: the myth that Głowacki piously acquiesced to the reality of social inequality.[16] Other commentators concurred. Only in the Soviet Union, "her true homeland," was Wasilewska able to write a play that provides a much-needed historical reassessment of Głowacki's biography.[17] By "unmasking lies" and presenting unwelcome truths about the past, her play has wrestled the Głowacki story from the cynical manipulations of Polish intellectual elites.[18] And in a publicity statement published the day before the opening night, Krasnowiecki advertised *Bartosz Głowacki* as an act of historical recovery, crucial to "the struggle for the communist education of the masses."[19] The Polski Theatre in Lwów "will have achieved its goal [of educating the masses]," he concluded, if Poles watching the play come to understand that "their own homeland, the Soviet Union," is the homeland of which Głowacki could only dream.[20]

Admittedly, some scenes, such as those between Bartosz and his cynical landlord, are freighted with the heavy-handed rhetoric of political propaganda. But what happens if we try to read *all* of the text before us?

To avoid schematic assumptions about the play, it is helpful to know that *Bartosz Głowacki* became the subject of intense controversy when Wasilewska submitted it for consideration at the Polski Theatre. Bronisław Dąbrowski, an actor and director then affiliated with the Polski Theatre, remembers that the acting company objected to what he calls euphemistically "certain polemical tendencies" in *Bartosz Głowacki*.[21] He suggests that the actors' concern was not so much with Wasilewska's revisionist approach per se, as with the appropriateness of presenting revisionist interpretations of national history in the harrowing circumstances of war, particularly at a time when Poland was subjected to a new partition. In other words, the actors' response implied that a stage production blaming Poland's defeat on the political blunders of the Polish ruling elite in the past was ill suited to the post-1939 realities. Rather than undermine national solidarity in wartime by flaunting divisive depictions of Polish history, it was imperative to foster feelings of patriotic bonding. Wasilewska, who participated in the debate about *Bartosz Głowacki* as a literary adviser to the Polski Theatre as well as the play's author, stood her ground. Eventually, however, she agreed to revise the script, and *Bartosz Głowacki* was cleared for production.[22]

In daring to criticize a prominent public figure who rubbed shoulders with high-ranking Soviet officials, the actors showed a great deal of courage, risking imprisonment and deportation, which were everyday occurrences in Soviet-occupied Lwów. And if that were not enough, they resisted the efforts of the Soviet authorities to co-opt them for reinventing Polish patriotism according to Soviet specifications. As Mieczysław Inglot has argued, "the principal goal of Soviet propaganda" in the occupied territories was to instill in Poles "new, Soviet patriotic sentiments."[23] With this goal in mind, Soviet propagandists sought to present prewar Poland as a backward, semifeudal state, to blame Poland's loss to Hitler's Germany in 1939 exclusively on the corrupted and dysfunctional Polish government, and to discredit the patriotic commitment to Poland's political independence as a smokescreen for class discrimination and oppression.[24] An enthusiastic apologist for a vision of the Soviet Union as a country that spreads freedom and social justice, Wasilewska became a leading crusader for a new, Soviet-oriented model of "true" patriotism. In her political vocabulary, genuine patriotism required allegiance and devotion to the Soviet Union, while false patriotism was identified with aspirations for national independence. In the debate about *Bartosz Głowacki*, however, she came to accept the actors' arguments that defied the Soviet propaganda campaign to remake Polish patriotism.[25]

Although it would be reasonable to describe *Bartosz Głowacki* as a socially engaged drama, the text owes more to imaginative literature than to any particular political ideology.[26] It bears emphasis that the play opened in Lwów under the title *A Tale of Bartosz Głowacki* (*Opowieść o Bartoszu Głowackim*). This title has been duly noted by several commentators. What has not been noted, however, is the implication of the term *tale* for a fuller understanding of Wasilewska's text. Thus it is not surprising that commentators have used the issue of historical accuracy as a major checkpoint to assess the play. While contributors to the *Czerwony Sztandar* praised the historical realism of *Bartosz Głowacki*, more recent commentators point out that Wasilewska tendentiously misrepresents the fundamental facts of Głowacki's biography.[27] In identifying *Bartosz Głowacki* as a tale, however, Wasilewska explicitly declares the affinity of her text with the anecdotal rather than the documentary tradition. The framework of the tale allows her considerable liberty by way of imaginative re-creation and dramatic evocation.

In act 1, Bartosz chooses nation above class. When Kościuszko assumes command of the 1794 insurrection, Bartosz follows his lead in championing cross-class solidarity against foreign occupation, and he appeals to fellow peasants to fight for Poland's freedom on the side of the gentry. Many villagers are skeptical. For them, the enemies of freedom are to be found closer to home. Consequently, the villagers are unwilling to overlook social wrongs and to fight their masters' war against tsarist Russia. Bartosz convinces them that the patriot should be above class because foreign oppression affects all Poles, regardless of their social status. The enemy can be overcome only through teamwork; therefore the peasantry should make common cause with the gentry to strive for the common good: Poland's independence. At the same time, Bartosz does not want peasants to be accused of holding the country to ransom; hence he resists the idea of bartering their military service for agrarian reforms while the uprising is still being fought. Confident that peasants, through their faithful fulfillment of patriotic duty on the battlefield, will accumulate a stash of moral capital that will later give them political leverage, he always makes his dream of a new Poland seem right, urgent, and irresistible. As he states with unbounded optimism in the opening line of the play, "Everything's going to change through and through."[28] Act 2 shows his anguish, frustration, and bitterness, as he unsuccessfully seeks to redeem Kościuszko's promise to relieve the plight of those peasants who have joined the insurrectionary army. Ultimately, his initial optimism and unquestioning enthusiasm change to detachment, and he becomes a skeptical and laconic watcher in the wings, keeping his own counsel. What triggers Bartosz's conversion is his own consciousness-raising.

Consciousness-raising begins, as it always does, by peering into the heart of darkness. When he returns from the military, Bartosz is puzzled that Kościuszko's proclamations are ignored: the manager of Mr. Szujski's country estate forces peasants to work double shifts to make up for the time when they served in the army. Uncooperative villagers meet with the overseer's vicious reprisals. Since Mr. Szujski has released him from serfdom, Bartosz is not affected by the violations of Kościuszko's decrees. However, he believes that as a freed man he ought to do more than attend to his own farm. Unlike Kruczkowski's Bartosz, Wasilewska's Bartosz takes on the role of a spokesman for the village community and an advocate of peasants' rights. In contrast to his argument in act 1, he now argues his case not in the treacly language of duty and sacrifice, but on the basis of justice: "[Kościuszko's] promises must be respected."[29] In other words, he intuitively follows the ideal of the citizen: he refuses to bow and scrape, he stands up to oppression, and he acts in common cause. Bartosz resolves to petition Mr. Szujski on the peasants' behalf, but he finds that the patriotism of the upper classes has its limits; therefore, even peasant patriots do not win arguments with them. As soon as Kościuszko loses the insurrection, Bartosz is deprived of his recently won freedom and arrested for inciting peasants to rebellion. He is given fifty lashes in front of the villagers and conscripted into an Austrian army.

But it is the play's epilogue that offers the most revealing insights into Wasilewska's break with the Głowacki story as it is reported in Kruczkowski's *Kordian and the Boor*. In the novel, Bartosz, along with the Austrian troops, is decamped abroad where all trace of him is lost. Not so in the play. In the epilogue, the action moves to Italy where General Jan Henryk Dąbrowski has organized the Polish Legions under French auspices in the hope that Napoleon would redraw the map of Europe and restore an independent Poland. The year is 1797. As the scene opens, the Legionnaires have just defeated an Austrian force, capturing several Polish peasants turned Austrian soldiers, Bartosz among them. The peasants are offered an opportunity to join the Legions. All but Bartosz enlist. Lieutenant Skórzewski, who recognizes him as the famous hero of Racławice, reminds Bartosz that it is a duty of every Pole, "regardless of his social status," to serve his homeland.[30] Yet Bartosz is unmoved. In the play's closing lines, he declares: "The road to the peasants' homeland is hard and long. And it's different, very different from the road to your homeland, sir. But I'll get there!"[31]

When the play was staged in Lwów in 1941, commentators interpreted Bartosz's final lines proleptically: he knows what he wants, even if what he wants is beyond his grasp, but his dream will come true in the Soviet Union, the ultimate homeland of working-class people.[32] Admittedly, Bartosz's statement reveals his hard-earned recognition that the serfdom system is not going to change merely because peasants have fought for Poland's freedom. He has seen his hopes for emancipation of the exploited and the disadvantaged crumble to dust. When power is solely in the hands of the upper classes, he now suggests, there can be no common cause. Peasants would always lose from cross-class solidarity because it is an unequal relationship as long as they are subject to the will of their masters. Disillusioned and embittered about the prospects of peasants' enfranchisement through patriotic war effort, he refuses to be reconverted to the idea of a common cause.

Yet the debate between Bartosz and Skórzewski is more complex than the commentators suggested. In the epilogue, Bartosz does not choose class over nation. Rather, he opts for something entirely different. Before discussing his decision, however, I want to examine two other aspects of the epilogue, which also complicate the standard reading of the play.

The epilogue first introduces a group of Legionnaires of the gentry class. Unlike Mr. Szujski, they are eager to advance political and social change in Poland, rather than protect upper-class privilege. As the Second Officer remarks, "There's much to do to set everything right. . . . Securing equal rights for townsmen, redressing old wrongs, correcting the errors of the past. . . . Everything will change for the better. Everything. But first, we need to drive the enemy out."[33] In asserting his belief in the rise of a new Poland, the Second Officer unwittingly echoes Bartosz's optimistic assumption in act 1 that the future could be made better by concerted effort. It would be naive, then, to conclude that the play's discursive domain is shaped by a schematic opposition of the "reactionary" upper classes and the "progressive" lower classes. By presenting noblemen who advocate political radicalization and democratic activism, the epilogue destabilizes such staple dividing lines.[34]

Moreover, the epilogue shows that Bartosz's peasant compatriots do not share his bitterness and disillusionment. In contrast to him, they readily sign up for the Legions. It is evident that they do not endorse his belief that "the road to the peasants' homeland is . . . very different from the road to [the nobles'] homeland." Although Bartosz has learned the hard way to be skeptical about cross-class solidarity, at the final curtain we see Legionnaires of different social backgrounds poised to fight side by side for Poland's freedom. The commentators on the play have either overlooked this moment or found it unacceptable and therefore left it unexamined. It is my argument that while the play portrays the sharp edge of the class system and demonstrates that social antagonisms erode patriotic solidarity, this is not the whole story.

In the epilogue, Bartosz is the only peasant who refuses to have anything to do with the Polish struggle for independence. The more Skórzewski flatters or taunts him, the further he tacks toward the margin. Moreover, Bartosz rejects loyalty to class when he abandons his peasant compatriots who have enlisted in the Legions. He does not attempt to empower them with his vision of "the peasants' homeland." He does not remind them that cross-class solidarity means solidarity on the terms of the gentry. He does not urge them to opt for a separatist agenda in order to make Poland safe for democracy. Instead of making an effort to attract them to his concept of "the peasants' homeland," he chooses apartness and insists on returning home. This is puzzling. His bitter experience with his landlord has resulted in his withdrawal from military service and patriotic commitment, yet he wants to go back to his village where his honor was worn raw by humiliation and injustice. As I have tried to show, moreover, one of the core values of Wasilewska's Bartosz is the ideal of being a free person. For Bartosz, the essence of being a free person is to be one's own man, unwilling to bend the knee to anyone at all. When he goes back, however, he will once again be subject to the domination of Mr. Szujski and dependent on his will. Yet Bartosz's attachment to his family outweighs the trauma he has suffered at the hands of his landlord.

If one regards Wasilewska as an outrider for vigorous political activism, then the epilogue is certainly a puzzle. Bartosz is portrayed as skeptical, politically disengaged, and expecting little of life. He is also depicted as introverted, private, and individualistic. For Bartosz, adherence to abstractions such as Homeland, Nation, or Class has no part in his complex of loyalties. He is now content with more particularist loyalties and alternative forms of belonging. His particularism is home- and family-oriented. Although it would be easy to argue that Bartosz's disillusionment has immunized him against patriotism, a different interpretation is possible. What looks like Bartosz's indifference to patriotism may be seen as opposition to the patriotism of warfare. His phrase "the peasants' homeland" suggests the kind of patriotism that involves the saving of life, instead of taking it. In short, what looks like Bartosz's indifference to patriotism is in fact an attempt to redefine the meaning of patriotism. This redefinition of patriotism puts him in opposition to those who preach either the primacy of national unity or the primacy of class struggle, but it does not put him in opposition to patriotism.

III.

The end of World War II saw the creation of a Poland whose geographic boundaries and political system were radically redrawn. Political power was now in the hands of communists installed by Moscow in 1944. Polish society was bitterly divided over the issue of the communist takeover, and underground opposition networks waged guerrilla warfare against communist forces throughout the latter half of the 1940s. The early postwar period also witnessed outbursts of hostility and violence against Jewish survivors who were returning to Polish towns and cities to reclaim their assets and to rebuild their lives.[35] On 4 July 1946, rumors circulating in Kielce about a

Christian child kidnapped by Jews unleashed the most bloody of the postwar pogroms.[36] To stage Otwinowski's *Easter* three months later, after forty-two people had been killed in the Kielce pogrom, was to become enmeshed in a thick web of anti-Jewish resentments, allegations, and recriminations, as well as self-defensive polemics about Polish attitudes and behavior toward Jews. Leon Schiller, a former inmate of Auschwitz and a major theatre artist recently appointed the director of the Polish Army Theatre in Łódź, took up the challenge. Schiller's production of *Easter* opened at the Polish Army Theatre on 1 October 1946. The play received another production, directed by Władysław Woźnik, at the Stary Theatre in Kraków on 4 December 1946.[37]

To understand more fully the challenge that Schiller faced, it is necessary to recognize that in the postwar Polish discourse on Poles' relations with the Jewish minority the dominant approach was to nationalize memories of the war through the narratives of collective Polish heroism and martyrdom, that is, to contend that "society as a whole had behaved in a righteous and honorable manner towards Jews" during the war, to stress that Poles risked their lives to rescue Jews, and to insist that only hoodlums denounced Jews to the Nazi occupiers.[38] With regard to the Kielce pogrom, as Joanna Michlic's research has demonstrated, Polish society at large perceived it "primarily . . . as an event that 'slandered the good name of Poland and its people' rather than a terrible tragedy that befell the Jewish survivors."[39] In these perceptions, Michlic adds, "Jews were accorded a secondary place."[40] Such views testified to the Polish inability to reflect on the anti-Jewish violence and to mourn the deaths of Jewish victims; this emotional and moral detachment from the Jewish community was "the result of a long-term exposure to thinking about Jews as aliens and enemies."[41] As Piotr Wróbel points out, "The Holocaust did not change the Polish stereotype of the Jew."[42]

Integral to this stereotype was the notion that Jews as a collectivity were supporters of communism and enemies of the Polish nation-state and its people.[43] After 1945, many Poles identified Jews with the country's unpopular communist regime and its brutal repressions against the anticommunist resistance movement that Polish society at large regarded as a heroic force fighting against overwhelming odds for freedom from foreign domination. Reinforced by new political conflicts, old prejudices, ressentiments, and animosities ossified. "It is therefore not surprising," remarks

Krystyna Kersten, "that the mental cliché, which linked Jews, the [communist] ruling group, and a threat to Polishness, enjoyed widespread popularity in Polish society."⁴⁴ Or, as Bożena Szaynok observes, "The frame of reference for Polish thinking about the Jewish people was overwhelmingly hostile."⁴⁵ As a result, there was no common ground, no common narrative, no possible area for a rapprochement between Poles and Jews. Even the notion of a common life shared on the same piece of land appeared unthinkable.

It is unavoidable to ask: Given this overwhelmingly hostile frame of reference, what dramaturgical and rhetorical strategies does Otwinowski use to reach his prospective audiences? How does his play under the richly resonant, perhaps even defiantly ironic title *Easter* grapple with the notion, circulating widely in postwar Polish society, that Others (primarily communists and Jews) are profoundly threatening to Polish identity? How does the play respond to the concept of Polishness that defines itself against those perceived as enemies of Polish values and traditions? What is at stake when the dramatic action brings together the Jewish revolt of 1943 and the Polish insurgency of 1794? Doesn't the play's multiple, and conflated, time structure betray the historical reality of the Holocaust? Isn't the title *Easter* a way of reassuring Polish audiences that the play's perspective is Christian, even though the dramatic action revolves around the Warsaw ghetto uprising that began during Passover?

Otwinowski spent the war years in occupied Warsaw. Although he was not Jewish, he experienced antisemitic prejudice firsthand when his facial features and dark hair began to attract attention on the streets. Afraid that he might be taken for a Jew and handed over to the police, he abandoned his work as a bookseller and went into hiding.⁴⁶ His personal experience, then, provided him with a glimpse into what it meant to be a Jew under German occupation. Then, on 19 April 1943, a force of some 500 poorly armed men and women in the Warsaw ghetto rose against Nazi troops. Convinced that there was no hope left because the entire population of the ghetto was about to be killed in a final roundup, they decided that it was better to go down fighting and die with dignity than submit to extermination. The unequal fight continued for three weeks, ending in a mass suicide at the resisters' headquarters on 8 May. To Otwinowski, the tragic ordeal of the ghetto became the source of a psychic wound that affected his life afterward.⁴⁷ He began writing *Easter* in June 1943, a month after the resistance of Warsaw Jews was broken and the ghetto reduced to rubble; he completed the play in 1945.[48]

The cast of *Easter* is made up of a broad variety of characters—noble and louche, religious and secular, old and young; intellectuals and salt of the earth; Poles and Jews. The plot is simple. Overwhelmed by German terror, Stanisław Łaski, a young Warsaw intellectual, leaves the city soon after the ghetto uprising breaks out on Monday of the Holy Week. He finds a peaceful retreat in the home of his uncle, Dr. Przypkowski, who lives in a small town near Warsaw. Just as both of them sit down to celebrate Easter, a Jewish woman, Ewa Freud, escapes from a local ghetto and comes to Przypkowski's house. Eager to help Ewa, Przypkowski suggests that the safest place for her would be Stanisław's apartment in Warsaw where no one knows her. Stanisław thus has an opportunity to put his high-minded liberal ideals into practice, but he vehemently refuses to risk his life in order to rescue Ewa. He has recently suffered a nervous breakdown, he says, and therefore he is unable to cope with the danger involved in sheltering a Jew. He eventually musters his courage and offers his apartment to Ewa, but his change of mind is not entirely voluntary. He is shamed into rescuing Ewa by a virulently antisemitic character, Siciński, who volunteers to put his own life on the line to save her, even though he wants Poland to be free of Jews.

As Stanisław's initial refusal to help Ewa suggests, *Easter* is not a manifesto of idealized Polish behavior during the war. Moreover, the play takes up the uncomfortable question of Polish accommodation and even collaboration under German occupation. Przypkowski's colleague, Twardowski, a pharmacist who serves as a liaison between Jewish resistance organizations in Warsaw and in the provinces, is shocked that so many Poles have chosen to turn a blind eye to the German extermination of Jews. This callousness, he says, shows how "horribly debased" the Polish population has become.[49] Stanisław defensively replies that Polish reactions vary, but he does note how successfully consciences can be silenced if a ruthless will drives a policy of violent repression: "Apathetic, disgusting silence. It's as if everybody expected these things to happen. Nobody is really surprised. There are even some who are pleased. . . . What is life in Warsaw like these days? It's back to normal. An amusement park is being set up on Krasiński Square [just outside the ghetto]—a carousel, some swings."[50] He remarks that one should not underestimate the extent of the moral degradation by the corrupting effects of war and German occupation. At the same time, however, he recognizes that many of those who might have attempted to aid Jews are held back by fear—not of Germans, but of their Polish neighbors: "Everybody is afraid of everybody else. People are afraid to help because provocateurs, informers, and extortionists are everywhere."⁵¹

While Twardowski, Przypkowski, and (eventually) Stanisław declare solidarity with, and support for, Jews, two of the characters—Siciński and Przypkowski's housekeeper—are openly antisemitic. Siciński, a spokesman for aggressive, hateful nationalism, is attracted to the Nazi vision of racial purity. Before the war, he embraced the Nazi racial theory and called for the expulsion of Jews from Poland. He now welcomes the Nazi extermination of Jews: "This, finally, will solve our major internal problem: the Jewish question."⁵² Whereas Siciński's antisemitism is grounded in nationalist and racist prejudices, the housekeeper's antisemitism is religiously motivated. She shares the belief, historically promulgated by the Catholic Church, that the responsibility for the crucifixion of Jesus lay with the Jewish people. And yet neither Siciński nor the housekeeper balks when Ewa asks for help. We are led to believe that people's beliefs and opinions are no prediction of their propensity to rescue Jews. In a critical moment, when Ewa needs a safe place to stay, antisemites act like philosemites, while the immediate reaction of a liberal-minded intellectual is an emphatic refusal to become involved.

What begins as an act of rescue becomes, by the final act, a love relationship between Ewa and Stanisław. The play, in other words, leaves us with a comforting image of the triumph of good over evil, hope over adversity, but it does so through a clichéd love plot. Admittedly, the plot line invites the audience to reflect on the possibility of courage, solidarity, friendship, and love in the most extreme and deadly circumstances. The problem is that the plot line threatens to reduce the play to a therapeutic, moralistic melodrama that naturalizes the Holocaust trauma into a conventionalized narrative.

To compound the problem, the plot line that puts us at ease is to a large extent predicated on a particular construction of Ewa and her family. The Freuds are assimilated Jews who no longer observe Jewish religious traditions.⁵³ And while they have no illusion that Jews (even Jews like themselves) can ever be smoothly integrated into Polish society, the Freuds refuse to emigrate when antisemitism intensifies in the 1930s. Ewa's mother answers Siciński's antisemitic grousing in 1938 by asserting her Polish belonging: "We were born here."⁵⁴ The Freuds, moreover, are presented as likable people: their personal qualities make them ideal good neighbors. In 1943, when Ewa needs help, Przypkowski makes the following argument to counter the presumptions of Siciński's antisemitic discourse that objectifies Jews as "the Jewish question" and Poland's "major internal problem": "[Ewa is] a smart and pleasant woman. Her whole family is like that. . . . A respectable family. They've always been kind to me. . . . They're not Poland's internal problem, but my next-door neighbors. They're not Jews, but people like us. Mrs. Freud [Ewa's mother] and I have lived here since childhood. Her maiden name is Rózia Margulies."[55]

This argument is undeniably moving. Przypkowski draws on his personal experience to show the ability of Poles and Jews to live with each other honestly and in comity. At the same time, however, Przypkowski's argument is deeply problematic. It is impossible to overlook slides in his reasoning. On the one hand, he locates the grounds for acceptance not in some abstract realm of liberal "tolerance," but in the constitution of a person's own identity: the Freuds are "people like us." On the other hand, he offers a representation of the Freuds that, while calling into question Siciński's dehumanizing, repressive discourse, nonetheless enforces its own repressive mode of expression. Przypkowski does not argue that there is no difference between Jews and Poles because we are all people. Instead, his acceptance of the Freuds depends on their character and behavior as individuals. He argues that the Freuds deserve respect and compassion because they have proven themselves as fully acculturated members of the Polish community. Such perceptions promote a construction of reality in which only Jews "like us" can be accepted by Polish society. By stressing this kind of commonality, Przypkowski's argument elides difference. In doing so, it precludes openness to those who are perceived as strangers because they are different. In order to be accepted, Przypkowski suggests, they would have to display qualities that overcome difference. Thus, he structures acceptance of Jews on a foundation that leaves dominant assumptions intact. His acceptance of the Freuds is synonymous not with acceptance of diversity, but with acceptance of those who do not challenge one's own self-fashioning.

This strategy of familiarizing the unfamiliar—that is, recasting the unfamiliar (and therefore threatening) in familiar terms, with which one can safely identify—is a conservative gesture. In adopting it, the play gives shelter to naive illusions of acceptance. One could argue, of course, that in the context of the mid-1940s, during a period marked by Polish violence against

Holocaust survivors, the play's message of eliding difference and "becoming one" was well suited to touch Polish audiences. But the construction of the Freuds' identity raises the question: Do any of the play's dramaturgical and rhetorical strategies allow for an articulation that does not confuse acceptance of difference with attempts to make others into facsimiles of oneself, but instead entails encounters or confrontations with others whose difference challenges one's own self-making? To address this question, it is necessary to consider the play's metastories.

Easter takes full advantage of the central theatrical paradox: a here-and-now that is not here and now. It transcends its place and time by deploying signs that metatheatrically orient us to a there-and-then. Chief among them is a statue of Kościuszko, located at the town's marketplace offstage. Invoked over and over again by the characters, the story of the statue becomes one of the play's major leitmotifs. We learn that it stands near an old well in which, according to legend, inebriated revelers drowned a Jewish man when he refused to yield to their abusive demands that he entertain them with his prayers. As Ewa puts it, the well is "a disturbing symbol of Polish-Jewish relations."[56] Built by the self-proclaimed democrat Twardowski in close proximity to the well, the Kościuszko monument has an agenda. Put simply, it is to counter the exclusionary nationalism of bigoted enemies of ethnic, cultural, and religious diversity by invoking the difficult task, often associated with Kościuszko, of fostering a distinctly radical and inclusive vision of democracy.

Given the prominence of the monument in the town's topography and cultural memory, moreover, it is not particularly surprising that the Polish characters, both major and minor, link the insurgency of 1943 with the events of 1794. "Just like back in 1794," says a local man about the launch of an uprising in the town's ghetto.[57] A local woman picks up the analogy: "He has stepped down from his monument."[58] And in the play's closing scene, Stanisław insists rather too insistently: "The Jewish people revived the Kościuszko tradition. . . . They burst the shackles of oppression."[59] From the perspective of the Polish characters, in other words, Jewish insurgents have been necessarily inspired by Kościuszko's heroism. And since the ghetto offensive unfolds to the sound of "La Varsovienne" ("Warszawianka"), a battle-song written and performed during the uprising of 1830, it is unavoidable to conclude that *Easter* consistently inscribes the ghetto revolt into the Polish insurgent tradition as a matter of course.[60]

As a result of these maneuvers, Otwinowski's text plays a risky game. On the one hand, *Easter* is an attempt to honor and commemorate the tragic heroism of ghetto fighters. By focusing on the resistance in a provincial ghetto, moreover, *Easter* expands cultural memory. That is to say, it challenges the widespread assumption that only the Warsaw ghetto rose up against Germans. On the other hand, *Easter* runs, indeed courts, the risk of ignoring a crucial difference between the circumstances in which the Jewish and Polish uprisings were fought: the exterminatory racism of Nazi ideology. In the Nazis' conception of Jews, they were not a regional obstacle to be swept out of the way, but a global enemy whose complete removal was vital to the very survival of the "Aryan" race. By situating the ghetto resistance firmly in the tradition of struggles for Poland's liberation, the play elides the incompatible and promulgates a polonocentric perspective. "If the Jewish people take up arms," declares Twardowski, "they will prove themselves heirs to Polish culture and history."[61] We are tacitly invited to complete this proposition: they did take up arms; therefore, they have earned the right to have the 1943 uprising regarded as a link in the chain of Polish freedom fighting.

Like the construction of the Freuds' identity, then, the construction of ghetto insurgents pivots on the notion of Jews "like us." Thus, *Easter* once again enforces a repressive mode of expression, a passing under extreme duress, so to speak. It diminishes the Jewishness of the ghetto uprising and instead subsumes the ghetto resistance under the Polish patriotic paradigm, represented by the Kościuszko monument and "La Varsovienne." *Easter*, in other words, makes acceptance of others deceptively easy because it represents them in terms that reinforce the Polish model.

I cannot leave this interpretation, however, without specifying the circumstances of Samuel Freud's death. Unlike his sister, Ewa, he refuses to seek shelter on the "Aryan" side. Instead, he resolves to remain in the town's ghetto where he has been involved in an underground organization. Once a deportation of Jews from the ghetto to a death camp is inevitable, he leads an attack against German troops, but is trapped in a space between the well and the Kościuszko monument, where he fights to the last. Rather than surrender or turn his gun upon himself, he jumps into the well and drowns. In doing so, he chooses to identify with an anonymous Jewish man, a victim of antisemitic prejudice. The scene at the well, in other words, restores to the tragic heroism of the ghetto uprising the specificity that can be lost when Jewish suffering and resistance are too glibly naturalized into Polish patriotic narratives.

As I have argued, one metastory of *Easter* attempts to establish continuity between the events of 1794 and 1943. This rhetorical and dramaturgical project is so insistent and suggestive, as well as flattering to Polish audiences, that one could miss the significance of Samuel's decision to control what is still his: the terms of his death. The play's other metastory depends on a baffling connection between the here-and-now and the Protestant Reformation.

Apart from Siciński, all the leading male characters are associated with the Reformation through either their ancestry or their intellectual interests. Stanisław is a descendant of Jan Łaski (1499–1560), a Polish-born Protestant churchman, theologian, and reformer, known in the West as John à Lasco. During the reign of Edward VI, à Lasco served as a superintendent at a Protestant church in London, achieving recognition as one of the earliest proponents of a more democratic form of church government. When the Reformation of Henry VIII and Edward VI gave way to Mary Tudor's Counter-Reformation on her accession to the throne in 1553, à Lasco's congregations disbanded, and he fled to the continent. His legacy, however, survived into the Elizabethan period, and his liturgy of public repentance has been absorbed into the Reformed, Presbyterian, and Puritan traditions.[62]

That *Easter* seeks to establish a connection between the here-and-now and the Protestant Reformation is also readable from the fact that the family lineage of Stanisław's uncle can be traced to Samuel Przypkowski (ca. 1592–1670), a member of the Polish Brethren, an antitrinitarian religious group within the Radical Reformation.[63] While the Brethren denied the divinity of Christ and abandoned the doctrine of the Trinity, they adopted "the Laskian emphasis on the threefold office of Christ" as prophet, priest, and king.[64] If one considers, moreover, that Stanisław, Twardowski, and Samuel Freud have done research on the history of the Protestant Reformation in Poland and that Stanisław is charged with completing Samuel's project after his death, it would be an understatement to say that the Protestant Reformation is important to a fuller understanding of the play.

On first reading, the reasons for this sustained attention to the Reformation are not difficult to identify. Because Poland's vigorous participation in the Reformation in the sixteenth and early seventeenth centuries has since fallen into obscurity, *Easter* reminds the audience, again and again, that Poland produced an internationally recognized religious reformer whose commitment to tolerance set an example for West Europeans.[65] The characters proudly acknowledge à Lasco's enduring contribution to the Reformation in Western Europe; Twardowski even insists that à Lasco is a household name in England. The story of à Lasco, in turn, serves as shorthand for a larger story of cultural and religious diversity. That is to say, the play reminds an audience increasingly forgetful of its multicultural and multireligious heritage about a plurality of cultural and religious traditions that characterized the Polish-Lithuanian Commonwealth. In doing so, the play attempts to harness this admirable aspect of a distant past to further an agenda for the future. Written at a time when Polishness continued to be perceived and defended as a fixed identity, in other words, *Easter* invites its Polish readers and spectators to consider that their heritage stems not simply from one taproot, but from a congeries of pasts. It is extremely reductive, the play suggests, to validate public and private memories and to construct self-identities solely through a single-minded obsession with one thread of the Polish past rather than through awareness of the whole patchwork quilt. Or, to put the same point somewhat differently, the play encourages the audience to view a static and monolithic concept of Polishness skeptically and instead to imagine Polishness in more dynamic terms, as a process of historical accumulation involving many different sites of identity. Within the play's particular discursive domain, then, to be a patriotic man or woman is to support values such as tolerance and respect for difference, rather than uphold a homogeneous and exclusivist notion of cultural identity.

Yet there is another side to Otwinowski's drama that complicates this interpretation. In a conversation with Stanisław, Samuel offers a potted account of à Lasco's activism, but he insists, curiously, on using a plural category: "à Lascoes," or reformers who "were compelled to emigrate for advocating universal democracy and absolute pacifism."[66] The historical record tells a different story: à Lasco neither supported "universal democracy and absolute pacifism" nor was persecuted for his ideas and expelled from Poland. These details, however, fit the history of the Polish Brethren. The Brethren were committed to social equality and in some cases freed their serfs, thus threatening the accepted social order. They also advocated pacifism, although they did make an exception for defending one's country against invasions. For their radical beliefs, religious as well as social, they experienced intolerance firsthand. In 1659, they were declared heretics and compelled to leave Poland on pain of death, or to convert to Catholicism. Samuel's category "à Lascoes," then, ties loosely together a bundle of discrete biographies to construct a composite image of nonconformists who were perceived as a theological, social, and cultural threat and who might have seen themselves as foreigners to others in the land they shared. This composite image, in turn, may even serve as a reminder that in the Catholic Church's arduous struggle to assert its religious hegemony, anti-Jewish stereotypes and accusations were regularly deployed to combat Protestants as well as Jews.[67] With the details about intolerance and persecution, the play retracts the gesture of appealing to the audience's sense of cultural pride, which it has extended through the characters' lines about à Lasco's achievements. But the fact that the text needs à Lasco both as a successful champion of tolerance and as a member of the persecuted "à Lascoes" makes it clear that Otwinowski was deeply suspicious of the Polish mystique of exclusive, unique, and superior heritage; therefore it was important to him not to elide the paradox involved in his construction of a usable past.

It is evident by now that *Easter* is a play that cannot be read except through multiple lenses, and in this respect it calls on readers to be extremely self-conscious about what they are bringing to the reading of the text. However, despite Otwinowski's elaborate rhetorical and dramaturgical maneuvers to address the vexed topic of Polish reactions to, and treatment of, the Jewish minority, to reclaim patriotism from chauvinist usurpations, and to engage his audiences, including those who were determined to see themselves solely as heroes and victims, in a self-critical inquiry into their national history and collective self-image, the persuasive powers of his play proved elusive when it was performed in 1946. In Łódź, *Easter* met with a mixed reception.[68] While some audience members applauded Otwinowski for addressing issues that all too often were passed over in silence, others, offended by the play, were keen to charge him with unfairness toward Poles. In the words of one spectator, *Easter* "is too critical of Poles.... I personally had many Jewish friends when I was young, and I am not antisemitic. Besides, I understand Jews very well. But I'm Polish, and I don't agree with many aspects of this play. They are unfair. We all make mistakes."[69] Still others hurled invectives at the author, the director, and the cast. Given Kościuszko's close association with Kraków, the city where he launched the 1794 insurrection, where he met with Jews in the Old Synagogue to appeal to their patriotism, and where he is buried, one would have thought that the Kościuszko theme would make *Easter* more acceptable to the audience in Kraków, but that was not the case.[70] The response was overwhelmingly hostile.[71]

In the immediate aftermath of the war, when Polish society was torn by political conflict, Otwinowski's ambitious project—his attempt to address uncomfortable issues, to restore complexity to Polish constructions of historical memory, understanding, and meaning, and to recover a concept of patriotism that refuses to assess the validity of a person's patriotic loyalty and engagement on the basis of his or her ethnicity or religion—fell largely on the deafest of deaf ears. The cataclysms of political life engendered, as they often do, a nostalgia for certainty and security—in this case, for the static closure of some idealistic vision of cultural purity, some essential Polishness, that would provide a reassuring shelter from flux. And so began a process by which *Easter* vanished from public conversation. First, it was sidelined and ignored. Then, the presumption of its artistic inferiority took hold. Erased from the literary history of the Holocaust, Otwinowski's play, along with his essays, has joined an invisible archive of the early literature on the destruction of European Jews. The continuing invisibility of this archive allows new generations of writers and readers "to feel profoundly scandalized by the presumed silence of those who came before."[72]

IV.

More than four decades later, Anna Bojarska structured her play, suggestively entitled *The Polish Lesson*, around a series of questions: What exactly is "my country" that patriots claim to love? What are the duties or practical implications of patriotism? Doesn't the sheer variety of ways to test patriotic sentiments (and of ways to cheat on a test) undermine rather than support the idea of a shared, stable, and knowable patriotism? Isn't it unpatriotic to insist that patriotic allegiance ought to be unquestioning and uncritical? Isn't it unpatriotic to bury disagreeable aspects of patriotic narratives under the shibboleths of national triumphalism and self-celebration? Isn't it unpatriotic to let selective memory prevail, deliberately deleting all mention of taboos? These are not comfortable questions, and *The Polish Lesson* is not a comfortable play. To explore these questions, Bojarska turned, rather provocatively, to Kościuszko, the quintessential Polish hero of liberty.

Before examining Bojarska's play, written in 1988, it may be helpful to comment briefly on a major attempt by another dramatist to enlist Kościuszko in a reconsideration of patriotism just ten years earlier: Jerzy S. Sito's *Polonaise (Polonez)*. Focusing on the circumstances of the second partition of the Polish-Lithuanian Commonwealth in 1793, *Polonaise* offers a powerful example of an application play, or a dramatic work that exists on two levels: that of the historical events represented and that of the current situation disguised as the past.[73] The final scene introduces the character of Kościuszko, who contends that the disaster of foreign occupation is not a cause but "a symptom" of Poland's ills.[74] While the other characters recite the old familiar charges about the wavering Stanisław August, the venal Polish magnates, and the imperialist designs of Catherine II and her advisers, Kościuszko insists that the time has come to put the blame for the partitions where it properly belongs: dysfunctional Polish society. He is ruthlessly honest in his assessment of his compatriots. No one is spared; everyone is held accountable for the fall of Poland. Kościuszko argues that the material and cultural inequalities of Polish society have created a space in which it is possible for those who have experienced marginalization and disempowerment to remain oblivious to the whole issue of Poland's sovereignty, while others have turned to Russia for military aid to suppress political and social reforms. To begin to confront Poland's unfreedom, then, it is necessary to break through the passivity and skepticism of peasants and other commoners and to battle against social prejudice for a more egalitarian Poland, or, as he puts it, to recognize that "the words *human being* refer to a king, a nobleman, and a peasant."[75] Until this recognition seeps through the groundwater of Polish culture, "it's best to bury our swords because they'll be useless."[76] And yet Kościuszko agrees to prepare for armed struggle against Russia to undo the partition of 1793. He is not optimistic about the outcome of the uprising, but he suggests that even a doomed insurgency can be a catalyst for social and political change. In short, the potential for a future victory "lies dormant even in the worst defeats."[77] *Polonaise*, however, is not a triumphalist assertion of the agency of the masses. In what is arguably the most compelling moment in the entire play, Kościuszko is alone on the stage, silently gazing at the audience, as if uncertain whether he can count on popular support for his radical commitment to democratic values and emancipatory politics.

First published in 1978, *Polonaise* was cleared for production only in the fall of 1980, when the Solidarity movement won a considerable relaxation of censorship restrictions. It opened at the Ateneum Theatre in Warsaw on 17 January 1981. The timing of the premiere, however, could not have been less fortuitous. The play's critique of a passive and indifferent population, along with its refusal to provide a comforting opposition of the virtuous "us" and the evil "them," found little favor among spectators during the heady months when the Solidarity movement was at its height.[78]

Sito's play presents a Kościuszko who is about to take the field against Russian occupation. For her own play, Bojarska has chosen what seems to be the least interesting part of Kościuszko's biography: his retreat from public life and his twilight years spent in obscurity. Like the historical Kościuszko, Bojarska's Kościuszko settles into austere retirement in Soleure, Switzerland, after the Congress of Vienna. *The Polish Lesson* shows a man who, until recently, believed that the fall of Napoleon created a congenial political situation to work toward full autonomy, under Russian protection, for the partitioned lands of the Polish-Lithuanian Commonwealth. Convinced that Alexander I may be sympathetic to this idea, he wrote him urgent letters during the Congress of Vienna, but was rebuffed. After the reactionary Holy Alliance has been launched by Alexander I at the Congress, Kościuszko withdraws from politics to cultivate his garden. For Bojarska's Kościuszko, cultivating his garden involves tutoring a young Swiss woman, Emilie Zeltner, and discovering or, rather, rediscovering love and passion. Much of the play focuses on this enigmatic relationship between them.[79]

At first glance, *The Polish Lesson* appears very modest. Written as an extended debate between Kościuszko and Emilie, it is a two-act drama with an epilogue, in a single domestic setting, in linear time. The play's mode is essentially realistic: there are no soliloquies, asides, alter egos, split or simultaneous scenes, or surreal effects. The only action is rearranging furniture, dancing a waltz, singing a few songs, making coffee, and embroidering. As I will argue, Bojarska may have chosen a conventional realistic frame for her characters, but it is no more than a frame. What matters is what is inside, and that is blazingly radical.

Completed by mid-1988, *The Polish Lesson* was accepted for production at the Powszechny Theatre in Warsaw.[80] Andrzej Wajda, who offered to direct it, and Tadeusz Łomnicki, who took the role of Kościuszko, convinced the company that the play should go into rehearsal without delay. In a society torn by political conflict and strained by economic hardships, they argued, the production would be extremely timely.[81] *The Polish Lesson* opened on 28 September 1988, a month after Poland's nearly bankrupt economy and a rising strike wave forced reformists in the Communist Party to meet with Solidarity representatives and bargain over trade-offs to stabilize the situation. Well received when it first opened, the production took on new relevance in the spring of 1989, after protracted round-table negotiations between the Communist Party and Solidarity cleared the way for a semifree parliamentary election in which only the Senate seats were to be freely contested, while 65 percent of the seats in the House of Representatives were set aside for the ruling coalition of the Communist Party and its satellite parties. The election was scheduled for 4 June. In May, Solidarity poured its energy into a vigorous election campaign. Tens of thousands of volunteers donated their time, services, and resources (e.g., cars and telephones).[82] One of the volunteers was Joanna Szczepkowska who played the female lead in *The Polish Lesson*. The production attracted packed houses. At many performances, the final curtain call served as an impromptu minirally, uniting actors, technical crew, and audience in a celebration of the recent triumphs of the opposition, epitomized by the relegalization of Solidarity on 17 April.

For the audiences who came to see *The Polish Lesson* in 1988–89, it was not easy to discard their ressentiments and to bracket off the play from the strains and stresses of Poland's political circumstances, past and present. They applauded heartily all the lines that were thought to characterize Poland as a victim of injustice and humiliation at the hands of foreign invaders, to express outrage about Russia's interference in Poland's affairs, and to deride the self-consciously calculating opportunism of the West. Kościuszko's caustic comment—"Poles are getting killed; West Europeans worry about job security"—was greeted with a particularly enthusiastic applause.[83] Emilie's rapturous address to Poland—"I'd like to learn Polish because I want to understand everything! You can't understand the world if you don't understand Poland"—often received a prolonged standing ovation.[84]

It would be tempting to attribute such effusions to the spectators' reductive understanding of the play: they missed the characters' hyperbole, irony, and self-parody, and therefore they construed *The Polish Lesson* to be about a Manichaean contest between good and evil in European politics. Wajda's staging, however, explicitly encouraged reductive reactions.[85] In particular, he either toned down or eliminated the play's inconvenient aspects that might have offended spectators used to the marmoreal luster of the received image of Kościuszko as Poland's national hero par excellence and accustomed to a glossier version of the cultural scripts that had come to define Polish identity. Examples abound. Bojarska's Kościuszko is a virtuoso of savage indignation whose belligerent lines are used to drily ironic effect. Wajda's production, in contrast, offered a gentler, unambiguously sympathetic Kościuszko: one of those rare beings, in other words, who are as likable as they are impressive. In the play, Kościuszko's Polish admirers who visit his home in Soleure after his death come across as blustering bigots: they nervously dismiss his private departures from the magisterial masculinity of the national hero, so that they can bask complacently in his reflected glory. In the production, the bigots were replaced with characters who are to be trusted and respected. In the play, Polish noblemen treat a Polish peasant with aristocratic hauteur. On the stage, the nobles were conscientiously unsnobbish. Moreover, the nobles and the peasant were equalized by virtue of wearing nondescript black dress, an emblem of their shared grief for Kościuszko, instead of class-specific costumes. The production thus conveyed a belief that at the heart of Polish culture there is a powerful bond—a sense of patriotic togetherness—that transcends the hierarchies of social status and authority. This belief was reinforced by projecting onto the backcloth, again and again, the solidaristic scene from the *Racławice* panorama—the scene that depicts Kościuszko leading his scythe-wielding peasant recruits in a bold attack on Russian batteries.

Interwoven with the theme of social solidarity was one of hope. While Bojarska's play offers a portrait of an idealist confronting, and ultimately defeated by, the minutiae of realpolitik, Wajda's staging repeatedly shifted the focus from the aged Kościuszko, whose hour on the stage of history is over, to the morale-boosting scene immortalized by the *Racławice* panorama. On the most obvious level, the dominant inscription of one of the most celebrated triumphs of the nation's glory within the act of theatre conveyed an upbeat affirmation of the national past. On a deeper level, the inscription vouchsafed hope by encouraging an optimistically totalizing reading of Polish patriotism. That is to say, the inscription of the *Racławice* panorama within the here-and-now of a theatrical performance invited spectators to understand their own leap for freedom in the 1980s as a way of honoring a cultural script of historical continuities that transmit the

Polish liberationist legacy, symbolized by Kościuszko's dazzling victory over foreign invaders.[86] To put this point yet another way, Wajda's production expressed a belief in the enduring virtues of Polish cultural heritage, uncorrupted even by communist indoctrination. And by juxtaposing the Poles' selfless and steadfast commitment to the cause of liberty with the Western pursuit of pragmatism and profit, the production amounted to a glowing tribute to Poland as the nonpareil of the nations in Europe.

The production's most obvious attraction, then, was Wajda's adroit expenditure from the man-myth Kościuszko's deposit account in the national memory to unite the true lovers of their country, to flatter them by playing into their romanticized self-image, and to fuel "the enveloping haze of patriotic self-congratulation" (to borrow E. P. Thompson's phrase).[87] He directed Bojarska's drama in quite express anticipation of the audiences' expectations that a work entitled *The Polish Lesson* would unequivocally show that there is something grand and enduring that makes Poland Polish. At a time when Solidarity began to reassert its leadership in oppositional politics, Wajda's concession to conventional expectations seemed unavoidable. Such concession, however, was bought at the price of strategic silences on the thorny issues posed by Bojarska's text. While the production catered to a glamorized version of Polish history, the play adopts a transgressive stance. While the production fostered collective pride and hope by offering an inspiring view of the national character and mission and by emphasizing the superiority of the Polish ethos over Western pragmatism and mercantilism, the play ironically deploys national iconography to encourage a radical expansion of vision. And while the production stressed the uplifting aspects of the Kościuszko story, the play attempts to break through the incense and routinized homage that have surrounded Kościuszko. By avoiding well-trodden ground, Bojarska offers to the audience an invitation to move beyond long-standing, and often dated and constricting, cultural templates and assumptions. The central question she addresses is not: What is uniquely Polish about Kościuszko and his patriotism? Rather, she asks: What is patriotism? What does it mean to be a patriot? She perhaps even goes so far as to ask: Is patriotism worth it?

The epilogue, in which a group of Poles visits Kościuszko's Swiss home after his death, provides a useful place to begin my analysis of the play. In this episode, Bojarska turns to satire, which enables her not only to mock facile opinions about Kościuszko but also to anatomize the opinionated.

This approach is perhaps most evident when the Polish visitors meet Emilie Zeltner. Flattered that the Zeltners maintain Kościuszko's home-turned-museum with loving care, they gloat: "The world knows about us. The world remembers us."[88] This line, of course, is a narcissistic overstatement. Given the context, it would be more accurate to say: "The world knows about Kościuszko. The world remembers Kościuszko." The slippage from Kościuszko to "us" reveals that the Polish visitors have cast him as an embodiment of the "collective soul" of the nation (to use a well-worn phrase). To their discomfort, however, Kościuszko's worshipful admirers learn from Emilie that he was not uncomplicatedly "masculine," as might be expected. Instead, he willingly identified across gender lines, taking up crocheting and embroidering. The Polish visitors might have concluded, say, that Kościuszko possessed a unique mix of "masculine" charismatic authority and "feminine" sensibility, but they defensively protest that he could not have practiced needlework. As their unease and scorn make it clear, they perceive needlework as an activity that does not become a man, let alone a national hero. Something else is at issue too. The Polish visitors have no need for a masculine-feminine Kościuszko because their vision of Polishness is defined in masculine terms, even though they insist on a Kościuszko who represents "us" or the Polish community in its entirety. In short, they are unable to make a spot for him on the more flexible terms of gender identity that he demands. This is one of the issues to which I return later.

The critical view of the self-aggrandizing investments in the national "we," conveyed through satire in the epilogue, is also the view that Kościuszko articulates in acts 1 and 2. He concedes that some segments of Polish society have warmed to the idea of patriotic service more readily than others, but he harbors no illusions about Polish patriotic devotion. In 1794, he insists, the duty of all true patriots to defend Poland should have remained absolute and unqualified even after he fell into Russian hands in the battle of Maciejowice. He found, however, that there were limits to Poles' willingness to make sacrifices for their country. More than twenty years later, he is still outraged by his compatriots, blaming them for the lost uprising and therefore for the fall of Poland: "It was still possible to turn everything around. We lost a battle, not the war. . . . And what did the Poles do? They wrote a new prayer! . . . They wept and prayed. . . . Does this country deserve to be free?! . . . Look how quietly Poland accepted foreign occupation! Who knows, maybe these people don't even care whether they're Poles or Russians."[89]

Balancing the books on the 1794 insurgency, Kościuszko concludes that history, at best, opens up opportunities that one does or does not grasp. He is convinced that those opportunities were squandered in Poland: even a national emergency could not rouse many Poles out of their self-absorbed lethargy. Looking ahead to the future, he sees yet another problem. There can be no impetus for Polish independence, he argues, unless all the oppressed peoples of Eastern Europe join forces to fight against tyranny, but this idea is not popular among Poles: they are unwilling or unable to recognize that they should look beyond their narrow political interests. The insurrection of 1794, he says, also taught him a few things about leadership: a leader must always be approachable and modest in demeanor; he must know how to act with affability and avoid all displays of hauteur and arrogance; he must never act contemptuously toward his social inferiors because this kind of behavior breeds hatred and often leads to unrest and rebellion. At the same time, however, he makes some very strange suggestions: that a compromise can be a good bargain; that honor may be a form of weakness; that ruthlessness may be a kind of probity, and in its clear-sightedness may even generate more public good than honor is likely to; that success and failure alter the moral dimensions of any worldly action. In short, "You should try to be a rat, if you can't be an eagle."[90] These suggestions seem more appropriate for a moral skeptic than a man who claims that he sought to rise above the compromises and corruptions of politics.

By now it is evident that Bojarska's Kościuszko, despite his aversion to tyranny and his commitment to liberty, is more spectacle than inspiration. It is true that, for all his finger-pointing, he is not interested in inflating himself to become a marble man. When his youthful love, Ludwika Sosnowska, sends him a ring engraved with the words "To Virtue, from Friendship," he shrugs his shoulders and puts it away.[91] Moreover, one might balance his harsh assessment of Polish society with his dark view of all human relationships: "Anyone can be a traitor. You can't trust anybody."[92] Admittedly, he is a man crippled by defeat. He lived history with a capital "H," but living history exacts a heavy emotional toll, especially when it does not appear to be moving one's way. His ordeals ravaged him, and his dashed hopes inevitably result in frustration, bitterness, and moral skepticism, if not outright cynicism. But his grievances are unduly acrimonious; his resentments, overly pedantic; his censure of Polish society, too rancorous and uncompromising; and his vision of human nature, too scornful and unsparing. In short, the play shows a misanthrope with a vocation for taking offense. For audiences who have learned to revere Kościuszko as an icon of Polish excellence, the effect can be chilling.

Bojarska's whole effort in *The Polish Lesson* can be understood as a series of double-edged strategies to perturb the smugness and self-admiration that undergird the cult of national heroes. The problem, of course, is that she seems to overdo her revisionist project. There is much to lose by presenting a frustrated, embittered, even cynical Kościuszko. It can be easy to shrug off his obsessive insistence that his compatriots' self-interest trumps patriotic self-sacrifice and to conclude that most of his set-piece speeches are no more than an old man's ranting. After all, even his clothing looks as if it were lifted from an old farce. One can therefore perhaps fault Bojarska for abiding by a relentlessly critical approach that does not allow for any possibility of constructive closure. This is an appropriate point at which to take up the question of Emilie's role in the play.

What did or did not happen between Kościuszko and his young student in the years when he rented a room in her parents' house? Bojarska is scrupulous in assuming no more about Kościuszko's relations with Emilie than the sparse evidence warrants, but she does ask us to imagine the limbo-like existence Emilie was now leading as a result of her father's botched career as the mayor of Soleure during the Napoleonic Wars. Francis Xavier Zeltner lost his fortune and his reputation, and the family suffered the humiliation of a downward social spiral. If we focus too closely on Kościuszko in *The Polish Lesson,* in other words, we might miss that much of the play is not about the venerated national hero, but about the younger generation, represented by his Swiss student. The insistent presence of this young woman suggests that the play's main concern is with intergenerational dynamics rather than with Kościuszko "as such." To develop my argument about the importance of intergenerational dynamics to a more complex understanding of *The Polish Lesson,* I want first to consider the full implications of Kościuszko's withdrawal from public life and responsibility in the play.

After the Congress of Vienna, Kościuszko becomes skeptical about European governments and the possibility of useful political change. Moreover, he becomes pessimistic about the possibility, at least in Europe, of large-scale changes in human attitudes. He sees the present not so much as a decline from the past, nor as the end of a cycle, but as a complete inversion of the ideals of civilization, a final uncreation of the good society. This perception means that he is unable to see any prospect of reversing this trend, any political action that would avert decay. Europe, in his view, is hopelessly disrupted. To Kościuszko in his last years, the only viable option left is personal retreat. Of the various solutions open to him, of the various means, such as accepting Jefferson's invitation to settle in America, of avoiding the consequences of what he sees as an incurable European society and its inverted values, he takes the path that involves an abandonment of a public role and a turn to privacy. His concerns become increasingly private, with the living of his own life on the terms he could maintain in spite of society, rather than with the reestablishment of a society in which his proper public role could be fulfilled.

While Kościuszko's rejection of a new Europe is rather predictable within the world of the play, the political solution he has created from this negative stance is shrouded by an enigma that awaits decoding. A key to this political solution can be found in Kościuszko's comment in act 2 that he has abandoned Rousseau for ancient Roman writers. Kościuszko makes this comment during an impassioned argument with Napoleon's devotee, General Franciszek Paszkowski. Kościuszko and Paszkowski disagree in their assessment of Napoleon. Kościuszko points out that he never welcomed Napoleon's rise to power precisely because he regarded him as "an arrogant careerist" who "crushed freedom" in Europe.[93] Paszkowski takes issue with Kościuszko's distrust of Napoleon, insisting that Napoleon was genuinely sympathetic to the full restoration of Polish independence. In the course of their political debate, Paszkowski asks Kościuszko, rather incongruously, whether he has heard from Sosnowska. Paszkowski has clearly touched a nerve, for Kościuszko overreacts. At first, he answers curtly that she has sent him a ring he never wears. Yet a moment later he plunges into an angry diatribe: "I no longer care for idyllic love stories. I'm no longer moved by romantic plots. I can no longer stand those books dripping with tears. Rousseau! I used to love Rousseau! I used to be moved to tears by Rousseau! Now I'm disgusted with him. . . . [I now read] ancient Roman writers."[94] It would be naive to take this outburst at face value. It is significant that Kościuszko admits to having received a ring from Sosnowska, yet he withholds from Paszkowski the fact of her sentimental journey to Soleure.[95] One senses, in other words, that Kościuszko's feelings about his unfulfilled youthful love for Sosnowska are necessarily ambivalent. Sosnowska has married another man; Kościuszko is in love with Emilie. But his outburst in response to Paszkowski's prying question suggests that Rousseau's *Julie, or the New Heloise* (*Julie, ou la nouvelle Héloïse*, 1761), Kościuszko's irritated denial notwithstanding, still has a powerful hold over him precisely because it reminds him of his own love wound that has never healed. In Rousseau's novel, Saint-Preux is in love with Julie d'Etanges, but when her father insists that she marry Monsieur de Wolmar, Julie sacrifices her love for Saint-Preux to her daughterly obedience. Years later, Saint-Preux returns to visit the couple, still cherishing his love for Julie.

While recognizing an all-too-obvious parallel between Saint-Preux and Kościuszko, however, I want to argue that for the Kościuszko of Bojarska's play, in his withdrawal from the public sphere, *Julie* resonates differently from the way it did when he was an impecunious young man tutoring Sosnowska, an aristocratic woman far beyond his modest social sphere, and suffering the pains of love for her. He may no longer have any need for the love plots of *Julie* and other "books dripping with tears," but he has internalized their deeply felt lesson in imagined empathy, along with a new model of human relations, a new phenomenology of self and other. As literary and cultural historians have pointed out, *Julie* and other epistolary novels of private lives and loves, such as Samuel Richardson's *Pamela* (1740) and *Clarissa Harlowe* (1747), encouraged readers to identify with a weak female character who struggled to preserve her autonomy and integrity against various forms of domestic oppression. Such novels allowed readers to peep over the shoulders of supposedly real letter-writers and to imagine themselves in their place. By creating strong bonds of empathy and identification between readers and female characters, the genre of the epistolary novel helped the former to understand that all humans resembled the latter on a fundamental level and that all humans intrinsically possessed natural, equal rights.[96]

Now that Bojarska's Kościuszko has turned his back on the world of political involvement, the "books dripping with tears" are a tool helping him define a new role for himself in a society he deplores. In other words, *The Polish Lesson* traces not only Kościuszko's turn to privacy, but also, and more importantly, his self-discovery. Kościuszko discovers himself by withdrawing from public life and responsibility and by breaking with inflexible imperatives such as freedom-or-death.[97] At the same time, he discovers that a private ethic—maintaining one's own integrity, living an honorable private life—is the only way to defeat, though in a necessarily limited and private manner, the effects of a disrupted society and an uncongenial political situation.

While Cato, the classic hero of liberty, used his suicide to communicate his exemplary dedication to the principle of liberty and to demonstrate his moral qualification, in the act of dying, to comment on the political condition of the Roman republic, Bojarska's Kościuszko uses his withdrawal to the provinces as a form of communication. Having spent a lifetime demonstrating his own courage to die on the battlefield, he now makes a deliberate choice to learn how to live in what he sees as an incurable Europe. His choice, in other words, involves a reversal of the Catonian treatment of death as the ultimate test of our courage or convictions. For Kościuszko in his winter years, it is life—and specifically, daily life, uneventful and tedious—that should be the ultimate test of our courage or convictions. Pessimistic about European society and the possibility of large-scale useful political change, he puts his faith in a private ethic and accepts the smallness of the individual's sphere of action. Where large solutions are unavailable, the only answer is a limited one: a commitment to effect good quietly in one's community.

In his self-created role at Soleure, while cultivating a private ethic, Kościuszko broadens the scope of his tutorials with Emilie, in whom he senses a kindred spirit: an ambitious, willful, even rebellious individual who thinks for herself and can never suppress her tendency to bluntness. At a time when girls were instructed to be sweet and gracious to powerful men, Emilie refuses to defer to Kościuszko. Instead, she challenges him to engage in a political debate with her. Boldly, brazenly even, she confronts him with hard, probing questions, sometimes articulating the same questions with which he was wrestling before he met her. Why did so many Poles collaborate with the enemy? Why didn't anyone attempt to rescue him after the Maciejowice disaster, when he was transported across eastern Poland to a prison in Russia? Didn't his compatriots want Poland to be free? In broaching these questions, Kościuszko formulates mentoring advice for Emilie. This advice may be summed up in five sentences: Don't make power an end in itself or use it excessively. Win allies and supporters by refusing to humiliate others, but be aware that anyone can be a traitor. Be determined and persistent, yet cautious. If you cannot use force, buy yourself crucial time by weighing other means of action, including political compromise. Remember that in a ruthlessly competitive world nothing succeeds like success.

The problem, of course, is that Kościuszko's advice is misaddressed. Ignoring the constraints of gender roles upon women, he mentors Emilie as if she were a young man destined for a political career. Not surprisingly, Emilie reminds him that her opportunities are extremely limited. One could argue, then, that by offering Emilie gender-blind mentoring, Kościuszko is myopically unaware of his society's dichotomous gender order. His mentoring advice serves only to highlight the possibilities that are beyond the reach of his student and other young women during his era.

But a different reading is possible as well. Kościuszko's mentoring of Emilie represents admirable striving against social prejudice, condescension, and limited expectations. What implicitly matters to him is not that the American revolutionaries did not even consider granting political rights to women, or that the French revolutionaries did consider this idea, only scornfully to deny it. For Bojarska's Kościuszko, the very idea of equal rights lays the groundwork for later liberation of those who have been denied those rights. Within the scope of his tutorials with Emilie, he establishes an "as if" alternative society. That is to say, he creates an alternative space where this young woman behaves as if she already lived in a society that does not discriminate on the basis of gender. In breaking with inflexible gender imperatives and in revising gendered social codes within the admittedly modest scope of his tutorials, he takes on a project whose significance extends beyond the present moment and the supposedly private, intimate sphere of home. Read in this context, the title, *The Polish Lesson,* becomes ironic. Instead of offering a lesson in what many have perceived as unique Polish virtues—honor, military courage, heroic sacrifice—embodied in the magisterially masculine Kościuszko, the play presents a Kościuszko who asserts his difference from a society in which masculinity has defined the norm.

V.

While *The Polish Lesson* continued to play in the spring of 1989, it remained an open question whether the deteriorating economy and social discontent constituted sufficient political capital to assure Solidarity a significant victory in the forthcoming parliamentary election. The semifree election, or what Wałęsa has aptly called "the thirty-five-percent democracy," was not necessarily an appealing option to voters who had lost confidence in the electoral process.[98] And yet the election, while less than fully democratic, provided an unprecedented opportunity to limit the Communist Party's control over the legislative process. As Wałęsa puts it,

> We had to do everything possible to squeeze through the crack that had opened for us, or else we would never break down the monolithic Communist rock and move beyond it.... In keeping with the principles agreed upon at the Round Table, ... the Senate would be in a position to reject any legislation that it judged harmful to the nation. There was leverage there.
>
> For such legislation to be enacted, it would first have to receive a two-thirds majority vote in the Sejm [i.e., the House of Representatives], or 66 percent. But it could not get that percentage if the 35 percent representing Solidarity voted against it.
>
> We had to win that 35 percent.[99]

In short, to win the 35 percent was to consolidate Solidarity's bargaining power beyond the round-table agreements.

Solidarity activists did not underestimate voters' skepticism and apathy or their disdain for electoral politics.[100] As Roger Boyes notes, "Solidarity was far from confident about the outcome of the election."[101] To win the 35 percent, then, it was imperative to convince voters that change could be effected through Poland's limited democracy, that Solidarity was indeed a viable alternative to the ruling coalition, and that it deserved their vote. To that end, Solidarity mounted a dynamic and well-organized election campaign. Since the communist establishment still controlled radio and television, Solidarity had to rely on other venues.

To publicize Solidarity candidates, Wałęsa had himself photographed with each of them. The photographs, used on election posters, gave instant recognition to all the members of what was widely called "Wałęsa's team." They also projected an attractive sense of solidarity within Solidarity. This sense of a unified community was Solidarity's "great trump card, which the movement exploited ceaselessly" during the election campaign.[102] To put these points differently, the posters of Wałęsa's team served to promote "the principle of dramaturgical unity" (to invoke Paweł Śpiewak's ironic phrase).[103] The insistence on the principle of dramaturgical unity, which the Solidarity campaign observed even at the cost of the democratic procedures that were within its reach, was most evident in the fact that the Solidarity leadership rejected the idea, proposed by some of its advisers (such as

Aleksander Hall and Tadeusz Mazowiecki), that Solidarity candidates compete with one another for every seat in Parliament allocated to the Solidarity movement; instead, there was only one Solidarity candidate for each available seat.

Wałęsa himself did not stand for a seat in Parliament, but he tirelessly crisscrossed the country, canvassing for Solidarity candidates with his typical élan and folksy humor. To secure a large voter turnout or, as he expressed it, "to prod anyone sitting on the fence into action," he also took part in "dozens of rallies."[104] Most of them were conventionally structured political mass meetings. By contrast, the rally he held on the Racławice battlefield on 14 May showed sweeping disregard for conventional constraints.[105] It was designed as a quasi-theatrical event, complete with role-playing, costumes, and props, yet it thrived on endless slippages between impersonation and self-presentation, simulation and antisimulation. The typically undisciplined structure of Wałęsa's public statements and their often knotted prose complicated matters further. In what follows, I examine the rally's rhetorical and performative strategies, along with its situational and emotional "truth."

For the Racławice rally Wałęsa dressed in an old-fashioned peasant coat, a replica of the *sukmana* that Kościuszko put on after the victory at Racławice to pay tribute to his peasant troops. Wałęsa arrived with panache, in an elegant landau drawn by two horses. A group of Solidarity activists accompanied him on horseback. Cast as Kościuszko's rural militiamen, they wore traditional peasant dress and hats adorned with peacock feathers. The arrival of Wałęsa and his entourage was loudly cheered and applauded by a loyal audience. Many audience members waved white-and-red Polish flags and Solidarity banners, and some carried placards with the 1988 strike slogan, "*Nie ma wolności bez Solidarności*" (There's no freedom without Solidarity), painted in the characteristic ink-blob script. Here and there in the crowd, however, one could hear dissenting voices. Wałęsa's doubters and detractors, critical of his power-sharing deal with the communist establishment during the round-table negotiations, sounded their disapproval: "Collaborationist! Sell-out!" But a whooping round of applause drowned out the protesters' charges.

After he greeted the cheering crowd, Wałęsa burst into a patriotic song. It was picked up by a group of men gathered around him and eventually by the other participants in the rally. One song followed after another. All of them were classics of the Polish patriotic repertoire, songs such as Alojzy Feliński's "Hymn" (1816) and Maria Konopnicka's "Oath of Allegiance" ("Rota," 1908). With impeccable timing, Wałęsa seized the most exuberant moment during the singing to make his case. He stressed the importance of winning 35 percent of the seats in the House and all the seats in the Senate by Solidarity candidates. At the same time, however, he cautioned the rally participants not to generalize about non-Solidarity candidates: "We can't just shrug our shoulders when it comes to the question what kind of candidates has been preapproved by the political parties. Some of them are better than others. It's crucial to choose the very best. We need to pay careful attention to the makeup of the whole Parliament."[106] Brandishing an upright scythe, the weapon of Kościuszko's peasant recruits, he also told the public: "It's time to replace scythes with ballots. . . . Never before did so much depend on you. The job of mobilizing society is in your hands. The government has granted us pluralism. . . . You must join the effort to build a new Poland, or else a new Poland will be built by others."[107] The audience agreed, and Solidarity activists whipped off their peacock-feathered hats. As before, a few skeptics here and there made sneering comments, only to be ignored. Wałęsa's lines grew barely audible over nearly continual applauding and cheering. Having stoked the fire of pro-Solidarity patriotism, he exited in his landau.

From this account it seems a short step to some preliminary conclusions. The extravaganza demonstrated not only Wałęsa's well-known rapport with audiences but also his flair for the performative aspects of public life. For this particular performance, he ransacked both history and cultural mythology for effective stratagems to reach the hearts of voters, to reinforce (or reinvigorate) their sense of community based on a set of shared values, symbols, and emotional attachments, and to enlist this strengthened sense of "we" for "a patriotic culture of citizenship" or, more precisely, for the Solidarity campaign in the cause of democratic reform.[108] In choosing the Racławice battlefield, Wałęsa took advantage of a major Polish *lieu de mémoire* where Poles can feel the strong beat of national pride.[109] He was, of course, well aware that the story of Kościuszko's victory over a Russian army at Racławice, magnified and distorted by a golden mist of time, became a Polish version of the eternal myth of the triumph of David over Goliath. In choosing the Racławice battlefield, Wałęsa also drew on the myth that attributes Kościuszko's victory to cross-class solidarity and national unity. And considering that Solidarity was intent on exposing corruption of the communist establishment and that, accordingly, morality was one of the words that dominated the Solidarity rhetoric, it is reasonable to assume that Kościuszko's reputation for absolute integrity made the Racławice battlefield doubly attractive during the election campaign. By virtue of its location, then, the rally mobilized both the symbolism of the Racławice battle and the hyper-moralized cult of its commander for a new kind of national unity to bring voters together under the Solidarity banner and to get them to the polling booths.

However, the rally is open to a different reading as well. This reading centers on the question: What does the Racławice framework reveal about the rally's implicit agenda for Poland's future? I will return to this question later. First, I want to consider the rally's tricks of temporality that engaged Racławice as a diachronic and synchronic site of memory and identity. What intrigues me in particular about the rally are the implications of the symbolic connection it sought to establish—through the uncanny spectacle of death and immortality, resurrection and apotheosis on the Racławice battlefield—between Kościuszko's battle and Solidarity's campaign. In the spring of 1794, Kościuszko's victory at Racławice was a powerful morale-booster for the population; ultimately, however, the insurrection ended in defeat, and a year later Poland ceased to exist altogether as a state. In the spring of 1989, Wałęsa's rally, held on the same fields that had been soaked with the blood of Kościuszko's soldiers, encouraged voters to view the Solidarity election campaign as a necessary sequel to Kościuszko's struggle for freedom and democracy. The enemy now was communism rather than Russia, but the round-table agreements offered an opportunity to complete Kościuszko's unfinished project and thus redeem the past. Rather than provide a simple, upbeat affirmation of a glorious moment from the national archive, in other words, the rally suggested that Solidarity's victory at the polls could secure a new, better Racławice. *Then* vanished into *now* in a grand, audacious gesture of political appropriation.

The most striking aspect of this appropriation was Wałęsa's impersonation of Kościuszko. An extraordinary performer with a sharp appreciation of the power of symbols in politics, Wałęsa seemed to claim a kinship with Kościuszko in order to romanticize the Solidarity Revolution of 1980–89 as a legitimate successor to Kościuszko's liberationist project. In truth, he crafted his public persona as a new, better Kościuszko. While the original Kościuszko urged peasants to beat scythes into weapons in order to defend their homeland and, through their apprenticeship in the struggle for Poland's independence, to earn citizens' rights in an unspecified future, the new Kościuszko reminded his audience what is required of citizens in democratic politics: "It's time to replace scythes with ballots." This kind of rhetoric may be inspiring, but Wałęsa's masquerade is not without problems. The rally was haunted by the paradox that Wałęsa's impersonation of Kościuszko signified within the framework of the 1989 election campaign: the rejection of the idea that political power be tied to specific individuals through membership in the Communist Party (that is, one kind of ideological heredity, so to speak) was legitimized by the reenactment of a specific individual, Kościuszko, who represents another kind of ideological heredity. Wałęsa's impersonation of Kościuszko, in other words, signified a reinstatement of the idea that political power be tied to specific individuals (although of a different ideological orientation). Ironically, then, the Racławice rally, driven by a commitment to democratize Polish politics, presented a stirring example of a man grounding political action in his immanent self—Wałęsa.

Wałęsa's masquerade may raise some eyebrows. It may be difficult to resist the conclusion that he exploited the man-myth Kościuszko to build up his own political capital. It may even be tempting to marshal additional evidence to support this conclusion. On 17 October 1990, during an election campaign for Poland's presidency, Wałęsa pressed the man-myth Kościuszko into his service again. To rally support for his candidacy, he held a public meeting in the Sukiennice Museum in Kraków, where he positioned himself directly in front of Matejko's painting, *Kościuszko at Racławice*.[110] That said, it is a commonplace of the practice of politics that political strategists use a variety of approaches to elicit in the electorate what they hope will be the right emotional response in order to advance their cause. As George E. Marcus argues, "Democratic politics cannot be solely a space of calm deliberation. It must also be a sensational place, one that attracts and engages spectators."[111]

While it is certainly possible to deplore the fact that the Racławice masquerade constituted an appropriation of the man-myth Kościuszko in the service of a shrewd politician, I submit that we might expand our understanding of Wałęsa's extravaganza by considering a striking simultaneity of historical time and (imagined) national time that the event generated. Here,

I turn to Benedict Anderson's famous formulation of modern national consciousness as being born out of (beside the rise of print culture and other factors) the invention of a new kind of simultaneous experience.[112] What is often forgotten about Anderson's idea of the simultaneously "imagined community," however, is that his notion of national temporality is explicitly borrowed from Erich Auerbach and Walter Benjamin.

Drawing on Auerbach's interpretation of the premodern mode of apprehending the world, Anderson notes that "the mediaeval Christian mind had no conception of history as an endless chain of cause and effect or of radical separations between past and present."[113] He goes on to quote Auerbach's point that from the medieval Christian perspective "the here and now . . . is *simultaneously* something which has always been, and will be fulfilled in the future."[114] Most significantly, Anderson appropriates the distinction between what Benjamin calls "Messianic time" and "homogeneous, empty time."[115] In Anderson's interpretation of this distinction, the former is a medieval notion characterized by "a simultaneity of past and future in an instantaneous present," while the latter is a newer form in which simultaneity depends on the concept of "meanwhile."[116] Simultaneity of the meanwhile type "is, as it were, transverse, cross-time, marked not by prefiguring and fulfillment, but by temporal coincidence, and measured by clock and calendar."[117] It is the empty, calendar time that Anderson associates with emergent national consciousness: "The idea of a sociological organism moving calendrically through homogeneous, empty time is a precise analogue of the idea of the nation, which also is conceived as a solid community moving steadily down (or up) history."[118]

In some ways (primarily by virtue of its location, a battlefield that has become the secular equivalent of the old holy places, its soil sanctified by the blood of heroic ancestors who thereby remain with the living, erasing boundaries between past, present, and future), the Racławice rally seemed to participate in a mythic consciousness that would be considered pre- national in Anderson's model; in other ways, the rally exemplified his simultaneously imagined modern community, defined by calendar time and temporal coincidence. The rally, then, could be understood as a manifestation of mythic temporality, but it was celebrated for its significance in the calendar of empty, homogeneous time and its enactment of bureaucratic randomness (in the sense that it fell on a Sunday three weeks before the election, rather than on 4 April, the anniversary of the Racławice victory).

In other words, 14 May was a calendrical coincidence or an empty date: a function of the slow progress of what one might call bureaucratic time.

In 1989, however, 14 May was not just a Sunday three weeks before the election. It was Whitsunday (Pentecost), a Christian festival observed on the seventh Sunday after Easter, commemorating the descent of the Holy Spirit on Christ's disciples. For Wałęsa, holding a rally on Whitsunday at the Racławice battlefield, the ground hallowed by Kościuszko's heroic dead, was a powerfully symbolic way of making the forthcoming election into a national monument that was both old and new, secular and holy. It was a way of refashioning national time—that is, marking the time of a rebirth of the imagined community of the nation. But it was also a way of reassuring his audience that the Polish imagined community is deeply rooted in noncalendrical time, beyond the steady onward clocking of homogeneous empty time. Or, to put this point slightly differently, the Racławice dead were exhumed, so to speak, to generate an encounter with the political sublime: the political as larger than life, as awesome and overwhelming.

This is an appropriate moment to return to the question I asked earlier: What does the Racławice framework reveal about the rally's implicit agenda for Poland's future?

To recapitulate my main points put forward thus far, I have been arguing that while the extravaganza was a spectacle in the theatrical sense, it was also a political spectacle in the sense of attracting and engaging voters' attention through sensational means to influence their political judgments. Noting that "spectacle has long been a hallmark of politics," Marcus offers the following distinction: "Although [political] spectacles can elicit a variety of emotional reactions, they tend to fall into one of two characteristic patterns. The first relies on the manufacture of enthusiasm for some purpose or cause, to strengthen allegiances, to bind a group more closely together—the processes that build and strengthen habits. The second intends to cause uncertainty or anxiety."[119] Wałęsa's political spectacle at Racławice appears to fall into the first category. It sought to bind large swathes of the electorate in support of Solidarity candidates by reinforcing certain habits (such as participation in commemorative celebrations) associated with integrative patriotic worship. Additionally, it seemed to assure voters that Wałęsa was running a positive election campaign, one that refrained from criticizing political opponents and asserted only positive claims.

A closer examination reveals that Wałęsa's political spectacle also represents Marcus's second category. While fostering positive emotions, the spectacle, paradoxically, introduced anxiety. This was most evident in Wałęsa's argument why voters should "join the effort to build a new Poland." Admittedly, he first assured them that support for Poland's democratization under the umbrella of Solidarity was fully legitimate: "The government has granted us pluralism." Rather than indulge in denigrating the communist system, moreover, he focused on the opportunity to work together, communists and noncommunists alike, in order to build a democratic polity.[120] This part of his speech was so unexpected that it provoked some audience members to sound their suspicion that the voice of Wałęsa was a ventriloquized trick of the communist establishment. To them, it was possible to hear in Wałęsa's speech some hidden interests of the communists, as channeled through his voice. It was only toward the end of the speech that Wałęsa's exhortatory rhetoric lost its positive momentum. He told the rally participants that if they boycott the election or renege on the fundamental obligation that the dutiful citizen has in democratic (or, for that matter, semidemocratic) politics, Poland's transformation will be performed "by others"—presumably communists and their allies. Regardless of his own rhetorical intention, Wałęsa's statement sounded like a warning, meant to generate anxiety in the electorate. In short, Wałęsa packaged his rally as a patriotic commemoration that relied on and reinforced habit, but he also alerted his audience that Solidarity might lose if habits remained in force.

Anxiety is typically placed in the category of negative emotions. In his study of the role of emotion in democratic politics, however, Marcus points out that anxiety, "too often disregarded and lumped in with other 'negative emotions,' . . . opens up new possibilities by inhibiting the ongoing course of action and by creating a willingness to learn, a willingness to question, and a willingness to consider new alternatives."[121] In the practice of politics, anxiety is useful precisely because it "releases us from the bonds of habits, of mind and behavior, for new possibilities, but how we execute the task of deliberation will depend on what alternatives are advanced by leaders and activists and how well they are challenged."[122] It is therefore necessary to ask: In introducing anxiety, what new alternatives did Wałęsa, in his capacity as the leader of Solidarity, present for voters' consideration?

In taking up this question, I want to examine the following lines from Wałęsa's speech: "The job of mobilizing society is in your hands. . . . You must join the effort to build a new Poland, or else a new Poland will be built by others." On first reading, Wałęsa's exhortation seems to rest on a juxtaposition of "you" (i.e., his audience) with "others," presumably political opponents of "you." A closer reading shows that, in fact, Wałęsa's speech introduces three categories of political actors: "you," "others," and "society." The third category refers to those who need to be recruited by "you." It follows from this that the specific purpose of the Racławice rally was not only to urge "you" to vote so that Solidarity could win 35 percent of the seats in the House, but also to mobilize "you" to build a more engaged electorate.

But who exactly are the "you" to whom Wałęsa entrusted the mobilization of "society" and who therefore held the keys to political change in Poland? To address this question, I want to consider the implications of the key prop used in the rally: an upright scythe that Wałęsa flourished before the audience. His scythe-brandishing may be viewed as an over-the-top gesture to drive his point home: it was time to abandon underground resistance to communist rule for peaceful, legal means. This interpretation, however, ignores the fact that the upright scythe is coded in the Polish National Symbolic as a class-specific weapon because it was used exclusively by Kościuszko's peasant troops. By deploying an upright scythe before "you," then, Wałęsa identified this "you" with farmers or, by metonymy, the working class. On one level, in other words, his political spectacle at Racławice appealed to an amalgamative concept of patriotism by invoking the precedent of the Kościuszko insurrection that has exerted a powerful hold on the Polish cultural imagination as an epitome of what cross-class consensus and solidarity can achieve in the struggle for Poland's liberation. On another level, his political spectacle drove a harsh wedge between different modes of collectivity: those who identify with the symbolism of the upright scythe and those who do not.

I have considered here an elaborately interlocking system of ambiguities, tensions, and audacities underpinning Wałęsa's extravaganza at the moment of the election campaign in 1989. The event provided one of the most striking (and illuminating) examples of the vitality and versatility of the man-myth Kościuszko in Polish culture, even though only a decade earlier his story had seemed to have lost much of its luster and popular appeal. This time, he was pressed into service as a Solidarity standard-bearer to help win votes in the election to Parliament. Embedded in a specific political occasion, the performance appeared to provide a basis for an affective bond that would reaffirm the vaunted solidarity of Solidarity, embracing performers and spectators, activists and nonactivists, rural and urban communities. The connection between cultural mythology and current political events seemed to fall into place, almost too easily.

Beneath the surface, however, there were intriguing contradictions. Again and again, Wałęsa called on the rally participants to cooperate in forging Poland's future. This is what his speech conveyed, but there was a nuanced message also, which can be summed up as follows: the solidarity of Solidarity needs to lose its cohesion and dissolve into various political groupings, driven by different interests and agendas. This message may be taken to bolster the argument that, as Jan Kubik contends in his study,

> Solidarity never sorted out in an organized, rational fashion its internal political tensions, veiled by the strong attachment to emotionally potent symbols.... In 1990, divisions within Solidarity, ranging from personal animosities through deeper programmatic and organizational differences, burst into the surface of the Polish political life with full force.
>
> The Solidarity movement, united by a common cultural-political vision developed throughout the late 1970s, was remarkably monolithic for only a brief moment—in the late summer and fall of 1980. The cracks in this monolith had already appeared by early 1981. By 1992 it had disappeared almost without a trace.[123]

While it is possible to feel a dark tinge of disappointment that the Solidarity monolith, along with its particular kind of dramaturgical unity, was short-lived, I want to suggest that the Racławice extravaganza, including Wałęsa's disquieting message, captured a realistic sense of a democratic polity—any democratic polity—as agonistic, conflictual, and processual, rather than unitary and static. In doing so, the rally provided a counterbalance to Solidarity's principle of dramaturgical unity just at the moment when this principle was scrupulously (and undemocratically) implemented by the Solidarity leadership, including Wałęsa himself, in the election campaign.

Transformations
An Epilogue

IN 1916, THE THIRD year of World War I, a Warsaw publisher reissued *A Conspectus of the National Catechism, or the Patriotic Principles for Polish Youth* (*Wykład katechizmu narodowego czyli prawidła patriotyczne do użycia młodzi narodowej*), originally published in 1791, the year of the first performance of Niemcewicz's *The Return of the Deputy*, Suchorzewski's burning speech to Parliament, and the modernizers' coup d'état to push the constitutional reform through the legislature.[1] Writing in an accessible format of questions and answers, the anonymous author of *A Conspectus* took moral measures to strengthen the patriotic character of Polish youth. The moral measures—recommendation of specific activities and types of behavior and proscription of other activities and types of behavior—rested on values: selfless devotion to the common good, courage, integrity, prudence, industriousness, steadfastness, and fortitude. Taken together, these values were understood to provide the underpinnings of true patriotism. The author of *A Conspectus*, in the moral provisions of the treatise, shifted attention from patriotism as an abstraction to patriotism as everyday behavior, designed a highly specific code of conduct, and identified compliance with the code as a statement of resistance to Poland's enemies and deviance from the code as a statement of sympathy for its enemies. In short, the author of *A Conspectus* simplified patriotic morality, limited its scope, and standardized it.

This program was devised to achieve a specific goal: to bring people together in a crisis and to save Poland. The failure of the program on a practical level in 1795, when the state was forced to cede its remaining territory to Austria, Prussia, and Russia, assured the program's success on a psychological level. As long as Poland was under foreign rule, Poles remained bound together by the moral imperative to resist oppression. Although many of them did not abide by the specific regulations put forth in codes of patriotic conduct such as *A Conspectus,* and although most of them had much on their minds besides emancipation from foreign rule, the tenacious durability of the moral imperative of resistance to Poland's oppressors enabled Poles to think of themselves as a virtuous people with a will and a character, regardless of their individual willingness or unwillingness to make sacrifices for Poland. In some segments of the population, the notion of virtuousness as a core element, indeed the pillar, of Polish identity has continued well into the 2000s.[2]

And yet the moral underpinnings of patriotism have an ephemeral quality. They can bring people together in a crisis, but they are not necessarily able to hold them together except by feeding into exercises in boastful national pride and heady cultural triumphalism. Claims such as "the world would be better off if other nations were more like the Poles" are pointed reminders of how easily a simplified and moralized version of patriotism can slide into self-congratulatory fictions, chauvinist enthusiasms, nationalist sloganeering, and xenophobic bigotry.[3] But the inclusion of both the Magna Carta and the words and music of the "Marseillaise" in *The Patriot's Calendar*, issued by a radical London publisher in the 1790s, is an equally pointed reminder of an alternative discourse of patriotism.

This book began partly because I became interested in exploring alternative conceptualizations of patriotism in Polish culture. To put it more broadly, I wanted to track counteractive patterns of culture, that is, "the elements of a culture's own negation [which] are, with greater or lesser force, included within it."[4] At the same time, I was curious about the ways in which the dramatic genre, and not just patriotic catechisms, participated in the process of defining and disseminating values, norms, and beliefs. I was also puzzled by plays that once were widely known but have since been declared unworthy of serious attention in scholarship and consigned to oblivion with barely a second glance. I wanted to make the other, less familiar traditions of Polish drama and theatre visible again, albeit in new ways. Accordingly, I set out to examine a broad range of plays, hoping to find out not only what patriotic commitments they recommend, but also what they can tell us about varieties of patriotism that are denied credibility in the effort to create a single discursive paradigm for modeling patriotic sentiments, attachments, idea(l)s, convictions, attitudes, and obligations. My goal was to identify alternatives—some consciously undervalued or denigrated, others barely recognized or hardly imaginable—that might be present at various levels in these works.

Presumably, few readers of this book had been familiar with plays such as Wybicki's *The Polish Woman*, Łubieńska's *Wanda, Queen of Poland*, or Bojarska's *The Polish Lesson;* therefore, one might be tempted to dismiss them outright on the grounds that they were simply statistical noise in terms of the general cultural pattern, defined by acknowledged masterpieces and canonized aesthetics. Admittedly, it is difficult for us nowadays to believe that audiences—readers and spectators alike—were once enthralled by plays that have since vanished from view. Their absence not just from the canon of Polish literature but also from mainstream scholarship does make one wonder, to be honest: "Don't they perhaps deserve it?"

An alternative approach, which I have adopted in this book, is to argue that plays such as *Wanda, Queen of Poland* were part of the same broad conversation among texts that gave rise to the more familiar tradition of celebrated classics and canonized aesthetics; hence they deserve to be made more available for critical discussion and classroom use. Although it is almost inevitable to see Polish cultural history through the lens of masterworks such as Mickiewicz's *Forefathers' Eve* and Wyspiański's *The Wedding,* which are now officially enshrined in the canon, it bears emphasis that their authors were never hermetically sealed off from the other traditions. As Piotr Mitzner has noted, a comparative reading of *Forefathers' Eve,* one of the foundational texts of Polish Romanticism, and Majeranowski's *Kościuszko's First Love* suggests that Mickiewicz modeled his protagonist's transformative self-making on Majeranowski's drama.[5] The now forgotten *Kościuszko's First Love* is thus an early touchstone for the private/public divide that would become a dominant paradigm in Polish literary discourse under foreign rule: the private man must die, so that the patriot rebel may be born. Or, to use another example, attention to Anczyc's *Kościuszko at Racławice*—a triumphantly successful and perennially popular drama that has had a prominent role in propagating and reinforcing a seductively attractive mythology of cross-class consensus and solidarity, along with all the presuppositions, appropriations, mystifications, stereotypes, and contradictions it involves—can deepen our understanding of the brash light-heartedness, the satirical cruelties, and the vertiginous audacities of *The Wedding*. In short, there is much to gain from extending our gaze beyond the master narrative of Polish drama and theatre.

The main remit of this book has been to investigate how and to what ends a specific body of dramatic writing—what I have called the drama of patriotism—engages with competing views of patriotic idea(l)s, principles, and concerns. I have concentrated on plays that feature the problematic figure of the patriot-hero or patriot-heroine who is "guilty" of combining unwavering allegiance and tireless dedication to the patriotic cause with the kind of rebellious nonconformity that his or her compatriots perceive as a threat to the hierarchies of gender and class. I do not claim, of course, that the patriotism/transgression nexus in support of democratic reform is the only subject in the preceding chapters. "Shadow" themes, surfacing from play to play and suggesting other rubrics under which the texts might be grouped, range from the contentious horizon between myth and history to the appropriation of patriot-heroes and patriot-heroines for wildly divergent ends. The clash between the demands of the individual self and those of the community, or the conflict between the desire for individual freedom and the obligation to further collective welfare, is also a recurring "shadow" theme. But the paradoxical convergence of patriotic devotion with transgressive nonconformity is an ongoing preoccupation in the plays I have selected for consideration. Attention to the audacity of a patriot's willfully transgressive insubordination provides an opportunity to take a fresh look at the seemingly self-evident concept of patriotism, at the boundaries that have provoked transgression of social or customary norms, and at the accommodations that have had to be made to "a patriotic culture of citizenship" if transgressive patriots were to become an accepted part of a shared tradition.[6]

I have designed each chapter as a self-contained narrative, using the lens of one particular selection from the archive to examine debates about the meaning of patriotism and controversies over "proper"/"improper" patriotic activism. Some of the dramatic texts I have chosen are "topical allusion plays," referring openly and unmistakably to current events, while others are "application plays," inviting audiences to see connections and draw parallels between events in the past and contemporary affairs.[7] Some are not shy about their edifying and consciousness-raising mission; others work hard to avoid moralistic high-handedness. Some charm and flatter audiences by resorting to the seductive thrills of national pride, while glossing over or blotting out class and gender inequalities; others recognize these inequalities but perform some delicate maneuvers to develop a solidaristic argument. In the latter group of plays, *Kościuszko at Racławice* stands out as the work of a gifted rhetorical strategist. In it, Anczyc famously attempts to knit together all segments of Polish society at a time of ominously revolutionary feeling by demonstrating that bonds of patriotic affection outweigh determinants of social class. The gaps, dissonances, and discontinuities in his play are thus a necessary side effect of the textual mechanisms deployed to fend off the threat of transgression, to buttress cultural investments in hierarchical taxonomies, and to reassure audiences that it is possible to build a patriotic community across class barriers while keeping the barriers intact.

Then there are plays that have a more open, exploratory disposition. Some authors (e.g., Mańkowska in *Tadeusz Kościuszko*) cautiously encourage us to venture into a territory that feels new, strange, "unnatural," as they grapple, dramaturgically and rhetorically, with the claim that the habit of treating patriotic devotion and transgressive nonconformity as hostile opposites is misguided. Ultimately, however, they tiptoe further and further away from transgressive challenges to the "natural" hierarchies of class and gender and take recourse to comfortable patriotic commonplaces. In contrast, plays such as Bełcikowski's *The Warsaw Street-Seller* are inquisitive and provocative texts, full of surprises. *The Warsaw Street-Seller* demonstrates that although patriotism may be perceived as a matter of "natural" obligation, transcending social distinctions and offering inclusiveness, the actual involvement in the patriotic cause makes many participants only too conscious of what divides them rather than what they share in common. Bełcikowski's play plants doubt right at the heart of the most fervently held conviction about patriotic agency and responsibility, as it imagines one of those who have been traditionally excluded from full citizenship attempting to carve out for herself a real if precarious place in the citizenship community.

Taken together, the plays demonstrate how protean, as well as how porous, the category *patriotism* has been. Although there can be few more obviously patriotic acts than to volunteer to defend one's country against the enemy, patriotic sentiments make their way into the plays through a variety of doors. Some of the doors are marked Political Intransigence, Armed Resistance, Performance in Battle, and Military Glory. Others are labeled Political Moderation, Parliamentary Sovereignty, Parliamentary

Opposition, Constitutional Reform, Civic Glory, Cross-Class Reconciliation and Solidarity, National Unity, Peace and Prosperity, Civil Disobedience, and Citizens' Rights and Liberties. Still others are designated as Armor of Righteousness and Cloak of Deceit. The construction of each of these many doors necessitates a constant battle over the traits by which to tell the "sincere" or "worthy" patriot from the "false."

The second point to be made in this context is that some plays open up a creative space for radical reconceptualizations of patriotism and that they do so in ways that may work in contradistinction to dominant or canonical materials that so often become the "truth" of a historical period. For example, while the titles of Wybicki's *The Polish Woman* and Bojarska's *The Polish Lesson* seem to frame their contents as a quintessentially Polish product, in fact both plays suggest that the category *patriotism* can exceed nationalist agendas for the pursuit of goals (e.g., a contestation of gender scripts) that lie beyond any national denomination or domain. Likewise, Otwinowski's *Easter* removes patriotic allegiance from the realm of the national and recodes patriotism as a contestation of constraints on cultural, religious, and ethnic diversity. In doing so, it seeks to widen the meaning of "us" by inviting audiences to understand and identify with those they would previously have regarded as other. At a time when it is still axiomatic that patriots feel a special bond of identification with their national community and that this community is the primary locus of their political allegiance, plays such as *The Polish Lesson* and *Easter* provide a voice of dissent, challenging the undemanding equation of nationalism and patriotism. Moreover, they reveal that there is more to the history of patriotic discourse in Poland than the all-too-familiar dichotomy between the heroic and thanatophilic patriotism of the Polish Romantics and the prudent and pragmatic patriotism of the Polish Positivists.

Third, while patriotism is neither a "masculine" nor a "feminine" concept, and (on the face of it) the patriotic stance appears to cut across the boundaries of masculinity and femininity, in the plays discussed here assumptions about "proper" patriotic activism are underpinned by the male/female binary. At the same time, gender is recoded over and over again, depending on whether it stamps unpatriotic men as effete, equates soldiering with masculinity, stigmatizes female soldiering as trespassing on male territory, brands women soldiers as defeminized, apotheosizes them as ethereal perfections, or identifies women's exceptional patriotic service as a claim for gender equality. It is thus not particularly surprising that so many of the plays on women's aspirations to gender-bending activism carry mixed messages. Although the perimeters of woman's sphere may be stretched to include brief stints at soldiering and although some female soldiers are celebrated as patriotic heroines, women's auxiliary or noncombatant service is clearly the norm. Female characters who refuse to perform support services and instead choose combat usually put an end to their experiment in gender-bending and revert to the traditional guarantors of female identity: romance, marriage, family. These characters are contradictory figures who open up new avenues for female self-expression, yet also reflect societal fears about female independence and ambition.

That said, several plays do offer rich material for new interpretive perspectives on the question of gender in Polish cultural history. It is usually assumed that pre-twentieth-century Polish drama is a man's world, decidedly unsympathetic to women's—especially ordinary women's—ambition to participate in politics. This commonly held assumption is overturned in Kublicki's *The Defense of Trembowla* and Wybicki's *The Polish Woman*. What makes them thrillingly new among Polish Enlightenment plays is that they speak to gender issues in a way that anticipates the now familiar idea of labile gender. That is to say, the most significant aspect of their dramaturgical and rhetorical projects is not necessarily the celebration of the patriot-heroine Zofia Chrzanowska and her challenge to the socially prescribed gender roles; rather, *The Defense of Trembowla* and *The Polish Woman* refuse to categorize masculinity and femininity as inherent qualities and polar opposites, embedded in biology. In doing so, both plays expose the false dichotomy undergirding constructions of gender identity itself. Instead of something natural, permanent, and preordained, gender emerges as something contingent, extemporaneous, and provisional.

At a time when biology was seen as the foundation of human character and behavior, and social roles were assigned by gender, *The Defense of Trembowla* and *The Polish Woman* disrupted such views. The evidence of these plays predates by almost two hundred years the idea that gender is not an essence, rooted in biological difference, but rather a sociocultural construct, the contours of which are continually in flux. In their insistence that gender is fluid rather than fixed, *The Defense of Trembowla* and *The Polish Woman* were directly at odds with those who invoked sexual difference to justify women's inferior social status. This may go some way toward explaining the subsequent eclipse of both plays. Recovered from obscurity, *The*

Defense of Trembowla and *The Polish Woman* invite us to rethink the history of feminism in Poland. They suggest the existence of an early strain of feminist discourse, albeit one whose radical potential was gradually closed down. They certainly prove that there is more to the problem of gender in the Polish Enlightenment than comic verses by writers such as Ignacy Krasicki, in which depictions of women come straight out of the well-stocked cabinet of misogynistic satiric conventions. Both plays also prove, among much else, that there is no shortage of evidence still to be retrieved from the archives and particularly from the tangled wasteland that is the literary miscellanies of the eighteenth century.

At first glance, history has validated the transgressions of boundaries, performed by my cast of characters. "Utopian" projects aimed at transforming class and gender relations seem to have succeeded. The hegemony of dominant groups over other groups excluded from full educational opportunities, political and social citizenship, and often basic respect has been broken. Girls are no longer reared on the doctrine of female docility and submission. And although the military had once been a male enclave, a woman can now join the army if she wishes; if she is a soldier in the US army, she can even fight on the front line. In other words, the transgressor, "guilty" of conflating the "legitimate" passion of patriotism with the "illegitimate" energy of transgressive nonconformity and determined to challenge long-held assumptions about gender- and class-coded identities and roles, has been vindicated. What has been disturbingly transgressive now belongs to the past and seems unimaginably distant.

In certain important respects, then, Bojarska's insistence in *The Polish Lesson* that the Kościuszko story, a rather antiquated *lieu de mémoire,* can illuminate some concerns in our own world might strike readers as ahistorical. As if anticipating such a charge, she has designed *The Polish Lesson* as an application drama (to invoke Robert D. Hume's terminology) that probes connections and parallels between the chronologically distant past and the present. On the most obvious level, *The Polish Lesson* suggests that the Solidarity Revolution of the 1980s created a need for a different way of thinking about patriotism, free from communist indoctrination. Bojarska, accordingly, took up the story of arguably the pivotal figure in the Polish pantheon—the revered patriot-hero who has left a deep imprint on the popular imagination. Her choice made perfect sense during the Solidarity Revolution, since Kościuszko's resistance to political oppression, his advocacy of democratic principles, and his human rights activism (to use a modern term) were part of the common stock of Polish knowledge. However, Bojarska was also keenly aware that Kościuszko was appropriated by devotees of Polish national mythology with its self-congratulatory cultural triumphalism. Part of her project in *The Polish Lesson*, then, is to critique inherited templates and deflate idealized accounts upheld by those with stars in their eyes. In contesting glossy narratives about the past, her application play also encourages an open-minded scrutiny of a mythology-in-the-making— a romanticized version of the Solidarity movement, which offers its own patriotic story lines populated by demigods. It is not just that heroic icons like Kościuszko (or Solidarity leaders) should be remembered for their blunders as well as their triumphs. The whole emphasis on hero worship is dated and constricting.

But there is more to Bojarska's application drama. In 1988, when women's concerns were marginalized by the reemerging Solidarity movement, and cultural ideas about women continued to be infused and informed by a view of motherhood as supremely defining of a woman, as the acme of femininity, she attempted to launch a public debate still needed today: Why is the deck stacked against women? This attempt entailed shifting the focus from Kościuszko as the public figure, enshrined in the Polish cultural imagination as a powerful symbol of national struggles against political oppression, to the private man. In the play, Bojarska gives a provocative twist to a relationship between Kościuszko and his Swiss student, Emilie Zeltner, joining them in an intimate bond that is desirous, aggressive, disturbing, and unstable, but also companionate, sustaining, and endlessly productive. Emilie has been locked into a traditional mold, within a limited range of options; her interaction with Kościuszko reveals her frustrations as an eloquent plea for equal opportunities for women. The historical Kościuszko has not been seen as a patron of feminist causes, but Bojarska finds just enough evidence in his biography to have him take a keen, sympathetic interest in the concerns of this young woman, to recognize the inequalities woven into the gender order, and to extend his advocacy of democratic principles to women. In incorporating the feminist themes of subversion and resistance into the play, Bojarska invites the audience to consider the idea that exposing the fictions of patriarchy, breaking with inflexible gender imperatives, dismantling binary oppositions that conceal hierarchies, and working to correct gender inequality can be forms of patriotic activism, but to recognize them as such requires a radical shift from localistic, nation-centered modes of thinking about patriotism toward an understanding of patriotism as civil disobedience for the transnational, borderless common good. At the same time, the play suggests that feminism may be viewed as more than a set of political goals.[8] Becoming a feminist means embracing a new identity that entails a revaluation of gender relations and the meaning of manhood (or womanhood) itself. Then, as now, this is a formidable challenge.[9]

The issue, however, is yet more complicated. Reading Bojarska's drama against Wajda's production, as I have done in my last chapter, brings back to light those aspects of the play that the theatrical enactment buried under comfortable patriotic commonplaces to avoid offending Polish sensibilities. Wajda's Kościuszko is one of Poland's greatest political exiles who continues to live in the world of the nation. For Bojarska's Kościuszko, by contrast, separation from his homeland occasions not so much a longing for his country as a wish to transcend nation. In his complex, ever-mutating world, he refuses to have his affinities and his passions focused on a single place and a particular national community. Reading Bojarska's play against Wajda's production, in other words, demonstrates that the lens of drama, although frequently displaced in criticism by the lens of stage performance, can provide keen insights into tendencies of cultural discord and dissension that gnaw at the principle of consensus and foster counterknowledge. The problem is that *The Polish Lesson* has never been published, which restricts public access to this unsettling, unflinching drama on the problem of patriotism, so timely in its postnational implications for the postcommunist era when patriotic sentiments have increasingly been associated with flag-waving and drum-beating and with the belief in the superiority of the patriot's own country to all others. Bojarska's play, which neither idolizes nor underestimates Kościuszko, stands strangely neglected, as if its questioning of patriotism in the conventional sense, as "a kind of loyalty to a particular nation which only those possessing that particular nationality can exhibit," has been deemed too subversive.[10]

In recovering lesser-known yet intriguing materials, this book has been designed to inform, to argue, and to stimulate further debate. I hope that it constitutes an invitation to continue dialogue about negotiations of patriotism in literature and the arts, without assuming that works on patriotic themes are always slaves to tradition and convention and without assuming that patriotism itself is static, monolithic, and self-evident.

Notes

For books published in the nineteenth century or earlier, publishers' names are omitted. In the titles of Polish sources, orthography has been standardized to modern usage.

Compass Points: A Prologue

1. See Ludwig Wittgenstein, *Philosophical Investigations*, trans. G. E. M. Anscombe, 3rd ed. (New York: Macmillan, 1968), 146.
2. Margaret R. Hunt, *Women in Eighteenth-Century Europe* (Harlow, UK: Longman, 2010), 337.
3. See Jan Lechoń, *Dziennik*, ed. Roman Loth, vol. 3 (Warsaw: Państwowy Instytut Wydawniczy, 1993), 257.
4. In eighteenth-century usage, the term *Polish Revolution* referred to the reformist legislation of the Four-Year Parliament that convened in Warsaw on 6 October 1788 and adjourned on 29 May 1792. See, e.g., Richard Butterwick, *The Polish Revolution and the Catholic Church, 1788–1792: A Political History* (Oxford: Oxford University Press, 2012); Richard Butterwick, "Political Discourses of the Polish Revolution, 1788–92," *English Historical Review* 120, no. 487 (June 2005): 695–731; Anna Grześkowiak-Krwawicz, *Czy rewolucja może być legalna? 3 maja 1791 w oczach współczesnych* (Warsaw: DiG, 2012), 7–46.
5. Benjamin Bennett, *Theater as Problem: Modern Drama and Its Place in Literature* (Ithaca, NY: Cornell University Press, 1990), 60.
6. See, e.g., Jan IJ. van der Meer, *Literary Activities and Attitudes in the Stanislavian Age in Poland (1764–1795): A Social System?* (Amsterdam: Rodopi, 2002), 105, 178–80; Józef Szczepaniec, "Gabinety i wypożyczalnie literatury w Polsce w drugiej połowie XVIII w.," *Ze Skarbca Kultury* 37 (1983): 7–108.
7. See Józef Szczepaniec, "*Teatr Polski* Piotra Dufoura," *Ze Skarbca Kultury* 1 (1955): 245–72. Other publishers continued Dufour's project into the nineteenth century.
8. This view, that Romanticism marked a crucial turning point in Polish culture, has been put forward most strongly by Maria Janion. See, e.g., Janion, "Romantyzm a początek świata nowożytnego," in *Narodziny i rozwój nowoczesnej kultury*

polskiej, ed. Jerzy Wojtowicz and Jerzy Serczyk (Wrocław: Zakład Narodowy im. Ossolińskich, 1976), 59–87. For the concept of the National Symbolic, which expands on Benedict Anderson's idea that nations are imagined communities, see Lauren Berlant, *The Anatomy of National Fantasy: Hawthorne, Utopia, and Everyday Life* (Chicago: University of Chicago Press, 1991), 20–21.

9. For this widespread claim, see, e.g., Barbara Einhorn, *Cinderella Goes to Market: Citizenship, Gender and Women's Movements in East Central Europe* (London: Verso, 1995), 228–29; Joanna Szwajcowska, "The Myth of the Polish Mother," in Ewa Mazierska and Elzbieta Ostrowska, *Women in Polish Cinema*, with a supplementary chapter by Szwajcowska (New York: Berghahn Books, 2006), 15–33, esp. 15, 20–23.

10. See Michel Foucault, *Aesthetics, Method, and Epistemology*, ed. James D. Faubion, trans. Robert Hurley et al. (New York: New Press, 1998), 289–90, 297–333.

11. Arlette Farge, *Fragile Lives: Violence, Power, and Solidarity in Eighteenth-Century Paris*, trans. Carol Shelton (Cambridge, MA: Harvard University Press, 1993), 5.

12. John Ashbery, *Other Traditions* (Cambridge, MA: Harvard University Press, 2000), 122.

13. I take the phrases "a cloak of deceit" and "an armor of righteousness" from Hugh Cunningham, "The Language of Patriotism," in *Patriotism: The Making and Unmaking of British National Identity*, ed. Raphael Samuel, 3 vols. (London: Routledge, 1989), 1:62.

14. The phrase "strong common identification" comes from Charles Taylor, "Why Democracy Needs Patriotism," in Martha C. Nussbaum et al., *For Love of Country: Debating the Limits of Patriotism*, ed. Joshua Cohen (Boston: Beacon Press, 1996), 120. The opinions about affinities of patriotism with nationalism are both taken from John H. Schaar, "The Case for Patriotism," in *Legitimacy in the Modern State* (New Brunswick, NJ: Transaction Books, 1981), 285. Schaar cites such opinions to show how successful the appropriation of patriotism for nationalist agendas and the cult of national power has been. For Polish debates about the relationship between patriotism and nationalism, see, e.g., Agnieszka Graff, *Rykoszetem: Rzecz o płci, seksualności i narodzie* (Warsaw: W.A.B., 2008), 214–23; Jerzy Jedlicki, "Nacjonalizm, patriotyzm i inicjacja kulturowa," *Znak* 49, no. 3 (March 1997): 51–61; Maria Karolczak, ed., *Maski i twarze patriotyzmu* (Kraków: Instytut Myśli Józefa Tischnera, 2012); Jan Józef Lipski, "Two Fatherlands, Two Patriotisms," in *Between East and West: Writing from Kultura*, ed. Robert Kostrzewa (New York: Hill and Wang, 1990), 52–71; Ewa Nowicka-Włodarczyk, ed., *Patriotyzm; tożsamość narodowa; poczucie narodowe* (Kraków: Międzynarodowe Centrum Rozwoju Demokracji, 1998).

15. Alasdair MacIntyre, *Is Patriotism a Virtue?* (Lawrence: University of Kansas, 1984), 3. Schaar offers a different assessment of patriotism during the 1960s: "It

is surely the understanding of patriotic duty that inspired the civil rights activity of the 1960s, and that for one glorious moment called more Harvard seniors to the Peace Corps than to the Business School." Schaar, "Case for Patriotism," 295.

16. For evidence that the term *patriotism* came into use in the Polish language only in the second half of the eighteenth century, see Konrad Górski, *Patriotyzm i nacjonalizm* (Toruń: Książnica Miejska im. M. Kopernika, 1988), 3.

17. See, e.g., Padhraig Higgins, *A Nation of Politicians: Gender, Patriotism, and Political Culture in Late Eighteenth-Century Ireland* (Madison: University of Wisconsin Press, 2010); Jacqueline Hill, *From Patriots to Unionists: Dublin Civic Politics and Irish Protestant Patriotism, 1660–1840* (Oxford: Clarendon Press, 1997); Francesca Morgan, *Women and Patriotism in Jim Crow America* (Chapel Hill: University of North Carolina Press, 2005); Cecilia Elizabeth O'Leary, *To Die For: The Paradox of American Patriotism* (Princeton, NJ: Princeton University Press, 1999). For an excellent attempt to disentangle the main meanings of patriotism in eighteenth-century Britain, see Christine Gerrard, *The Patriot Opposition to Walpole: Politics, Poetry, and National Myth, 1725–1742* (Oxford: Clarendon Press, 1994).

18. Gender is understood here as an arbitrary sociocultural construct or a complex of social and cultural conventions surrounding sexual difference. See, e.g., Joan W. Scott, *Gender and the Politics of History*, rev. ed. (New York: Columbia University Press, 1999).

19. Dustin Griffin, *Patriotism and Poetry in Eighteenth-Century Britain* (Cambridge: Cambridge University Press, 2002), 2–3.

20. In Greek and Roman antiquity, *patria* "referred chiefly, if not exclusively, to the city" or one's narrow local homeland. Ernst H. Kantorowicz, "*Pro Patria Mori* in Medieval Political Thought," in *Selected Studies* (Locust Valley, NY: J. J. Augustin, 1965), 310. Accordingly, "the [Roman] *imperium* was not called *patria* in the classical period . . . , whereas the *res publica* as well as the city of Rome were *patria* without restriction." Kantorowicz, *The King's Two Bodies: A Study in Mediaeval Political Theology* (Princeton, NJ: Princeton University Press, 1997), 233n120. In medieval usage, *patria* referred, on the one hand, to "the native hamlet, village, township, or province," and, on the other, to "the Kingdom of Heaven, the celestial city of Jerusalem," regarded as the Christian's true *patria* (ibid., 233–34). In modern times, *patria* has sometimes retained its original meaning as one's local homeland. For example, Schaar reminds us that "when George Washington said 'my country,' he meant Virginia, a usage which persisted until some time after the revolution of 1776," whereas Philipp Ziesche points out that, given the weakness of national sentiment and the constant threat of the disintegration of the American union, "many Americans continued to think of their home state as their 'country' well into the nineteenth century." Schaar, "Case for Patriotism," 299; Ziesche, *Cosmopolitan Patriots: Americans in Paris in the Age of Revolution* (Charlottesville: University of Virginia Press, 2010), 6.

21. Mary G. Dietz, "Patriotism," in *Political Innovation and Conceptual Change*, ed. Terence Ball, James Farr, and Russell L. Hanson (Cambridge: Cambridge University Press, 1995), 178. See also Sheldon S. Wolin, *Politics and Vision: Continuity and Innovation in Western Political Thought*, exp. ed. (Princeton, NJ: Princeton University Press, 2004), 73–74.

22. Griffin, *Patriotism and Poetry*, 3.

23. For a relevant excerpt from the essays, collected as *A Dissertation upon the Canon and Feudal Law*, see *The Political Writings of John Adams: Representative Selections*, ed. George A. Peek Jr. (Indianapolis: Bobbs-Merrill, 1954), 17. For the argument that patriotism has been imagined in the language of kinship and therefore perceived as a natural bond, see chapter 8 ("Patriotism and Racism") in Benedict Anderson, *Imagined Communities: Reflections on the Origin and Spread of Nationalism*, rev. ed. (London: Verso, 1991), 141–54. On the art of assimilating patriotism to kinship to make patriotic loyalties and obligations seem natural and inevitable, see Margaret Canovan, "'Breathes there the man, with soul so dead . . .': Reflections on Patriotic Poetry and Liberal Principles," in *Literature and the Political Imagination*, ed. John Horton and Andrea T. Baumeister (London: Routledge, 1996), 176–83.

24. Richard Price, *Political Writings*, ed. D. O. Thomas (Cambridge: Cambridge University Press, 1991), 178–79, 181. Somewhat analogously, Antoni Popławski, a contemporary of Price, cautioned in a 1775 treatise against "the love of one's mother country [that] tramples on concern with the needs of humanity and on the love of the human community." Popławski, *Pisma pedagogiczne*, ed. Stanisław Tync (Wrocław: Zakład Narodowy im. Ossolińskich, 1957), 56.

25. For a scathing critique of patriotism and patriotic attachments, see, e.g., George Kateb, *Patriotism and Other Mistakes* (New Haven, CT: Yale University Press, 2006), esp. 3–20.

26. The widely popular phrase, "our country, right or wrong," comes from a toast by a US naval officer, Stephen Decatur, in 1816. See Igor Primoratz, "Patriotism and Morality: Mapping the Terrain," in *Patriotism: Philosophical and Political Perspectives*, ed. Igor Primoratz and Aleksandar Pavković (Aldershot, UK: Ashgate, 2007), 20n9.

27. Kwame Anthony Appiah, "Cosmopolitan Patriots," in *Cosmopolitics: Thinking and Feeling beyond the Nation*, ed. Pheng Cheah and Bruce Robbins (Minneapolis: University of Minnesota Press, 1998), 112n8.

28. Joep Th. Leersen, "Anglo-Irish Patriotism and Its European Context: Notes towards a Reassessment," *Eighteenth-Century Ireland* 3 (1988): 7.

29. Linda Colley, "Radical Patriotism in Eighteenth-Century England," in *Patriotism*, ed. Samuel, 1:169.

30. Merle Curti, *The Roots of American Loyalty* (New York: Columbia University Press, 1946), viii.

31. Kateb, *Patriotism*, 17, 23. For the argument that patriotism is a precursor of nationalism, see Leonard W. Doob, *Patriotism and Nationalism: Their Psychological Foundations* (New Haven, CT: Yale University Press, 1964), 6. For the claim that nationalism is a "distinctive species of patriotism," see Ernest Gellner, *Nations and Nationalism* (Ithaca, NY: Cornell University Press, 1983), 138. For a dissenting view, concerned to dissociate patriotism from nationalism, see especially Dietz, "Patriotism"; Schaar, "Case for Patriotism"; Maurizio Viroli, *For Love of Country: An Essay on Patriotism and Nationalism* (Oxford: Clarendon Press, 1995). Characteristically, the title of Viroli's closing chapter is "Patriotism without Nationalism." For the argument that the term *patriotism* has anachronistically been burdened with nationalist connotations and credentials, see Leersen, "Anglo-Irish Patriotism," 8, 15.

32. Kateb, *Patriotism*, 11. On the relationship between, on the one hand, local attachments and solidarities based on group membership and, on the other, the universal moral commitments associated with liberal theory, see MacIntyre, *Is Patriotism a Virtue?*. For attempts to theorize and foster a nonnational form of patriotic loyalty that will be compatible with the universal principles of democracy, justice, and human rights, see especially Jürgen Habermas, "Citizenship and National Identity: Some Reflections on the Future of Europe," *Praxis International* 12, no. 1 (April 1992): 1–19; Jonathan M. Hansen, *The Lost Promise of Patriotism: Debating American Identity, 1890–1920* (Chicago: University of Chicago Press, 2003); Attracta Ingram, "Constitutional Patriotism," *Philosophy and Social Criticism* 22, no. 6 (November 1996): 1–18; Jan-Werner Müller, *Constitutional Patriotism* (Princeton, NJ: Princeton University Press, 2007); Viroli, *For Love of Country*. While Margaret Canovan doubts that such attempts can succeed, she nonetheless argues convincingly that "whatever their moral misgivings, theorists of politics need to pay more serious attention to patriotic sentiment." Canovan, "'Breathes there the man,'" 178. See also Canovan, "Patriotism Is Not Enough," *British Journal of Political Science* 30, no. 3 (July 2000): 413–32.

33. For information about *The Patriot's Calendar*, I am indebted to Colley, "Radical Patriotism," 182.

34. Dietz, "Patriotism," 188. See also a discussion of an influential Sheffield periodical, the *Patriot, or Political, Moral and Philosophical Repository*, in Albert Goodwin, *The Friends of Liberty: The English Democratic Movement in the Age of the French Revolution* (Cambridge, MA: Harvard University Press, 1979), 223–28. Launched in April 1792, the *Patriot* "found its way to Scotland, Ireland and America and was even translated into Welsh" (Goodwin, 224).

35. Dietz, "Patriotism," 188.

36. The quotation marks are meant to suggest how unstable and inefficient the boundaries between these categories are.

37. See, e.g., Jarosław Marek Rymkiewicz, *Wieszanie*, 2nd ed. (Warsaw: Sic!, 2011); Jarosław Marek Rymkiewicz, *Reytan: Upadek Polski* (Warsaw: Sic!, 2013); Jerzy Zawieyski, *Pomiędzy plewą i manną* (Warsaw: Czytelnik, 1971).

38. Robin May Schott, "The Gender of Enlightenment," in *What Is Enlightenment? Eighteenth-Century Answers and Twentieth-Century Questions*, ed. James Schmidt (Berkeley: University of California Press, 1996), 471. See also Anthony Pagden, *The Enlightenment and Why It Still Matters* (New York: Random House, 2013).

39. I do not wish to deny that research on the Polish Enlightenment has had a long and worthy tradition; my concern is with the tendency to ignore this period in poststructuralist literary and cultural studies. Scholarship on the Polish Enlightenment continues to grow, but it is political history, and especially the parliamentary, ministerial, and diplomatic dimensions of the politics of the period that galvanize scholars. See, e.g., Łukasz Kądziela, *Między zdradą a służbą Rzeczypospolitej: Fryderyk Moszyński w latach 1792–1793* (Warsaw: Volumen, 1993); Dariusz Rolnik, *Szlachta koronna wobec konfederacji targowickiej (maj 1792—styczeń 1793)* (Katowice: Wydawnictwo Uniwersytetu Śląskiego, 2000); Wojciech Szczygielski, *Referendum trzeciomajowe: Sejmiki lutowe 1792 roku* (Łódź: Wydawnictwo Uniwersytetu Łódzkiego, 1994).

40. See, e.g., Walter Berns, *Making Patriots* (Chicago: University of Chicago Press, 2001); Eric Liu and Nick Hanauer, *The True Patriot: A Pamphlet* (Seattle: Sasquatch Press, 2007). Given the persistence of regarding patriotic and nationalist positions as synonymous, particularly in the aftermath of the events of 11 September 2001, it is not surprising that the title of a 1996 volume of essays on patriotism, *For Love of Country*, acquired a skeptical question mark when the book was reissued in 2002. See Martha C. Nussbaum et al., *For Love of Country?* (Boston: Beacon Press, 2002).

41. For the argument that "national identity does in fact today exert a more potent and durable influence than other collective cultural identities" and that nationalism "provides the sole vision and rationale of political solidarity today, one that commands popular assent and elicits popular enthusiasm," see Anthony D. Smith, *National Identity* (Reno: University of Nevada Press, 1993), 175–76.

42. For exceptions to this general tendency, see, e.g., Jacek Kłoczkowski, ed., *Patriotyzm Polaków: Studia z historii idei* (Kraków: Ośrodek Myśli Politycznej, 2006); Arkadiusz Michał Stasiak, *Patriotyzm w myśli konfederatów barskich* (Lublin: Towarzystwo Naukowe Katolickiego Uniwersytetu Lubelskiego, 2005); Michał Syska, ed., *Ile ojczyzn? Ile patriotyzmów?* (Warsaw: Książka i Prasa, 2007); Andrzej Walicki, "The Three Traditions in Polish Patriotism," in *Polish Paradoxes*, ed. Stanislaw Gomulka and Antony Polonsky (London: Routledge, 1990), 21–39.

43. I borrow the phrase "the cultural liturgy" from Michal Jan Rozbicki, *Culture and Liberty in the Age of the American Revolution* (Charlottesville: University of Virginia Press, 2011), 109.

44. The phrase "a high voltage patriotism" is from Samuel L. Sharp, *Poland: White Eagle on a Red Field* (Cambridge, MA: Harvard University Press, 1953), 71. For studies invoking a parallel between Christ and Poland and attributing the concept of Poland as the martyred Christ to Adam Mickiewicz, the preeminent poet of the Romantic age in Poland, see, e.g., V. Kiernan, "Nationalist Movements and Social Classes," in *Nationalist Movements,* ed. Anthony D. Smith (New York: St. Martin's Press, 1977), 119; Smith, *National Identity,* 83. In truth, Mickiewicz emphatically declared that "the Polish nation is not a divinity like Christ." Mickiewicz, *Księgi pielgrzymstwa polskiego,* in *Dzieła,* ed. Zbigniew Jerzy Nowak et al., 17 vols. (Warsaw: Czytelnik, 1993–2005), 5:21. For an English translation, see Mickiewicz, *The Books of the Polish Pilgrimage,* in *Konrad Wallenrod and Other Writings,* trans. Jewell Parish et al. (Westport: Greenwood Press, 1975), 144.

45. For book-length contributions to the debate, see, e.g., Aleksander Hall, *Polskie patriotyzmy* (Gdańsk: Info-Trade, 1997); Wojciech Polak, *Patriotyzm dnia dzisiejszego* (Gdańsk: Finna, 2012); Dominik Zdort, ed., *Kompendium patiotyzmu* (Kraków: Wydawnictwo M, 2012).

46. Andrzej Nowak, "Wojna polsko-polska pod flagą biało-czerwoną," interview by Andrzej Brzeziecki and Michał Olszewski, *Tygodnik Powszechny,* 17 June 2012, 13.

47. In contrast, Stefan Żeromski's play, *The Rose* (*Róża,* 1909), for example, presents a patriotic ethos anchored in a set of twenty values and commitments, ranging from political independence to economic modernization, social betterment, and respect for those who have alternative views about serving their country. A century later, most of these values and commitments are no longer perceived as patriotic. For a discussion of the patriotic ethos in *The Rose,* see Małgorzata Fudalej and Janusz Goćkowski, "Los i ethos Polaków w drodze ku niepodległości," in *Narody: Jak powstawały i jak wybijały się na niepodległość?,* ed. Marcin Kula (Warsaw: Państwowe Wydawnictwo Naukowe, 1989), 229–46.

48. See, e.g., Wojciech Baliński, ed., *Wartości, rodzina, szkoła: Patriotyzm na co dzień i od święta* (Kraków: Księgarnia Akademicka, 2010). For an assessment of arguments for and against the teaching of patriotism in schools, see chapter 6 ("Should Schools Teach Patriotism?") in Harry Brighouse, *On Education* (London: Routledge, 2006), 95–114.

Introduction

1. Citizenship is understood here in its wider sense as membership in a community, which encompasses civil, political, and social rights. See, e.g., Barbara Hobson and Ruth Lister, "Citizenship," in *Contested Concepts in Gender and Social Politics,* ed. Barbara Hobson, Jane Lewis, and Birte Siim (Cheltenham, UK: Edward Elgar,

2002), 23–54. Like patriotism, the concept of citizenship is fraught with controversy. For an incisive discussion of debates about citizenship, see chapter 3 ("The Gendered Subject as Citizen") in Maro Pantelidou Maloutas, *The Gender of Democracy: Citizenship and Gendered Subjectivity*, trans. D. Koulouthros and Maloutas (London: Routledge, 2006), 64–85.

2. See Walter Benjamin, "N," trans. Leigh Hafrey and Richard Sieburth, in *Benjamin: Philosophy, History, Aesthetics*, ed. Gary Smith (Chicago: University of Chicago Press, 1989), 48.

3. My critical category, the drama of patriotism, is heuristic. That is to say, it is designed to facilitate interpretation. I use this broad classification for plays that share enough thematic coherence to be considered a subgenre.

4. I have adapted the methodological frameworks suggested by Lisa A. Freeman, *Character's Theater: Genre and Identity on the Eighteenth-Century English Stage* (Philadelphia: University of Pennsylvania Press, 2002); Louis Adrian Montrose, "The Purpose of Playing: Reflections on a Shakespearean Anthropology," *Helios* 7 (Spring 1980): 51–74; Robert Weimann, *Shakespeare and the Popular Tradition in the Theater: Studies in the Social Dimension of Dramatic Form and Function*, ed. Robert Schwartz (Baltimore: Johns Hopkins University Press, 1978).

5. I use the term *drame romantique* in its original meaning that applies to plays such as Victor Hugo's *Hernani* (1830) and Edmond Rostand's *Cyrano de Bergerac* (1897).

6. The origins of the Polish-Lithuanian Commonwealth lie in the late fourteenth century when political self-interest and dynastic accident led to the union of Poland and Lithuania in the persons of a daughter of the sonless Louis of Anjou, Hedwig (Jadwiga), Queen of Poland, and a Lithuanian duke, Jogaila (Władysław Jagiełło), in 1386.

7. The 1989 election was semi-free in the sense that 65 percent of the seats in the House of Representatives were reserved for a coalition of the Communist Party and its satellites; only the Senate was to be freely elected. Solidarity was both a trade union and a mass social movement. It grew out of a protest movement of the 1970s, asserted itself the during a strike in a Gdańsk shipyard in August 1980, and was licensed as an official organization in November 1980. Delegalized and forced underground in December 1981, Solidarity regained its legal status in April 1989.

8. Franco Moretti, *Atlas of the European Novel, 1800–1900* (London: Verso, 1999), 150. See also Patricia Meyer Spacks, *Boredom: The Literary History of a State of Mind* (Chicago: University of Chicago Press, 1995).

9. Defining the span of the Enlightenment in Poland continues to be a matter of debate. In earlier scholarship, the election of Stanisław Antoni (August) Poniatowski to the throne in 1764 and the fall of the Polish-Lithuanian Commonwealth in 1795 were typically used as convenient markers to stake out its chronological boundaries.

In more recent studies, different scholars date the beginnings of the Polish Enlightenment to 1730, 1740, or 1750, and its close to 1800, 1815, 1822, or 1830.

10. For the history of the Enlightenment, see especially Dan Edelstein, *The Enlightenment: A Genealogy* (Chicago: University of Chicago, 2010); Peter Gay, *The Enlightenment: An Interpretation*, 2 vols. (New York: Vintage, 1966–69); Margaret C. Jacob, *The Radical Enlightenment: Pantheists, Freemasons, and Republicans* (Boston: Allen and Unwin, 1981). For a discussion of modernity as an uncompleted project of the Enlightenment, see Jürgen Habermas, "Modernity: An Unfinished Project," trans. Nicholas Walker, in *Habermas and the Unfinished Project of Modernity: Critical Essays on "The Philosophical Discourse of Modernity,"* ed. Maurizio Passerin d'Entrèves and Seyla Benhabib (Cambridge, MA: MIT Press, 1997), 38–55. For debates about the Enlightenment and its legacy, see, e.g., Michael Baker and Peter Hanns Reill, eds., *What's Left of Enlightenment? A Postmodern Question* (Stanford, CA: Stanford University Press, 2001); John Bender, "A New History of the Enlightenment?," in *The Profession of Eighteenth-Century Literature: Reflections on an Institution*, ed. Leo Damrosch (Madison: University of Wisconsin Press, 1992), 62–83; Larry Wolff, *Inventing Eastern Europe: The Map of Civilization on the Mind of the Enlightenment* (Stanford, CA: Stanford University Press, 1994).

11. It should be added here that many Enlightenment thinkers and writers believed that women's limited education precluded their access to the full rights of citizenship; to address this deficiency, numerous pedagogical projects were launched across Europe during the second half of the century. On this issue, see, e.g., Martine Sonnet, "A Daughter to Educate," trans. Arthur Goldhammer, in *Renaissance and Enlightenment Paradoxes*, ed. Natalie Zemon Davis and Arlette Farge, vol. 3 of *A History of Women in the West*, ed. Georges Duby and Michelle Perrot (Cambridge, MA: Harvard University Press, 1993), 101–31. With regard to the rise of feminism, it bears emphasis that while voices protesting women's subordination and oppression within society go back hundreds of years, full-fledged feminist movements, with the necessary organizations and publications to assert feminist views, date from the 1830s, and the term *feminism* did not appear until the 1870s. See Karen M. Offen, *European Feminisms, 1750–1950: A Political History* (Stanford, CA: Stanford University Press, 2000).

12. Londa Schiebinger, *Nature's Body: Gender in the Making of Modern Science* (Boston: Beacon Press, 1993), 38.

13. Ibid.

14. Ibid., 37–38. See also Thomas W. Laqueur, *Making Sex: Body and Gender from the Greeks to Freud* (Cambridge, MA: Harvard University Press, 1990).

15. Joan W. Scott, *Only Paradoxes to Offer: French Feminists and the Rights of Man* (Cambridge, MA: Harvard University Press, 1996), x.

16. Schiebinger, *Nature's Body*, 38.

17. Dena Goodman, *Becoming a Woman in the Age of Letters* (Ithaca, NY: Cornell University Press, 2009), 55.

18. Karin Hausen, "Family and Role-Division: The Polarisation of Sexual Stereotypes in the Nineteenth Century—An Aspect of the Dissociation of Work and Family Life," trans. Cathleen Catt, in *The German Family: Essays on the Social History of the Family in Nineteenth- and Twentieth-Century Germany*, ed. Richard J. Evans and W. R. Lee (London: Croom Helm, 1981), 51. On the history of the dichotomization of character traits by sex, see also, e.g., Viola Klein, *The Feminine Character: History of an Ideology*, 3rd ed. (London: Routledge, 1989); Lieselotte Steinbrügge, *The Moral Sex: Woman's Nature in the French Enlightenment*, trans. Pamela E. Selwyn (New York: Oxford University Press, 1995).

19. Schiebinger, *Nature's Body*, 39.

20. See Emanuel Rostworowski, *Ostatni król Rzeczypospolitej: Geneza i upadek Konstytucji 3 maja* (Warsaw: Wiedza Powszechna, 1966), 158–71. On the instability of the concept of patriotism in the Polish Enlightenment, see also Barbara Grochulska, "'Patrioci prawdziwi i fałszywi': Historyczne kryteria patriotyzmu (II połowa XVIII—XIX w.)," in *Pamiętnik XIII Powszechnego Zjazdu Historyków Polskich, Poznań, 6–9 września 1984 roku*, vol. 2, ed. Hubert Izdebski (Wrocław: Zakład Narodowy im. Ossolińskich, 1988), 67–76; Dariusz Rolnik, *Portret szlachty czasów stanisławowskich, epoki kryzysu, odrodzenia i upadku Rzeczypospolitej w pamiętnikach polskich* (Katowice: Wydawnictwo Uniwersytetu Śląskiego, 2009), 224–330; Jerzy Snopek, *Prowincja oświecona: Kultura literacka Ziemi Krakowskiej w dobie Oświecenia 1750–1815* (Warsaw: Wydawnictwo Instytutu Badań Literackich PAN, 1992), 298–306.

21. The phrase "a certain amount of xenophobia" is from Snopek, *Prowincja oświecona*, 299. The celebration of the great noblemen of Poland's past was part of the flourishing cult of great men in eighteenth-century Europe, but the cult itself was hardly a modern invention. As David A. Bell notes, "It reached back to Roman and Greek antiquity, where it had held a central place in political life and had found its defining expression in one of the great classical works of history: Plutarch's *Lives*." The eighteenth-century cult of great men differed from its predecessors in "its scale, its relentless emphasis on patriotic pedagogy, and its definition of 'greatness.'" As a result, the eighteenth-century canon of great men included not only military heroes but also those regarded as true benefactors of humanity. Bell, *The Cult of the Nation in France: Inventing Nationalism, 1680–1800* (Cambridge, MA: Harvard University Press, 2001), 108–9.

22. The advocacy of improved education for women and a woman's right to select her life partner was part of the patriotic agenda promoted by the *Polish Patriot* (*Patriota Polski*), a short-lived journal expressly addressed to a middle-class readership and published in Warsaw in 1761.

23. For the locus classicus on patriotism, see Marcus Tullius Cicero, *On Duties*, trans. and ed. Miriam T. Griffin and E. Margaret Atkins (Cambridge: Cambridge University Press, 1991). A Polish translation, by Stanisław Koszutski, of *On Duties* was published in 1593 and reissued in 1766. Jan Kochanowski's *The Dismissal of the Greek Envoys* (*Odprawa posłów greckich*), first performed and published in 1578, is a particularly compelling example of the Ciceronian imperative of country before self in Polish dramatic literature. However, this drama fell on deaf ears, even though Kochanowski's contemporaries held him in high regard as a poet. It was rediscovered only in the 1840s, after more than two centuries of neglect.

24. I use the term *virtue* in its earlier, classical political meaning, referring to public spirit, that is, the willingness of citizens to engage actively in civic life and to put the common good over self-interest.

25. For a discussion of Charles-Louis de Montesquieu's comment in *The Spirit of the Laws* (*L'Esprit des lois*, 1748) that republics rest on the virtue of their citizens, see Howard Mumford Jones, *O Strange New World: American Culture, The Formative Years* (New York: Viking Press, 1964), 256–58. The first Polish translation of *The Spirit of the Laws*, by Mateusz Czarnek, was published in 1777. However, the credit for introducing *The Spirit of the Laws* to Polish readers belongs to the Warsaw *Monitor*, an essay periodical committed to disseminating Enlightenment thought to the remotest corners of the country. In 1768, the *Monitor* serialized Ignacy Krasicki's and Joachim Kalnassy's digests of Montesquieu's treatise.

26. For a reprint of Minasowicz's essay, see *"Monitor" 1765–1785: Wybór*, ed. Elżbieta Aleksandrowska (Wrocław: Zakład Narodowy im. Ossolińskich, 1976), 248–53.

27. Kołłątaj's pamphlet is reprinted in *Kołłątaj i inni: Z publicystyki doby Sejmu Czteroletniego*, ed. Łukasz Kądziela (Warsaw: Wydawnictwa Szkolne i Pedagogiczne, 1991), 131–50. It is typically (though not universally) asserted in scholarly commentary that Kołłątaj's virtuous patriot represents Stanisław August and that the pamphlet is a public relations piece to improve the king's image during the Four-Year Parliament. For this view, see, e.g., Anna Grześkowiak-Krwawicz, "U początków czarnej i białej legendy Stanisława Augusta," *Wiek Oświecenia* 15 (1999): 173–74.

28. Józef Szczepaniec, "Co to jest być prawdziwym patriotą? Jakobińska broszura z 1794 r.: Zagadnienia autorstwa i tekstu," *Ze Skarbca Kultury* 24 (1973): 26.

29. Kazimierz Hoszkiewicz, *Co to jest być prawdziwym patriotą?*, *Ze Skarbca Kultury* 24 (1973): 52. The attribution of this pamphlet to Hoszkiewicz has been established by Józef Szczepaniec. Earlier, Bogusław Leśnodorski attributed the pamphlet with some hesitation to Kołłątaj. See Leśnodorski, *Polscy jakobini: Karta z dziejów insurekcji 1794 roku* (Warsaw: Książka i Wiedza, 1960), 347; Leśnodorski, *Les Jacobins polonais* (Paris: Société des Études Robespierristes, 1965), 228. For other major contributions to the debate about patriotism in late eighteenth-century Poland, see, e.g., Józef Wybicki's *Patriotic Letters* (*Listy patriotyczne*, 1777–78), in which he argues that as long as the laws continue to favor a privileged minority, the

state will continue to decay. Patriotism was also a frequent subject of reflection in the newspaper and periodical press and in diaries and memoirs.

30. For an English translation, see Ignacy Krasicki, "Sacred Love of Our Cherished Homeland," in *Polish Baroque and Enlightenment Literature: An Anthology*, ed. and trans. Michael J. Mikoś (Columbus, OH: Slavica, 1996), 244.

31. For an English translation, see Adam Mickiewicz, "To a Polish Mother," in *Polish Romantic Literature: An Anthology*, ed. and trans. Michael J. Mikoś (Bloomington, IN: Slavica, 2002), 42–43. For controversies over this poem, see Halina Filipowicz, "Pojedynek Anny Schugt Terleckiej z Mickiewiczem," *Nowy Dziennik— Przegląd Polski*, 25 November 2005, 2; Jarosław Marek Rymkiewicz, Dorota Siwicka, Alina Witkowska, and Marta Zielińska, eds., *Mickiewicz: Encyklopedia* (Warsaw: Bertelsmann Media, 2001), 110–12. Anna Schugt Terlecka's rebuttal to Mickiewicz, in her poem "O, Polish Mother" ("O matko Polko," written ca. 1831), is especially interesting. She takes Mickiewicz to task for expecting Polish mothers to realize a deadly template of self-effacement and self-sacrifice—the traditional female roles that only reinforce gender stereotypes. Defying Mickiewicz in the name of a community of Polish mothers, she makes her case in terms of their contribution as educators, mentors, and activists. Unpublished until 1971, Terlecka's poem circulated widely in Poland in the 1830s.

32. Orlando Figes, *The Crimean War: A History* (New York: Henry Holt, 2010), 79. The scholarship on the fall of Poland-Lithuania is extensive. For a succinct account, see Jerzy Lukowski, *The Partitions of Poland: 1772, 1793, 1795* (London: Longman, 1999). For an interpretive narrative, see Tadeusz Cegielski and Łukasz Kądziela, *Rozbiory Polski 1772—1793—1795* (Warsaw: Wydawnictwa Szkolne i Pedagogiczne, 1990); Jerzy Lukowski, *Liberty's Folly: The Polish-Lithuanian Commonwealth in the Eighteenth Century, 1697–1795* (London: Routledge, 1991); Michael G. Müller, *Die Teilungen Polens: 1772—1793—1795* (Munich: C. H. Beck, 1984).

33. Juliusz Nowak-Dłużewski, *Studia i szkice* (Warsaw: Instytut Wydawniczy Pax, 1973), 177. See also Mieczysław Klimowicz, *Oświecenie*, 6th ed. (Warsaw: Wydawnictwo Naukowe PWN, 1998), 522; Juliusz Nowak-Dłużewski, *Z historii polskiej literatury i kultury* (Warsaw: Instytut Wydawniczy Pax, 1967), 95; Ryszard Przybylski, *Klasycyzm czyli prawdziwy koniec Królestwa Polskiego*, 2nd ed. (Gdańsk: Marabut, 1996), 119–48; Andrzej Wierzbicki, "Lelewel i ojczyzna," in *W kręgu historii, historiografii i polityki*, ed. Alina Barszczewska-Krupa et al. (Łódź: Wydawnictwo Uniwersytetu Łódzkiego, 1997), 39–40.

34. As Isabel Rivers notes in a different context, "The appeal to history [is] essential to patriotism." Rivers, *The Poetry of Conservatism, 1600–1745: A Study of Poets and Public Affairs from Jonson to Pope* (Cambridge: Rivers Press, 1973), 205. For a different version of this argument, see Bonamy Dobrée, "The Theme of Patriotism in the Poetry of the Early Eighteenth Century," *Proceedings of the British*

Academy 35 (1949): 49–65. Dobrée's point is that the emotion of patriotism can be "nourished by a sense of the past, or again by a vision of the future" (50).

35. As Dietz notes, "The powerful symbolism of heroic self-sacrifice for the glorious fatherland, so much a part of modern patriotism, had its roots in Roman history." Dietz, "Patriotism," 178. While Cicero's maxim has come to hold a permanent grip on the Polish cultural imagination both during and after the period of foreign rule, the force of his dictum has obscured the fact that in *On Duties* (I, 45, 159) he asks whether the fatherland is always and under any circumstances to be placed above the virtue of moderation. His answer is a clear no. As I argue later in this book, the Polish reception of the imperative to serve one's country and, if need be, lay down one's life for it can be more appropriately called Catonian (after the Roman senator Marcus Porcius Cato who opposed Julius Caesar's rise to the dictatorship of Rome and ultimately took his own life in protest) rather than unequivocally Ciceronian. For a comparison of Catonism with Ciceronianism, see Reed Browning, *Political and Constitutional Ideas of the Court Whigs* (Baton Rouge: Louisiana State University Press, 1982), 210–56.

36. Barbara Hodgdon, *The End Crowns All: Closure and Contradiction in Shakespeare's History* (Princeton, NJ: Princeton University Press, 1991), 16.

37. Written in 1797 and originally entitled "The Song of the Polish Legions in Italy" ("Pieśń legionów polskich we Włoszech"), Józef Wybicki's poem was renamed "A Patriotic Song" in 1806. For an English translation, see Wybicki, "The Song of the Polish Legions in Italy," in *Polish Baroque and Enlightenment Literature*, ed. Mikoś, 302–3.

38. L. P. Hartley, *The Go-Between* (New York: New York Review of Books, 2002), 17.

39. This concept of gender is often identified with the highly influential publications of Judith Butler, especially *Gender Trouble: Feminism and the Subversion of Identity* (New York: Routledge, 1990). In fact, it is closer to the position that the British poet-philosopher Denise Riley has advanced in her groundbreaking but now forgotten study, *"Am I That Name?": Feminism and the Category of "Women" in History* (Basingstoke: Macmillan, 1988).

40. For a fuller discussion of *The Defense of Trembowla*, see chapter 2.

41. John Stuart Mill, *On Liberty*, ed. David Bromwich and George Kateb (New Haven, CT: Yale University Press, 2003), 131, 134.

42. The corresponding sentence in *On Liberty* reads: "Precisely because the tyranny of opinion is such as to make eccentricity a reproach, it is desirable, in order to break through that tyranny, that people should be eccentric." Mill, *On Liberty*, 131.

43. The quotations are from James R. Thompson's review of *Thaddeus Kosciuszko: The Purest Son of Liberty* by James S. Pula, *Sarmatian Review* 20, no. 1 (January 2000): 680. For a depiction of Kościuszko as a model of upright character

and behavior, see, e.g., Francis Casimir Kajencki, *Discordant Trumpet: Discrimination of American Historians* (El Paso, TX: Southwest Polonia Press, 2003), esp. 28–29, 50, 53, 75–76.

44. On "the impulse to moralize reality," see Hayden White, *The Content of the Form: Narrative Discourse and Historical Representation* (Baltimore: Johns Hopkins University Press, 1989), 14. The term *thought-world* is from George Schöpflin, "The Functions of Myth and a Taxonomy of Myths," in *Myths and Nationhood*, ed. Geoffrey Hosking and George Schöpflin (New York: Routledge, 1997), 20.

45. Paul K. Longmore, *The Invention of George Washington* (Berkeley: University of California Press, 1988), ix. As Schöpflin, among others, points out, "Myth cannot be constructed purely out of false material; it has to have some relationship with the memory of the collectivity that has fashioned it." Schöpflin, "Functions of Myth," 26.

46. Lukowski, *Liberty's Folly*, 218.

47. For an example of this myth in scholarship, see Józef Andrzej Gierowski, *The Polish-Lithuanian Commonwealth in the XVIIIth Century: From Anarchy to Well-Organised State*, trans. Henry Leeming (Kraków: Polska Akademia Umiejętności, 1996), 203–5. Gierowski omits provincial theatres altogether from his discussion.

48. The National Theatre as a melting pot is a powerful metaphor, but the mingling of heterogeneous crowds at the National was much exaggerated by critics at the time, as it has been by many historians since. See, e.g., Zofia Wołoszyńska, "Teatr Narodowy (dzieje instytucji)," in *Słownik literatury polskiego oświecenia*, ed. Teresa Kostkiewiczowa, 2nd ed. (Wrocław: Zakład Narodowy im. Ossolińskich, 1991), 603–9.

49. For this claim, see, e.g., Rett R. Ludwikowski and William F. Fox Jr., *The Beginning of the Constitutional Era: A Bicentennial Comparative Analysis of the First Modern Constitutions* (Washington, DC: Catholic University of America Press, 1993), 134; Alex Storozynski, *The Peasant Prince: Thaddeus Kosciuszko and the Age of Revolution* (New York: St. Martin's Press, 2009), 146.

50. For attempts to set the record straight, see Gierowski, *Polish-Lithuanian Commonwealth*, 254; Jerzy Michalski, "Sejm w czasach panowania Stanisława Augusta," in *Historia Sejmu polskiego*, ed. Michalski, vol. 1 (Warsaw: Państwowe Wydawnictwo Naukowe, 1984), 405–6; Rostworowski, *Ostatni król*, 227.

51. For this view, see, e.g., Artur Śliwiński, *Powstanie Kościuszkowskie*, 2nd ed. (Warsaw: M. Arct, 1920), 68, 70; Daniel Stone, "Poland and the Lessons of the American Revolution," in *East Central European Society and War in the Era of Revolutions, 1775–1856*, ed. Béla K. Király (New York: Brooklyn College Press, 1984), 7. For a different assessment of the Racławice victory, see, e.g., Marian

Drozdowski, "Bitwa pod Racławicami na tle Insurekcji Kościuszkowskiej," in *Panorama Racławicka,* ed. Krystyn Matwijowski (Wrocław: Dolnośląskie Towarzystwo Społeczno-Kulturalne, 1987), 14–15; Jan Lubicz-Pachoński, *Bitwa pod Racławicami* (Warsaw: Państwowe Wydawnictwo Naukowe, 1984), 40–41, 46, 57, 67–74, 78–81. Drozdowski's and Lubicz-Pachoński's view, in short, is that the victory was the outcome of a chain of misjudgments and miscalculations on the Russian side and some quick action on the Polish side.

52. Among the many examples of this claim, perhaps the most notable are Małgorzata Fidelis, "'Participation in the Creative Work of the Nation': Polish Women Intellectuals in the Cultual Construction of Female Gender Roles, 1864–1890," *Journal of Women's History* 13, no. 1 (Spring 2001): 111; Maria Janion, "Szalona," *Twórczość* 44, no. 10 (October 1988): 73; Zofia Kossak, *Rok polski: Obyczaj i wiara,* 2nd ed. (Warsaw: Instytut Wydawniczy Pax, 1958), 104; Elzbieta Ostrowska, "Filmic Representations of the 'Polish Mother' in Post-Second World War Polish Cinema," *European Journal of Women's Studies* 5, nos. 3–4 (November 1998): 420; Krzysztof Tomasik, *Homobiografie: Pisarki i pisarze polscy XIX i XX wieku* (Warsaw: Wydawnictwo Krytyki Politycznej, 2008), 37; Sławomira Walczewska, *Damy, rycerze i feministki: Kobiecy dyskurs emancypacyjny w Polsce* (Kraków: eFKa, 1999), 41. For overviews of the historiography on the idea of separate spheres and for reassessments of the split between the public/political and private/domestic realms, see especially Dena Goodman, "Public Sphere and Private Life: Toward a Synthesis of Current Historiographical Approaches to the Old Regime," *History and Theory* 31, no. 1 (1992): 1–20; Joan B. Landes, ed., *Feminism, the Public and the Private* (Oxford: Oxford University Press, 1998); Johanna Meehan, ed., *Feminists Read Habermas* (London: Routledge, 1995); Amanda Vickery, "Golden Age to Separate Spheres? A Review of the Categories and Chronology of English Women's History," *Historical Journal* 36, no. 2 (June 1993): 383–414. For a summary of the debate about the separate spheres, see Robert B. Shoemaker, *Gender in English Society, 1650–1850: The Emergence of Separate Spheres?* (London: Longman, 1998), 6–10.

53. For a primary source on gender norms for Polish women, see especially Klementyna Tańska Hoffmanowa, *Pamiątka po dobrej matce, czyli ostatnie jej rady dla córki* (Warsaw, 1883). Originally published in 1819, *Pamiątka* (English title: *Keepsake of a Good Mother, or Her Last Advice to Her Daughter*) is a conduct book that codified standards of female behavior for many generations of Polish women. Tańska Hoffmanowa identified the following traits as the cardinal female virtues: "patience, sweetness, humility, a happy disposition, humanity, kindness, and constancy." Ursula Phillips, "The Upbringing and Education of Women as Represented in Novels by Nineteenth-Century Polish Women Writers," *Slavonic and East European Review* 77, no. 2 (April 1999): 207. Tańska Hoffmanowa's views were

enormously popular and influential in Polish society throughout the nineteenth century; at least eleven editions of *Keepsake* were published by 1901.

54. For a corrective to this fantasy, see, e.g., Wiesław Jamrozek and Dorota Żołądź-Strzelczyk, eds., *Rola i miejsce kobiet w edukacji i kulturze polskiej*, 2 vols. (Poznań: Instytut Historii Uniwersytetu Adama Mickiewicza, 1998–2001); Danuta Rzepniewska, "Rodzina ziemiańska w Królestwie Polskim," in *Społeczeństwo polskie XVIII i XIX wieku*, vol. 9., ed. Janina Leśkiewiczowa (Warsaw: Państwowe Wydawnictwo Naukowe, 1991), 137–200.

55. Eva Stachniak, "Why Did We Not Become Feminists? Women in Poland," *NWSA Journal* 7, no. 3 (Autumn 1995): 78.

56. By household theatres, I mean both semiprofessional facilities, maintained at aristocratic residences for the entertainment of family members and invited guests, and more modest arrangements at the homes of non-aristocrats, where a parlor or a dining room was temporarily converted into theatre space.

57. "Kolęda do polskiego wąsa" [1788], unpublished manuscript no. 131 (Jagiellonian University Library, Kraków), 98. The quotation is from a prayer-like litany of hateful deprecations that closes the poem. The full line reads: "May those feminine-masculine bastards, those hermaphrodites, perish [*Niech te basztardy kobieco-męskie, hermafrodyty przepadną*]."

58. See Katharine Eisaman Maus, *Being and Having in Shakespeare* (Oxford: Oxford University Press, 2013). For a related argument, based on an analysis of American fictional TV shows, see Susan J. Douglas, *Enlightened Sexism: The Seductive Message That Feminism's Work Is Done* (New York: Henry Holt, 2010).

59. Although in popular usage the term *gender relations* may mean only the way men treat women and vice versa, I use it in the sense of the complexities in power relations between the sexes within society and the structures through which these complexities are manifested and facilitated.

60. See Lechoń, *Dziennik*, 3:257.

61. Thomas Jefferson to Horatio Gates, 21 February 1798, in *The Papers of Thomas Jefferson*, vol. 30, ed. Barbara B. Oberg (Princeton, NJ: Princeton University Press, 2003), 123.

62. The term *lieu de mémoire* comes, of course, from Pierre Nora's essay that explicitly refers to classical mnemonics and its use of topoi. For an English translation, see Nora, "Between Memory and History: *Les Lieux de Mémoire*," trans. Marc Roudebush, *Representations* 26 (Spring 1989): 7–24. Natalie Zemon Davis and Randolph Starn's elaboration of Nora's (often misunderstood) term is helpful: "The literary confession, the nineteenth-century 'discovery' of the 'maladies of memory,' the commemorative monument, the ethnographical record—these are all 'places' where memories converge, condense, conflict, and define relationships between past, present, and future." Davis and Starn, "Introduction," *Representations* 26 (Spring 1989): 3.

63. After his return to Poland in 1784, Kościuszko continued to wear an American military uniform as a symbol of his commitment to the democratic ideals of the American Revolution. Ten years later, he dressed down by wearing a *sukmana*, a homespun peasant coat, in salute to his peasant troops.

Chapter 1

1. The playbill is quoted here from Jan Dembowski's letter to Ignacy Potocki, 20 February 1793, in Dembowski et al., *Tajna korespondencja z Warszawy do Ignacego Potockiego, 1792–1794*, ed. Maria Rymszyna and Andrzej Zahorski (Warsaw: Państwowe Wydawnictwo Naukowe, 1961), 148. Versions of the playbill have been published in Michał Janik, *Hugo Kołłątaj: Monografia z czterema podobiznami* (Lwów: privately printed, 1913), 293–94; Roman Kaleta, "Nawracanie posła: Biografia polityczna Jana Suchorzewskiego," in *Oświeceni i sentymentalni: Studia nad literaturą i życiem w Polsce w okresie trzech rozbiorów* (Wrocław: Zakład Narodowy im. Ossolińskich, 1971), 534–35; Jan Kott, ed., *Teatr Narodowy 1765–1794* (Warsaw: Państwowy Instytut Wydawniczy, 1967), 430. The reference to the year 1775 alludes to the adjournment of a rump Parliament that was called in 1773 to put a veneer of legality on the first partition of Poland-Lithuania.

2. The term *Revolutionary Parliament* was widely used at the time to describe the Parliament of 1788–92. See, e.g., Jan Dembowski's letter to Ignacy Potocki, 8 February 1794, in Dembowski et al., *Tajna korespondencja*, 318; Antoni Trębicki, *Opisanie sejmu ekstraordynaryjnego podziałowego roku 1793 w Grodnie; O rewolucji roku 1794*, ed. Jerzy Kowecki (Warsaw: Państwowy Instytut Wydawniczy, 1967), 60.

3. Quoted in Władysław Smoleński, *Konfederacja targowicka* (Kraków: privately printed, 1903), 28. For scholarly analyses of the Constitution, see, e.g., Jerzy Lukowski, "Recasting Utopia: Montesquieu, Rousseau, and the Polish Constitution of 3 May 1791," *Historical Journal* 37, no. 1 (March 1994): 65–87; Jerzy Michalski, "The Meaning of the Constitution of 3 May," trans. Janusz Duzinkiewicz, in *Constitution and Reform in Eighteenth-Century Poland: The Constitution of 3 May 1791*, ed. Samuel Fiszman (Bloomington: Indiana University Press, 1997), 251–86.

4. For a list of the signatories of the Act of Confederacy, see Smoleński, *Konfederacja targowicka*, 29. In scholarship, the debate about the origins and the consequences of the Targowica Confederacy and about the issue of culpability has spawned a historical literature of unrivaled moral intensity. See, e.g., Wacław Uruszczak, "Targowica—symbol narodowej zdrady," in *O prawie i jego dziejach księgi*

dwie, ed. Marian Mikołajczyk et al., 2 vols. (Białystok: Wydawnictwo Uniwersytetu w Białymstoku, 2010), 1:565–73.

5. Iakov Bulgakov, "Deklaracja dana w Warszawie maja 7/18 dnia 1792 roku," reprinted in Emanuel Rostworowski, *Popioły i korzenie: Szkice historyczne i rodzinne* (Kraków: Znak, 1985), 174.

6. Richard Butterwick, "The Enlightened Monarchy of Stanisław August Poniatowski (1764–1795)," in *The Polish-Lithuanian Monarchy in European Context, c.1500–1795*, ed. Butterwick (Basingstoke: Palgrave, 2001), 212.

7. Historians have examined Stanisław August's reign from a variety of angles, analyzing his strategies and compromises and attempting to evaluate what he achieved. To some, he is one of the most effective and attractive of Poland's rulers, distinguished by his "political wisdom, deeply felt patriotism, and exceptional services to Polish culture." Butterwick, *Polish Revolution*, 320. See also Richard Butterwick, *Poland's Last King and English Culture: Stanisław August Poniatowski, 1732–1798* (Oxford: Clarendon Press, 1998); Jean Fabre, *Stanislas-Auguste Poniatowski et L'Europe des Lumières: Étude de cosmopolitisme* (Paris: Les Belles Lettres, 1952); Jerzy Michalski, *Stanisław August Poniatowski*, ed. Wojciech Kriegseisen (Warsaw: Instytut Historii PAN, 2009). Others see him as a symbol of opportunistic calculation, abject servility, and fiscal irresponsibility. See, e.g., Tadeusz Korzon, *Wewnętrzne dzieje Polski za Stanisława Augusta (1764–1794): Badania historyczne ze stanowiska ekonomicznego i administracyjnego*, 2nd ed., vol. 3 (Kraków, 1897), 4–102; Jerzy Łojek, *Upadek Konstytucji 3 Maja: Studium historyczne* (Wrocław: Zakład Narodowy im. Ossolińskich, 1976); Jerzy Łojek, *Wokół sporów i polemik: Publicystyka historyczna* (Lublin: Wydawnictwo Lubelskie, 1991), 157–89; Krystyna Zienkowska, *Stanisław August Poniatowski* (Wrocław: Zakład Narodowy im. Ossolińskich, 1998).

8. The classic work on the subject is Robert Howard Lord, *The Second Partition of Poland: A Study in Diplomatic History* (Cambridge, MA: Harvard University Press, 1915).

9. Modeled on Joseph Addison and Richard Steele's *Spectator*, the *Monitor* was published over the course of twenty years (1765–85) under several editors, each of whom had a somewhat different editorial program. Its articles covered everything from politics to science, history to cultural criticism, and philosophy to theatre. All the topics were seasoned with pungent editorial comment and enlivened by the controversial views of some of the contributors, but the prevailing polemical tone of the *Monitor* was moderate. In contrast to the *Spectator*, for example, the *Monitor* often marginalized or trivialized women's concerns, addressed its programmatic articles exclusively to male readers, and, overall, paid little attention to its female readership. The exact reasons why the *Monitor* closed down are shrouded in mystery. Elżbieta Aleksandrowska has suggested that it folded under pressure from conservative circles. See Aleksandrowska, "Wstęp," in *"Monitor" 1765–1785*, cxxxii–cxxxiii. Given

that competition between papers for readership was intense, however, it is not improbable that the *Monitor* lost a foothold in the market, even though it displayed great ingenuity in circumventing, for much of the time, the obstacles placed in its way by existing prejudices.

10. The title was soon changed to *The Return of the Deputy*. The comedy was Niemcewicz's second play.

11. For example, Butterwick uncritically accepts Stanisław August's scornful designation of Suchorzewski as "that crank." Butterwick, *Polish Revolution*, 243.

12. See, e.g., Kaleta, "Nawracanie posła"; Jerzy Łojek, ed., *Rok nadziei i rok klęski 1791–1792: Z korespondencji Stanisława Augusta z posłem polskim w Petersburgu Augustynem Deboli* (Warsaw: Czytelnik, 1964), 207–8n7; Zbigniew Raszewski, *Bogusławski*, 2 vols. (Warsaw: Państwowy Instytut Wydawniczy, 1972), 1:240–42, 245, 263; Smoleński, *Konfederacja targowicka*, 24. For a notable exception, see Tadeusz Korzon, *Odrodzenie w upadku: Wybór pism historycznych*, ed. Marian Henryk Serejski and Andrzej Feliks Grabski (Warsaw: Państwowy Instytut Wydawniczy, 1975), 506. In a major biographical essay on Suchorzewski, Zofia Zielińska attempts to maintain a neutral tone, yet she approvingly cites Walerian Kalinka's contemptuous and dismissive opinion that Suchorzewski was "an unrelenting shouter" in Parliament. See Zielińska, "Suchorzewski Jan," in *Polski Słownik Biograficzny*, vol. 45 (Warsaw: Societas Vistulana, 2007–8), 316. Kalinka's phrase is from his *Sejm Czteroletni*, 5th ed., 2 vols. (Warsaw: Volumen, 1991), 1:161.

13. The description of Suchorzewski's parliamentary speeches as "hysterical outbursts" is from Butterwick, *Poland's Last King*, 305. The claim that Suchorzewski was "psychologically unbalanced" comes from Jerzy Łojek, *Ku naprawie Rzeczypospolitej: Konstytucja 3 Maja* (Warsaw: Interpress, 1988), 87.

14. The Parliament of the Polish-Lithuanian Commonwealth worked by consensus. By the mid-seventeenth century, the principle of consensus hardened into that of unanimity; the veto of a single member was enough to block any bill or indeed to cancel an entire session of Parliament.

15. The Commonwealth ceased to be a hereditary monarchy in 1572 when Parliament institutionalized an electoral system during an interregnum following the death of Zygmunt August, the last king of the Jagiellonian dynasty.

16. See, e.g., Benedykt Hulewicz to Stanisław Szczęsny Potocki, 19 January 1791, and Jan Świejkowski to Leonard Świejkowski, 18 January 1791, quoted in Kaleta, "Nawracanie posła," 513 and 511, respectively; Tadeusz Matuszewicz's letter to the editor, published in *Gazeta Narodowa i Obca* on 19 January 1791 and reprinted in *Teatr Narodowy 1765–1794*, ed. Kott, 290–91.

17. For this suggestion, see Augustyn Jendrysik, "*Powrót posła* przed sądem publiczności (W dwusetną rocznicę urodzin J. U. Niemcewicza)," *Nowe Sygnały*, 17 February 1957, 2.

18. My reconstruction of the session of Parliament on 18 January 1791 will draw on *Diariusz sejmu ordynaryjnego pod Związkiem Konfederacji Generalnej Obojga Narodów w podwójnym posłów składzie zgromadzonego w Warszawie od dnia 16 grudnia roku 1790*, vol. 1, part 2 (Warsaw, [1793]), 93–109; Stanisław Kublicki, "Z Warszawy w sobotę dnia 22 stycznia roku 1791," *Gazeta Narodowa i Obca*, 22 January 1791, 25; Julian Ursyn Niemcewicz, *Pamiętniki czasów moich*, ed. Jan Dihm, 2 vols. (Warsaw: Państwowy Instytut Wydawniczy, 1957), 1:323–24; Stanisław August's letter to Franciszek Bukaty, 19 January 1791, in Walerian Kalinka, *Ostatnie lata panowania Stanisława Augusta*, 2nd ed., 2 vols. (Kraków, 1891), 2:177–78; Stanisław August's letter to Augustyn Deboli, 19 January 1791, in *Rok nadziei*, ed. Łojek, 28–29; Stanisław August's letter to Girolamo Lucchesini, 19 January 1791, in Zdzisław Skwarczyński, "Wstęp," in Julian Ursyn Niemcewicz, *Powrót posła: Komedia w trzech aktach oraz wybór bajek politycznych*, ed. Skwarczyński, 10th ed. (Wrocław: Zakład Narodowy im. Ossolińskich, 1983), lxv; Benedykt Hulewicz's letter to Stanisław Szczęsny Potocki, 19 January 1791, quoted in Kaleta, "Nawracanie posła," 512–13; Jan Świejkowski's letter to Leonard Świejkowski, 21 January 1791, published in Kaleta, "Nawracanie posła," 511–12. For an English translation of a relevant excerpt from Stanisław August's letter of 19 January 1791 to Deboli, see Laurence Senelick, ed., *National Theatre in Northern and Eastern Europe, 1746–1900* (Cambridge: Cambridge University Press, 1991), 199–200.

19. On Suchorzewski's annual income, see Korzon, *Wewnętrzne dzieje Polski*, 10.

20. This paragraph represents my interpretation of the evidence available in the following works: *Diariusz sejmu ordynaryjnego pod Związkiem Konfederacji Generalnej Obojga Narodów w Warszawie rozpoczętego*, 2 vols. (Warsaw, [1789–92]); *Diariusz sejmu ordynaryjnego pod Związkiem Konfederacji Generalnej Obojga Narodów w podwójnym posłów składzie zgromadzonego w Warszawie od dnia 16 grudnia roku 1790*, vol. 1, parts 1 and 2 (Warsaw, [1791–93]); Kaleta, "Nawracanie posła"; Kalinka, *Sejm Czteroletni*; Bernard Krakowski, *Oratorstwo polityczne na forum Sejmu Czteroletniego: Rekonesans* (Gdańsk: Gdańskie Towarzystwo Naukowe, 1968); Andrzej Stroynowski, *Opozycja sejmowa w dobie rządów Rady Nieustającej: Studium z dziejów kultury politycznej* (Łódź: Wyższa Szkoła Studiów Międzynarodowych, 2005); Józef Szczepaniec, "Sejm Wielki wobec zagadnień cenzury i wolności słowa," *Prace Literackie* 31 (1991): 156–84.

21. See Klimowicz, *Oświecenie*, 448; Krakowski, *Oratorstwo polityczne*, 111. For an excellent introduction to the elements of classical rhetoric and an extremely helpful discussion of the rhetorical arts as an indispensable nursery for politicians, see Quentin Skinner, *Reason and Rhetoric in the Philosophy of Hobbes* (Cambridge: Cambridge University Press, 1996), 40–51, 66–211.

22. Jan Suchorzewski, *Głos Jaśnie Wielmożnego Jmci Pana Suchorzewskiego, posła kaliskiego, na sesji sejmowej dnia 18 stycznia 1791 roku miany* [Warszawa],

[1791?], 2. Ryx held the theatrical monopoly from 1776 to 1791. On Ryx's business practices, see, e.g., Zbigniew Raszewski, *Teatr na placu Krasińskich* (Warsaw: Krąg, 1995), 30–34, 36–47.

23. Suchorzewski may have alluded to Kublicki's antimonopoly bill. Submitted in December 1788, it was passed only on 4 April 1791. In the following year, the Targowica Confederacy restored the theatre monopoly.

24. For such views, see, e.g., an untitled article by an anonymous author, published in the *Monitor* on 24 February 1781 and reprinted in Stanisław Ozimek, *Udział "Monitora" w kształtowaniu Teatru Narodowego (1765–1785)* (Wrocław: Zakład Narodowy im Ossolińskich, 1957), 196–99; the anonymous pamphlet *Byłem u pana podstolego* (Warsaw, [1792?]), 23–26; [Szczęsny Czacki?], *Listy z okoliczności "Monitorów" od przyjaciela do przyjaciela pisane*, an unpublished manuscript partly printed in Ozimek, *Udział "Monitora,"* 200–205; Franciszek Salezy Jezierski, *Wybór pism*, ed. Zdzisław Skwarczyński ([Warsaw]: Państwowy Instytut Wydawniczy, 1952), 196–99.

25. Suchorzewski, *Głos*, 2–3. By the 1780s, "'Muscovite' (*Moskal*) became the worst of all insults." Butterwick, *Polish Revolution*, 58.

26. Suchorzewski, *Głos*, 4. His statement was not rhetorical guff. In the Four-Year Parliament, he was the first to condemn, in his speech of 18 December 1788, exploitation and mistreatment of serfs. On 14 April 1791, moreover, he introduced a bill to extend certain rights (e.g., the right of protection against arbitrary arrest) to burghers. With some modifications, the bill was passed on 18 April 1791. Known as the Law on Royal Towns, it later became part of the Constitution of 3 May 1791.

27. In the play, Walery describes the French as a "valiant nation" that "burst the shackles of oppression and founded a free government on the ruins of tyranny." Julian Ursyn Niemcewicz, *Powrót posła: Komedia w trzech aktach oraz wybór bajek politycznych*, ed. Zdzisław Skwarczyński, 10th ed. (Wrocław: Zakład Narodowy im. Ossolińskich, 1983), 48. All subsequent quotations from *The Return of the Deputy* will be taken from this edition. It should be added here that Niemcewicz completed the play before the French Revolution disintegrated into the Reign of Terror.

28. This line of Suchorzewski's argument inescapably brings to mind John Locke's famous idea, expressed in the second of his *Two Treatises of Government* (1690): "Wherever law ends, tyranny begins." *The Selected Political Writings of John Locke*, ed. Paul E. Sigmund (New York: W. W. Norton, 2005), 106. The second *Treatise* was to establish a new movement in political thought, formulated most impressively by Montesquieu's *The Spirit of the Laws* and concerned with the containment of power by law and the protection of the individual against arbitrary power. Suchorzewski may have been familiar with the second *Treatise* through a French translation published in 1701 or, secondhand, through César Félicité Pyrrhis

de Varille's *A Political Compendium, or a Short Dissertation on Various Forms of Political Authority in Poland* (*Compendium politicum, seu Brevis dissertatio de variis Poloni imperii vicibus*, 1760) that draws heavily on Locke. De Varille, a French teacher working in Poland, was an intimate of a circle of reformist thinkers and writers in Warsaw. For information about de Varille and his *Compendium*, I am indebted to Irena Stasiewicz-Jasiukowa, *Człowiek i obywatel w piśmiennictwie naukowym i podręcznikach polskiego Oświecenia* (Wrocław: Zakład Narodowy im. Ossolińskich, 1979), 56–67.

29. Suchorzewski, *Głos*, 5–6. In the first sentence quoted here, he refers to the incidents in the Parliament of 1767–68, when Catherine II's ambassador in Warsaw used Russian troops to break parliamentary opposition and to push through the legislation demanded by the empress. Some members of Parliament were repeatedly detained, and four of them were arrested and deported to Russia, where they remained until 1773.

30. Suchorzewski had a point. The National Theatre never staged Kniaźnin's *The Spartan Mother*, and Józef Wybicki's *The Polish Woman*, also known as *The Motherland and Her Only Son* (*Ojczyzna z jednym synem*) and *Kazanowska*, was produced only in 1807. On Izabela Czartoryska's unsuccessful efforts to have *The Spartan Mother* performed at the National Theatre, see Alina Aleksandrowicz, "Sejm Czteroletni i Konstytucja 3 Maja w kręgu Puław," in *"Rok Monarchii Konstytucyjnej": Piśmiennictwo polskie lat 1791–1792 wobec Konstytucji 3 Maja*, ed. Teresa Kostkiewiczowa (Warsaw: Instytut Badań Literackich PAN, 1992), 197.

31. Suchorzewski, *Głos*, 5. By invoking the inviolable terms of the king's coronation oath, Suchorzewski reminded his listeners that in 1764, like every monarch-elect before him, Stanisław August swore to respect the rightful liberties and privileges of the nobility and to observe a set of legally binding regulations known as the *pacta conventa*. The *pacta conventa* set clear limits on the exercise of the royal prerogative. Regarded as almost a formal constitutional contract, they were the condition by which the newly elected king was accepted by the nobility.

32. Of the fifty-five regional assemblies that met in November 1790, only nine—three in Poland and six in Lithuania—supported hereditary succession to the throne. See Butterwick, *Polish Revolution*, 220–23; Zofia Zielińska, *"O sukcesyi tronu w Polszcze" 1787–1790* (Warsaw: Wydawnictwo Naukowe PWN, 1991), 207–20. For an incisive analysis that helps contextualize the statistical data, see Wojciech Szczygielski, "Z badań nad świadomością polityczną prowincjonalnej szlachty w dobie Sejmu Wielkiego (1790 r.)," in *W kręgu historii*, ed. Barszczewska-Krupa et al., 245–65.

33. As Stanisław August noted in his letter of 19 January 1791 to Deboli, "Yesterday, Suchorzewski was partly reading, partly speaking for a long time." *Rok nadziei*, ed. Łojek, 29. This comment also makes it clear that Suchorzewski repeatedly, as was his custom as an orator, departed from a prepared text.

34. *Diariusz sejmu ordynaryjnego pod Związkiem Konfederacji Generalnej Obojga Narodów w podwójnym posłów składzie zgromadzonego w Warszawie od dnia 16 grudnia roku 1790*, vol. 1, part 2 (Warsaw, [1793]), 98–99.

35. Jendrysik, "*Powrót posła* przed sądem," 2.

36. See, e.g., Jan Świejkowski's letter to Leonard Świejkowski, 21 January 1791, published in Kaleta, "Nawracanie posła," 511–12; Maria Wirtemberska's undated letter to an unidentified recipient, in *Teatr Narodowy 1765–1794*, ed. Kott, 655.

37. The phrase "Poland's historical demonology" is from Lukowski, *Liberty's Folly*, 205.

38. For evidence that the constitutional bill was forced through by means of a coup, see especially Bartłomiej Szyndler, *Czy Sejm Czteroletni uchwalił Konstytucję 3 maja? (Na tropie mitów narodowych)* (Warsaw: DiG, 2010). For additional details, see Jan Dihm, *Trzeci maj* (Kraków: Wydawnictwo Literacko-Naukowe, 1932), esp. 22, 34; Kalinka, *Sejm Czteroletni*, 2:506–30; Krakowski, *Oratorstwo polityczne*, 172–75; Łojek, *Ku naprawie*, 82–88; Rostworowski, *Ostatni król*, 231–36. On skeletons in the constitutional closet, see also Jerzy Kowecki, "Relacja o przewrocie trzeciomajowym czy dokument akcji prokonstytucyjnej?," in *Francja—Polska XVIII–XIX w.: Studia z dziejów kultury i polityki*, ed. Antoni Mączak et al. (Warsaw: Państwowe Wydawnictwo Naukowe, 1983), 81–96. For a corrective to the view, widely accepted in both scholarly and popular venues, that the constitutional bill was passed by acclamation, see Stanisław August's letter to Augustyn Deboli, 7 May 1791, in *Rok nadziei*, ed. Łojek, 49–50. For Suchorzewski's account of the coup, see his 1791 pamphlet, *Odezwa do Narodu, wraz z Protestacją dla śladu gwałtu i przemocy, do której w całym prawie Sejmie zbliżano, a w dniu trzecim maja 1791 dokonano*, reprinted in Leon Wegner, *Dzieje dnia trżeciego i piątego maja 1791* (Poznań, 1865), 269–75. For vivid, although not entirely reliable, accounts of the coup in English, see Ludwikowski and Fox, *Beginning of the Constitutional Era*, 136–37; Adam Zamoyski, *The Last King of Poland* (London: Jonathan Cape, 1992), 337–40.

39. Suchorzewski's speech of 30 August 1790, quoted in Kalinka, *Sejm Czteroletni*, 2:375. Suchorzewski returned to the question of hereditary succession in September. For a discussion of a speech he gave on 30 September, see Dariusz Złotkowski, "Stanisław August Poniatowski wobec sukcesji tronu na Sejmie Czteroletnim," in *Cztery lata nadziei: 200 rocznica Sejmu Wielkiego*, ed. Henryk Kocój (Katowice: Uniwersytet Śląski, 1988), 166. According to Złotkowski, Suchorzewski presented arguments that attest to his clear-sightedness and political nous, but Parliament's "blind enthusiasm" for hereditary kingship swept his "very wise position" aside.

40. Karyna Wierzbicka-Michalska, *Teatr w Polsce w XVIII wieku* (Warsaw: Państwowe Wydawnictwo Naukowe, 1977), 235; Kaleta, "Nawracanie posła," 497, 509, 518. These or similar phrases also occur in other publications.

41. Roman Kaleta, "*Wolność ojczysta:* Antytargowickie argumenty tragedii," *Archiwum Literackie* 9 (1965): 199; Anna Grześkowiak-Krwawicz, "Konstytucja 3 Maja—narodziny mitu," in *Ku reformie państwa i odrodzeniu moralnemu człowieka: Zbiór rozpraw i artykułów poswięconych dwusetnej rocznicy ustanowienia Konstytucji 3 Maja 1791 roku*, ed. Piotr Żbikowski (Rzeszów: Wydawnictwo Wyższej Szkoły Pedagogicznej, 1992), 145. "Zealot" is a standard term of opprobrium in commentaries on Suchorzewski. See, e.g., Łukasz Kądziela, "Wprowadzenie," in *Kołłątaj i inni*, ed. Kądziela, 33; Kaleta, "Nawracanie posła," 497; Raszewski, *Bogusławski* 1:245; Bartłomiej Szyndler, *Stanisław Nałęcz Małachowski 1736–1809* (Warsaw: Wydawnictwo Ministerstwa Obrony Narodowej, 1979), 129.

42. See an account entered by Antoni Siarczyński into parliamentary records and published anonymously as *Dzień trzeci maja roku 1791* (Warsaw, 1791), 14–30. This scene is also captured in Jean-Pierre Norblin's painting, *The Third of May* (*Dzień Trzeciego Maja*, 1806), based on his 1791 drawing.

43. See, e.g., Michał Czacki, *Wspomnienia z roku 1788 po 1792* (Poznań, 1862), 72; Julian Ursyn Niemcewicz, *Pamiętniki czasów moich* (Leipzig, 1868), 117; Niemcewicz, *Pamiętniki czasów moich* (1957 ed.), 1:335–36; Michel Oginski, *Mémoires de Michel Oginski sur la Pologne et les Polonais, depuis 1788 jusqu'a la fin de 1815*, vol. 1 (Paris, 1826), 123. For a visual representation of the incident, see Jan Matejko's painting, *The Constitution of 3 May* (*Konstytucja 3 Maja*, 1891). In it, Matejko has moved the attempted filicide from Parliament to a public square outside St. John's Cathedral.

44. See Jan Suchorzewski, *Przymówienie się Jaśnie Wielmożnego Jmci Jana Suchorzewskiego, posła kaliskiego, na sesji dnia 12 października 1790 roku* (Warsaw, [1790]), 6.

45. In April and again in November 1788, Suchorzewski pledged to make annual payments toward the augmentation and upkeep of the troops. In October 1788, he supported a proposal to expand the army from 30,000 to 100,000 men. He also campaigned to raise taxes in order to increase the army and offered, in November 1789, to pay a double income tax for this purpose.

46. Suchorzewski's decision to withdraw from the Targowica plot in the spring of 1793 seems to confirm Jerzy Kowecki's point that by mid-1793 brutal self-interest and out-and-out cynicism began to prevail within the Confederacy. See Kowecki, "Wstęp," in Trębicki, *Opisanie sejmu*, 22.

47. See Kaleta, "Nawracanie posła," 541.

48. Bernard Bailyn, *The Ideological Origins of the American Revolution* (Cambridge, MA: Harvard University Press, 1967), 44. The adjective *Catonic* is not a modern invention; it was used in the eighteenth century. See Browning, *Political and Constitutional Ideas*, 9n12.

49. The widespread resonance of the imperative of liberty-or-death in Polish culture has been attributed to the charismatic authority and pervasive influence of

Polish Romantic literature and its quasi-religious cult of self-sacrifice at the altar of Christ-like Poland. My argument, in contrast, is that the liberty-or-death imperative has a history that goes back considerably further than the Romantic era.

50. See Joseph Addison, *Cato*, ed. Laura J. Rosenthal, in *The Broadview Anthology of Restoration and Early Eighteenth-Century Drama*, ed. J. Douglas Canfield (Peterborough, ON: Broadview Press, 2001), 199, 212. For the argument that Henry made a different speech on 23 March 1775 and that his celebrated "Liberty or Death" oration was probably invented by his biographers many years later, see, e.g., Ray Raphael, *Founding Myths: Stories That Hide Our Patriotic Past* (New York: New Press, 2004), 145–56. The intense political resonance of the *Cato*-inspired slogan "Give me liberty or give me death!" continued into the twentieth century. In 1913, for example, British suffragettes printed it on their banners for a funeral of Emily Wilding Davison, who was killed while attempting to attach to the bridle of George V's horse a sash with the "Votes for Women" inscription. See Lisa Tickner, *The Spectacle of Women: Imagery of the Suffrage Campaign, 1907–14* (Chicago: University of Chicago Press, 1988), 138.

51. Józef Andrzej Załuski's translation of Cato's soliloquy in act 5, scene 1—the longest single speech in Addison's drama—was published in 1754. The publication of Józef Epifani Minasowicz's partial translation of the play followed in 1756. See Grzegorz Sinko, "Próby dramatyczne Józefa Andrzeja Załuskiego," *Pamiętnik Literacki* 41, nos. 3–4 (1950): 808–9; Ludwik Bernacki, *Teatr, dramat i muzyka za Stanisława Augusta*, 2 vols. (Lwów: Zakład Narodowy im. Ossolińskich, 1925), 2:214.

52. In his speech of 18 January 1791, Suchorzewski does invoke "the example of the virtuous and determined republicans—Romans, Greeks, Athenians," whom he wants "to emulate." Suchorzewski, *Głos*, 3. Is it a mere coincidence that he lists Romans before Greeks?

53. Catharine Edwards, *Death in Ancient Rome* (New Haven, CT: Yale University Press, 2007), 115, 100.

54. Browning, *Political and Constitutional Ideas*, 10.

55. Ibid., 19.

56. Richard Butterwick, "Positive and Negative Liberty in Eighteenth-Century Poland," in *Liberté: Héritage du Passé ou Idée des Lumières?*, ed. Anna Grześkowiak-Krwawicz and Izabella Zatorska (Kraków: Collegium Columbinum, 2003), 66.

57. Ibid.

58. Lukowski, *Liberty's Folly*, 8; Butterwick, "Positive and Negative Liberty," 69.

59. Quentin Skinner, *Hobbes and Republican Liberty* (Cambridge: Cambridge University Press, 2008), 211–12.

60. See Władysław Smoleński, *Ostatni rok Sejmu Wielkiego*, 2nd ed. (Kraków, 1897), 29.

61. Anna Grześkowiak-Krwawicz, "Zdrada Trzeciego Maja? Malkontenci wobec Ustawy Rządowej," in *Bo insza jest rzecz zdradzić, insza dać się złudzić:*

Problem zdrady w Polsce przełomu XVIII i XIX w., ed. Grześkowiak-Krwawicz (Warsaw: Wydawnictwo Instytutu Badań Literackich PAN, 1995), 55. In particular, the Roman-republicans objected to Article VII, "The King; the Executive Power" ("Król; władza wykonawcza"), of the Constitution. In their reading of Article VII, the monarch was granted full control over the government and hence unlimited executive power in the state. To the Roman-republicans, this represented a fundamental threat to liberty.

62. See Grześkowiak-Krwawicz, "Zdrada Trzeciego Maja?," 58. In a subsequent study, Grześkowiak-Krwawicz has modified her interpretation; the revised version is replete with heavy-handed moralizing. See Grześkowiak-Krwawicz, *Regina libertas: Wolność w polskiej myśli politycznej XVIII wieku* (Gdańsk: Słowo/obraz terytoria, 2006), 327.

63. Jerzy Michalski, "Z problematyki republikańskiego nurtu w polskiej reformatorskiej myśli politycznej w XVIII wieku," *Kwartalnik Historyczny* 90, no. 2 (1983): 334. See also Janusz Tazbir, "Próby zrozumienia racji targowiczan," in *Trudne stulecia: Studia z dziejów XVII i XVIII wieku*, ed. Łukasz Kądziela, Wojciech Kriegseisen, and Zofia Zielińska (Warsaw: Wydawnictwo Naukowe Semper, 1994), 235–44. In other scholarly commentaries, the Roman-republicans' idea that without liberty Poland-Lithuania had no purpose is typically dismissed outright as a "manic" delusion. See, e.g., Zofia Zielińska, "Seweryn Rzewuski—pułapki republikanizmu," in *Bo insza jest rzecz zdradzić*, 46.

64. See Marian Brandys, *Z dwóch stron drzwi* (Warsaw: NOWA, 1982), 22.

65. See Jarosław Maciejewski, *Teatry poznańskie w latach panowania króla Stanisława Augusta* (Warsaw: Państwowe Wydawnictwo Naukowe, 1986), 228.

66. For example, of the three provincial theatricals invoked by Suchorzewski, Raszewski mentions only the Puławy production of *The Spartan Mother*. He argues that Suchorzewski referred to this production to make political capital out of the fact that Niemcewicz performed in it. According to Raszewski, Suchorzewski wanted to remind Parliament of Niemcewicz's close ties to the Czartoryskis who, until recently, were bitterly anatagonistic toward the king. In Raszewski's interpretation, Suchorzewski insinuated that a man who enjoyed the Czartoryskis' patronage and who was elected to Parliament as their protégé only to go on to curry favor at the royal court could not be trusted. See Raszewski, *Bogusławski*, 1:241.

67. Montrose, "Purpose of Playing," 68.

68. Steele's essay no. 167 (4 May 1710), reprinted in Joseph Addison and Richard Steele, *The Tatler*, ed. Donald F. Bond, 3 vols. (Oxford: Clarendon Press, 1987), 2:423. In the same essay, Steele adds: "Young Men, who are too unattentive to receive Lectures, are irresistibly taken with Performances" (2:423).

69. William Dunlap, *History of the American Theatre*, vol. 1 (New York: Burt Franklin, 1963), 133.

70. In *A Treatise of Human Nature* (1739–40), David Hume makes a bold and provocative claim that "reason is, and ought only to be the slave of the passions, and can never pretend to any other office than to serve and obey them." Hume, *A Treatise of Human Nature*, ed. David Fate Norton and Mary J. Norton (Oxford: Oxford University Press, 2000), 266. On Hume's influence on the thought and values of the Enlightenment, see Craig Taylor and Stephen Buckle, eds., *Hume and the Enlightenment* (London: Pickering and Chatto, 2011).

71. Denise S. Sechelski, "Garrick's Body and the Labor of Art in Eighteenth-Century Theater," *Eighteenth-Century Studies* 29, no. 4 (Summer 1996): 377.

72. Graham Ley, "The Significance of Diderot," *New Theatre Quarterly* 11, no. 44 (November 1995): 349. *The Paradox of the Actor* was published only in 1830, but its contents and tenor were apparently known to a limited circle of Diderot's contemporaries even before it appeared in print.

73. Diderot, *Paradoxe sur le comédien*, quoted in Ley, "Significance of Diderot," 352; Ley's translation.

74. Diderot, *Paradoxe sur le comédien*, quoted in Ley, "Significance of Diderot," 350; Ley's translation, slightly modified.

75. Ley, "Significance of Diderot," 353.

76. See Sechelski, "Garrick's Body." See also, e.g., Alan S. Downer, "Nature to Advantage Dressed: Eighteenth-Century Acting," *PMLA* 58, no. 4 (December 1943): 1002–37; Joseph R. Roach, *The Player's Passion: Studies in the Science of Acting*, 2nd ed. (Ann Arbor: University of Michigan Press, 1993); Earl R. Wasserman, "The Sympathetic Imagination in Eighteenth-Century Theories of Acting," *Journal of English and Germanic Philology* 46 (1947): 264–72.

77. Sechelski, "Garrick's Body," 378.

78. Ibid., 377, 379.

79. Ibid., 379.

80. Suchorzewski, *Głos*, 5.

81. Sechelski, "Garrick's Body," 378.

82. For example, Czacki, who saw the original production of *The Return of the Deputy*, recorded in his memoirs that the "cold" acting style of the player cast as Mr. Justice clashed with the performances by Karol Świerzawski as Mr. Windbag, Agnieszka Truskolaska as Mrs. Windbag, and Wojciech Bogusławski as Mr. Charming. Czacki found it disconcerting that "the important role of Mr. Justice, an exemplary Pole who loves his native land with his soul and heart," received such a "cold" treatment. Czacki, *Wspomnienia*, 121. Czacki could not recall the name of the actor who played Mr. Justice, and theatre historians have been unable to establish his identity.

83. Marie-Hélène Huet, *Rehearsing the Revolution: The Staging of Marat's Death, 1793–1797*, trans. Robert Hurley (Berkeley: University of California Press, 1982), 34.

84. Garry Wills, *Cincinnatus: George Washington and the Enlightenment* (Garden City, NY: Doubleday, 1984), 102.

85. Ibid.

86. Hunt, *Women*, 337.

87. The play's subtitle, *An Opera*, is misleading. *The Spartan Mother* belongs to the hybrid genre of music drama in which passages sung to music constitute only a small percentage of the entire text. This generic classification also applies to Wybicki's *The Polish Woman* and Kublicki's *The Defense of Trembowla*.

88. The critical understanding of the eighteenth-century concept of sensibility has undergone major shifts. See especially G. J. Barker-Benfield, *The Culture of Sensibility: Sex and Society in Eighteenth-Century Britain* (Chicago: University of Chicago Press, 1992); Jerome McGann, *The Poetics of Sensibility: A Revolution in Literary Style* (Oxford: Oxford University Press, 1996); Janet Todd, *Sensibility: An Introduction* (London: Methuen, 1986). It may say something for the strength of the cult of sensibility that it generated a jeering counterdiscourse that reveled in human suffering and physical affliction. On this issue, see Simon Dickie, *Cruelty and Laughter: Forgotten Comic Literature and the Unsentimental Eighteenth Century* (Chicago: University of Chicago Press, 2011).

89. Franciszek Dionizy Kniaźnin, *Matka Spartanka*, in *Utwory dramatyczne: Wybór*, ed. Augustyn Jendrysik (Warsaw: Państwowy Instytut Wydawniczy, 1958), 72.

90. See Aleksandrowicz, "Sejm Czteroletni," 209–10.

91. Czartoryska's research notes include a comment that Lycurgus, a legendary Spartan lawgiver, did away with the sheltered upbringing of women and opened up athletic training to them. This comment has led Aleksandrowicz to suggest that Czartoryska read Ignacy Krasicki's *A Compendium of Useful Information* (*Zbiór potrzebniejszych wiadomości*, 1781) that has an essay on Sparta. See Aleksandrowicz, "Sejm Czteroletni," 210–11. Aleksandrowicz's probing study, however, does not consider the possibility that both Czartoryska's notes and Krasicki's essay are based on Plutarch's *Life of Lycurgus* from his *Lives of Noble Greeks and Romans*, a standard source of familiar claims about Sparta. Yet another possible source for Czartoryska's notes is Rousseau's *Emile, or On Education* (*Émile, ou de l'éducation*, 1762) that draws on Plutarch's *Sayings of Spartan Women* as well as *Life of Lycurgus*, including the story of Spartan women's physical education. In recent times, scholars have done a great deal of work in attempting to separate what is trustworthy in the ancient sources from that which is a product of the Spartan mirage, but this work has not removed all doubt. For an assessment of historical evidence about the lives of Spartan women, see Barton Kunstler, "Family Dynamics and Female Power in Ancient Sparta," *Helios* 13, no. 2 (Fall 1986): 31–48; Sarah N. Pomeroy, *Spartan Women* (Oxford: Oxford University Press, 2002).

92. See Kniaźnin's letter to Stanisław Kłokocki, 23 April 1786, reprinted in Tadeusz Mikulski, *Ze studiów nad Oświeceniem: Zagadnienia i fakty* (Warsaw: Państwowy Instytut Wydawniczy, 1956), 274–79. Lessel's music for *The Spartan Mother* is now lost.

93. See Izabela Czartoryska's letter to Maria Wirtemberska, 14 June 1786, quoted in Aleksandrowicz, "Sejm Czteroletni," 199.

94. For a concise overview of the evidence, see Aleksandrowicz, "Sejm Czteroletni," 197, 229; Augustyn Jendrysik, "Wstęp," in Kniaźnin, *Utwory dramatyczne*, 39–40.

95. The phrase "strangely beautiful" is from Ignacy Potocki's letter to Seweryn Rzewuski, 16 June 1786. The letter is quoted in Emanuel Rostworowski, *Sprawa aukcji wojska na tle sytuacji politycznej przed Sejmem Czteroletnim* (Warsaw: Państwowe Wydawnictwo Naukowe, 1957), 270.

96. See Tadeusz Mikulski, *W kręgu Oświeconych: Studia, szkice, recenzje, notatki* (Warsaw: Państwowy Instytut Wydawniczy, 1960), 498.

97. See Aleksandrowicz, "Sejm Czteroletni," 229; Jendrysik, "Wstęp," 62.

98. Józef Wybicki, *Wiersze i arietki*, ed. Edmund Rabowicz and Tadeusz Swat (Gdańsk: Wydawnictwo Morskie, 1973), 159; Kniaźnin, *Matka Spartanka*, 69.

99. One exception is Aleksandrowicz's "Sejm Czteroletni."

100. Jendrysik, "Wstęp," 39.

101. Ibid., 40, 39. Likewise, Mikulski contends that *The Spartan Mother* is "rather lackluster" and "anemic." Mikulski, *W kręgu Oświeconych*, 495, 499.

102. Jendrysik, "Wstęp," 42. For evidence that in truth Kniaźnin's play had a crucial presence in the public discourse of the early 1790s, see Aleksandrowicz, "Sejm Czteroletni," 229, 241.

103. See, e.g., Kaleta, "'Spartanka': Nieznany poemat Stanisława Trembeckiego," in *Oświeceni i sentymentalni*, 413–49; Mikulski, *W kręgu Oświeconych*, 495–500.

104. Lukowski, *Liberty's Folly*, 220.

105. See Elizabeth Rawson, *The Spartan Tradition in European Thought* (Oxford: Clarendon Press, 2002), 137–57. This view of Sparta was shared by the leaders of the American Revolution. "It may seem strange," Paul A. Rahe admits, "that the American Founding Fathers should single out Lacedaemon for admiration, for there were other ancient communities that future generations would think better suited to liberal democratic taste." It is Rahe's argument, however, that "the accomplishments of the legendary Lycurgus were indelibly impressed on the minds of the men who initiated the American Revolution and subsequently wrestled with the difficulties involved in the establishment of republican government in the New World." Rahe, *Republics Ancient and Modern: Classical Republicanism and the American Revolution* (Chapel Hill: University of North Carolina Press, 1992), 186, 185.

106. Aleksandrowicz, "Sejm Czteroletni," 196, 230.

107. See also Andrzej Wyrobisz's survey of normative pronouncements about women by sixteenth- and seventeenth-century Polish authors: "Staropolskie wzory rodziny i kobiety—żony i matki," *Przegląd Historyczny* 83, no. 3 (1992): 405–21. The exemplary Polish woman, propagated by these authors, is a dutiful and subservient helpmate whose life revolves around her family and household. Although born with a weaker mind, she strives to make up for this deficiency by being obedient, deferential, complaisant, self-effacing, morally irreproachable, hard-working, prudent, and mostly silent. Despite their strong local flavor, such normative pronouncements were not, of course, unique to Poland.

108. Quoted in Aleksandrowicz, "Sejm Czteroletni," 204. The same point is made earlier in the play, during a polemic between two Trojan women. Deidania persuades her female companions to take up arms and join the war, but Teano sends them back home, arguing that men and women have different obligations.

109. For a related argument that there are few positive female characters in Polish Enlightenment literature, see Zdzisław Libera, *Wiek Oświecony: Studia i szkice z dziejów literatury i kultury polskiej XVIII i początków XIX wieku* (Warsaw: Państwowy Instytut Wydawniczy, 1986), 59–60.

110. Rawson, *Spartan Tradition*, 1.

111. Ibid., 10.

112. Charles Seltman, *Women in Antiquity* (London: Thames and Hudson, 1956), 66.

113. Ibid.

114. Ibid., 67.

115. Kniaźnin, *Matka Spartanka*, 64. To put Kniaźnin's point slightly differently, Sparta is "the land of the free and the home of the brave." These words come, of course, from Francis Scott Key's "The Star-Spangled Banner," but, as Rahe reminds us, Key adopted "a phrase which his countrymen had hitherto reserved for ancient Lacedaemon." Rahe, *Republics Ancient and Modern*, 185.

116. Julian Ursyn Niemcewicz, "Do Polek," reprinted in Kniaźnin, *Matka Spartanka*, 97.

117. Kniaźnin, *Matka Spartanka*, 74.

118. Rawson, *Spartan Tradition*, 136.

119. Kniaźnin, *Matka Spartanka*, 69, 76.

120. Ibid., 81.

121. Ibid., 70.

122. See Jendrysik, "Wstęp," 38.

123. Quoted in Sarah B. Pomeroy, *Spartan Women* (Oxford: Oxford University Press, 2002), 60.

124. Niemcewicz, *Pamiętniki czasów moich* (1868 ed.), 112.

125. For the argument that Kalinka's close attention to the role of public opinion broke new ground in the historiography on the Four-Year Parliament, see Jerzy

Michalski, "Na marginesie reedycji *Sejmu Czteroletniego* Waleriana Kalinki," in Michalski, *Studia historyczne z XVIII i XIX wieku,* ed. Wojciech Kriegseisen and Zofia Zielińska, 2 vols. (Warsaw: Stentor, 2007), 2:512.

126. Kalinka, *Sejm Czteroletni,* 1:198.

127. On 20 October 1788, for example, the public galleries in Parliament erupted in thunderous applause in response to Michał Walewski's proposal to increase the army to 100,000 men. Ovations were led by elite women who waved their shawls and shouted hurrahs. The cheering and applauding drowned out the voices of skeptics, and on 22 October the proposal was unanimously approved. It was the first piece of legislation passed by the Four-Year Parliament. See Kalinka, *Sejm Czteroletni,* 1:148–51, 203; Szyndler, *Czy Sejm,* 29.

128. Stanisław Kot, "Wstęp," in Julian Ursyn Niemcewicz, *Powrót posła: Komedia w trzech aktach oraz wybór bajek politycznych z epoki Sejmu Wielkiego,* ed. Kot, 6th ed. (Wrocław: Zakład Narodowy im. Ossolińskich, 1950), xv–xvi.

129. On Niemcewicz's activism in the Four-Year Parliament, see Jan Dihm, *Niemcewicz jako polityk i publicysta w czasie Sejmu Czteroletniego* (Kraków: Kasa im. J. Mianowskiego, 1928).

130. On the dating of the composition of *The Return of the Deputy,* see Augustyn Jendrysik, "Wokół daty powstania *Powrotu posła,*" *Pamiętnik Literacki* 68, no. 2 (1977): 181–93. Jendrysik also makes a convincing case to correct the publication history of the play; he argues that it was first published only in mid-January 1791, rather than in November 1790.

131. Niemcewicz, *Powrót posła,* 23.

132. Jan Dihm, "Wstęp," in Niemcewicz, *Pamiętniki czasów moich* (1957 ed.), 1:10. Likewise, Kalinka remarked more than a century earlier that *The Return of the Deputy* is "a product of political pamphleteering rather than a work of literary art." Kalinka, *Sejm Czteroletni,* 2:438.

133. Van der Meer, *Literary Activities,* 313.

134. Roy Porter, *The Enlightenment,* 2nd ed. (Basingstoke: Palgrave, 2001), 1.

135. Niemcewicz, *Powrót posła,* 5.

136. See Dihm, *Niemcewicz jako polityk,* 84; Witold Kośny, "Nochmals zu Niemcewicz und Griboedov," in *Studien zur polnischen Literatur-, Sprach- und Kulturgeschichte im 18. Jahrhundert,* ed. Ilse Kunert (Köln: Böhlau Verlag, 1993), 239.

137. See especially Mr. Justice's cutting riposte to Mr. Windbag: "We ourselves are to blame for our own misfortunes! . . . We thought of ourselves and never of our country." Niemcewicz, *Powrót posła,* 18.

138. According to van der Meer, for example, two conspicuous features of *The Return of the Deputy* are "the lack of [sexually] bold and frivolous elements and, in relation to this, the still very much restricted part played by female characters," whom he describes as "completely passive," "superficial," and "colourless." Van der Meer, *Literary Activities,* 312, 314–15.

139. Ibid., 314.

140. Ibid.

141. Ibid., 312; see also 310, 315–16, 322. In contrast, Dobrochna Ratajczakowa argues that "all the characters have a neo-classical genealogy." Ratajczakowa, *Komedia oświeconych 1752–1795* (Warsaw: Wydawnictwo Naukowe PWN, 1993), 337.

142. Van der Meer, *Literary Activities*, 314.

143. John Adams to James Sullivan, 26 May 1776, in *The Papers of John Adams*, ed. Robert J. Taylor, vol. 4 (Cambridge, MA: Belknap Press of Harvard University Press, 1979), 208.

144. Van der Meer, *Literary Activities*, 314-15.

145. See Jean-Jacques Rousseau, *Emile, or On Education*, trans. Allan Bloom (New York: Basic Books, 1979), 358, 365. Mary Wollstonecraft responded to *Emile* with *A Vindication of the Rights of Woman* (1792), in which she critically examined the prejudices that served to exclude women from serious education; in doing so, she laid the philosophical foundation for feminism. On female responses to Rousseau's educational theories more generally, see Jean Bloch, *Rousseauism and Education in Eighteenth-Century France* (Oxford: Voltaire Foundation, 1995), 215–22.

146. Niemcewicz, *Powrót posła*, 26.

147. Mieczysława Miterzanka has suggested that Mr. Justice's views on female upbringing and education reflect those of Adam Kazimierz Czartoryski in pedagogical works such as *The Letters of Mr. Wisdom* (*Listy J.Mci Pana Doświadczyńskiego*, 1782). It is her argument that Niemcewicz, Czartoryski's assistant and protégé, was eager to disseminate his mentor's educational ideas; therefore, he conceived Mr. Justice as Czartoryski's mouthpiece. See Miterzanka, *Działalność pedagogiczna Adama ks. Czartoryskiego, generała ziem podolskich* (Warsaw: Naukowe Towarzystwo Pedagogiczne, 1931), 255. In sharp contrast to Mr. Justice, however, Czartoryski came out strongly against the patriarchal system, blaming the deficient state of girls' upbringing and education on the men who were satisfied to tolerate and even encourage female ignorance instead of assisting women to improve themselves. "Men," he argued, "have seized control of both the domestic and civic spheres, therefore men are to blame when something goes wrong in either of these spheres. . . . I repeat: men have made themselves the legislators of both spheres, therefore they are to blame for flaws in female education." Czartoryski, *Listy J.Mci Pana Doświadczyńskiego*, in *Pisma i projekty pedagogiczne doby Komisji Edukacji Narodowej*, ed. Kamilla Mrozowska (Wrocław: Zakład Narodowy im. Ossolińskich, 1973), 325, 338.

148. See van der Meer, *Literary Activities*, 314.

149. See Niemcewicz, *Powrót posła*, 91.

150. Ibid., 26.

151. Van der Meer, *Literary Activities*, 314-15.

152. Niemcewicz, *Powrót posła*, 16.

153. Goodman, *Becoming a Woman*, 275. On the rise of the companionate marriage in Western Europe, see Daniel Roche, *France in the Enlightenment*, trans. Arthur Goldhammer (Cambridge, MA: Harvard University Press, 2000), 521–30; Lawrence Stone, *The Family, Sex, and Marriage in England 1500–1800* (London: Weidenfeld and Nicolson, 1977), 325–36. On the advocacy of the companionate marriage in Poland, see especially Ksawery Zubowski's letter to the editor, published in the *Monitor* on 18 March 1778 and reprinted in *"Monitor" 1765–1785*, ed. Aleksandrowska, 485–88. In the letter, Zubowski cites a confession by a young woman who is about to marry a man she loves. She attributes widespread marital misery to the lack of freedom in choosing a life partner, the absence of mutual affection, and the insistence on wifely subjection. She envisions her own marriage as an affectionate union of like-minded individuals, respectful of each other's human dignity: "I will never forget that I am a human being; therefore I will not accept the yoke of oppression and the burden of servitude" (488). Zubowski uses this presumably fictitious confession to support the novel idea that conjugal and domestic happiness can result only from a marriage based on the free choice of individuals following their hearts.

154. On the connection between the companionate marriage and a fundamental reassessment of power relations between husband and wife, see Stone, *Family, Sex, and Marriage*, 325–26; James F. Traer, *Marriage and the Family in Eighteenth-Century France* (Ithaca, NY: Cornell University Press, 1980), 15–21, 70–78.

155. Scholars are divided on the question whether there was a major change in child-rearing attitudes and practices in the eighteenth century. For the argument in support of this thesis, see Philippe Ariès, *Centuries of Childhood*, trans. Robert Baldick (Harmondsworth: Penguin Books, 1973). In contrast, Linda A. Pollock argues that "although there may be changes in feeding practices . . . , and some slight changes in attitudes, there is no dramatic transformation in child-rearing practices in the 18th century." Pollock, *Forgotten Children: Parent-Child Relations from 1500 to 1900* (Cambridge: Cambridge University Press, 1983), 271.

156. Niemcewicz, *Powrót posła*, 44.

157. See ibid., 26.

158. Ibid., 39.

159. Ibid., 91.

160. On this issue, Mrs. Justice's position differs from that of Wollstonecraft. While arguing that women are capable of other achievements as well, Wollstonecraft stresses in *A Vindication of the Rights of Woman* that "the rearing of children, that is, the laying [of] a foundation of sound health both of body and mind in the rising generation, has justly been insisted on as the peculiar destination of woman." Wollstonecraft, *A Vindication of the Rights of Men; A Vindication of the Rights of Woman*, ed. D. L. Macdonald and Kathleen Scherf (Peterborough, ON: Broadview Press, 2001), 337.

316 | *Notes to Pages 110–117*

161. In scholarship on educational reforms in eighteenth-century Poland, Franciszek Bieliński is credited with being the first to formulate, in his epistolary treatise, *On Education* (*Sposób edukacji,* 1775), a comprehensive proposal for gender-blind education. See, e.g., Mieczysława Mitera-Dobrowolska, "Zainteresowanie Komisji Edukacji Narodowej sprawą wychowania dziewcząt," in Łukasz Kurdybacha and Mieczysława Mitera-Dobrowolska, *Komisja Edukacji Narodowej* (Warsaw: Państwowe Wydawnictwo Naukowe, 1973), 176. In truth, Bieliński assigns a reduced version of a boys' curriculum to girls from the gentry class and insists that girls from the lower classes merely master the rudiments of reading, writing, and arithmetic. Moreover, he cautions that moral instruction is what girls need most of all. See Bieliński, *Sposób edukacji w XV listach opisany,* in *Pisma i projekty pedagogiczne,* ed. Mrozowska, 118, 67. Bieliński was not alone in discounting girls' educational needs. Essay periodicals published in Poland between 1764 and 1795 provide copious evidence that many of the old biases surrounding female education still lingered. For example, although the ostensibly progressive *Monitor* argued that the minds of women and men have the same intellectual potential, it minimized the importance of a serious academic curriculum for female students and instead emphasized instruction in practical skills to prepare them for their future roles as wives, mothers, and housekeepers. Additionally, the *Monitor* upheld piety as a woman's most valued trait. See Eugenia Podgórska, "Sprawa wychowania kobiet w znaczniejszych czasopismach polskich drugiej połowy XVIII wieku," in *Rozprawy z dziejów oświaty,* ed. Łukasz Kurdybacha, vol. 4 (Wrocław: Zakład Narodowy im. Ossolińskich, 1961), 19–33; Zofia Sinko, *"Monitor" wobec angielskiego "Spectatora"* (Wrocław: Zakład im. Ossolińskich, 1956), 144–63.

162. Linda K. Kerber, "The Republican Mother: Women and the Enlightenment, an American Perspective," *American Quarterly* 28, no. 2 (Summer 1976): 204. Or, as Jacqueline Rose has pointed out recently, "Having a child ushered the woman on a path that led to something other than motherhood itself—an idea which modern times seem progressively to have lost." Rose, "Mothers," *London Review of Books* 36, no. 12 (19 June 2014): 17.

163. See Niemcewicz, *Pamiętniki czasów moich* (1957 ed.), 1:71; Jan Świejkowski to Leonard Świejkowski, 21 January 1791, published in Kaleta, "Nawracanie posła," 511–12.

164. Wojciech Bogusławski, *Dowód wdzięczności narodu* (Warsaw, 1791), 51.

Chapter 2

1. The most famous of American female soldiers, Sampson Gannett enrolled to serve in the Continental Army for the term of three years in May 1782, but was discharged in October 1783, a month after Congress accepted a peace treaty. The

bounty receipt appears to be signed by "Robert Shurtlieff," but the signature may also be read as "Robert Shurtliff." Her 1797 petition for a pension was denied. It was only in 1805 that Congress awarded her a pension, retroactive to 1803. For the most recent and thorough treatment of Sampson Gannett, see Alfred F. Young, *Masquerade: The Life and Times of Deborah Sampson, Continental Soldier* (New York: Alfred A. Knopf, 2004).

2. See Mary S. Austin, *Philip Freneau, the Poet of the Revolution: A History of His Life and Times*, ed. Helen Kearny Vreeland (New York: A. Wessels, 1901).

3. Philip Freneau, "Ode XIII: On Deborah Gannet," in *The Poems of Philip Freneau*, ed. Fred Lewis Pattee, vol. 3 (Princeton, NJ: Princeton University Library, 1907), 182. However, the phrase "a heroine in a bold career" does not appear in the original newspaper version, published in 1797. Freneau added this phrase in an expanded but somewhat softened version that was first published in a collection in 1815. For the 1797 text, see Freneau, "On Deborah Gannet," in *The Newspaper Verse of Philip Freneau: An Edition and Bibliographical Survey*, ed. Judith R. Hiltner (Troy, NY: Whitston, 1986), 605–6. It is the original newspaper text that I will discuss here.

4. Freneau, "On Deborah Gannet," 605.

5. Ibid., 606.

6. The distinction between sex and gender is at times attributed to Judith Butler. In fact, it was first formulated by Robert Stoller in the 1960s and developed for feminist theory by Gayle Rubin in the 1970s. For a history of the sex/gender distinction, see Toril Moi, *What Is a Woman? And Other Essays* (Oxford: Oxford University Press, 1999), 3–120. For a reprint of Rubin's path-breaking essays written in the 1970s, see Gayle S. Rubin, *Deviations* (Durham, NC: Duke University Press, 2011).

7. In the subtitle of his play, Kublicki uses the word *męstwo*, which I have translated as *manly courage*. Sharing its root with *mężczyzna* (a man) and *męskość* (manliness, manhood, masculinity, virility), *męstwo* etymologically excludes women. The intrinsic maleness of the term *męstwo* conveys the idea that there is a particular type of bravery that is characteristic of, or associated with, men as distinguished from women.

8. Hobson and Lister, "Citizenship," 27.

9. Ibid., 25, 27.

10. Lukowski, *Liberty's Folly*, 233.

11. For example, the question of female education received scant attention. Although the Commission for National Education (1773–95), one of the most progressive institutions of the Polish Enlightenment, was charged with modernizing the entire school system in Poland-Lithuania, it did little to improve girls' education, apart from appointing Adam Kazimierz Czartoryski to develop guidelines for private schools in 1774 and sponsoring Maksymilian Prokopowicz's beginning textbook in 1790. In the guidelines, Czartoryski argues that "girls ought to be constantly

reminded that women have not been put on this earth to be an inactive part of the nation; on the contrary, women, along with men, owe civic duty to their homeland." At the same time, however, he supports a segregated and strictly limited system of female education. He excludes Latin and ancient history from a girls' curriculum, bans books such as such Plutarch's *Lives of Noble Greeks and Romans* from libraries at girls' schools, and emphasizes training in household skills. Czartoryski, "Przepisy od Komisji Edukacji Narodowej pensjo-mistrzom i mistrzyniom dane," in *Ustawodawstwo szkolne za czasów Komisji Edukacji Narodowej: Rozporządzenia, ustawy pedagogiczne i organizacyjne (1773–1793)*, ed. Józef Lewicki (Kraków: M. Arct, 1925), 73. As I have argued above, Czartoryski took a different approach to the issue of female upbringing and education in his later work, *The Letters of Mr. Wisdom*.

12. For a discussion of Mniszech's proposal, see Jerzy Michalski, "Gdyby nami rządziły kobiety (Poglądy Amelii Mniszchowej na reformę Rzeczypospolitej)," in *Studia historyczne z XVIII i XIX wieku*, 2:97–108. Whether or not Lubomirska is the author of two anonymous proposals is a contested issue. Władysław Konopczyński argues in favor of her authorship; Michalski remains cautious, noting that evidence is inconclusive. See Konopczyński, *Kiedy nami rządziły kobiety* (London: Veritas, 1960), 169–71; Michalski, "Gdyby nami rządziły kobiety," 107.

13. For examples of mocking invective and verbal venom, see "I ja też," an anonymous pamphlet originally published ca. 1790 and reprinted in *Kołłątaj i inni*, ed. Kądziela, 173; Jędrzej Kitowicz, *Pamiętniki, czyli Historia polska*, 2nd ed., ed. Przemysława Matuszewska (Warsaw: Polski Instytut Wydawniczy, 2005), 488; Juliusz Nowak-Dłużewski, *Satyra polityczna Sejmu Czteroletniego* (Kraków: Kasa im. J. Mianowskiego, 1933), 23–28, 53–56; Trębicki, *Opisanie sejmu*, 206; Stanisław Trembecki, "Spartanka," in Kaleta, *Oświeceni i sentymentalni*, 442–49.

14. This involvement did not materialize because Catherine II rejected Stanisław August's offer in 1788.

15. The quotation is from Zamoyski, *Last King of Poland*, 315.

16. I have taken information for this account from Aleksander Czołowski, "Wojna polsko-turecka 1675 r.," *Kwartalnik Historyczny* 8, no. 4 (1894): 593–626; Zbigniew Kuchowicz, *Wizerunki niepospolitych niewiast staropolskich XVI–XVIII wieku* (Łódź: Wydawnictwo Łódzkie, 1972), 267–77; Kazimierz Piwarski, "Chrzanowska Anna Dorota" and "Chrzanowski Jan Samuel," in *Polski Słownik Biograficzny*, vol. 3 (Kraków: Polska Akademia Umiejętności, 1937), 458–60.

17. Wybicki, MP in 1767–68 and 1784–85, did not stand for a seat in the Parliament of 1788–92 but became involved in negotiations over legislative initiatives to foster urban renewal. Like Kublicki, MP in 1788–92, he was also an outspoken critic of serfdom. For studies of Wybicki's life and work, see Andrzej Bukowski, ed., *Józef Wybicki: Księga zbiorowa* (Gdańsk: Zakład Narodowy im. Ossolińskich, 1975); Irena Kadulska, Piotr Kąkol, and Józef Włodarski, eds., *Nuta wolności w pismach i*

działalności Józefa Wybickiego (Gdańsk: Wydawnictwo Uniwersytetu Gdańskiego, 2013); Adam M. Skałkowski, *Józef Wybicki, 1747–1795* (Poznań: Księgarnia Uniwersytecka, 1927); Władysław Zajewski, *Józef Wybicki*, 3rd ed. (Warsaw: Książka i Wiedza, 1989); Władysław Zajewski, "Józef Wybicki i sprawa Konstytucji 3-go Maja 1791 r.," in *Konstytucja 3 Maja: Prawo—polityka—symbol,* ed. Anna Grześkowiak-Krwawicz (Warsaw: Polskie Towarzystwo Historyczne, 1992), 91–98. A full-length biography of Kublicki has yet to be written. For a short introduction to his life and work, see Bernard Krakowski, "Kublicki Stanisław," in *Polski Słownik Biograficzny,* vol. 16 (Wrocław: Zakład Narodowy im. Ossolińskich, 1971), 34–37.

18. On this issue, see, e.g., Ian Donaldson, *The World Upside-Down: Comedy from Jonson to Fielding* (Oxford: Clarendon Press, 1970), 14.

19. Maria Bogucka, *Women in Early Modern Polish Society, against the European Background* (Aldershot, UK: Ashgate, 2004), 105, 122.

20. Jezierski, *Wybór pism,* 190.

21. Ibid., 143.

22. See ibid., 143–44, 192, 233, 226.

23. Bogucka, *Women,* 122.

24. For this approach, see Jendrysik, "Wstęp," 61–62; Roman Kaleta, "Wstęp," in Józef Wybicki, *Utwory dramatyczne,* ed. Kaleta (Warsaw: Państwowy Instytut Wydawniczy, 1963), 35–36; Edmund Rabowicz, "Józef Wybicki—literat," in *Józef Wybicki,* ed. Bukowski, 93.

25. See Kaleta, "Wstęp," 48–49. A notable exception is Irena Kadulska's recent survey of Wybicki's representations of patriotic Polish women. See Kadulska, "Obrońców ojczyzny jest więcej: Józef Wybicki o patriotycznych postawach Polek," in *Nuta wolności,* ed. Kadulska et al., 73–83. Written from a woman-centered perspective, Kadulska's article nevertheless leaves unexplored the problem of gender as an arbitrary social and cultural construct.

26. Kaleta, "Wstęp," 49.

27. Ibid.

28. Quoted in Kaleta, "Wstęp," 49.

29. Stanisław Kublicki, *Obrona Trembowli, czyli Męstwo Chrzanowskiej,* 2nd ed. (Warsaw, 1789), 10–11.

30. On the Enlightenment's polarization of the sexes, see especially Hausen, "Family and Role-Division."

31. Marion W. Gray, "Enlightenment Vocabulary and Female Difference: Two Women Writers' Search for Inclusive Language," in *Gender in Transition: Discourse and Practice in German-Speaking Europe, 1750–1830,* ed. Ulrike Gleixner and Marion W. Gray (Ann Arbor: University of Michigan Press, 2006), 246.

32. Sara Ellen Procious Malueg, "Women and the *Encyclopédie,*" in *French Women and the Age of Enlightenment,* ed. Samia I. Spencer (Bloomington: Indiana University Press, 1984), 262. See also chapter 2 ("Dividing the Human Race: The

Anthropological Definition of Woman in the *Encyclopédie*") in Steinbrügge, *Moral Sex*, 21–34. As Malueg points out, "such obvious disdain for the fair sex and such one-sided reporting" in Joseph Desmahis's entry on "Femme" infuriated a number of thinkers of the period, including Voltaire (262). The overall treatment of the subject of women in the *Encyclopédie* is far from uniform. Contributed by different authors, the views on women are a mixture of contradictory attitudes: traditional, openly misogynistic assertions (exemplified by the stereotypes in Desmahis's article) and enlightened ideas (e.g., a clear statement of the equality of the sexes in marriage in an article by Louis Jaucourt). However, the encyclopedists offer no program for educating women and no plan to improve their position. With regard to the social role of woman, the encyclopedists agree on a notion that is hardly avant-garde: motherhood is the most important function of women.

33. Maurice Bloch and Jean H. Bloch, "Women and the Dialectics of Nature in Eighteenth-Century French Thought," in *Nature, Culture and Gender*, ed. Carol P. MacCormack and Marilyn Strathern (Cambridge: Cambridge University Press, 1980), 32. On Kant's views about women, see Schott, "Gender of Enlightenment," 474–76. For analyses of Rousseau's ideas about women, see, e.g., Jean Bethke Elshtain, *Public Man, Private Woman: Women in Social and Political Thought*, 2nd ed. (Princeton, NJ: Princeton University Press, 1993), 148–70; Lynda Lange, "Rousseau: Women and the General Will," in *The Sexism of Social and Political Theory: Women and Reproduction from Plato to Nietzsche*, ed. Lorenne M. G. Clark and Lynda Lange (Toronto: University of Toronto Press, 1979), 41–52; Susan Moller Okin, *Women in Western Political Thought* (Princeton, NJ: Princeton University Press, 2013), 97–194; Joel Schwartz, *The Sexual Politics of Jean-Jacques Rousseau* (Chicago: University of Chicago Press, 1984).

34. Józef Wybicki, *Utwory dramatyczne*, ed. Roman Kaleta (Warsaw: Państwowy Instytut Wydawniczy, 1963), 306.

35. Ibid.

36. Ibid., 330.

37. Ibid., 334.

38. Ibid.

39. Ibid., 350.

40. Kublicki, *Obrona Trembowli*, 21.

41. Wybicki, *Utwory dramatyczne*, 319.

42. Ibid., 336.

43. See Wybicki to Augustyn Gorzeński, 30 January 1789, in *Archiwum Wybickiego*, vol. 1, ed. Adam M. Skałkowski (Gdańsk: Towarzystwo Przyjaciół Nauki i Sztuki, 1948), 139–40. In the letter, Wybicki also writes about his ambivalence about submitting *The Polish Woman* for consideration at the National Theatre. He is concerned that the play might put his political career at risk by embroiling him in yet

another controversy. He makes it clear that the earlier controversy was over *Observations on the Life of Jan Zamoyski* (*Uwagi nad życiem Jana Zamoyskiego*, 1787). This political treatise presents a trenchant critique of Poland-Lithuania's political, social, and economic system and offers a series of proposals on how to achieve a just (or at least a less unjust) society. Thus, for example, nobles should claim no monopoly on political rights, burghers should be given greater opportunities for direct participation in public affairs, and peasants should be guaranteed legal protection. Published anonymously, the treatise was immediately attributed to Wybicki because its arguments in support of a new relationship between individuals and the body politic resembled, in the opinion of many, those of his *Patriotic Letters*. In fact, *Observations* was written by Stanisław Staszic.

44. See Maciejewski, *Teatry poznańskie*, 228.
45. Rabowicz, "Józef Wybicki—literat," 93–95.
46. In January 1790, rehearsals of Kublicki's play were suddenly abandoned in Warsaw, even though playbills had been posted. Maciejewski has suggested that the play might have been performed by Mateusz Witkowski's touring company sometime in 1790. See Maciejewski, *Teatry poznańskie*, 270.
47. See Kaleta, "Wstęp," 62–63, 66.
48. Stanisław Grzeszczuk and Danuta Hombek, *Książka polska w ogłoszeniach prasowych XVIII wieku: Źródła*, vol. 2, ed. Zbigniew Goliński (Kraków: Universitas, 1995), 272.

Chapter 3

1. See Laura Mulvey, "Visual Pleasure and Narrative Cinema," in *Feminist Film Theory: A Reader*, ed. Sue Thornham (New York: New York University Press, 1999), 62; Sue-Ellen Case, *Feminism and Theatre* (Basingstoke, UK: Macmillan, 1988), 119. Mulvey's essay was originally published in 1975. For Mulvey's revised argument, see her 1981 essay, "Afterthoughts on 'Visual Pleasure and Narrative Cinema' Inspired by King Vidor's *Duel in the Sun* (1946)," in *Feminist Film Theory*, 122–30.

2. Ignacy Dembowski, *Wanda* (Kraków, 1810), v.

3. Norman Davies, *God's Playground: A History of Poland*, 2 vols. (New York: Columbia University Press, 2005), 1:52. For a survey of the Wanda myth in Polish literature and culture, see Albina I. Kruszewska and Marion M. Coleman, "The Wanda Theme in Polish Literature and Life," *American Slavic and East European Review* 6, nos. 1–2 (May 1947): 19–35; Katarzyna Marciniak, "Królewna Wanda—pierwsza polska 'feministka'?," in *Kobieta epok dawnych w literaturze, kulturze i społeczeństwie*, ed. Iwona Maciejewska and Krystyna Stasiewicz (Olsztyn: Littera,

2008), 89–98; Hanna Mortkowiczówna, *Podanie o Wandzie: Dzieje wątku literackiego* (Warsaw: Księgarnia Towarzystwa Wydawniczego, 1927). Of all the myths about Poland's pre-Christian past, as Julian Maślanka observes, the Wanda myth has been the most popular and generative. See Maślanka, *Literatura a dzieje bajeczne* (Warsaw: Państwowe Wydawnictwo Naukowe, 1984), 6.

4. See Snopek, *Prowincja oświecona*, 176–81.

5. Since the dating of the first production of Wężyk's *Wanda* bears on my discussion, I want to address this issue here. Kazimierz Bartoszewicz avers that Wężyk's drama was first performed in 1807; however, the production information he supplies makes it clear that he means Łubieńska's *Wanda, Queen of Poland*. See Bartoszewicz, *Szkice i portrety literackie*, vol. 1 (Kraków: Gebethner i Wolff, 1930), 262. Other scholars claim that Wężyk's play premiered in 1818. See Barbara Czwórnóg-Jadczak, *Klasyk aż do śmierci: Twórczość literacka Franciszka Wężyka* (Lublin: Wydawnictwo Uniwersytetu Marii Curie-Skłodowskiej, 1994), 85; Kruszewska and Coleman, "Wanda Theme," 28; Marian Szyjkowski, *Dzieje nowożytnej tragedii polskiej: Typ pseudoklasyczny, 1661–1831* (Kraków: Akademia Umiejętności, 1920), 277, 301; Dobrochna Ratajczakowa, "Wanda w świątyni dziejów," *Studia Polonistyczne* 8 (1981): 103; Józef Ujejski, "Wstęp," in Tekla Łubieńska, *Wanda*, ed. Ujejski (Warsaw: Związek Artystów Scen Polskich, 1927), 37. However, Mortkowiczówna has established that the 1818 production was a revival of Łubieńska's drama. See Mortkowiczówna, *Podanie o Wandzie*, 115–16.

6. Davies, *God's Playground*, 2:222.

7. Łubieńska's letter of 14 June 1806, written to her son, Tomasz Łubieński, suggests that she completed the play the previous winter, possibly even earlier. For a relevant excerpt from the letter, see Ujejski, "Wstęp," 6.

8. Tekla Łubieńska, *Wanda*, ed. Józef Ujejski (Warsaw: Związek Artystów Scen Polskich, 1927), 132–33. On the evidence that survives, the paean did meet with an enthusiastic response. See Ujejski, "Wstęp," 11.

9. Łubieńska, *Wanda*, 92, 84, 92.

10. John Loftis, *The Politics of Drama in Augustan England* (Oxford: Clarendon Press, 1963), 5.

11. Łubieńska's correspondence suggests that it was Ludwik Osiński, a critic and dramatist, who made it possible for her to secure a foothold in the playwrighting profession. See Ujejski, "Wstęp," 6–7.

12. In introducing the Wanda-Rytygier love plot, Łubieńska's play shows an intriguing similarity with Zacharias Werner's *Wanda, Queen of Sarmatians* (*Wanda, Königin der Sarmaten*), first produced by Goethe's theatre in Weimar in 1808. Ujejski rules out the possibility that Werner, a Prussian civil servant who left Poland in 1805, was familiar with Łubieńska's play when he set out to write his in 1807. See

Ujejski, "Wstęp," 17–19. For a different view, see Kruszewska and Coleman, "Wanda Theme," 33.

13. The play was rescued from obscurity by Ujejski who published it from a manuscript deposited in the Library of Municipal Theatres in Warsaw. However, the front page of Ujejski's edition gives only an abbreviated title of the play. For the full title, *Wanda, królowa polska,* see the first page of the play itself (page 61 in Ujejski's edition).

14. While I have no intention of discounting the valuable work of scholars who have written on Łubieńska's and Wężyk's dramas, I want to propose that when gender is used as an analytical category, other, more troubling readings of the plays emerge.

15. See Wincenty Kadłubek, *Kronika Polska,* trans. and ed. Brygida Kürbis (Wrocław: Zakład Narodowy im. Ossolińskich, 1992), 17–19. For an analysis of Kadłubek's narrative about Wanda, see Jacek Banaszkiewicz, *Polskie dzieje bajeczne mistrza Wincentego Kadłubka* (Wrocław: Leopoldinum, 1998), 65–153.

16. See Ignacy Krasicki, *Historia,* ed. Mieczysław Klimowicz (Warsaw: Państwowy Instytut Wydawniczy, 1956), 157.

17. Wojciech Bogusławski, *Cud albo Krakowiaki i Górale,* ed. Mieczysław Klimowicz (Wrocław: Zakład Narodowy im. Ossolińskich, 2005), 130. The play is also known as *Cud mniemany albo Krakowiaki i Górale* (*The Alleged Miracle, or Cracovians and Highlanders*).

18. Wiktor Brumer, *Służba narodowa Wojciecha Bogusławskiego* (Warsaw: Księgarnia F. Hoesicka, 1929), 88.

19. Napoleon attended a performance of Ludwik Osiński's allegorical drama, *Perseus and Andromeda* (*Perseusz i Andromeda*), at the Warsaw National Theatre on 18 January 1807. For a description of the performance, see Bartoszewicz, *Szkice,* 1:258–62; Brumer, *Służba,* 89–95; Raszewski, *Bogusławski,* 2:117.

20. Józef Bachórz, "O Emilii Plater i *Śmierci pułkownika:* Narodziny i dzieje legendy," in *Jak pachnie na Litwie Mickiewicza i inne studia o romantyzmie* (Gdańsk: Słowo/obraz terytoria, 2003), 49.

21. For example, Mortkowiczówna describes nineteenth-century Polish freedom fighters as "Wanda's heirs." Mortkowiczówna, *Podanie o Wandzie,* 24.

22. For further discussion of this issue, see Mortkowiczówna, *Podanie o Wandzie,* 24; Ratajczakowa, "Wanda," 114.

23. Ratajczakowa, "Wanda," 109, 111.

24. Ibid., 106.

25. Ursula Phillips, "Polish Women Writers in the Nineteenth Century: 1800–50," in *A History of Central European Women's Writing,* ed. Celia Hawkesworth (Basingstoke, UK: Palgrave, 2001), 65. By "the national situation,"

Phillips means more than a century of foreign domination and political nonexistence (1795–1918).

26. Ibid., 65–66.

27. For example, Katarzyna Marciniak contents herself with describing Łubieńska's Wanda as an ideal ruler who is fully devoted to the welfare of her people. Marciniak thus continues the earlier scholarly tradition of failing to recognize that Wanda's decision to kill herself counters her seemingly inexhaustible commitment to serve the public good. See Marciniak, "Królewna Wanda," 93.

28. Loftis, *Politics of Drama*, 5.

29. Brygida Kürbis, "Wstęp," in Wincenty Kadłubek, *Kronika Polska*, trans. and ed. Kürbis (Wrocław: Zakład Narodowy im. Ossolińskich, 1992), iii. The theme of Wanda's suicide was introduced by a later medieval chronicler, in an untitled work known as *The Wielkopolska Chronicle (Kronika Wielkopolska)*. Its anonymous author depicts Wanda's suicidal leap into the Wisła as a votive offering to the gods for a victory over Germans troops.

30. Łubieńska, *Wanda*, 121.

31. Franciszek Wężyk, *Wanda* (Kraków, 1826), 55.

32. Ibid., 89.

33. For this reading of Wężyk's play, see Kruszewska and Coleman, "Wanda Theme," 28.

34. Wężyk, *Wanda*, 4.

35. Ibid., 11.

36. Ibid., 18.

37. Elizabeth I, *Elizabeth I: Collected Works*, ed. Leah S. Marcus, Janel Mueller, and Mary Beth Rose (Chicago: University of Chicago Press, 2000), 97.

38. Ibid., 326. In fact, it is quite likely that she never said anything of the sort. There is no script from her hand or that of her speechwriter, and no eyewitness account. The canonical version comes from the letter of an unreliable commentator, written almost forty years later. For the argument that the Tilbury speech was probably a seventeenth-century invention, see Felix Barker, "If Parma Had Landed," *History Today* 38, no. 5 (May 1988): 34–41.

39. She wanders alone near a battlefield in search of an enemy who would kill her. When that fails, she leaps into the Wisła.

40. Łubieńska, *Wanda*, 71.

41. Ibid., 72.

42. Ibid., 109.

43. Wężyk, *Wanda*, 45.

44. Łubieńska, *Wanda*, 117.

45. Ujejski, "Wstęp," 24–25.

46. For this view, see Ratajczakowa, "Wanda."

Chapter 4

1. Natalie Zemon Davis, "Women on Top: Symbolic Sexual Inversion and Political Disorder in Early Modern Europe," in *The Reversible World: Symbolic Inversion in Art and Society*, ed. Barbara A. Babcock (Ithaca, NY: Cornell University Press, 1978), 154.

2. To compound the problem, the biographical evidence remains tantalizingly incomplete for many areas of Plater's life. A standard source for accounts of her life is a pseudobiographical compilation by Joseph Straszewicz, her relative and companion-in-arms, who often appears to build a house of straw rather than bricks. See Straszewicz, *Émilie Plater, sa Vie et sa Mort* (Paris, 1835). For an English translation, see Straszewicz, *The Life of the Countess Emily Plater*, trans. J. K. Salomonski (New York, 1842). For subsequent publications that draw on Straszewicz's account, see, e.g., Donata Ciepieńko-Zielińska, *Emilia Plater* (Warsaw: Książka i Wiedza, 1966); Dioniza Wawrzykowska-Wierciochowa, *Sercem i orężem ojczyźnie służyły: Emilia Plater i inne uczestniczki powstania listopadowego 1830–1831* (Warsaw: Wydawnictwo Ministerstwa Obrony Narodowej, 1982), 128–266; Małgorzata Żaryn, *Emilia Plater* (Warsaw: DiG, 1998).

3. Straszewicz, *Life*, 166.

4. Quoted in Straszewicz, *Life*, 37. Bouboulina commanded the fleet of the island of Spetses during the Greek struggle for independence in the 1820s.

5. Mill, *On Liberty*, 131, 134.

6. Bachórz's reading of historical evidence leads him to conclude that Plater was given only an honorary command and that her military importance has been exaggerated. See Bachórz, "O Emilii Plater," 31.

7. Plater, of course, was not the only female soldier whose transgression of gender norms triggered concerns about her sexual conduct. For example, in justifying its decision to award Deborah Sampson Gannett military service wages never paid during the Revolutionary War, the Massachusetts House of Representatives argued in 1792 that she "exhibited an extraordinary instance of female heroism by discharging the duties of a faithful gallant soldier, and at the same time preserving the virtue & chastity of her sex unsuspected & unblemished." Such concerns about whether or not female soldiers committed sexual improprieties reveal just how unsettling their unconventional mode of patriotic activism was to their contemporaries. For a reprint of the 1792 resolution by the Massachusetts legislature, see Emil F. Guba, *Deborah Samson [sic] alias Robert Shurtliff, Revolutionary War Soldier* (Plymouth, MA: Jones River Press, 1994), 80.

8. See, e.g., Wojciech Goczałkowski, *Wspomnienia lat ubiegłych*, 2 vols. (Kraków, 1862), 2:52.

9. See Henryk Golejewski, *Pamiętnik*, ed. Irena Homola, Bolesław Łopuszański, and Janina Skowrońska, 2 vols. (Kraków: Wydawnictwo Literackie, 1971), 1:401.

10. Kazimiera Iłłakowiczówna, "Ogródek Emilii Plater," in *Trazymeński zając: Księga dygresji* (Kraków: Wydawnictwo Literackie, 1968), 15.

11. Goczałkowski, *Wspomnienia*, 2:53. Bachórz contends that the use of "Mr. Plater" as a form of address for her was merely a joke. See Bachórz, "O Emilii Plater," 32.

12. See, e.g., Bachórz, "O Emilii Plater," 32–33; Goczałkowski, *Wspomnienia*, 2:17; Wiktor Gomulicki, *Kłosy z polskiej niwy* (Warsaw: S. Orgelbrand, [1912]), 22–23.

13. Attempts to bolster a threatened worldview by linking women's military service with promiscuity have not vanished. For example, Henryk Piecuch claims that the Emilia Plater Women's Battalion was organized in 1943 solely to provide sexual services to officers. See Piecuch, *Akcje specjalne: Od Bieruta do Ochaba* (Warsaw: Wydawnictwo 69, 1996), 94–97. The veterans of the Plater Battalion charged Piecuch with slander and brought a lawsuit against him. As a result of the lawsuit, he issued a public apology. Claims such as Piecuch's are not, of course, confined to Polish culture. For an excellent discussion of a slander campaign against the Women's Army Corps in the United States, see Leisa D. Meyer, *Creating GI Jane: Sexuality and Power in the Women's Army Corps during World War II* (New York: Columbia University Press, 1996), esp. 33–50.

14. Marcia Holly, "Consciousness and Authenticity: Toward a Feminist Aesthetic," in *Feminist Literary Criticism: Explorations in Theory*, ed. Josephine Donovan, 2nd ed. (Lexington: University Press of Kentucky, 1989), 38.

15. At the Women's Theatre Festival in Boston in 1985, the Omaha Magic Theatre presented *Mud*, written and directed by Maria Irene Fornes. In the play, a young working-class woman, Mae, is driven to suicide when she can no longer bear sexist abuse. During a public discussion after one of the performances in Boston, women in the audience took Fornes to task for presenting Mae as a victim. None of them was willing to admit that the play might prompt some viewers to imagine how Mae's life could have been different.

16. Margaret Fuller, *Woman in the Nineteenth Century* (Columbia: University of South Carolina Press, 1980), 36, 159. Fuller's account of Plater's military career relies on Straszewicz's *Life*, which was in Elizabeth Peabody's library in Boston. Fuller accepts Straszewicz's "homage" to Plater at face value, attributing it solely to "a brotherly devotion," selfless and generous (35). In the earlier, shorter version of *Woman in the Nineteenth Century*, published under the title *The Great Lawsuit* in the Boston *Dial* in July 1843, Fuller does not mention Plater.

17. Fuller, *Woman*, 33.

18. Margaret Fuller to Caroline Sturgis, 13 March 1845, in *The Letters of Margaret Fuller*, ed. Robert N. Hudspeth, vol. 4 (Ithaca, NY: Cornell University Press, 1987), 59.

19. Margaret Fuller, *"These Sad But Glorious Days": Dispatches from Europe, 1846–1850*, ed. Larry J. Reynolds and Susan Belasco Smith (New Haven, CT: Yale University Press, 1991), 223.

20. Thomas J. Pniewski, "Mickiewicz and America," *Kosciuszko Foundation Newsletter* 44, no. 2 (Fall 1998): 7.

21. Wollstonecraft, *Vindication of the Rights of Woman*, 197.

22. See Jaroslaw Maciejewski, *Mickiewicza wielkopolskie drogi: Rekonstrukcje i refleksje* (Poznań: Wydawnictwo Poznańskie, 1972), 346–48. The reference to Plater as "the true Polish woman" is from an article published in *Gazeta Wielkiego Księstwa Poznańskiego* on 3 August 1831 and reprinted in Maciejewski, *Mickiewicza wielkopolskie drogi*, 347.

23. See, e.g., *Histoire d'Émilie Plater, héroïne de la Pologne, 1831* (Bordeaux, 1831); Adam Mickiewicz, *Livre des pélerins polonais*, trans. Charles de Montalembert (Paris, 1833); Michel Pietkiewicz, *La Lithuanie et sa dernière insurrection* (Brussels, 1832); Straszewicz, *Émilie Plater*; Joseph Straszewicz, *Les Polonais et les Polonaises de la Révolution du 29 Novembre 1830* (Paris, 1832–36). The anonymous *Histoire d'Émilie Plater* is believed to have been written by Cezary Plater. Mickiewicz's *Livre des pélerins polonais* (*The Books of the Polish Pilgrimage*), a translation of his 1832 *Księgi pielgrzymstwa polskiego*, includes a long introductory essay by the translator, an extreme Catholic publicist, and "Hymne à la Pologne" ("Hymn to Poland") by the priest and writer Félicité de La Mennais.

24. The most thorough and illuminating discussion of the poem can be found in Bachórz, "O Emilii Plater"; Bogdan Zakrzewski, "'Ach, to była dziewca . . .' O Mickiewiczowskiej Platerównie," in *"Palen dla cara": O polskiej poezji patriotycznej i rewolucyjnej XIX wieku* (Wrocław: Zakład Narodowy im. Ossolińskich, 1979), 7–34.

25. In Mickiewicz's poem, "Ordon's Stronghold" ("Reduta Ordona," 1833), by contrast, Julian Konstanty Ordon, another hero of the uprising of 1830, dies in battle, although the historical Ordon survived.

26. Adam Mickiewicz, "Śmierć Pułkownika," in *Dzieła*, 1:347. For an anonymous English translation, see "The Death of the Colonel," *Harper's New Monthly Magazine* 10 (January 1855): 279.

27. In his lecture, given at the Collège de France in Paris on 17 June 1842, Mickiewicz presents a version of Plater's biography that returns her to the aristocratic fold: "This young and delicate maiden from an aristocratic family launched an

insurgency in her county [*w swym powiecie*] and took part in many battles." Mickiewicz, "Wykład XXX," in *Dzieła*, 9:386.

28. Straszewicz, *Life*, 28–29, 35.

29. See ibid., 267.

30. These accounts are: Felicja Boberska, "O Polkach, które się szczególniej zasłużyły Ojczyźnie w powstaniu listopadowym," in *Pisma* (Lwów, 1893), 29–59; Bolesław Limanowski, "Emilia Platerówna: Szkic biograficzny," in *Szermierze wolności* (Kraków: Książka, 1911), 1–26; Kazimierz Żurawski, *Dziewica-bohater: Życiorys Emilii Platerówny, kapitana 1 kompanii 25 pułku (1 litewskiego) piechoty liniowej wojsk polskich 1831 roku* (Lwów: Koło Towarzystwa Szkół Ludowych im. Emilii Plater, 1913). Boberska's and Żurawski's essays originated as lectures given in Lwów in November 1880 and December 1911, respectively.

31. As Toril Moi points out, one of the strategies used to control women in a patriarchal society is to impose "certain social standards of femininity on all biological women, in order precisely to make us believe that the chosen standards for 'femininity' are *natural*. Thus a woman who refuses to conform can be labelled both *unfeminine* and *unnatural*." Moi, *Sexual/Textual Politics: Feminist Literary Theory* (London: Routledge, 1991), 65.

32. In Limanowski's and Żurawski's accounts, the cousins confide their plans to Plater, and she offers to help them.

33. "However, she remained compassionate and tender of heart, and local peasants often benefited from her sympathy and assistance." Boberska, "O Polkach," 49.

34. Ibid.

35. Ibid., 48.

36. Ibid., 49.

37. See Fidelis, "'Participation,'" 113. The popularity of the *Bluszcz* continued until 1939 when the outbreak of World War II forced the magazine to close down.

38. Ibid., 121.

39. Żurawski, *Dziewica-bohater*, 46.

40. See Limanowski, *Szermierze wolności*, i. On Limanowski's socialism, see Kazimiera Janina Cottam, *Bolesław Limanowski (1835–1935): A Study in Socialism and Nationalism* (Boulder, CO: East European Quarterly, 1978).

41. For a generous source of information about women's involvement in patriotic resistance in nineteenth-century Poland, see Jadwiga Prendowska, *Moje wspomnienia*, ed. Eligiusz Kozłowski and Kazimierz Olszański (Kraków: Wydawnictwo Literackie, 1962).

42. Mickiewicz, "Wykład XXX," in *Dzieła*, 9:385–86. Mickiewicz echoes Straszewicz's assertions in *Life*, 28–29, 34–35.

43. Wiktoria Śliwowska, "Polskie drogi do emancypacji (o udziale kobiet w ruchu niepodległościowym w okresie międzypowstaniowym 1833–1856)," in *Losy*

Polaków w XIX–XX w., ed. Barbara Grochulska and Jerzy Skowronek (Warsaw: Państwowe Wydawnictwo Naukowe, 1987), 221, 236.

44. For such views, see, e.g., Aleksander Mac, "Dowodziłem kobiecym batalionem," and Irena Sztachelska, "Mówiłyśmy, o jaką Polskę walczymy," in *Platerówki*, ed. Eleonora Syzdek (Wrocław: Zakład Narodowy im. Ossolińskich, 1988), 196, 200. Although they pay tribute to the soldiers of the wartime Emilia Plater Women's Battalion, both Mac and Sztachelska emphatically insist that women's proper place is in auxiliary forces, such as medical services, rather than in combat troops.

45. On the growing mistrust of Russia in Western Europe and the fears of the Russian threat to Western civilization, see, e.g., Figes, *Crimean War*, 78–88. On the rise of anti-Russian sentiments in France, see Raymond T. McNally, "The Origins of Russophobia in France: 1812–1830," *American Slavic and East European Review* 17, no. 2 (April 1958): 173–89. For a history of the cult of Joan of Arc and an analysis of its ideological underpinnings, see Marina Warner, *Joan of Arc: The Image of Female Heroism* (New York: Alfred A. Knopf, 1981). Warner, however, does not consider the connection between Joan and Plater.

46. Straszewicz, *Life*, 217.

47. Well aware that initially Joan had no success in persuading the commander of French forces to take her mission seriously, Straszewicz does not mince words about the reasons why Plater was rebuffed by a citizens' committee in Wilno: "She forgot that she was a woman, and that men affect an exclusive monopoly in politics, courage, and wisdom. Her sex excluded her from that confidence which her enterprising character and extensive designs ought to have secured to her." Straszewicz, *Life*, 165.

48. See ibid., 171.

49. Justin Maurice, "Élégie," in Straszewicz, *Émilie Plater*, 337, 339. "Élégie" was originally published in 1834, in *Le Polonais: Journal des Intêrets de la Pologne*, a Paris-based periodical edited by Władysław Plater.

50. Pierre Simon Ballanche, "Préface," in Straszewicz, *Émilie Plater*, xiii.

51. The precedent of Joan of Arc is invoked not only in Mickiewicz's "The Death of the Colonel," but also in Gaszyński's "A Poem" and Antoni Edward Odyniec's "The Kovno Meadow: A True Story" ("Smug kowieński: Zdarzenie prawdziwe," written in 1832). Gaszyński's and Odyniec's poems are reprinted in Zakrzewski, *"Palen dla cara,"* 36–39. Although the phrase "virgin-hero" in Mickiewicz's poem links Plater with the Maid of Orleans, Bachórz nevertheless argues that Mickiewicz seeks to lock the Plater story "in her native realm," therefore "no allusions" to her foreign predecessors "detract from the atmosphere of Polishness in the poem." Bachórz, "O Emilii Plater," 46.

52. The poems include "On the Commemoration of the Events of 29 November, Celebrated on 29 July in Warsaw" ("Na obchód 29 listopada, urządzony 29 lipca w Warszawie," 1831) by an anonymous author, "Miss Plater: On the

Seventieth Anniversary of the Death of the Heroine" ("Platerówna: W siedemdziesiątą rocznicę śmierci bohaterki," 1901) by Ferdynand Kuraś, and "In Livonia" ("Na Żmudzi," 1904) by Maria Konopnicka, as well as those by Mickiewicz, Gaszyński, and Odyniec. The anonymous poem was published in the newspaper *Zjednoczenie* on 1 August 1831. Kuraś's poem is reprinted in Żaryn, *Emilia Plater*, 76-78. For Konopnicka's poem, see her *Śpiewnik historyczny* (Lwów: Polskie Towarzystwo Nakładowe, 1905), 171-72.

53. For a study of Gąsiorowski's novel, see Barbara Gołębiowska, "Rzeczywistość i fikcja w *Emilii Plater* Wacława Gąsiorowskiego," *Prace Polonistyczne* 28 (1972): 97-107. For a discussion of the poems, see Bachórz, "O Emilii Plater"; Zakrzewski, *"Palen dla cara"*; Janina Znamirowska, *Liryka Powstania Listopadowego* (Warsaw: Kasa im. Mianowskiego, 1930).

54. I have not been able to locate Eustachy Czekalski's *Emilia Plater* (written ca. 1917) and the full text of Adam Znamirowski's *Emilia Plater* (written ca. 1915). Only a short excerpt (act 2, scene 4) from Znamirowski's play appears to be extant. See Znamirowski, "Emilia Plater," *Ilustrowany Tygodnik Polski*, 28 November 1915, 286. Wawrzykowska-Wierciochowa has identified Ludwika Broel-Plater's *The Chosen Woman* (*Wybrana*, 1903) as yet another play about Plater. See Wawrzykowska-Wierciochowa, *Sercem i orężem*, 259. However, *The Chosen Woman* deals with Joan of Arc rather than Plater.

55. Stefan Kiedrzyński, *Zaręczyny pod kulami* (Warsaw: I. Rzepecki, 1938), 15.
56. Bronisław Bakal, *Bitwa pod Łowczówkiem* (Warsaw: I. Rzepecki, 1938), 16.
57. Ibid.
58. Ibid., 17.
59. Ibid.
60. Zygmunt Nowakowski, *Gałązka rozmarynu* (Lwów: Atlas, 1938), 23.
61. Ludwik Stolarzewicz, *W gronie dziewcząt* (Łódź: Wydawnictwo Drukarni Państwowej, [1935]), 17.
62. Ibid., 19.
63. The other portraits are those of Maria Skłodowska Curie and the writers Maria Konopnicka and Eliza Orzeszkowa.
64. Davies, *God's Playground*, 2:170.
65. Janina Sedlaczek, *Pod sztandarem kobiety* (Poznań, 1895), 3.
66. Władysław Winiarski, *Mogiła więcej* (Kraków: G. Gebethner, 1912), 29.
67. Sedlaczek, *Pod sztandarem kobiety*, 4; Tadeusz Orsza Korpal, *Emilia Plater: Panny w r. 1831* (Miejsce Piastowe: Towarzystwo św. Michała Archanioła, 1937), 71.
68. Korpal, *Emilia Plater*, 46.
69. Winiarski, *Mogiła więcej*, 22.
70. Wanda Brzeska, *Emilia Plater*, in *Powstanie listopadowe*, ed. Maria Ojerzyńska (Poznań: Zjednoczenie Młodzieży Polskiej, 1927), 93.

71. Ibid., 91.
72. Ibid., 93.
73. For accounts of Michał Plater's attempted commemoration and its far-reaching consequences, see Józef Twardowski's letters to Adam Jerzy Czartoryski, in "Korespondencja 1822–24," ed. J. Ogończyk, *Roczniki Poznańskiego Towarzystwa Przyjaciół Nauk* 26 (1900), 320–35; Maria Dernałowicz, Ksenia Kostenicz, and Zofia Makowiecka, *Kronika życia i twórczości Mickiewicza: Lata 1798–1824* (Warsaw: Państwowy Instytut Wydawniczy, 1957), 411–12; Juliusz Kleiner, *Mickiewicz*, rev. ed., 2 vols. (Lublin: Towarzystwo Naukowe Katolickiego Uniwersytetu Lubelskiego, 1995), 1:459–60.
74. Cheri Register, "American Feminist Literary Criticism: A Bibliographical Introduction," in *Feminist Literary Criticism*, ed. Donovan, 20. Register is quoting Wendy Martin, "The Feminine Mystique in American Fiction," in *Female Studies*, ed. Florence Howe, vol. 2 (Pittsburgh: KNOW, 1970), 33.

Chapter 5

1. Although Kościuszko's career has generated enough commentary to fill a small library, a full-scale, in-depth biography remains to be written. As Tadeusz Rawski notes, the challenge of such an undertaking is compounded by the fact that nearly all aspects of Kościuszko's life are open to "diametrically opposed interpretations." Rawski, "Kościuszko—wódz," *Studia i Materiały do Historii Wojskowości* 1 (1968): 160–230. For an overview of his life, see Bartłomiej Szyndler, *Tadeusz Kościuszko 1746–1817* (Warsaw: Bellona, 1991). Storozynski's *Peasant Prince* offers a lively, popular account but contains a variety of errors and apocrypha.
2. Thompson, review of *Thaddeus Kosciuszko*, 680. For a survey of views about Kościuszko, see Krystyna Śreniowska, *Kościuszko, bohater narodowy: Opinie współczesnych i potomnych 1794–1946* (Warsaw: Państwowe Wydawnictwo Naukowe, 1973), and, for a contrasting perspective, Adam Galos, "Tradycje Naczelnika powstania Kościuszkowskiego i Racławic w XIX w.," in *Panorama Racławicka*, ed. Matwijowski, 17–35.
3. For this portrait of Kościuszko, see, e.g., Adam Próchnik, *Demokracja Kościuszkowska* (Warsaw: Wiedza, 1946); Storozynski, *Peasant Prince*.
4. See, e.g., Maria Janion and Maria Żmigrodzka, *Romantyzm i historia*, 2nd ed. (Gdańsk: Słowo/obraz terytoria, 2001), 287; Tadeusz Korzon, *Kościuszko: Życiorys z dokumentów wysnuty* (Kraków, 1894), 453; Jerzy Kowecki, "The Kościuszko Insurrection: Continuation and Radicalization of Change," trans. Jerzy Kolodziej and Mary Helen Ayres, in *Constitution and Reform*, ed. Fiszman, 515; Adam Próchnik, *Kim był Tadeusz Kościuszko* (Warsaw: Wiedza, 1946), 28–29; Władysław Smoleński, *Znaczenie Tadeusza Kościuszki w dziejach polskich* (Warsaw: Gebethner i Wolff,

[1917]), 10; Andrzej Walicki, *The Enlightenment and the Birth of Modern Nationhood: Polish Political Thought from Noble Republicanism to Tadeusz Kościuszko*, trans. Emma Harris (Notre Dame: University of Notre Dame Press, 1989), 111. In arguing that the 1794 uprising opened a new chapter in Polish history because it enabled the emergence of "a modern concept of nation, encompassing all social classes," Łukasz Kądziela goes so far as to make a sweeping claim that the insurgency "marked a final break with the gentry's monopoly on political life and armed struggle." Kądziela, "The 1794 Kościuszko Insurrection," trans. Robert Strybel, *Polish Review* 39, no. 4 (1994): 391. Likewise, Perry Anderson contends that "the radicalism of the Polish Insurrection of 1794 pronounced the death-sentence on the *szlachta* [gentry] State." Anderson, *Lineages of the Absolutist State* (London: NLB, 1974), 297.

5. Jefferson to Gates, 21 February 1798, in Jefferson, *Papers*, 123.

6. Franciszek Dionizy Kniaźnin, "Do Tadeusza Kościuszka" and "Na rewolucją [*sic*] 1794," in *Wiersze wybrane*, ed. Andrzej K. Guzek (Warsaw: Państwowy Instytut Wydawniczy, 1981), 171, 185.

7. As Catharine Edwards points out, "Traditionally the term *virtus* has been most often linked to performance in battle," but it has also been used "as an all-embracing ethical term" that "generally has the sense of bravery, both physical and mental." Edwards, *Death in Ancient Rome*, 90, 78.

8. Monica M. Gardner, *Kosciuszko: A Biography* (London: George Allen and Unwin, 1920), 111. In claiming Kościuszko as the epitome of Polishness, Gardner asserts that he was "a devout Catholic" (116). In truth, Kościuszko was a strictly rational deist.

9. On this issue, see especially Franciszek Ziejka, *Panorama Racławicka* (Kraków: Krajowa Agencja Wydawnicza, 1984), 80–97.

10. Damian Walford Davies, *Presences That Disturb: Models of Romantic Identity in the Literature and Culture of the 1790s* (Cardiff: University of Wales Press, 2002), 95.

11. Ibid., 108. For a historically grounded overview of the popularity of Cato as a patriotic model, see James William Johnson, *The Formation of English Neo-Classical Thought* (Princeton, NJ: Princeton University Press, 1967), 95–105.

12. Ibid., 96.

13. Ibid., 98–99.

14. On the reception of Addison's drama, see, e.g., Lincoln B. Faller, *The Popularity of Addison's "Cato" and Lillo's "The London Merchant," 1700–1776* (New York: Garland, 1988), 5–87; Frederic M. Litto, "Addison's *Cato* in the Colonies," *William and Mary Quarterly*, 3rd series, 23, no. 3 (July 1966): 431–49. On the play's impact on the political rhetoric in British North America, see Bailyn, *Ideological Origins*, 43–44.

15. The attacks by Addison's contemporaries were directed not so much against the love scenes per se as against the presence of women in the play. See Freeman, *Character's Theater*, 101.

16. Ibid., 255n39.

17. John Lash, *The Hero: Manhood and Power* (London: Thames and Hudson, 1995), 27.

18. Quoted in Jerzy Kowecki, *Pospolite ruszenie w insurekcji 1794 r.* (Warsaw: Wydawnictwo Ministerstwa Obrony Narodowej, 1963), 67.

19. In contrast, "The patriotism of the gentry . . . did not include an understanding that far-reaching social reforms were essential if the Polish state were to survive," or a recognition "that the peasants must receive much more than that vague 'protection of the state' promised in the constitution [of 3 May 1791] if they were to fight and die for independent Poland." Andrzej Zahorski, "The Attitudes of the Polish Estates toward the Kościuszko Insurrection," in *East Central European Society and War in the Era of Revolutions, 1775–1856*, ed. Béla K. Király (New York: Brooklyn College Press, 1984), 80.

20. As Emanuel Rostworowski points out, "Under Polish law only nobles, Christian burghers, and vagrants were accepted into the army," although exceptions did occur. The reasons for the exclusion of peasants are not difficult to identify: "The enlistment of peasants was seen not only as a loss of manpower on the land but also as a significant threat to the principle of serfdom." Rostworowski, "War and Society in the Noble Republic of Poland-Lithuania in the Eighteenth Century," in *East Central European Society and War in the Pre-Revolutionary Eighteenth Century*, ed. Gunther E. Rothenberg, Béla K. Király, and Peter F. Sugar (Boulder, CO: Social Science Monographs, 1982), 171–72. See also Jerzy Kowecki, "The General Levy in Eighteenth-Century Poland," in the same volume, 189–97.

21. For the text of the Połaniec Proclamation, see *Uniwersał Połaniecki*, ed. Jerzy Topolski (Lublin: Wydawnictwo Lubelskie, 1984), 49–54. For an English translation, see "Połaniec Manifesto 1794," trans. M. B. Biskupski, in *Polish Democratic Thought from the Renaissance to the Great Emigration: Essays and Documents*, ed. M. B. Biskupski and James S. Pula (Boulder, CO: East European Monographs, 1990), 189–93. The implementation of the Połaniec Proclamation was largely unsuccessful because "the vast majority" of the nobles opposed it and found ways to "sabotage" its provisions. Emanuel Halicz, *Polish National Liberation Struggles and the Genesis of the Modern Nation: Collected Papers*, trans. Roger A. Clarke (Odense: Odense University Press, 1982), 24; Zahorski, "Attitudes," 80. For a more extended treatment of resistance to the Połaniec Proclamation, see Jerzy Kowecki, *Uniwersał Połaniecki i sprawa jego realizacji* (Warsaw: Państwowe Wydawnictwo Naukowe, 1957).

22. On this issue, see, e.g., Szymon Askenazy, "Przedmowa," in *Akty powstania Kościuszki*, ed. Askenazy and Włodzimierz Dzwonkowski, vol. 1 (Kraków:

Akademia Umiejętności, 1918), vi; Kowecki, *Pospolite ruszenie*, 274; Adam M. Skałkowski, *Z dziejów insurekcji 1794 r.* (Warsaw: Gebethner i Wolff, 1926), 18.

23. While the jacquerie, in which over one thousand nobles lost their lives, undoubtedly played into the hands of Austrian officials who manipulated social tensions to their political advantage, "there is no evidence to show that [peasants] were encouraged by the Austrian government." R. F. Leslie, *The Polish Question: Poland's Place in Modern History* (London: Historical Association, 1971), 18.

24. In Polish: "*Kościuszko to był wariat, // Co buntował proletriat!*" Adam Asnyk, "Historyczna nowa szkoła," in *Poezje* (Warsaw: Państwowy Instytut Wydawniczy, 1974), 635.

25. See, e.g., Stefan Bratkowski, *Z czym do nieśmiertelności* (Katowice: Śląsk, 1977), 216–24; Korzon, *Kościuszko,* 100–1; Storozynski, *Peasant Prince,* 13–16. The framing premise of Storozynski's book is that Kościuszko's experience of having been rejected "as a suitor for the daughter of an aristocrat was the pivotal moment in his life" (xiv; see also 286). For a dissenting view, see Feliks Koneczny, *Tadeusz Kościuszko: Życie, czyny, duch,* 2nd ed. (Poznań: Wielkopolska Księgarnia Nakładowa Karola Rzepeckiego, 1922). Koneczny argues that Kościuszko's dedication to "larger, higher, and more serious" goals was too absolute to brook any competing demands on his attention (118).

26. For the hypothesis that Kościuszko hoped to marry Sosnowska for financial gain, see Szyndler, *Tadeusz Kościuszko,* 61.

27. Storozynski, *Peasant Prince,* 14. See also Franciszek Paszkowski, *Dzieje Tadeusza Kościuszki, Pierwszego Naczelnika Polaków* (Kraków, 1872), 13–14; Trębicki, *Opisanie sejmu,* 213–14. For an opposite view, see Korzon, *Kościuszko,* 593.

28. Korzon, with a brilliant mixture of amused irony and razor wit, makes mincemeat of the rumors about the elopement. See Korzon, *Kościuszko,* 101–2, 592–93. Storozynski has evidently missed Korzon's irony because he cites the Polish historian's anti-elopement argument as proof that the abduction did take place. See Storozynski, *Peasant Prince,* 286n6.

29. See, e.g., Gardner, *Kosciuszko,* 34–35; Lucjan Siemieński, *Żywot Tadeusza Kościuszki* (Kraków, 1866), 39; Storozynski, *Peasant Prince,* 16–17. In truth, Kościuszko's enlistment in the Continental Army was, as much as anything, a career move. It is Konstanty Majeranowski's play *Kościuszko's First Love* (*Pierwsza miłość Kościuszki,* 1820) that has firmly impressed on the public imagination the image of a lovelorn Kościuszko who leaves Poland because he is forbidden to marry the woman he loves. I discuss *Kościuszko's First Love* in section II of this chapter.

30. Jan Dihm, *Kościuszko nieznany* (Wrocław: Zakład Narodowy im. Ossolińskich, 1969), 315.

31. Julian Ursyn Niemcewicz, *Notes sur ma captivité a Saint-Pétersbourg, en 1794, 1795 et 1796* (Paris, 1843), 23. See also Niemcewicz, *Pamiętniki czasów moich*

(1957 ed.), 2:115. *Notes sur ma captivité* was originally written in French. Alexander Laski, who translated *Notes* into English in 1844, missed the difference between the primary meanings of the French verb *embrasser* and the English verb *embrace;* hence he rendered the scene stiffly decorous: "I embraced the General, who had not yet recovered his senses." Niemcewicz, *Notes of My Captivity in Russia in the Years 1794, 1795, and 1796,* trans. Alexander Laski (Edinburgh, 1844), 29.

32. The corresponding sentence in Furtwangler's study reads: "Our image of Washington may never be completely free of our sense of him as a hero fixed at the center of a tableau or a series of tableaux." Furtwangler, *American Silhouettes: Rhetorical Identities of the Founders* (New Haven, CT: Yale University Press, 1987), 83.

33. See, e.g., Wiktor Hahn, *Kościuszko w polskiej poezji dramatycznej* (Poznań: Księgarnia Św. Wojciecha, 1918), 55; Piotr Mitzner, *Teatr Tadeusza Kościuszki: Postać Naczelnika w teatrze 1803–1994* (Warsaw: Wydawnictwo Uniwersytetu Kardynała Stefana Wyszyńskiego, 2002), 17–44, esp. 43; Zofia Ordyńska, *To już prawie sto lat: Pamiętnik aktorki* (Wrocław: Zakład Narodowy im. Ossolińskich, 1970), 16; Adam Grzymała Siedlecki, "W. L. Anczyc i jego *Kościuszko pod Racławicami,*" *Tygodnik Ilustrowany,* 16 October 1915, 610; Tadeusz "Boy" Żeleński, *Reflektorem w serce, romanse cieniów: Wrażenia teatralne* (Warsaw: Państwowy Instytut Wydawniczy, 1968), 197.

34. For this argument, see, e.g., Jan Stanisław Kopczewski, "Tadeusz Kościuszko," in *Życiorysy historyczne, literackie i legendarne,* ed. Zofia Stefanowska and Janusz Tazbir, 3 vols. (Warsaw: Państwowe Wydawnictwo Naukowe, 1980–92), 1:170–80.

35. In an otherwise illuminating study of the rise of the Kościuszko cult in the nineteenth century, Adam Galos claims that it was only the centennial commemoration of the 1794 insurrection that established the image of Kościuszko as a facilitator of social solidarity and national unity. See Galos, "Tradycje Naczelnika," 29–30. For a similar argument, see Patrice M. Dabrowski, *Commemorations and the Shaping of Modern Poland* (Bloomington: Indiana University Press, 2004), 114–15, 124–25. However, Anczyc's influential play, *Kościuszko at Racławice,* created and propagated the unifying figure of Kościuszko fourteen years earlier.

36. For an overview of plays on the Kościuszko theme, see Hahn, *Kościuszko w polskiej poezji dramatycznej;* Mitzner, *Teatr Tadeusza Kościuszki;* Dobrochna Ratajczakowa, *Obrazy narodowe w dramacie i teatrze* (Wrocław: Wiedza o Kulturze, 1994). Mitzner also provides archival evidence to document censors' objections to the plays, including those discussed in this chapter.

37. For information about the 1820 production, see Mitzner, *Teatr Tadeusza Kościuszki,* 22. The opening night, on 16 October, was part of a public fete to launch the construction of the commemorative Kościuszko Mound.

38. Konstanty Majeranowski, *Pierwsza miłość Kościuszki* (Kraków, 1820), 25.

39. In his commentary on the play, Hahn notes that Kościuszko's nervousness and insecurity make him a rather disagreeable figure. See Hahn, *Kościuszko w polskiej poezji dramatycznej*, 18.

40. In *Kościuszko on the Seine,* Majeranowski takes this idea one step further by contrasting Kościuszko with Napoleon.

41. Majeranowski, *Pierwsza miłość Kościuszki,* 20.

42. In writing this segment on the popularity of the pro-Russian stance after 1815, I have drawn on Galos, "Tradycje Naczelnika," 19–21. For additional information about the Kościuszko funeral, I have consulted Mirosław Francić, "Kopiec Kościuszki—historia znaczeń," in *Kościuszce w hołdzie,* ed. Mieczysław Rokosz (Kraków: Secesja, 1994), 185–237.

43. Stanisław Bratkowski, *Akademik warszawski* (Warsaw, [1831?]), 13.

44. See Galos, "Tradycje Naczelnika," 22–23.

45. Aleksander Świętochowski, "Wskazania polityczne," in *Publicystyka okresu pozytywizmu 1860–1900: Antologia,* ed. Stanisław Fita (Warsaw: Wydawnictwo Instytutu Badań Literackich PAN, 2002), 189. For a slightly different translation of this excerpt, see "Political Directions," in *For Your Freedom and Ours: Polish Progressive Spirit through the Centuries,* ed. Manfred Kridl, Władysław Malinowski, and Józef Wittlin, trans. Ludwik Krzyżanowski (New York: Frederick Ungar, 1943), 132. First published in 1882, Świętochowski's article is a major programmatic statement of Polish Positivists.

46. For a discussion of the ideology of the Polish Positivism, see, e.g., Stanislaus A. Blejwas, *Realism in Polish Politics: Warsaw Positivism and National Survival in Nineteenth-Century Poland* (New Haven, CT: Yale Concilium on International and Area Studies, 1984); Maciej Janowski, *Polish Liberal Thought before 1918,* trans. Danuta Przekop (Budapest: Central European University Press, 2004), 147–88; Andrzej Jaszczuk, *Spór pozytywistów z konserwatystami o przyszłość Polski 1870–1903* (Warsaw: Państwowe Wydawnictwo Naukowe, 1986).

47. *The Governor's Equal* opened in Lwów in 1866. The title is a shorthand for a Polish proverb, "*Szlachcic na zagrodzie równy wojewodzie*" (The nobleman on his little acre is the governor's equal).

48. The historical Kościuszko was inducted into the Cincinnati shortly before his return to Poland in 1784.

49. Joseph J. Ellis, *His Excellency: George Washington* (New York: Alfred A. Knopf, 2006), 158.

50. Jefferson to Washington, 14 November 1786, quoted in Ellis, *His Excellency,* 159.

51. On the controversy over the Society of the Cincinnati, see Ellis, *His Excellency,* 158–60; John E. Ferling, *The First of Men: A Life of George Washington* (Knoxville: University of Tennessee Press, 1988), 347–48; Wills, *Cincinnatus,* 138–48.

52. Józef Ignacy Kraszewski, *Równy wojewodzie* (Poznań, 1868), 158.

53. Although Kraszewski was not affiliated with the Positivist movement, Positivist writers and thinkers recognized him as their ideological precursor who had repudiated armed struggle and violent revolutionary change in favor of a concerted effort toward economic, social, and cultural modernization. An 1874 article, attributed to Świętochowski, a leading figure in the Positivist movement, is a compelling tribute by the Positivists to Kraszewski. The article, "Józef Ignacy Kraszewski," is reprinted in *Józef Ignacy Kraszewski*, ed. Wincenty Danek (Warsaw: Państwowe Zakłady Wydawnictw Szkolnych, 1965), 200–206.

54. Published anonymously in 1880, Mańkowska's play was first performed in Poznań in 1917. Anczyc's play opened in Kraków in 1880; it was published in the following year.

55. Bogusława Mańkowska, *Tadeusz Kościuszko, czyli cztery chwile życia tego bohatera* (Poznań, 1880), 17, 19.

56. For information about Sobieski's sword, I draw on Szyndler, *Tadeusz Kościuszko*, 321.

57. Mańkowska, *Tadeusz Kościuszko*, 41, 72.

58. See, e.g., Dobrochna Ratajczakowa, "*Kościuszko pod Racławicami* Anczyca—arcydzieło patriotycznej sceny popularnej," in *Kościuszko—powstanie 1794 r.—tradycja: Materiały z sesji naukowej w 200-lecie powstania kościuszkowskiego 15–16 kwietnia 1994 r.*, ed. Jerzy Kowecki (Warsaw: Biblioteka Narodowa, 1997), 285–304.

59. Władysław Ludwik Anczyc, *Kościuszko pod Racławicami*, in *Życie i pisma*, ed. Marian Szyjkowski, vol. 4 (Kraków: privately printed, 1908), 185. Kościuszko's lines in this scene are a slightly modified version of the oath by the historical Kościuszko. For a facsimile of the original oath, along with a translation into English, see Kowecki, "Kościuszko Insurrection," 503.

60. As Jan Lubicz-Pachoński points out, there is no evidence to support the widely held view that Kościuszko ennobled Głowacki. In making this point, he revises his earlier claim that the ennoblement did take place but was never ratified by Parliament because Poland ceased to exist in 1795. See Lubicz-Pachoński, *Wojciech Bartosz Głowacki: Chłopski bohater spod Racławic i Szczekocin* (Warsaw: Państwowe Wydawnictwo Naukowe, 1987), 26–28, 71–78. In contrast, Patrice Dabrowski avers, without evidence, that after the Racławice battle "Kościuszko proceeded to ennoble several peasant scythemen." See Dabrowski, *Commemorations*, 115.

61. Anczyc, *Kościuszko pod Racławicami*, 231.

62. In his preface to the first edition of *Kościuszko at Racławice*, Anczyc remarks that in the earlier version of the play, completed in 1870, patriotic sentiments were "too exalted and therefore implausible." Anczyc, *Kościuszko pod Racławicami*, 286.

63. The song is a collage of excerpts, slightly modified, from Teofil Lenartowicz's poem, "The Battle of Racławice" ("Bitwa racławicka," 1859). Compare

Anczyc, *Kościuszko pod Racławicami*, 218–21, and Lenartowicz, *Bitwa Racławicka / the Battle of Racławice*, trans. Noel Clark (Wrocław: Polskie Stronnictwo Ludowe, 1994), 18–21, 24–26, 28–35, 52–55.

64. For a comparison of both versions, see Piotr Mitzner, "*Kościuszki pod Racławicami* droga na scenę," in *Dramat i teatr pozytywistyczny*, ed. Dobrochna Ratajczakowa (Wrocław: Wiedza o Kulturze, 1992), 103–4.

65. Anczyc, *Kościuszko pod Racławicami*, 243–44.

66. Ibid., 244.

67. Ibid., 162.

68. In creating the character of Magda, Bełcikowski draws on the story of one Magdalena Granasowa, recorded in Kazimierz Władysław Wójcicki's semidocumentary works, *The Memoirs of a Child of Warsaw* (*Pamiętniki dziecka Warszawy*, 1870) and *The Warsaw Community at the Beginning of Our Century, 1800–1830* (*Społeczność Warszawy w początkach naszego stulecia, 1800–1830*, 1875–76). However, there are significant differences between the two street-sellers turned wartime spies. In Wójcicki's account, Granasowa is a middle-aged widow when she offers to spy on the Prussian forces in 1794; she dies of old age some twenty years later. In Bełcikowski's drama, Magda is young and single; she dies shortly after her spying mission is over. Moreover, Wójcicki identifies Granasowa's late husband as Kazimierz (Casimir) Pułaski's soldier in the campaign of 1768–72, known as the Confederacy of Bar. Thus Wójcicki suggests that Granasowa's patriotic passion is not entirely spontaneous because she follows in her husband and Pułaski's footsteps. See Wójcicki, *Pamiętniki dziecka Warszawy i inne wspomnienia warszawskie*, ed. Juliusz W. Gomulicki and Zofia Lewinówna, 2 vols. (Warsaw: Państwowy Instytut Wydawniczy, 1974), 1:59, 2:133–34.

69. These consciousness-raising aspects of Bełcikowski's drama were not lost on the Russian censor in Warsaw. While it was possible to publish and perform *The Warsaw Street-Seller* in the Austrian partition, which had won political autonomy as a result of the Austro-Hungarian Compromise of 1867, the play was banned in the Russian partition until 1912 on the grounds that it was an open invitation to political incendiaries. Likewise, Anczyc's *Kościuszko at Racławice* was first performed in the Russian partition only in 1915.

70. For two productions in 1912, the play was renamed *The Siege of Warsaw* (*Oblężenie Warszawy*). This suggests that theatre directors were skeptical about the marketing value of the original title.

71. Małgorzata Czyszkowska-Peschler, "She Is—a Nobody without a Name: The Professional Situation of Polish Women-of-Letters in the Second Half of the Nineteenth Century," in *Women in Polish Society*, ed. Rudolf Jaworski and Bianka Pietrow-Ennker (Boulder, CO: East European Monographs, 1992), 134.

72. Hahn, *Kościuszko w polskiej poezji dramatycznej*, 32.

73. Rather predictably, Kościuszko addresses Magda as "my child." Adam Bełcikowski, *Przekupka warszawska*, in *Dramata i komedie*, vol. 5 (Kraków, 1898), 279.
74. Ibid., 281.
75. Ibid.
76. Ibid., 326.
77. I am indebted here to a methodological framework developed in Moi, *What Is a Woman?*, 3–120.

Chapter 6

1. Kościuszko to Jefferson, 15 September 1817, in Tadeusz Kościuszko and Thomas Jefferson, *Korespondencja 1798–1817*, ed. Izabella Rusinowa, trans. Agnieszka Glinczanka and Józef Paszkowski (Warsaw: Państwowy Instytut Wydawniczy, 1976), 145. The voluminous secondary literature on Kościuszko obscures the fact that all the key moments in his life raise questions that have yet to be adequately examined. For challenges to the complacent notion that Kościuszko is a familiar figure, see Bratkowski, *Z czym do nieśmiertelności*, esp. 5–29; Łojek, *Wokół sporów*, 192–207.
2. See Tomasz Szarota, *Karuzela na placu Krasińskich: Studia i szkice z lat wojny i okupacji* (Warsaw: Rytm, 2007), 27–29.
3. See Józef Świętorzecki to Ignacy Potocki, 12 January 1793, in Dembowski et al., *Tajna korespondencja*, 128. For scholarly commentary on these materials, see especially Krystyna Maksimowicz, "Poetycka legenda Tadeusza Kościuszki (lata 1792–1794)," *Wiek Oświecenia* 11 (1995): 65–82; Waldemar Okoń, "Ikonografia Tadeusza Kościuszki—wybrane zagadnienia," in *Wtajemniczenia: Studia z dziejów sztuki XIX i XX wieku* (Wrocław: Wydawnictwo Uniwersytetu Wrocławskiego, 1996), 7–26; Bolesław Oleksowicz, *Legenda Kościuszki: Narodziny* (Gdańsk: Słowo/obraz terytoria, 2000); Zdzisław Maciej Zachmacz, "Wokół 'Pieśni na wjazd Kościuszki,'" *Wiek Oświecenia* 11 (1995): 83–101.
4. Kopczewski, "Tadeusz Kościuszko," 157.
5. Mila Szczecina, Marek Pieniążek, and Victor Adorjan, "The Panorama Racławicka: A Battleground for Identity," *Performer* 5 (2012). Grotowski.net. Instytut im. Jerzego Grotowskiego. Web. 6 January 2014.
6. For accounts of the postwar controversy over the *Racławice* panorama, see Magdalena Micińska, "The Myth of Tadeusz Kościuszko in the Polish Mind (1794–1997)," *European Review of History* 5, no. 2 (Autumn 1998): 196; Barbara Törnquist Plewa, *The Wheel of Polish Fortune: Myths in Polish Collective Consciousness during the First Years of Solidarity* (Lund: Lund University, 1992), 193; Ziejka, *Panorama Racławicka*, 80–97.

7. See Mitzner, *Teatr Tadeusza Kościuszki*, 176.

8. See, e.g., Adam Ciołkosz, *Wanda Wasilewska: Dwa szkice biograficzne* (London: Polonia Book Fund, 1977); Jacek Trznadel, *Kolaboranci: Tadeusz Boy-Żeleński i grupa komunistycznych pisarzy we Lwowie 1939–1941* (Komorów: Wydawnictwo Antyk Marcin Dybowski, 1998); Bohdan Urbankowski, *Czerwona msza albo uśmiech Stalina* (Warsaw: Alfa, 1995). For a more nuanced view, see, e.g., Jan T. Gross, *Revolution from Abroad: The Soviet Conquest of Poland's Western Ukraine and Western Belorussia* (Princeton, NJ: Princeton University Press, 2002), 147; Marci Shore, *Caviar and Ashes: A Warsaw Generation's Life and Death in Marxism, 1918–1968* (New Haven, CT: Yale University Press, 2006). esp. 372–74; Joan S. Skurnowicz, "Soviet Polonia, the Polish State, and the New Mythology of National Origins, 1943–1945," *Nationalities Papers* 22 (1994): 103; Julian Stryjkowski, *Ocalony na Wschodzie: Z Julianem Stryjkowskim rozmawia Piotr Szewc* (Montricher, Switzerland: Editions Noir sur Blanc, 1991), 161, 179–81. A comprehensive biography of Wasilewska has yet to be written.

9. See Wanda Wasilewska, "Ku nowym dniom," *Czerwony Sztandar*, 17 September 1940, 4. Excerpts from Wasilewska's speech are reprinted in Trznadel, *Kolaboranci*, 399–401.

10. See, e.g., Wasilewska, "Ku nowym dniom"; Wasilewska, "Za wolność swoją i za wolność świata," *Czerwony Sztandar*, 25 June 1941, 3.

11. Quoted in Raphael Samuel, "British Marxist Historians, 1880–1980: Part One," *New Left Review* 120 (March–April 1980): 48.

12. For a comparison of the Lwów production of *Bartosz Głowacki* with the 1946 production in Kraków, see Jacek Frühling, "*Bartosz Głowacki* we Lwowie i w Krakowie," *Odrodzenie* 15 (1946): 11. In Frühling's view, the Lwów production was the better of the two.

13. See Tadeusz "Boy" Żeleński, *1001 noc teatru: Wrażeń teatralnych seria osiemnasta* (Warsaw: Państwowy Instytut Wydawniczy, 1975), 456. Żeleński's review was originally published in *Nowe Widnokręgi*, a Moscow-based Polish literary magazine, in June 1941.

14. Żeleński, *1001 noc teatru*, 457. For a different assessment of *Bartosz Głowacki*, see Mieczysław Inglot, *Polska kultura literacka Lwowa lat 1939–1941; Ze Lwowa i o Lwowie: Lata sowieckiej okupacji w poezji polskiej—Antologia utworów poetyckich w wyborze* (Wrocław: Towarzystwo Przyjaciół Polonistyki Wrocławskiej, 1995), 173–77, 195–96. Inglot builds his argument around his claim that the play is available only in the Russian translation, published in Moscow in 1955 (see 177). According to Inglot, the fact that Polish publishers ignored *Bartosz Głowacki* even during the communist period proves that it is hackwork, unworthy of any serious attention. In truth, the play was published in communist Poland in 1956.

15. Władysław Krasnowiecki, "O teatr socjalistycznego realizmu," *Czerwony Sztandar*, 31 August 1940, 3.

16. Ibid.

17. Jerzy Putrament and Z. Dobrucki, "*Opowieść o Bartoszu Głowackim*," *Czerwony Sztandar*, 27 March 1941, 5.

18. Ibid.

19. Władysław Krasnowiecki, "Przed premierą *Bartosza Głowackiego*: Teatr historycznej prawdy," *Czerwony Sztandar*, 23 March 1941, 4.

20. Ibid.

21. Bronisław Dąbrowski, *Na deskach świat oznaczających*, vol. 1 (Kraków: Wydawnictwo Literackie, 1977), 161.

22. This paragraph summarizes my interpretation of the evidence available in Dąbrowski, *Na deskach*, 161; Jan Kreczmar, "Teatr lwowski w latach 1939–1941: Wspomnienie," *Pamiętnik Teatralny* 12, nos. 1–4 (1963): 240; Małgorzata Szejnert, *Sława i infamia: Rozmowa z Bohdanem Korzeniewskim* (London: Aneks, 1988), 40.

23. Inglot, *Polska kultura*, 174, 89.

24. See ibid., 89, 174–75. See also Mieczysław Inglot, "Spór o Wrzesień w poezji polskiej lat 1939–1941 we Lwowie," *Pamiętnik Literacki* 81, no. 1 (1990): 205–40.

25. For a different view, see Inglot, *Polska kultura*, 175. Using the Russian translation of *Bartosz Głowacki* as his evidence, Inglot argues that the play besmirches Polish patriotism.

26. According to Michał Borwicz, for example, the play silently draws on Wojciech Skuza's narrative poem, "Kumac: A Story of Wojciech Bartos Głowacki" ("Kumac: Rzecz o Wojciechu Bartosu Głowackim," 1933). See Borwicz, *Ludzie, książki, spory . . .* (Paris: Księgarnia Polska, 1980), 40–42.

27. See Inglot, *Polska kultura*, 173–74; Urbankowski, *Czerwona msza*, 89.

28. Wanda Wasilewska, *Bartosz Głowacki*, in *Pisma zebrane*, vol. 2 (Warsaw: Wydawnictwo Ministerstwa Obrony Narodowej, 1956), 721.

29. Ibid., 775.

30. Ibid., 810.

31. Ibid., 814.

32. See, e.g., Krasnowiecki, "Przed premierą."

33. Wasilewska, *Bartosz Głowacki*, 804–5.

34. That the epilogue incorporates Wasilewska's major revisions is at least a reasonable conjecture. Kreczmar remembers that it was especially the play's tendentious interpretation of the Polish Legions that drew fire from the actors when *Bartosz Głowacki* was considered for production at the Polski Theatre. See Kreczmar, "Teatr lwowski," 240.

35. See Jan T. Gross, *Fear: Anti-Semitism in Poland after Auschwitz; An Essay in Historical Interpretation* (New York: Random House, 2006), esp. chapter 2; Alina Skibińska, "Powroty ocalałych," in *Prowincja noc: Życie i zagłada Żydów w dystrykcie warszawskim*, ed. Barbara Engelking, Jacek Leociak, and Dariusz Libionka (Warsaw: Wydawnictwo Instytutu Filozofii i Socjologii PAN, 2007), 505–81.

36. For accounts of the Kielce pogrom, see Łukasz Kamiński and Jan Żaryn, eds., *Reflections on the Kielce Pogrom*, trans. Aleksandra Matulewska (Warsaw: Institute of National Remembrance, 2006); Bożena Szaynok, *Pogrom Żydów w Kielcach 4 lipca 1946* (Warsaw: Bellona, 1992).

37. After the two productions, however, interest in *Easter* waned. Since 1946, the play has not been performed or reprinted. It has also been neglected in scholarship, although Schiller's production has inspired several studies. See, e.g., Anna Kuligowska-Korzeniewska, "Między zagładą a pogromem: *Wielkanoc* Stefana Otwinowskiego w reżyserii Leona Schillera," in *Żydzi w lustrze dramatu, teatru i krytyki teatralnej*, ed. Eleonora Udalska (Katowice: Wydawnictwo Uniwersytetu Śląskiego, 2004), 203–29.

38. Joanna B. Michlic, "The Holocaust and Its Aftermath as Perceived in Poland: Voices of Polish Intellectuals, 1945–1947," in *The Jews Are Coming Back: The Return of the Jews to Their Countries of Origin after WW II*, ed. David Bankier (Jerusalem: Yad Vashem, 2005), 220.

39. Ibid., 223. See also Joanna B. Michlic, "'Old Wine in a New Bottle': The Jews as Perceived in Post-war Communist Poland, 1945–47," in *The Phoney Peace: Power and Culture in Central Europe 1945–49*, ed. Robert B. Pynsent (London: School of Slavonic and East European Studies, 2000), 87–99.

40. Michlic, "Holocaust," 223.

41. Ibid., 226.

42. Piotr Wróbel, "Double Memory: Poles and Jews after the Holocaust," *East European Politics and Societies* 11, no. 3 (Fall 1997): 569. See also a classic study by Michael C. Steinlauf, *Bondage to the Dead: Poland and the Memory of the Holocaust* (Syracuse, NY: Syracuse University Press, 1997).

43. This notion, inherited from virulently nationalist rhetoric before the war, was disseminated in most of the underground press during the early postwar period. See Michlic, "Holocaust," 210.

44. Krystyna Kersten, "Wstęp," in Bożena Szaynok, *Pogrom Żydów w Kielcach 4 lipca 1946* (Warsaw: Bellona, 1992), 9. See also Krystyna Kersten, *Polacy—Żydzi—komunizm: Anatomia półprawd 1939–68* (Warsaw: Niezależna Oficyna Wydawnicza, 1992), 152.

45. Bożena Szaynok, "Polacy i Żydzi lipiec 1944—lipiec 1946," in *Wokół pogromu kieleckiego*, ed. Łukasz Kamiński and Jan Żaryn (Warsaw: Instytut Pamięci Narodowej, 2006), 15.

46. See Stefan Otwinowski, "Wspólny los," *Odrodzenie* 37 (1945): 6. See also Otwinowski, *Niedyskrecje i wspomnienia* (Kraków: Wydawnictwo Literackie, 1957), 127; Włodzimierz Maciąg, ed., *Sceptyk pełen wiary: Wspomnienia o Stefanie Otwinowskim* (Kraków: Wydawnictwo Literackie, 1979), 119.

47. See Stefan Otwinowski, *Wielkanoc* (Kraków: Centralny Komitet Żydów Polskich, 1946), 17.

48. My account of Otwinowski's work on *Easter* is based on his prefatory notes to the play and on Stanisława Mrozińska's interview with him. See Otwinowski, *Wielkanoc*, 16–18; Mrozińska, *Trzy sezony teatralne Leona Schillera: Łódź 1946–1949* (Wrocław: Zakład Narodowy im. Ossolińskich, 1971), 48. In addition to *Easter*, Otwinowski's contributions to postwar debates about Polish relations with the Jewish minority and about the meaning of Polish patriotism include essays such as "Common Fate" ("Wspólny los," 1945), "Letter 1" ("List pierwszy," 1946), "Letter 3" ("List trzeci," 1946), and "Neighbors: In Lieu of a Programmatic Article" ("Sąsiedzi: Zamiast artykułu programowego," 1947). "Common Fate," "Letter 1," and "Letter 3" are reprinted in Otwinowski, *Niedyskrecje*, 85–91, 7–15; "Neighbors" is included in *Martwa fala: Zbiór artykułów o antysemityzmie*, by Jerzy Andrzejewski et al. (Warsaw: Spółdzielnia Wydawnicza, 1947), 51–59.

49. Otwinowski, *Wielkanoc*, 41.

50. Ibid. 39–40.

51. Ibid., 40.

52. Ibid., 45.

53. In the prologue, set in 1938, the dramatic action pivots on the fact that the Freuds, who run a small hotel, work during the Sabbath.

54. Otwinowski, *Wielkanoc*, 29.

55. Ibid., 49.

56. Ibid., 33.

57. Ibid., 67.

58. Ibid.

59. Ibid., 91.

60. Written in French by Casimir Delavigne and translated into Polish by Karol Sienkiewicz, with music by Karol Kurpiński, "La Varsovienne" urges Poles to tear off their fetters in a decisive move that will bring either freedom or death.

61. Otwinowski, *Wielkanoc*, 62.

62. For background information about John à Lasco, I am indebted to Oskar Bartel, *Jan Łaski: Część I, 1499–1556*, ed. Janusz Maciuszko (Warsaw: Neriton, 1999); Halina Kowalska, *Działalność reformatorska Jana Łaskiego w Polsce 1556–1560* (Warsaw: Neriton, 1999); Dirk W. Rodgers, *John à Lasco in England* (New York: Peter Lang, 1994); Rodgers, "John à Lasco's Liturgy of Public Repentance: A Contribution to the Reformed, Presbyterian, and Puritan Traditions," in *Pulpit, Table, and Song: Essays in Celebration of Howard G. Hageman*, ed. Heather Murray Elkins and Edward C. Zaragoza (Lanham, MD: Scarecrow Press, 1996), 1–32; George Huntston Williams, *The Radical Reformation*, 3rd ed. (Kirksville: Northeast Missouri State University, 1992).

63. On the distinction between the Radical Reformation and the classical Reformation, see Williams, *Radical Reformation*, 9–10.

64. Ibid., 1143. For additional information about the Polish Brethren, I have drawn on Aleksander Brückner, *Różnowiercy polscy: Szkice obyczajowe i literackie*, ed. Lech Szczucki (Warsaw: Państwowy Instytut Wydawniczy, 1962), 97–198; Ludwik Chmaj, *Bracia Polscy: Ludzie, idee, wpływy* (Warsaw: Państwowe Wydawnictwo Naukowe, 1957); Stanislas Kot, *Socinianism in Poland: The Social and Political Ideas of the Polish Antitrinitarians in the Sixteenth and Seventeenth Centuries*, trans. Earl Morse Wilbur (Boston: Starr King Press, 1957).

65. This idea is central to an American play on à Lasco. Its author, Edwin G. York, pays him the following tribute: "The sixteenth century was not a time of widespread religious tolerance, yet it was a time when a champion of religious tolerance—the Polish churchman Jan Laski—influenced many countries to take that path." York, *Jan Laski, Champion of Religious Tolerance* (Milford, NJ: privately printed, 2001), 36.

66. Otwinowski, *Wielkanoc*, 32.

67. On this issue, see especially Magda Teter, *Jews and Heretics in Catholic Poland: A Beleaguered Church in the Post-Reformation Era* (New York: Cambridge University Press, 2006).

68. See Mrozińska, *Trzy sezony*, 48, 53–54.

69. Quoted in Mrozińska, *Trzy sezony*, 54.

70. A commemorative plaque at the Old Synagogue, contributed by the United Jewish Appeal Young Leadership—Morasha "Heritage" Mission to Poland in 1990, carries the following excerpt from a speech that Kościuszko gave there in March 1794: "The Jews proved to the world that whenever humanity can gain, they would not spare their lives."

71. See Maciąg, *Sceptyk*, 226–27; Otwinowski, *Niedyskrecje*, 26–27. Otwinowski recalls that a group of right-wing nationalist students turned up at the opening night and repeatedly disrupted the performance with their whistling. Having decided that the play's author must be a Jew, they attempted to attack Otwinowski after the performance.

72. David G. Roskies and Naomi Diamant, *Holocaust Literature: A History and Guide* (Waltham: Brandeis University Press, 2012), 126.

73. I borrow the term *application plays* from Robert D. Hume, *Henry Fielding and the London Theatre, 1728–1737* (Oxford: Clarendon Press, 1988), 78.

74. Jerzy S. Sito, *Polonez*, 2nd ed. (Warsaw: Czytelnik, 1991), 180.

75. Ibid., 168.

76. Ibid.

77. Ibid., 184.

78. For a related point that the production of *Polonaise* attracted little attention, see Kazimierz A. Lewkowski, "Trzeci Maja w dramacie polskim," in *Konstytucja 3 maja w tradycji i kulturze polskiej*, ed. Alina Barszczewska-Krupa (Łódź: Wydawnictwo Łódzkie, 1991), 570.

79. The historicity of this love plot is not my concern here. When the historical Kościuszko was in his waning years, some of his contemporaries were inclined to believe that he was in love with Angelique Zeltner, the wife of Emilie's uncle. See, e.g., Wirydianna Fiszerowa, *Dzieje moje własne i osób postronnych: Wiązanka spraw poważnych, ciekawych i błahych,* trans. Edward Raczyński (London: privately printed, 1975), 244, 249. Bojarska, however, takes her cue from Kościuszko's will of 10 October 1817, in which he designated Emilie Zeltner, along with his former secretary, Franciszek Paszkowski, as his principal beneficiary. For a facsimile of the will, see Szyndler, *Tadeusz Kościuszko,* 364.

80. *The Polish Lesson* grew out of Bojarska's essay, "The Death of Kościuszko" ("Śmierć Kościuszki"), completed in May 1983 and first published in January 1984. In the mid-1980s, Tadeusz Łomnicki adapted the essay for the stage and performed it to great acclaim as a forty-minute monodrama. Subsequently, Łomnicki and Andrzej Wajda encouraged Bojarska to develop the essay into a full-length play. See Maria Bojarska, *Król Lear nie żyje* (Warsaw: Polski Dom Wydawniczy, 1994), 162; Tadeusz Łomnicki, *Spotkania teatralne,* ed. Maria Bojarska (Warsaw: Tchu, 2003), 310. For the essay, see Anna Bojarska, "Śmierć Kościuszki," *Więź* 27, no. 1 (January 1984): 57–81, and *Pięć śmierci* (Warsaw: Krąg, 1990), 32–64. However, the play remains unpublished. Bojarska's sources include Dihm, *Kościuszko nieznany;* Józef Drzewiecki, *Pamiętniki Józefa Drzewieckiego (1772–1852)* (Kraków, 1891); Tadeusz Kościuszko and Józef Pawlikowski, *Czy Polacy wybić się mogą na niepodległość,* ed. Emanuel Halicz (Warsaw: Wydawnictwo Ministerstwa Obrony Narodowej, 1967); Julian Ursyn Niemcewicz, "Dziennik mojej podróży," in Józef Tretiak, *Finis Poloniae! Historia legendy maciejowickiej i jej rozwiązanie* (Kraków: Krakowska Spółka Wydawnicza, 1921), 58–88; Paszkowski, *Dzieje Tadeusza Kościuszki;* and Kościuszko's letters to Jefferson and Paszkowski.

81. See Łomnicki, *Spotkania teatralne,* 311.

82. See Andrzej Friszke, *Rok 1989: Polska droga do wolności / Nineteen Eighty-Nine: Polish Path towards Freedom,* trans. Aleksandra Rodzińska-Chojnowska (Warsaw: Wydawnictwo Sejmowe, 2009), 151–52; Andrzej Małkiewicz, *Wybory czerwcowe 1989* (Warsaw: Instytut Studiów Politycznych PAN, 1994), 21. According to some estimates, the number of volunteers involved in the Solidarity campaign was close to 100,000.

83. Anna Bojarska, *Lekcja polskiego* (1988), unpublished manuscript (Library of the Powszechny Theatre, Warsaw), 42.

84. Ibid., 3.

85. On this issue, see, e.g., M. Bojarska, *Król Lear,* 160–61.

86. A precedent for drawing a symbolic connection between the Kościuszko insurrection and the Solidarity movement was established in May 1981 when Wałęsa came to Kraków to repeat the 1794 oath in which Kościuszko pledged his commitment to the cause of Poland's sovereignty.

87. E. P. Thompson, *The Making of the English Working Class* (London: Penguin Books, 1991), 86.

88. Bojarska, *Lekcja polskiego*, 54.

89. Ibid., 16–17, 44. The final sentence is from Kościuszko's letter to Franciszek Paszkowski, 15 October 1816. See Kościuszko, "Listy Kościuszki ze spuścizny po gen. Paszkowskim (1791–1817)," ed. Adam M. Skałkowski, *Kwartalnik Historyczny* 43, no. 1 (1929): 41; Paszkowski, *Dzieje Tadeusza Kościuszki*, 245–46.

90. Bojarska, *Lekcja polskiego*, 42.

91. Ibid., 44.

92. Ibid., 2.

93. Ibid., 40.

94. Ibid., 44.

95. In the closing scene of act 1, Sosnowska unexpectedly pays Kościuszko a brief and surreptitious visit.

96. For the argument about the epistolary novel's deeply felt instruction in imagined empathy, I am indebted to Lynn Hunt, *Inventing Human Rights: A History* (New York: W. W. Norton, 2007).

97. Launching the insurrection in 1794, the historical Kościuszko insisted that it was an all-or-nothing wager. In his speech to the troops on 24 March 1794, he said: "Dear colleagues, I take as our motto 'Death or victory!' I put my trust in you and in this nation that would rather die than suffer the disgraceful yoke." Kościuszko, *Listy, odezwy, wspomnienia*, ed. Henryk Mościcki (Warsaw: Gebethner i Wolff, 1917), 46.

98. Lech Walesa, *The Struggle and the Triumph: An Autobiography*, trans. Franklin Philip (New York: Arcade, 1992), 200.

99. Ibid., 202, 204.

100. Concerns about voters' wait-and-see attitudes and outright indifference were not unjustified. Despite the historic nature of the 1989 election, only 62 percent of the electorate exercised their voting rights. For especially keen insight into the reasons why the round-table negotiations and agreements met with distrust in society at large, see especially Paweł Śpiewak, "Po Okrągłym Stole," *Res Publica* 11, no. 4 (1989): 24–29. Written soon after the round-table talks officially ended on 5 April 1989, Śpiewak's article was rejected by the daily press as too pessimistic; he subsequently submitted it to the monthly *Res Publica*.

101. Roger Boyes, *The Naked President: A Political Life of Lech Walesa* (London: Secker and Warburg, 1994), 186. See also, e.g., Andrzej W. Lipiński, *Plebiscyt i odmowa: Studium terenowe reakcji wyborczej 1989 roku* (Warsaw: n.p., 1990), 61; Frances Millard, *The Anatomy of the New Poland: Post-Communist Politics in Its First Phase* (Aldershot, UK: Edward Elgar, 1994), 64; Andrzej Paczkowski, *The Spring Will Be Ours: Poland and the Poles from Occupation to Freedom*, trans. Jane Cave (University Park: Pennsylvania State University Press, 1998), 504.

102. Paczkowski, *Spring*, 504. On this issue, see also, e.g., Friszke, *Rok 1989 / Nineteen Eighty-Nine*, 149–51.

103. Paweł Śpiewak, "Narodziny polskiej demokracji (Wiosna 1989–jesień 1990)," in *Bitwa o Belweder*, ed. Mirosława Grabowska and Ireneusz Krzemiński (Kraków: Wydawnictwo Literackie, 1991), 202.

104. Walesa, *Struggle*, 203, 201.

105. For reports on the rally, see "Wałęsa pod Racławicami," *Gazeta Wyborcza*, 16 May 1989, 1; Lidia Wójcik, "Grać czy nie grać?," *Teatr* 44, no. 9 (September 1989): 4–5.

106. Quoted in "Wałęsa pod Racławicami," 1.

107. Quoted in Wójcik, "Grać czy nie grać?," 4.

108. The phrase "a patriotic culture of citizenship" is from Simon Schama, *Citizens: A Chronicle of the French Revolution* (New York: Alfred A. Knopf, 1989), xv.

109. On the concept of *lieu de mémoire*, see my note 62 in the introduction.

110. For a photograph of the meeting, see Antoni Dudek, *Historia polityczna Polski 1989–2005* (Kraków: Arcana, 2007), 123.

111. George E. Marcus, *The Sentimental Citizen: Emotion in Democratic Politics* (University Park: Pennsylvania State University Press, 2002), 148.

112. See Anderson, *Imagined Communities*, 24–36.

113. Ibid., 23.

114. Quoted in Anderson, *Imagined Communities*, 24.

115. Walter Benjamin, *Illuminations,* ed. Hannah Arendt, trans. Harry Zohn (New York: Schocken Books, 1969), 263–64.

116. Anderson, *Imagined Communities*, 24.

117. Ibid.

118. Ibid., 26.

119. Marcus, *Sentimental Citizen*, 99.

120. The day before the first round of the election, Wałęsa made an even more explicit statement. Appearing on television, he announced his support for all but one of the candidates on the so-called national list. He was referring to a separate, nationwide ballot, listing thirty-five leaders of the communist establishment. See Antoni Dudek, "Decydujące miesiące: Polska, kwiecień—sierpień 1989," in *Polska 1986–1989: Koniec systemu*, vol. 1, ed. Paweł Machcewicz (Warsaw: Trio, 2002), 131; Millard, *Anatomy of the New Poland*, 66.

121. Marcus, *Sentimental Citizen*, 146.

122. Ibid., 139.

123. Jan Kubik, *The Power of Symbols against the Symbols of Power: The Rise of Solidarity and the Fall of State Socialism in Poland* (University Park: Pennsylvania State University Press, 1994), 268–69. On the disintegration of the Solidarity myth, see also Marcin Frybes and Patrick Michel, *Après le communisme: Mythes et légendes de la Pologne contemporaine* (Paris: Bayard Éditions, 1996).

Transformations: An Epilogue

1. For a reprint of *Wykład katechizmu narodowego,* see Henryk Mościcki et al., *Trzeci maj* (Warsaw: Gebethner i Wolff, 1916), 121–35.

2. The persistence of this belief and its deep imbeddedness in Polish identity politics are readable, for example, from a public outcry against Jan T. Gross's *Neighbors: The Destruction of the Jewish Community in Jedwabne, Poland* (*Sąsiedzi: Historia zagłady żydowskiego miasteczka,* 2000).

3. The quotation comes from interviews conducted for a comparative research project. See Krzysztof Koseła, "Choroba na Polskę," *Tygodnik Powszechny,* 19 June 2005, 4.

4. Clifford Geertz, *The Interpretation of Cultures: Selected Essays* (New York: Basic Books, 2000), 406.

5. See Mitzner, *Teatr Tadeusza Kościuszki,* 24.

6. Schama, *Citizens,* xv.

7. Both terms, *topical allusion plays* and *application plays,* come from Hume, *Henry Fielding,* 78.

8. For this view in contemporary feminist theory, see Nancy Cott, *The Grounding of Modern Feminism* (New Haven, CT: Yale University Press, 1987); Linda Nicholson, *Identity before Identity Politics* (Cambridge: Cambridge University Press, 2008).

9. Given that antifeminism continues to have deep appeal to many, it is not particularly surprising, for example, that at the Democratic Party's 2012 convention, "First Lady Michelle Obama's otherwise powerful speech discounted her entire professional life in favor of her role as 'mom in chief.' . . . Understanding why [this kind of rhetoric] is still necessary means understanding what continues to drive the [antifeminist] backlash. And it demonstrates that, if the sexual counterrevolution is ever over, the unfinished work of the original revolution is still waiting." Kathryn Joyce, "Women Who Want to Be Women," *Women's Review of Books* 30, no. 1 (January—February 2013): 7.

10. MacIntyre, *Is Patriotism a Virtue?,* 4.

Plays Cited

For plays published in the nineteenth century or earlier, publishers' names are omitted.

Addison, Joseph. *Cato*. Edited by Laura J. Rosenthal. In *The Broadview Anthology of Restoration and Early Eighteenth-Century Drama*, edited by J. Douglas Canfield, 186–216. Peterborough, ON: Broadview Press, 2001.
Anczyc, Władysław Ludwik. *Kościuszko pod Racławicami*. In *Życie i pisma*, edited by Marian Szyjkowski, 4:149–283. Kraków: privately printed, 1908.
Bakal, Bronisław. *Bitwa pod Łowczówkiem*. Warsaw: I. Rzepecki, 1938.
Bałucki, Michał [Jan Załęga, pseud.]. *Kiliński*. Kraków, 1893.
Bełcikowski, Adam. *Przekupka warszawska*. In *Dramata i komedie*, 5:267–338. Kraków, 1898.
Bogusławski, Wojciech. *Cud albo Krakowiaki i Górale*. Edited by Mieczysław Klimowicz. Wrocław: Zakład Narodowy im. Ossolińskich, 2005.
———. *Dowód wdzięczności narodu*. Warsaw, 1791.
Bojarska, Anna. *Lekcja polskiego*. [1988] Unpublished manuscript. Library of the Powszechny Theatre, Warsaw.
Bratkowski, Stanisław. *Akademik warszawski*. Warsaw, [1831?].
Brzeska, Wanda [Eminus, pseud.]. *Emilia Plater*. In *Powstanie listopadowe*, edited by Maria Ojerzyńska, 85–93. Poznań: Zjednoczenie Młodzieży Polskiej, 1927.
Bunikiewicz, Witold. *Piosnki ułańskie*. Lwów: Wydawnictwo Polskie, 1919.
Dembowski, Ignacy. *Wanda*. Kraków, 1810.
Fornes, Maria Irene. *Mud*. In *Plays*, 13–40. Preface by Susan Sontag. New York: PAJ Publications, 1986.
Kiedrzyński, Stefan. *Zaręczyny pod kulami*. Warsaw: I. Rzepecki, 1938.
Kniaźnin, Franciszek Dionizy. *Utwory dramatyczne: Wybór*. Edited by Augustyn Jendrysik. Warsaw: Państwowy Instytut Wydawniczy, 1958.
Kochanowski, Jan. *The Dismissal of the Greek Envoys*. In *Polish Renaissance Literature: An Anthology*, translated and edited by Michael J. Mikoś, 214–39. Columbus, OH: Slavica, 1995.
———. *Odprawa posłów greckich*. Edited by Tadeusz Ulewicz. 10th ed. Wrocław: Zakład Narodowy im. Ossolińskich, 1962.
Konczyński, Tadeusz. *Emilia Plater*. Warsaw: Biblioteka Groszowa, [1933].

Korpal, Tadeusz Orsza. *Emilia Plater: Panny w r. 1831*. Miejsce Piastowe: Towarzystwo św. Michała Archanioła, 1937.
Kraszewski, Józef Ignacy. *Równy wojewodzie*. Poznań, 1868.
Kublicki, Stanisław. *Obrona Trembowli, czyli Męstwo Chrzanowskiej*. 1788. 2nd ed. Warsaw, 1789.
Łubieńska, Tekla. *Wanda*. Edited by Józef Ujejski. Warsaw: Związek Artystów Scen Polskich, 1927.
Majeranowski, Konstanty. *Kościuszko nad Sekwaną*. Kraków, 1821.
———. *Pierwsza miłość Kościuszki*. Kraków, 1820.
Mańkowska, Bogusława. *Tadeusz Kościuszko, czyli cztery chwile życia tego bohatera*. Poznań, 1880.
Mickiewicz, Adam. *Dramaty*. Edited by Zofia Stefanowska. Warsaw: Czytelnik, 1995. Vol. 3 of *Dzieła*, edited by Zbigniew Jerzy Nowak et al. 17 vols. 1993–2005.
Niemcewicz, Julian Ursyn. *Powrót posła: Komedia w trzech aktach oraz wybór bajek politycznych*. Edited by Zdzisław Skwarczyński. 10th ed. Wrocław: Zakład Narodowy im. Ossolińskich, 1983.
———. *Powrót posła: Komedia w trzech aktach oraz wybór bajek politycznych z epoki Sejmu Wielkiego*. Edited by Stanisław Kot. 6th ed. Wrocław: Zakład Narodowy im. Ossolińskich, 1950.
Nowakowski, Zygmunt. *Gałązka rozmarynu*. Lwów: Atlas, 1938.
Otwinowski, Stefan. *Wielkanoc*. Introduction by Michał Maksymilian Borwicz. Kraków: Centralny Komitet Żydów Polskich, 1946.
Reis, Zygmunt. *Strzelecka miłość*. Miejsce Piastowe: Towarzystwo św. Michała Archanioła, 1933.
Sedlaczek, Janina. *Pod sztandarem kobiety*. Poznań, 1895.
Segel, Harold B., ed. *Polish Romantic Drama: Three Plays in English Translation*. Amsterdam: Harwood, 1997.
Sito, Jerzy S. *Polonez*. 1978. 2nd ed. Warsaw: Czytelnik, 1991.
Stolarzewicz, Ludwik. *I my dziewczęta wojować będziemy*. Łódź: Wydawnictwo Drukarni Państwowej, [1935].
———. *W gronie dziewcząt*. Łódź: Wydawnictwo Drukarni Państwowej, [1935].
Wasilewska, Wanda. *Bartosz Głowacki*. In *Pisma zebrane*, 2:717–814. Warsaw: Wydawnictwo Ministerstwa Obrony Narodowej, 1956.
Wężyk, Franciszek. *Wanda*. Kraków, 1826.
Winiarski, Władysław [Marian Ładysławski, pseud.]. *Mogiła więcej*. Kraków: G. Gebethner, 1912.
Wybicki, Józef. *Samnitka*. Poznań, 1787.
———. *Utwory dramatyczne*. Edited by Roman Kaleta. Warsaw: Państwowy Instytut Wydawniczy, 1963.

Wyspiański, Stanisław. *The Wedding.* Trans. Noel Clark. Introduction by Jerzy Peterkiewicz. London: Oberon Books, 1998.
——. *Wesele.* Kraków: Wydawnictwo Literackie, 1958. Vol. 4 of *Dzieła zebrane,* edited by Leon Płoszewski et al. 16 vols. 1958–71.
York, Edwin G. *Jan Laski, Champion of Religious Tolerance.* Milford: privately printed, 2001.
Ździebłowski, Antoni Stefan. *Bohaterka z Powstania 1863 roku.* Chicago, 1893.
Żeromski, Stefan. *Róża: Dramat niesceniczny.* Warsaw: Czytelnik, 1975. Vol. 20 of *Dzieła,* edited by Stanisław Pigoń. 23 vols. 1973–75.

Index

acting, 37, 51, 79–80, 81–82
Adams, John, 6, 102
Addison, Joseph: *Cato*, 69–70, 197, 307nn50–51, 333n15
Aleksandrowicz, Alina, 90–91, 310n91
Alexander I, 205, 252
American Revolution, 41, 70, 117, 194, 202, 207–8, 212, 227, 311n105
Anczyc, Władysław Ludwik: *Kościuszko at Racławice*, 1, 18, 42, 201, 202, 209, 211, 213–17, 218, 220, 228, 229, 231, 233, 275, 277, 335n35, 337n54, 337n62, 338n69
Anderson, Benedict, 12, 268, 284n8
Anderson, Perry, 332n4
antisemitism, 43, 239–46, 249, 344n71
antitrinitarians. *See* Polish Brethren
Aristotle, 97
Ashbery, John, 4
Asnyk, Adam, 199
Ateneum Theatre, 252
Auerbach, Erich, 268

Bachórz, Józef, 329n51
Bakal, Bronisław: *The Battle of Łowczówek*, 182–83, 184–85
Ballanche, Pierre, 181
Bałucki, Michał: *Kiliński*, 220
Bartoszewicz, Kazimierz, 322n5
Bełcikowski, Adam, 150; *The Warsaw Street-Seller*, 33, 42, 202, 219–26, 277, 338nn68–70
Benjamin, Walter, 16, 268
Bennett, Benjamin, 2, 16
Bentham, Jeremy, 41
Bieliński, Franciszek, 316n161
Bluszcz, 176
Boberska, Felicja, 174, 175–77, 179

Bogucka, Maria, 125
Bogusławski, Wojciech, 50, 82, 113, 141, 309n82; *The Miracle*, 149; *The Nation's Grateful Tribute*, 113–16
Bojarska, Anna, 10, 44, 45; *The Polish Lesson*, 1, 44, 229, 230, 250–51, 252–62, 275, 278, 280–82, 345nn79–80
Bouboulina, Laskarina, 167, 175, 325n4
Boyes, Roger, 263
Brandys, Marian, 75
Branicki, Franciszek Ksawery, 48
Bratkowski, Stanisław: *The Warsaw Student*, 205
Broel-Plater, Ludwika: *The Chosen Woman*, 330n54
Browning, Reed, 70, 71
Brumer, Wiktor, 149
Brzeska, Wanda: *Emilia Plater*, 39, 188–90, 191–92
Brzozowski, Stanisław, 35
Bunikiewicz, Witold: *The Uhlan Songs*, 182–83
Burke, Edmund, 2, 6
Butler, Judith, 295n39, 317n6

Caesar, Julius, 70
Canovan, Margaret, 287n32
Case, Sue-Ellen, 143, 144
Catherine II, 22, 35, 47–48, 53, 121, 251
Cato, Marcus Porcius (and Catonism), 69–71, 196–97, 261, 295n35
Child, Lydia Maria, 169
Chrzanowska, Anna Dorota. *See* Chrzanowska, Zofia
Chrzanowska, Zofia, 26, 28–29, 32, 33, 34, 37–38, 120–24, 129, 131, 279. *See also* Kublicki, Stanisław; Wybicki, Józef: *The Polish Woman*

Chrzanowski, Jan Samuel, 122–23, 129, 137, 142
Cicero, Marcus Tullius, 21, 25, 97, 106, 186, 295n35
Cincinnatus, Lucius Quinctius, 207
citizenship, 7, 16, 22, 33, 99, 101, 120–21, 198, 221, 277, 289n1
class, 30–32, 42–44, 115, 141, 177, 195, 198, 201, 211–12, 214, 216, 220, 232, 235, 237–39, 251, 271, 277, 280
Coleridge, Samuel Taylor, 196
communism, 13, 43, 229, 231, 232, 240, 266
Confederacy: Bar, 22, 338n68; Targowica, 47–48, 67–69, 71, 74, 85, 194, 299n4, 306n46
Congress of Vienna, 150, 204–5, 218, 252, 258
Conspectus of the National Catechism, The, 273
Constitution of 3 May 1791, 30, 47, 65, 71, 114, 189, 218, 303n26
Copernicus, Nicholas, 228
corvée, 198, 214, 215
Cunningham, Hugh, 284n13
Curie, Maria Skłodowska, 330n63
Curti, Merle, 8
Czacki, Michał, 309n82
Czartoryska, Izabela, 1, 76, 85, 87, 89–90, 93, 126, 308n66, 310n91
Czartoryski, Adam Jerzy and Konstanty, 87
Czartoryski, Adam Kazimierz, 76, 85, 87, 89–90, 93, 126, 308n66, 314n147, 317n11
Czekalski, Eustachy: *Emilia Plater*, 330n54
Czerwony Sztandar, 233, 235
Czyszkowska-Peschler, Małgorzata, 220

Dąbrowski, Bronisław, 234
Dąbrowski, Jan Henryk, 237
Dabrowski, Patrice M., 337n60
D'Alembert, Jean Le Rond, 130
Dąmbska, Helena, 61, 76
Davies, Damian Walford, 196
Davies, Norman, 145, 188
Davis, Natalie Zemon, and Randolph Starn, 298n62

Decatur, Stephen, 286n26
Derrida, Jacques, 1
Diderot, Denis, 79, 81, 130
Dietz, Mary G., 295n35
Dihm, Jan, 200
Dobrée, Bonamy, 294n34
drama, genres: application drama, 251, 276, 280–81, 344n73, 348n7; domestic drama, 17, 223; *drame romantique*, 17, 18, 290n5; Jesuit school drama, 102; melodrama, 17, 219, 243; music drama, 17, 149, 310n87; neoclassical tragedy, 17, 33, 39, 144, 146, 147, 153, 163, 197, 314n141; political drama, 99, 100; romantic comedy, 17, 53, 98; satirical comedy, 17, 97; thesis play, 17; topical allusion drama, 276, 348n7
drama, popularity in Poland, 2–4, 17–18, 274. *See also* theatre
Dubienka, battle of, 194, 227
Dufour, Pierre, 3
Dunlap, William, 77–78
Dziennik Literacki, 177

education, 110–12, 316n161, 317n11
Edwards, Catharine, 332n7
Elizabeth I, 159–60, 162, 324n38
emotion vs. reason, 78–79, 81, 83–84, 86, 309n70
Enlightenment, 2, 10–11, 18–22, 29, 33, 37–38, 48, 50–52, 64, 76, 77–78, 98–99, 112, 119, 195, 197; Polish, 11, 26–27, 33, 35–37, 72, 76, 126, 149, 288n39, 290n9; women and the, 11, 19, 37–38, 91, 121, 125–26, 129–30, 140, 280, 291n11, 319n32, 320n32

Farge, Arlette, 4
Feliński, Alojzy, 265
femininity, 6, 11, 20, 26–27, 38, 40, 96, 116, 119–20, 123–24, 133, 135, 137–38, 159, 168–69, 191, 226, 278, 279, 281, 328n31
feminism, 19, 20, 33, 38, 101, 107, 111, 112, 118–19, 121, 124, 139–40, 169, 170–72, 175, 177, 189, 190, 191–92, 221, 280, 281–82, 291n11, 314n145, 317n6, 348n9

Fornes, Maria Irene, 326n15
Foucault, Michel, 4
Four-Year Parliament. *See under* Parliament: 1788–92
Frederick, W. *See* Frederick William II
Frederick William II, 46, 48
French Revolution, 2, 198, 219, 303n27
Freneau, Philip, 117–20, 317n3
Fuller, Margaret, 169, 170–71, 326n16
Furtwangler, Albert, 201, 335n32

Galos, Adam, 335n35
Gannett, Deborah Sampson, 117, 316n1, 325n7
Gąsiorowski, Wacław, 182
Gaszyński, Konstanty, 180, 329n51
Gazeta Warszawska, 57, 142
gender: boundaries, 17, 26–27, 32, 39, 41, 44, 96, 123, 135, 137, 140, 160, 175, 184, 187, 191–192, 223, 256, 278, 280; definitions, 119, 174, 226, 279, 285n18; equality, 26, 31, 40, 101, 111, 125, 138, 163, 170, 177, 179, 182, 191–192, 222, 262, 278, 281, 320n32; hierarchies, 91, 125, 151, 169, 218, 276, 277, 281; norms, 6, 19, 29, 31, 40, 85, 101, 103, 109, 118–19, 122, 124, 131–32, 138–39, 157, 164, 167–68, 182, 186, 191, 210, 297n53, 325n7; relations, 37, 115, 192, 225, 280, 282, 298n59; roles and identities, 26, 29, 37–38, 102, 110–11, 113, 119–20, 124, 125, 127, 131, 134–38, 140, 150, 160, 161, 165–72, 174–76, 178, 185–86, 189–90, 210, 218, 220, 223, 225, 256, 262, 279–80, 294n31; transgression (insubordination, nonconformity), 26, 38, 39–40, 96, 120, 122–23, 129 131–33, 138, 140, 142, 156–57, 165, 167–68, 170, 172–74, 177–75, 179, 186, 188–89, 191–92, 211, 325n7. *See also* education; femininity; feminism; masculinity; sexuality; women; *and under* Enlightenment; patriotism
Gierowski, Józef Andrzej, 296n47

Głowacki, Wojciech Bartosz, 43, 213, 230, 232–33, 337n60. *See also under* Wasilewska, Wanda
Goethe, Johann Wolfgang von, 322n12
Gombrowicz, Witold, 35
Goodman, Dena, 107
Goodwin, Albert, 9
Gorzeńska, Ludwika, 61, 76
Granasowa, Magdalena, 338n68
Griffin, Dustin, 6
Grześkowiak-Krwawicz, Anna, 74, 308n62

Hahn, Wiktor, 222, 336n39
Hall, Aleksander, 264
Hartley, L. P., 26
Hausen, Karin, 20
Henry, Patrick, 69–70, 307n50
Hill, Aaron, 79–80, 81
Hobson, Barbara, and Ruth Lister, 120
Hodgdon, Barbara, 25
Hoffmanowa, Klementyna Tańska, 175, 297n53
Holocaust, 11, 13, 43, 240, 245, 250
homoeroticism, 200, 227
Horace, 115
Hoszkiewicz, Kazimierz, 23–24, 293n29
Huet, Marie-Hélène, 82
Hulewicz, Benedykt, 73
Hume, David, 78, 309n70
Hume, Robert D., 280
Hunt, Leigh, 196
Hunt, Margaret R., 1, 85

Ilnicka, Maria, 176
Inglot, Mieczysław, 234, 340n14, 341n25

Jan III Sobieski, 212–13
Janion, Maria, 10
Jefferson, Thomas, 41, 193, 208, 227, 259
Jendrysik, Augustyn, 89
Jewish minority, 239–47, 249, 344n70
Jezierski, Franciszek Salezy, 125–26
Joan of Arc, 172, 180–81, 329n47, 329n51
John Paul II, 228
Johnson, James Williams, 196

Joyce, Kathryn, 348n9
Juliusz Słowacki Theatre, 231

Kaczyński, Lech, 28
Kadłubek, Wincenty, 148, 154–55
Kadulska, Irena, 319n25
Kądziela, Łukasz, 332n4
Kaleta, Roman, 68, 126–27
Kalinka, Walerian, 97, 301n12, 312n125, 313n132
Kant, Immanuel, 98, 130
Kara Mustafa, Merzifonlu, 212
Kasprowicz, Wilhelmina, 179, 181
Kateb, George, 8
Kazanowska. See Wybicki, Józef: *The Polish Woman*
Keats, John, 196
Kerber, Linda K., 111
Kersten, Krystyna, 240–41
Kiedrzyński, Stefan: *Engaged on a Battlefield*, 182, 187
Kielce pogrom, 239–40
Kniaźnin, Franciszek Dionizy, 10, 49, 52, 85, 87–89, 91, 95–96, 194; *The Spartan Mother*, 1, 10, 37, 49, 51, 61, 76, 81, 85–96, 126, 304n30, 308n66, 310n87, 312n108
Kochanowski, Jan: *The Dismissal of the Greek Envoys*, 293n23
Kołłątaj, Hugo, 23, 24, 88, 293n27
Konczyński, Tadeusz: *Emilia Plater*, 188
Koneczny, Feliks, 334n25
Konopnicka, Maria, 35, 265, 330n52, 330n63
Korpal, Tadeusz Orsza: *Emilia Plater*, 188–89
Korzon, Tadeusz, 334n28
Kościuszko, Tadeusz, 18, 23, 28–29, 30, 31, 34, 41–43, 44, 69, 193–225, 227–30, 249–50, 258–59, 264–67, 331n1, 332n8, 334n25, 334nn28–29, 337nn59–60, 339n1, 345n79; clothes symbolism, 32, 198, 211–12, 264, 299n63; Kościuszko Uprising (*see* uprisings: 1794); plays about, 1, 18, 42, 201–26, 228–29, 235–36, 245–46, 250–62, 280–82, 335n36
Kossak, Wojciech, 201
Kossakowski, Szymon, 48

Kot, Stanisław, 97
Krak, 147
Krasicki, Ignacy, 24, 121, 149, 280, 310n91
Krasnowiecki, Władysław, 233–34
Kraszewski, Józef Ignacy, 337n53; *The Governor's Equal*, 202, 206–9, 217, 336n47
Kruczkowski, Leon, 232–33, 236–37
Kubik, Jan, 272
Kublicki, Stanisław, 126, 318n17; *The Defense of Trembowla*, 26–27, 38, 88, 119–22, 124–32, 137–42, 279, 317n7, 321n46
Kuraś, Ferdynand, 329n52

Łaski, Jan (John à Lasco), 44, 247–49, 344n65
Law on Royal Towns, 30, 67, 303n26
Lenartowicz, Teofil, 337n63
Leśnodorski, Bogusław, 293
Lessel, Wincenty, 87, 311n92
Lesser, Aleksander, 150
Ley, Graham, 79
liberty, 18, 22, 23–24, 28, 41, 54, 71–74, 84; Suchorzewski and, 49, 59–60, 62, 66–67, 69–71, 72–73
liberum veto, 54, 65, 98, 301n14
lieu de mémoire, 42, 265, 280, 298n62
Limanowski, Bolesław, 174–75, 177
Locke, John, 30, 103, 303n28
Loftis, John, 146, 153
Łomnicki, Tadeusz, 252, 345n80
Longmore, Paul K., 29
Lubicz-Pachoński, Jan, 337n60
Łubieńska, Tekla, 33, 45, 145–47, 322n11; *Charlemagne and Witykind*, 147; *Wanda, Queen of Poland*, 33, 39, 144–47, 149, 150–56, 161–65, 275, 322n5, 322n7, 322–23n12–14
Łubieński, Feliks, 145
Lubomirska, Zofia, 121, 318n12
Lubomirski, Józef, 199, 210
Łuskina, Stefan, 57

Maciejowice, battle of, 194, 200, 218, 227, 256, 261
MacIntyre, Alasdair, 5

Madison, James, 41
Majeranowski, Konstanty: *Kościuszko on the Seine*, 201, 207, 336n40; *Kościuszko's First Love*, 42, 201, 202–5, 209, 217–18, 222, 228, 275, 334n29
Małachowski, Stanisław, 56, 63
Mańkowska, Bogusława: *Tadeusz Kościuszko*, 202, 209–13, 217, 277, 337n54
Marciniak, Katarzyna, 324n27
Marcus, George E., 267, 269–70
marriage and family, 3, 31, 39, 99–101, 104, 107–10, 152, 156–58, 163, 189, 221, 239, 279, 315nn153–55, 316n162
"Marseillaise, La," 274
masculinity, 6, 11, 26–27, 38, 40, 119, 123–24, 135, 137, 168–69, 191, 203–4, 226, 254, 262, 278–79, 317n7
Matejko, Jan, 201, 267
Maurice, Justin, 181
Maus, Katharine Eisaman, 34
Mazowiecki, Tadeusz, 264
Mercier, Louis-Sébastien, 113
Michlic, Joanna, 240
Mickiewicz, Adam, 3, 151, 172, 178–79, 181, 188, 289n44, 327n27. WORKS: "The Death of the Colonel," 169, 172–73, 181, 329n51; *Forefathers' Eve*, 151, 275; *Grażyna*, 151; *Konrad Wallenrod*, 151; "Lecture XXX," 178–79; "Ordon's Stronghold," 327n25; *Pan Tadeusz*, 196; "To a Polish Mother," 24, 294n31
Mill, John Stuart, 27–28, 167, 295n42
Minasowicz, Józef Epifani, 22, 24
Miterzanka, Mieczysława, 314n147
Mitzner, Piotr, 275
Mniszech, Amelia, 121
modernization, 18, 21, 23, 36, 50, 54, 64–65, 89, 97–98, 114, 206, 273
Moi, Toril, 317n6, 328n31
monarchy, 21, 36, 60, 72, 73, 301n15, 308n61
Monitor, 22, 48, 87, 293n25, 300n9, 316n161
Montesquieu, Charles-Louis de, 22, 24, 30, 72, 193, 293n25

Moretti, Franco, 18
Mortkowiczówna, Hanna, 322n5, 323n21
Motherland and Her Only Son, The. See Wybicki, Józef: *The Polish Woman*
Mulvey, Laura, 143, 144
myth, historical, 29, 296n45

Napoleon, 145, 149, 164, 195, 204–5, 252, 259, 323n19
National Symbolic, 3, 202, 228, 271, 284n8
National Theatre, 29–30, 32, 36, 48–49, 50, 52, 54–56, 58–62, 64–65, 75, 76–77, 82, 84, 87, 113, 141, 296n48, 304n30
Niemcewicz, Julian Ursyn, 63, 65–66, 77–78, 83–84, 87, 97–99, 101–2, 200, 227, 308n66; *The Return of the Deputy*, 1–2, 18, 36–37, 49, 51–56, 60–63, 64–66, 74–75, 76, 77–78, 81–83, 88, 89, 97–116, 273, 303n27, 309n82, 313n130, 313n132, 313nn137–38; "To Polish Women," 88
nobility, the, 21, 22, 29, 60, 71, 72, 114, 214, 304n31
Nora, Pierre, 298n62
Norwid, Cyprian Kamil, 150
Nowak-Dłużewski, Juliusz, 24
Nowakowski, Zygmunt: *A Sprig of Rosemary*, 39, 182–83, 184–85, 186

Obama, Michelle, 348n9
Odyniec, Antoni Edward, 329n51
Omaha Magic Theatre, 326n15
Orzeszkowa, Eliza, 35, 330n63
Osiński, Ludwik, 322n11; *Perseus and Andromeda*, 323n19
Otwinowski, Stefan, 241–42, 343n48; *Easter*, 11, 43–44, 45, 230–31, 240–50, 278, 342n37, 344n71

Paine, Thomas, 41
Parliament: 1767–68, 304n29; 1788–92, 18, 27, 30, 47, 50, 53, 56, 64, 65, 67–68, 88, 89, 97, 112, 120, 121–22, 126, 273, 299n2; 1989–91, 229, 253, 263–64, 265, 272

partitions of Poland-Lithuania, 24, 47–48, 53, 82–83, 179, 194, 197, 251–52, 299n1
Paszkowski, Franciszek, 259, 345n79
Patriot Act, 8
Patriota Polski, 292n22
patriotism, 5–9, 14, 15–17, 21–26, 33, 34–35, 42, 44, 54, 69, 83, 115, 122, 128, 196, 221, 231, 239, 250, 255–56, 273–78, 282, 286n23, 333n19; gender and, 6, 122–23, 127, 137, 167, 173, 182, 188, 221–22, 278–79, 281; nationalism and, 7–8, 16, 245, 249, 274, 278, 284n14, 287n31, 288nn40–41; *patria* and, 5–6, 24, 69, 86, 150, 173, 188, 221, 226, 285n20; Roman models of, 69–70, 115, 196–97, 207, 261, 295n35, 307n52; self-sacrifice and, 90, 150, 166, 173, 174, 175–76, 187, 258, 295n35, 307n49; theatre and, 76, 83–84, 143–44; transgressive nonconformity and, 10, 15–16, 25–28, 31–32, 35, 40, 191, 198–200, 217–18, 225–26, 276–77, 325n7; "true" vs. "false," 10, 14, 16–17, 35–38, 36, 42–43, 49, 80, 96, 126, 224, 278
Patriot's Calendar, The, 8–9, 274
Pawlikowski, Józef, 72
peasants, 32, 41, 172, 188, 193, 195, 198, 212–13, 215, 218, 236–39, 251, 254, 267, 321n43, 333nn19–20, 334n23
Permanent Council, 22, 30, 35
Phillips, Ursula, 151
Piecuch, Henryk, 326n13
Pietkiewicz, Michał, 172
Piłsudski, Józef, 183, 228
Piotrowski, Maksymilian A., 150
Plater, Cezary, 172
Plater, Emilia, 28–29, 34, 39–40, 166–92, 220, 222, 325n2, 325nn6–7, 329n47; novel about, 182; plays about, 39–40, 170, 182, 188–92, 330n54; poems about, 329nn51–52
Plater, Michał, 189–90, 331n73
Plater, Władysław, 172
Plutarch, 85, 92, 96, 310n91, 318n11
Połaniec Proclamation, 198, 333n21
Polish Army Theatre, 240

Polish Brethren, 247, 248–49
Polish-Jewish relations. *See* antisemitism; Jewish minority
Polish Revolution (1788–92), 2, 18, 22, 30, 36, 283n4
Polish-Russian War (1792), 211, 227
Polish-Soviet War (1920), 182, 187
Polish Theatre, The, 3
Pollock, Linda A., 315n155
Polski Theatre, 233–34
Poniński, Adam, 227
Popławski, Antoni, 286n24
Porter, Roy, 98–99
Positivism, 174, 188, 206, 208–9, 278, 337n53
Potocka, Józefa, 126
Potocka, Klaudyna, 175
Potocki, Ignacy, 88, 311n95
Potocki, Stanisław Szczęsny, 46–48, 67, 87–88, 126
Powszechny Theatre, 252
Price, Richard, 6–7
Prószyńska, Maria, 179, 181
Przypkowski, Samuel, 247
Pułaski, Kazimierz, 228, 338n68

Quintilian, Marcus Fabius, 97, 106

Racławice, battle of, 30–31, 41, 193–95, 198, 210, 211, 213, 230, 232, 264, 265–66, 268–69
Racławice panorama, 201, 230, 254
Rahe, Paul A., 311n105, 312n115
Raszanowicz, Maria, 179–80, 181
Raszewski, Zbigniew, 308n66
Ratajczakowa, Dobrochna, 150–51
Rawson, Elizabeth, 91–92, 93
Reeve, Joseph, 197
Reformation, 247–48
Reis, Zygmunt: *Love of a Rifleman*, 183, 185, 187
Revolutionary Parliament, 47, 299n2
Richardson, Samuel, 260
Riley, Denise, 295n39
Rivers, Isabel, 294n34
Romanticism, 3, 10–11, 278, 283n8, 307n49
Rose, Jacqueline, 316n162
Rostworowski, Emanuel, 333n20

Rousseau, Jean-Jacques, 37, 90, 100–101, 104, 130, 204, 259–60, 310n91, 314n145
Rozbicki, Michal Jan, 288n43
Rubin, Gayle S., 317n6
Ryx, Franciszek, 58, 62

satire, political, 46–47, 48, 68. *See also* Niemcewicz, Julian Ursyn: *The Return of the Deputy*
Schaar, John H., 1, 284nn14–15, 285n20
Schiebinger, Londa, 19, 20
Schiller, Leon, 240, 342n37
Schöpflin, George, 296nn44–45
Scott, Joan W., 20
Sczaniecka, Emilia, 175
Sechelski, Denise S., 79, 82
Sedlaczek, Janina: *Rallying under a Woman's Banner*, 188
sensibility, 86, 204, 310n88
serfdom, 60, 114, 197, 198, 237, 248, 303n26, 318n17, 333n20
sexuality, 19–20, 29, 38, 52, 59, 95, 100, 101, 104, 107–8, 110, 111, 119, 133, 134–35, 139, 140, 141, 143, 144, 156, 158, 160, 165, 168, 186, 211, 223, 225–26, 279, 285n18, 317n6, 325n7
Sharp, Samuel L., 289n44
Siarczyński, Antoni, 67
Sienkiewicz, Henryk, 25
Sito, Jerzy S.: *Polonaise*, 251–52, 344n78
Skórkowski, Albin Kazimierz, 73
Śliwowska, Wiktoria, 179
Smith, Anthony D., 288n41
Smoleński, Władysław, 73
Snopek, Jerzy, 292n21
Society of the Cincinnati, 207–8, 336n48
Solidarity, 18, 44, 229, 252–53, 255, 263–67, 270–72, 280–81, 290n7, 345n86
Sołtan, Stanisław, 63
Sosnowska, Ludwika, 199–200, 209–10, 227, 259–60
Sosnowski, Józef, 199, 209–10
Sparta, 85, 87, 90–94, 310n91, 311n105, 312n115
Spectator, 300n9
spectatorship, 37, 51, 55–56, 82, 83–84, 143
Spenser, Edmund, 166

Śpiewak, Paweł, 263
Stachniak, Eva, 31
Stanisław August, 22, 29, 35, 47–48, 53, 55, 57, 62, 89, 113–14, 121, 126, 199, 251, 293n27, 300n7, 304n31
Stary Theatre, 240
Staszic, Stanisław, 88, 321n43
Steele, Richard, 77, 308n68
Stolarzewicz, Ludwik: *Girlfriends*, 183, 185–86, 189; *We, Women, Will Also Take Up Arms*, 39, 183, 185–87, 189
Stoller, Robert, 317n6
Storozynski, Alex, 331n1, 334n25, 334n28
Straszewicz, Józef, 172–74, 175, 180–81, 188, 325n2, 326n16, 329n47
Styka, Jan, 201
Suchorzewski, Jan, 36–37, 47, 48–52, 56–85, 91, 96, 273, 301nn12–13, 303n26, 304n31, 304n33, 305n39, 306nn45–46, 307n52
Świerzawski, Karol, 113–14, 309n82
Świętochowski, Aleksander, 337n53
Sygiert, Józef, 144
Szaynok, Bożena, 241
Szczekociny, battle of, 232
Szczepaniec, Józef, 293n29
Szczepkowska, Joanna, 253
Szymonowic, Szymon, 91

Tasso, Torquato, 166
Tatler, 77, 208n68
Taylor, Charles, 284n14
Terlecka, Anna Schugt, 294n31
theatre: functions, 49, 51–52, 62, 76, 77–78, 84, 96, 149; metatheatricality, 146, 245, 247; objections to, 59–60, 75; provincial (and household), 75–77, 81, 83–84, 298n56; theatre house conditions, 55–56; Warsaw theatregoers, 61, 80–81. *See also* acting
Thelwall, John, 196
Thompson, E. P., 255
Thompson, James R., 28, 295n43
Tomaszewska, Antonina, 179, 181
transgression. *See under* gender; patriotism

treason, 65, 67, 85
Truskolaska, Agnieszka, 309n82

Ujejski, Józef, 323n13
uprisings: 1794, 11, 18, 23, 30–31, 44, 69, 149, 193, 194–95, 197–98, 205, 211, 213–15, 220, 227, 232, 235, 241, 245, 251, 256–57, 265–66, 271, 296n51, 331n4, 345n86, 346n97; 1830–31, 40, 167, 173, 180, 205, 232, 245; 1846 Galician, 198–99, 215; 1863–64, 175–76, 183–84, 187, 205, 206; Warsaw ghetto, 11, 43, 231, 241–42, 245–47

van der Meer, Jan Ij., 98, 101–3, 105, 313n138
Varille, César Félicité Pyrrhis de, 303n28
"Varsovienne, La," 245–46, 343n60
Vienna, battle of, 212–13
Voltaire, 212

Wajda, Andrzej, 1, 229, 230, 252–55, 282, 345n80
Wałęsa, Lech, 10, 229, 230, 263–72, 345n86, 347n120; Racławice pageant, 10, 229, 230, 264–72
Walewski, Michał, 313n127
Wanda, 28–29, 33, 34, 39, 144, 147–51, 164, 166, 173, 324n27, 324n29; plays about (*see* Łubieńska, Tekla; Werner, Zacharias; Wężyk, Franciszek)
Warsaw, siege of (1794), 194, 219, 222–23, 338n70
Washington, George, 41, 201, 207–8, 285n20, 335n32
Wasilewska, Wanda, 231–32, 233–35, 239; *Bartosz Głowacki*, 43, 230–39, 340n14, 341n24, 341n34
Wawrzykowska-Wierciochowa, Dioniza, 330n54
Werner, Zacharias: *Wanda, Queen of Sarmatians*, 322n12
Wężyk, Franciszek, 144; *Wanda*, 39, 144–45, 147, 150–161, 162, 164–65, 322n5

Wielkopolska Chronicle, 324n29
Wills, Garry, 83
Winiarski, Władysław: *Yet Another Grave*, 188–89
Witkowski, Mateusz, 321n46
Wittgenstein, Ludwig, 1, 34
Wójcicki, Kazimierz Władysław, 338n68
Wollstonecraft, Mary, 2, 171, 314n145, 315n160
women, 19–21, 26–27, 31–33, 37–41, 87, 117–25, 129–30, 166–82, 278–82, 285n18, 291n11, 297n53, 312n107, 314n145, 316n161, 317n11, 326nn13–15, 328n31, 348n9; in *The Defense of Trembowla* and *The Polish Woman*, 124–42, 278–80; in the Plater plays, 182–92, 223–24; in *The Polish Lesson*, 262, 278, 281–82; in *The Return of the Deputy*, 100–113, 115–16, 314n147; in *The Spartan Woman*, 91, 93–94, 96, 312n108; in *Tadeusz Kościuszko*, 210–11; in the *Wanda* plays, 144, 147, 150–65; in *The Warsaw Street-Seller*, 220–25
Wordsworth, William, 196
Woźnik, Władysław, 240
Wróbel, Piotr, 240
Wybicki, Józef, 318n17. WORKS: *The Nobleman as Bourgeois*, 141; *Patriotic Letters*, 293n29; "A Patriotic Song," 26, 88, 295n37; *The Polish Woman*, 37, 38, 51, 61, 76, 81, 88, 119–22, 124–37, 138, 139–41, 275, 278–79, 304n30, 320n43; *Political Thoughts on Civil Freedom*, 72; *The Samnite Woman*, 126–27; "The Song of the Polish Legions in Italy" (*see* "A Patriotic Song")
Wyspiański, Stanisław: *The Wedding*, 42, 218–19, 275–76

York, Edwin G., 344n65

Ździebłowski, Antoni Stefan: *A Heroine of the Uprising of 1863*, 187–88, 191–92

Żeleński, Tadeusz ("Boy"), 233
Zeltner, Angelique, 345n79
Zeltner, Emilie, 345n79
Zeltner, Francis Xavier, 258
Żeromski, Stefan: *The Rose*, 289n47
Zielińska, Zofia, 301n12
Ziesche, Philipp, 285
Znamirowski, Adam: *Emilia Plater*, 330n54
Zubowski, Ksawery, 315n153
Żurawski, Kazimierz, 174–75, 176–77

www.ingramcontent.com/pod-product-compliance
Lightning Source LLC
Chambersburg PA
CBHW050613300426
44112CB00012B/1479